WHAT LIFE
HAS TAUGHT ME

Dr. Siaka Stevens

© Siaka Probyn Stevens 1984

Photos:
Cover (colour): Count Walter B. Kramer di Griffon.
Text pages: the author's private collection, Sierra Leone Ministry of Information (photographic section), courtesy of the Royal Commonwealth Society Library pp. 22, 23, 24 (bottom), 36, 37, 42, 44-45 (bottom), 211 (bottom); agencies 211 (top), 252, 253.

British Library Cataloguing in Publication Data.

Stevens, Siaka
    What Life Has Taught Me
    1. Stevens, Siaka   2. Sierra Leone --
    Presidents -- Biography
    I. Title
    966'.404'0924   DT516.82.S73

    ISBN 0-946041-12-1

Published by the Kensal Press
Kensal House, Abbotsbrook, Bourne End, Bucks. England

Designed and produced in Great Britain by
IMPADS Associates,
267, Kensal Road, London W.10 5DB

Contents

4

INTRODUCTION

My first memory of Siaka Stevens goes back to January 1966. He was at one of the low points of his political career, sitting with two other All People's Congress (A.P.C.) parliamentarians alone and strikingly isolated from the crowd of largely Sierra Leone People's Party (S.L.P.P.) M.P.s in the lounge of Parliament. The A.P.C., then the major opposition party, was under assault from many quarters. Some of its parliamentary members had crossed the carpet to join the governing S.L.P.P. in hopes of finding greener pastures; others were being enticed to do so. The party itself was rife with rumours and questions about the loyalty of some of those who remained, its coffers were empty, and its prospects seemed poor. Albert Margai, the Prime Minister, and his supporters were enthusiastic about the idea of a one-party state — which if implemented would cause the demise of the A.P.C. The Prime Minister's pressures were often far from subtle, ranging from statements in Parliament that "if you do not join us now you won't even get a bone" to comments about force and reminders about who controlled the power. There were some in the A.P.C. who thought the party leadership should bargain with the S.L.P.P. to get as many positions and as much power for party activists as they could and then join the S.L.P.P. And on that day, as I interviewed Siaka Stevens, I wondered if the pressure wouldn't be so great that the A.P.C. leadership would do just that. Stevens was clearly dispirited, feeling the pressure from both within the A.P.C. and from the outside. Yet as we talked, he seemed to revive. When I asked him how the negotiations were progressing with the S.L.P.P. on the subject of the one-party state he replied: "It is nothing. They never should have brought it up for their own good. They should have gone about their business of organising and said nothing. They made too much noise about it. There has got to be an election, and we are ready for it, we are strong." Those seemed brave words at the time, yet they were prophetic. The issue of establishing a one-party state backfired on the S.L.P.P., engendering both strong public criticism and opposition within its own ranks.

By March 1967, Stevens was criss-crossing the country in support of his party's candidates to tumultuous crowds which often stood hours in the sun along roads which seemed to be choked by billowing clouds of powdered red earth as each vehicle went by. Then came elections day and the country waited. As the results began to be tallied, it was clear that the A.P.C. had won the largest number of seats and the largest total vote. On March 21st, several days after the election, I interviewed a tired and dusty Siaka Stevens just back from the Provinces where he had secured the support of enough victorious Independent M.P.s to guarantee a majority in a vote of confidence. He was as elated as his supporters dancing in the streets, and as we talked, word came that the Governor General wanted him to come to State House to be sworn in as Prime Minister — the first leader of an opposition party in Africa to become Head of Government.

An examination of the last half-century of the history of Sierra Leone has a great deal to teach us. There are the problems of integration of an indigenous population with a resettled one, compounded by migrations from other parts of Africa which continue to this day. There are the effects of European influence, the consequences of colonialism, and nationalism such as we have seen in much of the rest of Africa. There are also some very important areas in which Sierra Leone was a pioneer including an active, critical, lively press. That tradition has continued in spite of periodic repression of the press both before and after independence. Sierra Leone has had a long history of mass political participation and representation including its inspiration as the "Land of Freedom" in 1787, in which a complex system of representation was designed and briefly implemented, elections to the Freetown Municipal Council since 1895, and the election of three Colony representatives to the Legislative Council from 1924. Sierra Leoneans participated more broadly with the extention of the franchise to the Protectorate in 1957, after which suffrage became universal for all adults. Sierra Leone was the first African country in which an opposition party came to power by electoral means. It also is one of the few nations in history in which a military regime was removed by its own enlisted men who returned control to the duly elected civilian authorities. Sierra Leone is also a country in which the judiciary has played an important role in safeguarding the fairness of elections. Over the years a good many electoral results have been reversed as a consequence of election petitions.

Sierra Leone has taken on an importance far beyond its small size. It first became known to westerners as a home for slaves returned to Africa by the English, whether by private organisations, investors hoping for a profit, or on their own. The area around Freetown became a haven for these settlers, soon to be called Creoles. In time they were to dominate the Peninsula, which became known as the Colony under British authority, while the rest of Sierra Leone became the Protectorate.

The relationship between Creoles and the tribal people was not always cordial and the British Colonial government acted to prevent Creole domination in the early post-World War II years; thus avoiding the kind of split which has haunted Liberia into the 1980s. Sierra Leone was known to many Americans and Europeans during World War II because of its port, one of the largest in the world. It also has one of the oldest universities in Africa, Fourah Bay College, which has trained many generations of Sierra Leone leaders as well as large numbers from Nigeria, Ghana, Gambia, and other parts of West Africa.

Like much of the rest of the Third World, Sierra Leone has suffered from the economic crises of the late 1970s and early 1980s, including the rising cost of oil, the falling prices of raw materials and agriculture products, and the rising cost of imports. Its major exports are from the mining sector, primarily diamonds, iron ore and rutile, with a small amount from the agricultural sector. Diamond mining in particular caused great dislocations in the economy from migration to the mining areas, illegal mining, smuggling, corruption, and so on. At the same time the large scale migrations to the urban areas hurt the agricultural economy. Agricultural production fell due both to the migration of farmers and the low prices paid for agricultural products (in part to keep food prices low in the cities). By the early 1980s the economy was in serious trouble especially since the market for diamonds and iron ore was very poor as a result of the idle industrial capacity in much of the industrial world and because the prices of raw materials were often below the cost of production. Yet unlike in some African states, efforts were made to increase producer prices paid to the farmers and to encourage food production — efforts which saw some success in 1983. Attempts to control the Government budget were also more successful than in previous years. Goods continued to be found in the shops although prices rose. Like the rest of Africa and much of the Third World, Sierra Leone suffered much more severely than the industrial nations which made the headlines. President Stevens and his Minister of Finance, Salia Jusu-Sheriff could do some things to bolster the country's economy, but their ground for maneouver was severely circumscribed by international political and economic factors over which they had no control.

The career of Siaka Stevens encompasses some of the most important of these events, spanning more than fifty years of Sierra Leone's history including the introduction and development of trade unions, the nationalist period, political opposition and imprisonment by the colonial government, independence, political competition in a democratic multi-party system, the coming to power of an opposition party, republican status, the one-party state, the national and international economic crisis of the late 1970s and the early 1980s. In most of these events his role was that of a major participant. It is thus important to have his perspective on this period, his reflections on the significance of what occurred, and often useful new information on many of the major events and decisions of this period. While not every one will remember or interpret these events exactly as Siaka Stevens does, that is to be expected. What is important is that we have his views of fifty years of history, views often filled with surprise and self-criticism, as well as with satisfaction and awe.

This is also the story of a quite remarkable self-made man. Like many other rural Africans, he received his primary and secondary education away from home through the sacrifices of his family and friends and with the aid of a Creole family in Freetown. Although his formal education stopped after graduation from the Albert Academy (except for a very important stay at Ruskin College, Oxford in 1947) his education did not. Stevens read widely, taught himself to type while working at the mines, learned the techniques of broadcasting by memorising BBC broadcasts, and most importantly learned to read, understand, and lead people. As one can see in this work, the education of Siaka Stevens continues in his late 70s.

One of the refreshing aspects of this autobiography is that Siaka Stevens does not paint himself as an heroic figure. While delighted about his success and proud of his achievements, he also talks about mistakes, errors in judgement, and weaknesses. His comments on the colonial period and nationalist responses demonstrate an openness that clarifies and instructs. He is hurt and stung by the injustices of colonialism, identifies with the nationalism of the Haidara rebellion, yet is struck by what he learned from colonial officials and citizens. Stevens is no apologist for colonialism. He writes:

> *It is hard for anyone outside the continent to understand what being African means to me and to millions of my brothers. It means being the heir to a stifled civilisation. It means being half-deprived of identity. It means having nothing to show and everything to prove. It means being a victim of rape and robbery and slavery. It means a slow stirring from shock — the numbing, sometimes crippling shock, of a culture controverted by generations of colonialism and racialism. It means having to face apparently insuperable problems, apparently impossible odds. (p. 94).*

Yet Stevens is generous in his praise of European help and friendship. He speaks of his stay at Ruskin College as "one of the happiest periods of my life" noting that "never once was there any suspicion of condescension in their attitude towards me as an African" (p. 122). Of his arrival at Ruskin he recalls:

> *Before I knew it I found myself the centre of a group of white faces, all eager to introduce themselves and to learn my christian name. Within minutes the warmth that emanated from them began to penetrate my smoke screen and melt my defensive shield, and to my great surprise I felt the tension within me relax as I naturally responded to the atmosphere of cordiality and helpfulness that is found only among genuine friends. Effortlessly they drew me out of my self-imposed isolation and treated me as one of themselves. (p. 122).*

We also gain insights into the first stirrings of trade unionism in West Africa. Stevens writes about the terrible conditions of Sierra Leone miners in the 1930s, paid 7½ cents a day "plus two cups of rice and a pinch of salt". He recalls, "They were little better than slaves. They soon developed the weary attitude of hopelessness. They cultivated a resignation born of despair, spirits, crushed, bellies empty." (p. 96) We get glimpses of the attitude of the mining company, workers organisation, the eventual willingness of the colonial government to tolerate trade unions with the pressure of war breaking out in Europe, the registration of the Mine Workers' Union in Marampa in 1939, and the actions, miscommunication, reactions, frustration, and anger which led to the first strike. Stevens was very much involved as an observer, an activist and later the mineworkers' first full-time paid union official.

In the pages which follow you will also find interesting glimpses of chieftaincy from the perspective of a trade unionist, leader of the opposition, Prime Minister, and President. Stevens discusses polygamy with an eye to helping the reader understand it; ethnicity and its effect on political life; education and its benefits and costs; workers and farmers, intellectuals who have "no sense" and illiterates who do.

Like many others active in politics during the nationalist period and thereafter, Stevens spent time in jail on several occasions. He was jailed by the colonial government, by the S.L.P.P., and by the military. These were important experiences eliciting stories about prison life and thoughts about what detention does to the spirit and to the body. Yet there is little romanticism here. While one sees the differences between political prisoners and those guilty of other crimes, more striking is a recognition of the fine line between those politicians within the walls and those without.

Siaka Stevens used to talk about his prison experiences, what he learned about courage from I.T.A. Wallace-Johnson and other prisoners, and how difficult prison life could be. In his autobiography he shares his thoughts. The periods in prison clearly played a major role in shaping Stevens' attitudes about adversity. He speaks here about what he learned from others in prisons and what he learned about himself. He recalls:

> *It seems to me an odd paradox... that I should have learned some of my deepest and truest lessons about freedom when I was behind bars as a political prisoner. There I discovered that freedom is a state of mind — something a man can create inside himself, whatever the circumstances. Even in prison — especially in prison, I felt free inside. Nobody could take my inner freedom away, whatever they tried to do to me. (p. 193).*

Siaka Stevens also played a vital part in that period of lively and open political competition which flowered with particular vigour in Sierra Leone between independence and the military coup of March 1967. During this period we see Stevens as populist, teacher, story teller, activist, nationalist party leader. He is championing the masses against elites, he is instructing party workers against violating election laws lest victory by nullified by unlawful practices, he is trying to raise bail for the imprisoned editor of the party newspaper *We Yone*. He can speak eloquently in Parliament against abuse of power, create a sense of obligation when seeking funds to keep his party's campaign vehicles in petrol, and convulse an audience in laughter with a Krio proverb critical of S.L.P.P. policies.

During the 1967 election campaign I travelled with Siaka Stevens (as I also did with the two S.L.P.P. candidates, Salia Jusu-Sheriff, then Minister of Education and S.L. Matturi, an M.P. and former Resident Minister under Milton Margai). Stevens campaigned from before sunrise to late in the evening and although he was at least twenty years older than anyone with him he never flagged. At seventy eight, one sees much of that same energy today. Part of his success then was his ability to communicate. He could explain why voters should not let chiefs tell them how to vote, discuss the differences between the powers of chiefs and that of the central government in ways they could understand, and urge people to vote for the A.P.C. He might say, as he did in Makeni in 1967:

> *Now the paramount chiefs have power too. When the English-*

man left he left two keys. He gave one to the country, one to the chief. Now if you have a strongbox with money in it and you have two keys, you give one key to your wife. You don't give two keys to your wife. [laughter] So here there is one key to the chief and you keep one key. If you let the chief tell you how to vote, you have given him two keys.

He might then go on to talk about what elections meant and why they were important, as he did in Kabala during that campaign:

Now the big power of the central government is only for five years because it is so great. So people only have power five years at a time because the power is so important. When the five years is up, we get to consider how those in power have done — whether we agree with the way the S.L.P.P. ran the government or whether we want a change. So if you don't like the way the S.L.P.P. has done things, when you see the palm tree (S.L.P.P. symbol), say, 'no thank you pa' and vote for the rising sun — for the A.P.C.

One of the issues which helped Stevens and the A.P.C. win a victory in 1967 was their skillful use of wide-spread opposition to the idea of a one-party state, proposed earlier by the S.L.P.P. There were other issues: equal justice for people in chiefdoms in court, fair access to the nation's mineral resources, national control of the foreign owned diamond mines, improving the economy and the condition of workers and farmers, limiting the power of chiefs, and improving educational opportunities.

The one-party issue was to return as a major political question after Siaka Stevens came to power. In an interview with him as Prime Minister in 1970 he commented: "I was opposed to an imposed one-party state. On the other hand, if the one-party state is voluntary, if the people by a gradual process decide that they want a one-party state, then that is all right with me." Stevens discusses his changing views about competitive parties in some detail in the chapters which follow — along with thoughts about the conditions for effective competition. The debate about the one-party state in Sierra Leone was a long one. When the one-party state came into being in 1978 it brought to an end one phase of Sierra Leone's political history and opened another. It did not end political competition, however. Most seats were contested in the 1982 Parliamentary elections. Among those contesting, 52% of the incumbent M.P.s lost their seats as did four of the nine Ministers who ran for re-election in contested seats.

There is much in these pages to interest anyone — thoughts about the temptations of corruption, views on ideologies, and free speech. Siaka Stevens talks about his supporters and his opponents. He remembers the first Prime Minister, Sir Milton Margai, with reverence and respect — even when he reflects on his imprisonment during that period. Perhaps most revealing of Stevens (and especially interesting to scholars for its new information and perspectives) is his assessment of the military, attempts on his life, coups he tried to forestall by gentle warnings to potential perpetrators, those that were attempted and failed, as well as the one that succeeded in 1967. Stevens brings this period vividly to life and in the process poses difficult questions about how one controls a military bent on intervention in political affairs. Siaka Stevens has been more successful than many political leaders in this regard and as such his thoughts, concerns, and actions are particularly important — especially in the context of yet another coup in Nigeria. This book is important in addition because it reveals much more than the life of Siaka Stevens. It is also about the process of development, decolonisation, and the dynamics of nation-building.

I do not wish to summarise this story for you — for Siaka Stevens can tell it far, far better than I can retell it or summarise. Indeed, I found this book difficult to put down, especially as Stevens talked and thought about the post-independence years. There is something very compelling about *What Life Has Taught Me: The Autobiography of President Siaka Stevens of Sierra Leone*. In part it is the insights into the thoughts, feelings, and actions of the man; in part the doubts, unresolved issues, and self-criticism; and also new information and fresh perspectives. Most important of all, Siaka Stevens gives us both a sense of this vital period in the history of Sierra Leone and a bit of the flavour of his role in it.

Fred M. Hayward

Madison, Wisconsin
February 3, 1984

SITTING AT MY DESK AT STATE HOUSE SOON AFTER I BECAME PRIME MINISTER IN 1968 AND....(see next page)

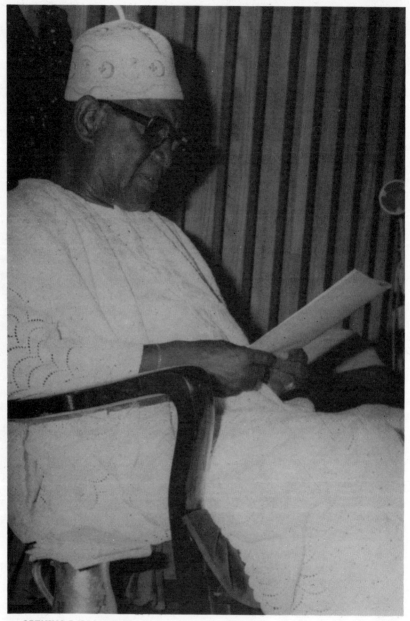

....OPENING PARLIAMENT SOME 14 YEARS LATER.

CHAPTER ONE

My Home

Recently I came home to Freetown after a busy visit in Europe. There had been too many meetings, too many people to see, too much sitting in the limited confines of an aeroplane. I was exhausted but happy because much had been achieved. I went to bed early that night, every limb aching with fatigue. As I lay there waiting for sleep to come, it was almost as if seventy years had dissolved before my eyes: I was a small boy again, lying on my straw mattress, my feet sore and my back weary. And again I was satisfied that my day had been a full one — a day of helping my father with errands, a day of companionship with my family and neighbours, a day of learning. Over the years the setting has changed. I more often travel by car or plane than walk barefoot as I did as a child. I no longer feel the hunger, or sense the relish, for food I remember from my boyhood. And although I still often meet the people from the villages, many of my acquaintances are world statesmen. Yet through this transformation I have brought with me the values of the village; and indeed, village life seems never far away from me. The standards of sincerity, hard-work and friendship that I learnt when young have proved to be true and lasting. I am grateful to my parents for the childhood they gave me. Unlike many statesmen, I had no birthright to guarantee me an important place in society.

I was born into the mud-and-straw world of the masses of the ordinary people of my country. My first patriotism was felt for the small rural community in which my values were moulded and my character formed. All my experience as a politician and a President have taken me back to those peasant ways — and African ways — of making society work by harnessing human compassion, making virtues of necessities and adhering to the great principle of mutual help. My childhood home and village life are models of the basic goodness which I have striven all my life to help Sierra Leone and Africa to re-capture on a larger scale. This is the theme of my story. By turning to our

15

African experience with reverence and love we can find the sources for the kind of society we want to build today in Africa and bequeath to the future. The peasant communities of my childhood had no material advantages. They were contented because they knew no other way of life, and hard-working because their very survival depended on the amount and quality of the food they could produce.

The village was like one large family, each household pooling its labour resources to work one another's farms in turn. The men planted and harvested the rice, the women weeded and watered it. While there was precious little money most of the year, nobody lacked the necessities of life, nobody in trouble was without help and sympathy, and in times of bad harvest, what little food there was was shared equally among the families. Hoarding, stealing, uncooperative or anti-social behavour were rare. Disputes there were, of course, human nature being what it is, but if these could not be settled amicably among the parties concerned, there was always the Chief to resort to, with the overall guidance the community gave through custom and the sheer necessity of mutual dependence.

My earliest memories are of little things — the sights and smells and tastes of childhood spent exploring elementary experience with a wonder I can still vividly recall. I remember my family at prayers. I remember the awesome steam trains, their disciplined pounding and wild screams and the smell of hot metal and steam in my nostrils. I remember our neighbours' smiles. I remember meals and the warming taste of our savoury rice and the feel of it in my belly, all my taste-buds and gastric senses alert with boyish hunger. Most of all I remember the love of my family and the wisdom and goodness of my father.

By worldly standards my father was a modest, simple man, but he filled the little world of our household and his orders and example dominated our lives. He was illiterate; but, thanks to the efforts and sacrifices he made, I became the first of his line to get a formal education. His goodness and uprightness gave him a wisdom — a kind of insight and human understanding which most educated people lack. He had what you might call a popular learning, a learning he had picked up by observing and listening and reaping the lore and traditions of rural life. Piety and unstinting toil earned him a place of respect in society and work and thrift gradually brought him the basis of a modest sufficiency: as a result I was able to go to school and get a good start in life. He seemed to inherit all the best virtues of his tribe, the Limbas.

The Limba tribe is one of the most important in Sierra Leone and is divided into a number of sub-tribes, such as the Tonko-Limbas, Brewa-Limbas and Saffroko Limbas. The people have earned themselves a reputation for palm wine tapping, honesty and fidelity. They are very rarely involved in court cases, and are in great demand in positions of trust.

The Limbas were not a self-seeking or deliberately ambitious people, and few of them sought contact with the Europeans and Creoles on the coast. Other tribes regarded them as backward and somewhat simple-minded. They remained cut off from the southern tribes for a long time, for there was little in Limba country to attract outsiders; the land was not particularly fertile, there were no large-scale mining operations, no industries, no railway connections and poor road links. Those that did not migrate to Freetown and other towns tended to live together under their own headmen, retain their tribal dress and customs and seemed slower than most tribes to integrate with city life.

Because of the stigma attached to them, many Limbas who came from the north-west of the territory bordering on Temne land passed themselves off as Temnes in the belief that this would add to their prestige. I was amused early in my Presidency when I was told that a certain countryman of mine who had long posed as a Temne went to the headmaster of the school where his son was a pupil and asked that the records be changed to show his son as a Limba. "After all," he said, "things are different now that we have a Limba as President."

The Gallinas tribe to which my mother belonged inhabit the extreme south-east of Sierra Leone near the border with Liberia where many of them live and they pass from one country to the other regardless of the boundary. On my mother's side, I was related to King Siaka of Geindayma (Gendama) who was a powerful man in Gallinas country in the 1890s. He even corresponded with Queen Victoria. Gendama today still bears traces of its historic importance — the old road (a rare thing in the Protectorate in the old days), the ancient cannon guarding the line of the creek which leads up from the Atlantic, and the reminders of the slave trade that once brought an obnoxious prosperity to the little town. When I paid a visit to Gendama in 1974 the old people performed some of their atavistic ceremonies in honour of the dead. In the middle of these echoes of the past I landed by helicopter — a nice juxtaposition of tradition and technology which is typical of modern Sierra Leone. I warmed to the old-timer who told me on my walk-about, "I wish King Siaka could get up from his grave and see what is happening in Gendama today!"

Perhaps the most outstanding thing about the Gallinas is the fact that it is the only tribe in this part of Africa which developed a writing of its own, the Vai Alphabet. It is said that it originated when an elder of the tribe observed that a European trader made some marks on a piece of paper as a commercial transaction was being negotiated and later referred to his notes to recall facts and figures with great accuracy. The elder then decided to devise his own system of recording relevant facts — a system which was eventually developed by members of the tribe into a full alphabet. One would have expected such an improvised system of writing to be ideographic, as most of the early systems were, with various signs standing for objects, concepts or figures. The remarkable thing about the Vai alphabet is that the elder who conceived it hit straight away on the idea of a phonetical system with signs standing for various sounds used in the tribal dialect. If I ever get some time for leisure in my life, I would like to do some research on the old Vai culture.

I have often said that I am a true representative of my country: my father came from the far north and my mother from the south east. I was born in the centre, at Moyamba, and spent much of my childhood there among the Mende people. Later, I was educated in Freetown and worked among the Creoles there. I represented the Freetown West constituency in Parliament, and I married a girl of Temne-Susu origin from the north west. I am proud to have such a mixed background. I think it has helped me in understanding my countrymen. Divisiveness has been one of the key problems in Sierra Leone; too many people have let tribal, ethnic or religious loyalties come between them and their neighbours. It has often surprised me that people do not always put their fellow beings first. In the village where I grew up, helping other people was one of the first first lessons that every child learnt. My father was a strong upholder of the values of kindliness to others — always, in the case of his children, tempered with firmness!

My father's family, like most people living in the northern region of Sierra Leone, were farmers as had been their forebears for generations past. Their main crop was upland rice which was grown with great physical hardship on the steep hills north and east of the territory, some of which rose to heights of 2,000 ft. On the plains, 400 ft. above sea level, much of which was swamp, other crops were grown such as groundnuts, millet, cassava, sweet potatoes and maize. But whatever the crop, nothing grew without sheer hard work and the constant attention of the farmers and their families.

My father's neighbours were peace-loving, honest men and women who derived pleasure after a day's hard labour from one another's companionship around a calabash of palm wine, relaxing with their children or playing Warri — a game for two people who use a special board and some pebbles. When we were adolescents, my father enjoyed telling us about the earlier years of his life. He used to recall that after the evening meal, and when he had finished the various chores expected of him, he would join the group of older men who gathered each evening to chat about the state of the crops, local happenings and the latest news gleaned from people who had returned from places further afield. He listened to their grouses about the injustice of the Protectorate hut tax and heard how rumour had it that the monies so collected were being used for developing Freetown and the Colony instead of the Protectorate where schools, hospitals, roads, railways and bridges were desperately needed. He heard mention of fascinating jobs that some local boys had landed in Freetown and the complaints that the opportunities there were attracting the cream of Protectorate youth away from the land.

My father was a man who liked to see things for himself and he was interested to see what was going on in the Colony. So, as he had an adventurous spirit and, at that time, litle responsibility, he set off on the long trek to Freetown — a distant, terrifying metropolis by the standards of my father's world. But because he had never had the opportunity of an education he found when he got there that the only openings that were available to him were in poorly paid labouring jobs. He decided that if it was a question of living below the bread line he would rather do that back home, where at least food and lodging would be assured. But just as he was about to leave he caught sight of a recruiting poster for the Royal West African Frontier Force which somebody interpreted for his benefit. It seemed the very job for him. He presented himself at the headquarters and was immediately accepted.

The Sierra Leone Battalion, which was formerly known as the Police Frontier Force, numbered in those days 629 men, 550 of whom were privates. Its officers and men had recently been highly commended for the part they played in the Ashanti War in the Gold Coast in 1900 when, as scouts for the advancing column that went to the relief of Kumasi, they discovered the enemy and fought with such courage that one of their number, Private Amadu, was promoted sergeant on the spot and was later awarded the Distinguished Service Order. In those days, of course, it was common practice for the colonial powers to use troops from one Colony to conquer another, or to put down a rebellion.

Unfortunately, Africans innocently lent themselves to this practice as the spirit of African unity and solidarity had not yet swept the Continent.

As a raw recruit my father was paid 6d. a day which was raised to 9d. upon his appointment being confirmed. He was also issued with trousers and boots. This may seem so normal a procedure for an army recruit that people may wonder at my bothering to mention it. But in fact had my father joined up a few years later, in 1909, he would have been ordered to walk barefoot and wear khaki shorts. Nobody could give a reason for this extraordinary action on the part of the authorities, but our army boys marched bootless for thirty years or more until "agitators" like the late I. T. A. Wallace-Johnson brought pressure to bear and got the issue of boots re-introduced.

I remember my father telling me of the time he was sent to Liberia. The soldiers did not get paid on time, so one day they raised such hell that the Liberian government had to ask Freetown to recall them! When he was back in Freetown he took his turn mounting guard at Government House, the official residence of the British Colonial Governor. I often wonder what he would have said had he known that one day his own son would become the lawful occupier of Government House. I know he would have been very happy and perhaps a little surprised that a guard's son should become President. Whenever I think of him standing on guard outside the very building in which I now labour as Chief Executive of my country, I feel a surge of pride in my roots and a renewed sense of oneness with my people.

Sir Leslie Probyn, who was Governor at that time, must have made a very favourable impression on my father, for when I was born he named me Siaka Probyn. My name of Probyn was not the only reminder of Dad's army career, for our family name was permanently changed as a result of this period of his life. He enlisted as James Tibin and was discharged as James Stevens. It seemed that when the European officers yelled 'Tibin!' it sounded like 'Steven', so much so that many people thought his name actually was Steven or Stevens, and as he raised no objection, it stuck and he continued to use it from then on.

Before long my father was posted to Moyamba, about 75 miles from Freetown, as part of a military expedition launched by the British Administration. There he became orderly to a sergeant major called Norman, whose grand-daughter, Miatah Massaquoi, was staying with him. My father married her and later she became my mother.

From Moyamba my father was posted to Gbonjeima which was at that time a stronghold of the Mende tribal warriors. The Mendes were, and are, one of the largest tribes in Sierra Leone. They were more fortunate than other tribes in the hinterland in that when Western education eventually began to penetrate inland from the Creole-populated strip of coastland known as the Colony, schools were established in their territory some little time before they were in the more northerly parts of the country. As a result, the Mendes became the first of all other tribes in Sierra Leone to be able to challenge the Creoles for the so-called 'white collar' jobs which had previously been the sole preserve of the educated Creoles.

Soon after my brother Kortu was born, the period for which my father had signed on for military service expired. Instead of re-enlisting for another nine years he asked to be discharged. Undoubtedly, the increasing responsibilities of marriage coupled with fatherhood had had a settling effect on him and made him anxious to establish roots, to be his own boss and master in his own house. Maybe, too, his boots were wearing out and he had heard the rumour that he would shortly be expected to march barefoot!

With his gratuity from the army of £20 he bought a supply of liquor, tobacco and provisions and set up a small shop in Gbonjeima. Whenever the stock needed replenishing my mother had to travel a distance of ten miles each way to Sembehun on the Bagru River to buy what was necessary from the large commercial firms there. It is really only in retrospect that I am able to appreciate fully how tough was the fight for survival in those days. At the time it seemed no hardship that our women should trudge miles on end down dusty tracks under the scorching sun, weighted down either by pregnancy or a baby strapped to the back, or both, plus an enormous head-load of items they hoped to trade for a few miserable pennies profit. It was all a part of the everyday scene, all we had ever known. There was no easy way to keep body and soul together.

My father took two other wives, Mabondo and Memuna, both of whom belonged to leading families in Gbonjeima. This was a great help to my mother who now had others with whom she could share her work load. My mother was a devout Muslim and my father was a Christian. He had chosen Christianity because he sincerely believed in its doctrine, even though it is not a religion ideally suited to the traditional African way of life. It had gained the title of the 'white man's religion', and, like all European ideas and ways of doing things, it was un-African and quite

SIR LESLIE PROBYN, THE BRITISH GOVERNOR OF SIERRA LEONE, WITH MEMBERS OF HIS STAFF IN 1904. MY MIDDLE NAME, PROBYN, WAS GIVEN TO ME BY MY FATHER IN HONOUR OF THE MAN WHOM HE HAD SERVED AS A GUARD AT GOVERNMENT (NOW STATE) HOUSE IN THE YEAR BEFORE I WAS BORN.

SIR EDWARD MEREWETHER, THE BRITISH COLONIAL GOVERNOR AT THE TIME WHEN I BECAME A SCHOOLBOY IN MOYAMBA. HE IS SEATED IN THE CENTRE OF A GROUP IN THE GARDEN OF GOVERNMENT HOUSE WHERE SOME OF MY OFFICIAL RECEPTIONS ARE NOW HELD. THE GARDEN HAS HARDLY CHANGED SINCE THIS PHOTOGRAPH WAS TAKEN NEARLY THREE QUARTERS OF A CENTURY AGO.

THE COLONIAL GOVERNOR INSPECTS A GUARD OF HONOUR. BOOTS AND SPATS WERE STILL BEING ISSUED FOR CEREMONIAL OCCASIONS WHEN THIS PHOTOGRAPH WAS TAKEN IN 1911...

.BUT THE FULL KIT OF THE ORDINARY SOLDIER IN THE WEST AFRICAN REGIMENT, AS LAID OUT FOR THE PURPOSE OF THESE PHOTOGRAPHS, DID NOT INCLUDE SUCH LUXURY ITEMS.

*MY FATHER IN THE LATE 1920s,
AT A TIME WHEN PHOTOGRAPHY
WAS STILL FAR FROM PERFECT
IN THE PROVINCIAL TOWNS OF
SIERRA LEONE.*

*THE TOMBSTONE ON MY FATHER'S
GRAVE IN MOYAMBA. THE INSCRIP-
TION READS:*

*Here Lie the Remains of
Our Dear Father
Alimamy James Stevens
Sgt 711 S.L. BWA - FFS 1891-1908
Regimental Sgt Major
Liberian Frontier Force 1908-1909
Native Tribal Ruler Moyamba
Kaiyamba Chiefdom Medalist S.L.
1898-1899
Who Departed This Life on
Easter Day 1st April 1941
R.I.P.
By His Children
Siaka, Momodu, M'Balu & Edward*

MY FATHER'S HOUSE IN MOYAMBA WHERE I WAS BORN IN 1905. THE TWO-STOREY HOUSE TO THE RIGHT OF OURS DID NOT EXIST IN MY CHILDHOOD AND NO CAR HAD EVER BEEN SEEN IN OUR TOWN.

TOWER HILL BARRACKS IN FREETOWN IN 1908. AT THE TIME WHEN MY FATHER WAS IN THE COLONIAL ARMY ONLY WHITE SOLDIERS WERE STATIONED THERE. THE BUILDING HAS SURVIVED AND IS STILL IN USE.

alien to us. Because of these difficulties many Africans, although attracted by the fundamental precepts of the Christian church, have been unwilling to participate because it would go against their traditional life style. One of the stumbling-blocks for any African considering Christianity is that of monogamy versus polygamy. This was certainly a problem for my father, for although he was a devout Christian, he saw nothing wrong with polygamy.

The fact that he officiated in church as a sidesman made his practice of polygamy doubly hard for the clergy to suffer, but no matter how often the pastor admonished him for the number of wives he had, it had no effect whatsoever. I well remember the day when the pastor brought to our two-storey mud-brick house the bishop of the Mission, an American who was visiting Sierra Leone. Together they tackled my father on the subject of polygamy and a fierce argument ensued in an upstairs room. Then my father called to me to bring up my mothers. There were five of them and they stood dutifully in line before him. "Now this one," he said, indicating my real mother, "is Siaka's mother. This one, as you can see, is suckling her newly born child. This one next to her is about to give birth to her second child. This one has year-old twins and this one was put in my care by my dying father. Now I would like you to choose from among them the one I ought to keep and those I must drive away." The two church dignatories shook their heads in bewilderment and were forced to concede defeat. "As I have said many times before," my father said, "you may take Siaka and Kortu and do with them what you like, but please leave me in peace to live with my wives."

The human usefulness of polygamy for my father's household and for the society in which it was embedded shows how the African has always evolved the social conventions best suited to his environment, without interference from outside. The attitude of the church authorities shows how alien dogmas, insensitively applied, however well intentioned, are a negative — even destructive — influence on Africa. If polygamy dies out— and already many husbands find the economic advantages of monogamy irresistible — it will be because of changes in the total social and economic context and, in particular, because of the changing role and aspirations of women. It will not be because of the strength of European ethical conventions, or because there is anything morally wrong with polygamy. I have always been amused at outsiders' attitudes to this highly organised African custom. The parting words from a kindly Cockney butcher to me when I left London in 1948 were,

"So yer'll be returnin' 'ome to yer nine wives, lad". I could do nothing but reply with a wink (while I laughed inwardly at the note of envy in his voice), "How right you are! But what can a man do? You see, we have no brothels in Africa!"

Polygamous marriages are entered into in such a serious manner that the rights of each wife, from the most senior to the most junior are highly protected. Far from each wife being jealous of the others, they are usually very companionable together, sharing household duties and becoming firm friends. Indeed often a wife may be selected by the senior wife who, in any case, must always be consulted before a marriage takes place. Each woman knows her place and what is expected of her. It is the senior wife alone who receives orders from her husband to be passed on to the other women, and it is she who decides which of them shall share the man's bed each night. It is the duty of the wife whose turn it is to sleep with the husband to cook his food that day and prepare his room.

To my mind the African has far more wisdom and honesty than the European in his attitude towards relationships between men and women, for it is often unrealistic to advocate one woman for one man. Harmony and happiness in a monogamist's household often depend very much on the man's success at secrecy coupled with the wife's willingness to turn a blind eye. One might say that in every monogamist there is the natural polygamist struggling to get out, and the fact that in non-African countries brothels abound, divorce courts are overworked and paternity orders are hotly contested suggests that monogamy is not so blissful as its supporters would have us believe.

The African Christian gets round the difficult question of monogamy demanded by the Christian Church by marrying one wife according to the rites of the Church and other wives according to native customs. Coming from a home both Christian and Muslim I feel I have gained an insight into each of these religions and, although I am nothing more than a layman on religious topics, I do have very decided views. It has always seemed to me that Islam has much to commend it as religion for the African. The few demands it makes on him are straightforward and only concerned with practical religion. It does not interfere with his customs and traditional way of life. In the case of Christianity, however, worship does not seem to be so simple. The differences between sects of the Christian Church may be impossible to bridge, whereas although there are as many as 72 sects in the Muslim faith, members of any sect can worship quite happily in the same mosque.

But a Roman Catholic may be unwilling to attend a Methodist service and an Anglican would feel unfamiliar with a Greek Orthodox service. Christians seem, then, separated rather than united, even when they belong to the same country and race as Catholics and Protestants do in Northern Ireland.

I believe that the simpler the demands made on man by any religion the more likelihood there is of him leading a saintlier life. This is not to decry the virtues of love, charity, tolerance and humility, but rather to emphasise that so long as a man lives decently and properly there should be no question of his private affairs being interefered with by any authoratative body, religious or otherwise. And I know that in his own way my father fulfilled his obligations. He loved and cared for all his wives and children; he was a good father and good husband and a valuable member of the community. He sought God with a sincere heart in depth of faith, which is the essence of all true religion. And yet all the pastor could do was complain that my father was a polygamist!

My father's army training had made him into a disciplinarian. Sometimes my brother and I were a little afraid of him, although we always respected him. As soon as we were able to walk we had to join the menfolk and lend a hand with the cultivation of crops, the care of animals, the building of shelters — in short, the art of survival. We were all expected to pull our weight, whatever our age.

But it was not all work and no play. Kortu and I were mischievous young boys and sometimes we tried to escape from the daily chores so that we could run off into the woods and hunt small animals, climb trees, play rowdy games or search for fruit and berries to eat. But when we returned home punishment awaited us in the form of a good spanking and extra tasks to perform.

Some of the pranks we got up to caused my parents much anxiety, for we were highly adventurous and scared of nothing. One day my father bought a bull which be believed was securely tethered in the compound. Kortu, who was very young at the time, wandered outside on his own and became interested in this fierce looking beast, going up close and no doubt teasing it. Suddenly a piercing yell from Kortu brought everybody rushing out of the house in alarm. The bull had broken loose, charged at his tormentor and made a deep ugly gash on his forehead. It was lucky for Kortu that he lived to tell the tale and was left with no more than a scar as a permanent reminder of his foolhardiness.

My father, who had never received a formal education, was very anxious that his own children should be educated. In fact, he had managed to pick up a little bit of reading and counting in the army, but not enough to satisfy him. I remember how he used to struggle with reading his Bible on Sunday afternoons. Because of this he was more determined than ever that his children should have the benefit of education. He was also greatly egged on by a neighbour of ours, Margaret Barber, affectionately known as Mammy Barber, who always said "Sergeant Stevens, sen dem pikin go school O!"

He told me once how hard he prayed when in Gbonjeima that he might get something to do in Moyamba so that he could send us to school. His prayer was answered, for in 1911, with the help of his army discharge certificate, he was appointed as contractor to supply food to the central prison in Moyamba.

Although I had been born in Moyamba I could remember nothing about it, for I was only an infant when we left. Now, at the age of 6 or so, I returned to my birth place as a stranger, and a very astonished stranger at that. Gbonjeima, the only place I had ever known, had seemed very big to my childish eyes and the idea that bigger places might exist never entered my head. Suddenly, as I found myself in this large, busy and important-looking town, Gbonjeima shrivelled into insignificance in my mind. Two and even three storied houses lined the streets; there were two schools, a number of big commercial firms, the Circuit Court which was the Supreme Court of the Protectorate, the central prison and the gallows which the colonial administration found to be very necessary in those days.

Within a very short time of our arrival in Moyamba the town was colourful with flags and bunting to celebrate the coronation of King George V of Great Britan and Ireland, the British Dominions beyond the seas, Defender of the Faith, Emperor of India and under whose sovereignty we also were. I had no idea what all the excitement was about but I remember being given a china mug which stunned me at the time because it was the first gift of such splendour I had ever received. When the message somehow got through to me that this glistening coloured object was mine, I clutched it possessively to my chest, afraid that somebody who hadn't got one themselves might take it from me. We sat at long tables in the Market Place and stuffed ourselves with food, much of which I had never tasted before.

I soon became very well acquainted with the central prison because every day of my father's contract I helped carry heavy loads of cassava, greens and other food and deliver them at the prison gates. I shall never forget those daily journeys as long as I live. It is not the memory of the loads I carried nor the distance I had to travel that huants me, because my home was not that far from the prison, but the torture I suffered from tiny flea-like insects called jiggers which jump about in the dust and settle on human flesh, especially between the toes and on the soles of the feet. Once they attach themselves to you they never let go, but burrow their way into the flesh and remain there, sucking the blood and growing bigger and bigger until the pain they cause becomes unbearable. It was impossible to avoid these jiggers because the tracks we had to use were infested with them. There were no tarred roads at that time and no heavy lorries to crush the sharp stones, so that trying to negotiate that gritty uneven surface while jiggers burrowed their way painfully into the soles of my feet became a positive nightmare. A woman in our household who was given the job of removing these pests from my feet made the pain doubly worse by treating the sores with limes.

I always associate jiggers with *akarah*, a sort of cake made from a mixture of banana and rice which is fried in palm oil after having been allowed to ferment for a while. It was delicious and was made by a Mammy Tigidah, who was our next-door neighbour. After these jiggers had sucked blood from my toes all night, I used to wake up in the morning feeling so hungry that the one longing I had was to fill my stomach with *akarah*. I promised myself that when I became an engine driver and got a salary at the end of each month, I would buy lots of Mammy Tigidah's *akarah*.

To be an engine driver was my greatest ambition. On every possible occasion I used to rush to the railway station to watch the daily passenger train arrive. With hero worship in my eyes, I gazed at the engine driver going through his routine: refreshing himself from a bottle, checking a valve, moving a brass lever, touching this gadget and that, waiting for the guard's whistle and then touching his oily cap in a farewell greeting as he brought his steaming, hissing monster to life. To me he was no ordinary man, but somebody very special, the ultimate in manhood. How could a boy aspire to be anything less?

I began my education at the mission school of the Evangelical United Brethren. The present Harford boarding school for girls was then a day school and the girls used to join us in the school building for lessons and return home after school. I remember many of them — Virginia and Beatrice Morgan, Laura Dove, Hawa Jumu, Amanda and Nellie Weaver and Flora Caulker, and several U.B.C. missionaries, such as Eta Odle and Miss Shanklin, who used to invite us to their mission home on Sunday afternoons and give us sweets. Because of my association with the Harford, I am sometimes tempted to describe myself as an old boy of the Harford Girls' School!

It is common practice in Sierra Leone for a man living in the more remote areas to send his children to live with friends in the principal towns so that they can attend the schools there. As soon as my father moved to Moyamba many of his friends took advantage of the situation. Quite suddenly our household increased by about 15 boys! For Kortu and me it was the greatest fun having so many companions with whom to play and share the work, but I cannot imagine how my parents retained their sanity, especially at mealtimes when pandemonium broke loose. The food was put into two big bowls each of which was allocated to seven or eight boys. Immediately the bowls appeared on the mud floor they were pounced upon by a ravenous, shouting hoard, each boy shoving and elbowing his way to get nearest to the food, some grabbing portions of rice and stuffing them into whatever container was most handy, others cramming as much as they could into their mouths.

Fortunately for my parents our days were so planned that there was little time for us to fool around and get up to mischief. My military-minded father saw to that. We had to be up at 6 a.m. to take food to the prison. On our return we had a bath and breakfast and then went to school. Our afternoons were taken up buying the prisoners' food for the following day, fetching wood for the fire, running errands and doing any other job that my parents asked us to do. When all these chores were properly completed, we were free to swim in the river and enjoy ourselves. Our pleasures were simple and we were so thrilled with the little that was offered us. Bits of wood, a rusty wheel rim, old boxes, pebbles, all kinds of junk were converted into playthings and highly prized. I never possessed a toy from a shop. To spend hard-earned money on such trivia when there were stomachs to fill and bodies to clothe would have been unthinkable.

My father established contact with a lot of prominent people all over Sierra Leone during these years because Moyamba was the centre for what was known as the circuit court, which was the highest court in the Protectorate as it then was. Now and again chiefs and other prominent people from as far away as Kabala, Kenema and Kailahun would meet in Moyamba for sessions of the court, as well as prominent lawyers from Freetown, such as Pa Barrett. I used to accompany my father when he visited the Paramount Chief or some other big personality in the evening, and I would sit down in a corner to listen to their conversation. This is customary, and it gives a child, even at that early age, an insight into what is going on. The District Commissioner was often the subject of conversation at these pow-wows and he seemed to me, in my childish way, to be a bogeyman. The D.C. was held in dread all over the country — so much so that when my father called us to prayers he would readily add "And save us, O Lord, from the trouble of the D.C."! I suppose all children have a figure in their imagination that they hold in fear and dread, but perhaps the District Commissioner was a more unusual choice than the customary witches and goblins that have a place in most people's recollections.

As I look back on my childhood, I am often surprised that it is the small and seemingly unimportant incidents that are most vivid in my mind. In retrospect I can see that often these events were more special than one gave credit for at the time. One such incident I remember in particular. My mother, being of the Islamic faith, dressed Kortu and me in Muslim dress when we first went to school. I liked this type of garment very much because under the flowing gown we wore satin shirts which had two very useful pockets. As we passed through my father's shop on our way to school we used to pick up biscuits and smuggle them out in these concealed pockets. We thought it was a huge joke to trick my father, who was always so smart and alert. Then one morning he called us back. "Come here a minute," he said, his hands immediately alighting on the tell-tale bulges in our top pockets. "So this is what you get up to when my back is turned, is it?"

My father taught me humility and honesty, disciplined me, but never to excess. His punishments always fitted our crimes, and I admired him for his sense of fairness. His determination to do right for his sons impressed me, so that even now, years later, I can look back on my childhood with warmth and affection, remembering it with happiness —apart, of course, from the jiggers!

CHAPTER TWO

My Schooling

When I was nine years old my father decided that the time had come to send me to Freetown where I would have the chance of a higher standard of education and an opportunity to mix with boys from many different tribes and social backgrounds. For children at school in Sierra Leone today it is hard to imagine what education was like when I was a boy. The subjects taught in schools then were not geared towards producing good African citizens, knowledgeable about their culture and heritage, but rather merely to produce men who would be capable of holding administrative posts in the colonial regime. Children found themselves learning about British history and politics, while they knew very little about their own country. It was only recently that I learnt the name of one of our major rivers, at a time when the Thames, the Seine and the Tiber were names already familiar to me. This has struck me as being absurd and I have consistently campaigned for a more African orientated syllabus in our schools. But in my young days it was not only the lessons that left much to be desired; the emphasis was on educating the Colony — the small colonial enclave around Freetown — not the Protectorate, where the vast majority of the people lived; and in the Protectorate those who did receive a formal education were usually of chiefly and other leading families. I need hardly say that this was a very undesirable situation. On a personal level, however, it makes the determination and doggedness of my father all the more remarkable. I was not the son of a chief and my family was poor; my prospects of an education in the Colony were far from bright. If it had not been for the sacrifices my father made I probably would not even have learnt to spell my name! But he had set his heart on sending me to Freetown, and his wish eventually came true. He spent some time looking for a reliable guardian for me, for Freetown was no place for a young and inexperienced country lad to roam around where he pleased. Fortunately an old army friend of my father had a son, a train guard called Mr.

Smith. He and his wife Okeke lived in Kissy, which was then a little village a few miles outside of Freetown, and they kindly agreed to take me under their wing.

Clutching my few possessions, I set out with my father to board the train from Moyamba to Kissy. It was my first parting from my family, but I was so excited about the prospect of this great adventure and so full of hopes and plans for the future, that any feelings of sadness I might have had were temporarily numbed. And above all, awaiting me was the tremendous thrill of five-and-a-half to six hours journey on a train. The railway was still quite a novelty even for my father, for the whole project was only begun eighteen years previously and was not completed until 1906.

I can remember feeling very glad that my father was to accompany me on the train journey, for although I was thrilled at the thought of independence and a new school in a huge and exciting town, I was also a little anxious. At each stop there were crowds of people standing on the station platforms, greeting newly arrived friends or waving goodbye to departing relatives. There were women traders who tried to sell their wares to the hungry and thirsty passengers. Most of all I remember the feeling of butterflies in my stomach as we crawled at a snail's pace across a deep ravine. I peered down far below me at the swirling water. I recall with shame how I half prayed for some dreadful catastrophe that would send us hurtling down the ravine. That would have been a real adventure! It seems impossible to me now that a nine year-old boy should be so unaware of death and destruction. And yet one cannot help but admire the simplicity of youth which sees only adventure in even the most desperate situations.

It seemed as if all too soon we arrived at Waterloo Station, which was only about twenty five miles away from Freetown. We were told that the train would wait there for some considerable time. "In that case," my father said to our carriage companions, with whom he had made friends, "we might as well get out and stretch our legs." As he intended to combine this exercise with a drink of palm wine, he told me to wait patiently where I was until he returned. After a while I felt the carriage give a jolt, then to my horror the train started to move off. I leant out of the window, shouted and gesticulated, but there was no sign of my father and I could not stop the train. It was late when the train pulled into Kissy station and it was a somewhat anxious and subdued youngster who clambered down from the carriage and with a very crushed bundle tucked under one arm, stood timidly and apprehensively on the platform to take stock of the lonely situation in which he found himself. "Are you lost, boy?" a kindly official asked me. I explained to him what had happened and he took care of me until my father arrived some hours later to claim me and take me to my new home.

Before he left me to return to Moyamba he impressed upon me my good fortune in being able to attend school in the capital, in having Mr. and Mrs. Smith to care for me and in the great future that lay within my grasp if I made the utmost of every opportunity that would come my way. "Remember, son," he said, "whatever you do here will reflect on us at home and I know you won't discredit us by shirking your duties either in school or in the house. Do whatever you are asked to do willingly and to the best of your ability. If you get into a mess that is not of your own making I will always stand by you, but I'll never lend a hand to a sloven or a sloth." He stressed that whilst it was important to be proud of my own tribe, my home and my parents, I must respect the fact that strangers I would meet would feel equally proud of theirs, that I must never let these feelings turn to arrogance or allow them to come between me and my friends, that I must learn to be tolerant and understanding of other people's customs and ideas.

As I take stock of what now seems to be an increasingly intolerant world, I cannot but be grateful for my father's advice. It was good advice and I have always tried to practise it. If only more people could have heard Dad's words of wisdom!

I tried to be as helpful as possible in the Smith household. My day began at 5 a.m. when I would light the fire and sweep the compound. Once the fire was hot enough I would warm up the stew or palaver sauce which had been prepared the previous evening, and on Mondays, Wednesdays and Fridays I would pack some of this with rice in a 'chop box' which I carried to Kissy railway station for Mr. Smith to take with him on his train journey up country. On my return to the house at about 7 a.m. it was time to escort Mrs. Smith to Freetown to help carry the large bundles of merchandise which she traded there. As soon as I off-loaded these, I rushed back to Kissy as fast as my legs would carry me to bath and prepare myself for school which was the Wesleyan Primary School in Kissy. Even when school finished at 3 p.m. there was no time for me to hang around, chat and play games with my schoolmates for my schedule was so tight that it simply did not allow for it. Instead I had to rush back home, cook a pot of rice for the evening meal, sweep the yard again to rid it of mango leaves and other rubbish that had collected during the day, and then leave for Freetown once more to collect Mrs.

FREETOWN AT THE TURN OF THE CENTURY AND ALSO AS IT WAS SOME 15 YEARS
LATER WHEN I FIRST ARRIVED IN THE CITY AS A NINE-YEAR OLD. THIS PHOTOGRAPH
BY DIONYSIUS LEOMY WAS TAKEN FROM THE TOWER OF ST. GEORGE'S CATHEDRAL
LOOKING EASTWARD OVER HOWE STREET. THE TALLER BUILDING ON THE LEFT IS
THE BACK OF WHAT WAS THEN THE VICTORIA HOTEL.

COLONIAL OFFICIALS AND THEIR LADIES MOVED AROUND THE CITY IN HAMMOCKS
CARRIED BY BAREFOOTED SIERRA LEONEAN PORTERS.

THE KING JIMMY SLAUGHTER HOUSE AND MARKET AS IT WAS IN THE DAYS WHEN, AS A BOY SERVANT, I WAS HELPING MY "MISSUS" WITH HER SHOPPING AND HAD MY FIRST ENCOUNTER WITH THE FREETOWN ROGUES.

THE PUBLIC WASH HOUSE IN FREETOWN WHICH WE USED BEFORE PIPE-BORNE WATER BECAME AVAILABLE.

Smith and her wares which now included a supply of fresh fish or meat and other provisions that she had bought for our supper. On Tuesdays, Thursdays and Saturdays my next duty was to meet Mr. Smith at the railway station and carry back his empty food container. After I had eaten my meal and washed the dishes it was time for bed, and I was certainly ready for it!

Alternatively, sometimes after school I would go out selling kerosene by the bottle and we had a special way of shouting 'Ker-ro-sene-ya' at the top of our voices. We liked hawking kerosene: we young rascals could get together and swap news. Heaven only knows what we discussed in those days but we were always chattering away.

It was only now that I learnt to talk Krio. Coming from up-country I did not know much Krio and the boys used to laugh at me, but soon I was luxuriating in phrases like, 'You sabbi but you nor know!' or 'Gi am fedder!' To me it was a delightful language, full of the opulent creativity and imagination of the Creole people. It had a bit of French, a bit of Portuguese, a bit of Yoruba in it. It was as rich as a patchwork of divers bits of the history of Sierra Leone.

Saturday was always a particularly busy day, because it was laundry day. In addition to my normal chores I had to help with the washing. Mrs. Smith did not go to Freetown on Saturdays and spent most of her time preparing food for the following day. I can still remember the taste of that food: groundnut stew, pepper soup, the famous Creole palaver sauce, peppery beef, tripe, bologie leaves, palm oil and dried 'bonga'. There was also foo-foo, which we helped to make by pounding softened cassava with a pestle and mortar. It was a boring job, but my efforts were always rewarded when I sat down to eat the delicious food. I did not resent my heavy work load, for I was grateful for the kindness the Smiths had shown me by taking me in, but one thing that did annoy me was the attitude of many Creole families towards children from the Protectorate who were put into their care. My position in the household was that of a servant. I was even something of a slave to the children! With me around to fetch and carry, sweep and clean, they were free to play, study or do whatever they liked. At my home in Moyamba everybody in the house was expected to pull their weight until too old or infirm to do so. Sometimes during those days in Kissy I had firmly to repeat to myself my father's advice always to be willing and helpful. Often it was these words alone that helped me to check my tears, for I felt like crying at what seemed to me such injustice. Although at the time I would never have guessed that one day I would be grateful for this training, I now see that this self-discipline was an invaluable lesson. I often think that if it had not been for this I would still be somewhere at the bottom of the ladder. Moreover, because my playtime was so limited it became all the more precious to me, and I learnt to use it well, not wasting one minute of it. My days in Kissy taught me the basis of successful living: how to work hard and how to play hard, and, most important of all, how to keep the two separate.

Kissy in those days was cut off from Freetown by thick bush and during the day people went there to gather firewood, search for fruit and trap small animals for the stewpot. Gradually over the years more and more of the bush was cleared to make way for buildings and roads until the village of Kissy and the city of Freetown became so linked that it was difficult to tell where one ended and the other began. A house that marked the boundary between the two places was owned at one time by an ex-telegraph inspector I knew, called Mr. Leigh.

When I first visited Freetown I thought it was a terrifying place and whenever I accompanied Mrs. Smith with her loads during my first few weeks there I kept close behind her for fear of getting lost among the pushing, jostling crowds of people. There were so many streets to confuse me, such high buildings hemming me in, hazards to watch for, like bicycles and hammocks barging their way through the congested thoroughfare, with traders noisily touting their wares and hosts of beggars squatting hopefully outside the large stores. One worry was spared me at least, for there were no cars in those days to add to my confusion.

On my first visit to Freetown, I returned home to my 'Missus' — as I called Mrs. Smith — with cuts all over my feet. I was so busy looking up awestruck at the tops of buildings, the like of which I had never seen before — instead of watching the road — that I stepped on some sharp pieces of broken glass. The tallest building I had ever seen was a Syrian trader's house in Moyamba, with sleeping quarters above the shop. I had never imagined the rest of the world could be so different.

I found it very difficult to get used to the number of rogues that abounded in Freetown. At home in Moyamba most people did what they could to help one another and few would think of taking something that was not theirs by right. In spite of Mrs. Smith's frequent warnings to me to be on my guard, I still found it hard to mistrust people.

A few months after I had arrived in the capital, Mrs. Smith sent me to buy a glass for a kerosene lamp from a French store called Perineaux, near the Sawpit Wharf steps. As I was standing in the street, gazing in bewilderment into the store and wondering if it was the right place, a man came up to me. He was wearing the usual threadbare trousernine and an old black jacket. "Can I help you?" he asked me kindly, no doubt aware that I was a stranger in town. I told him what I wanted and showed him the money I had in my hand. "Give me the money and wait here a minute," he said, "I'll go in and get it for you." I was impressed by his friendliness and gladly handed over the cash, for being somewhat shy by nature, big stores overwhelmed me as they still do. As the time went by and he did not appear I began to be anxious and timidly peered into the shop to see if I could see him. There was no sign of him and the store was preparing to shut down for the night. My heart sank into my stomach and tears of anger and disappointment welled up in my eyes. Now my problem was: how to return home? I could not dare tell my Missus I'd been gulled. I was hiding in the compound in the dark and before long Mrs. Smith spied me and asked what had happened. I told her that I had met a man at the shop and had given the money to him. I prefer not to recall the language that she used, but I think I remember one sentence: "Dis kossoh dog!" She then gave me a good hiding.

It was a hard lesson to learn, and, to a small trusting boy, it was impossible to imagine that such dishonesty abounded. My training up-country in farm work, in hunting and trapping animals and in keeping a weather eye open for dangers in the bush had developed my powers of observation and keeness of sight to a high degree. On the Saturday morning following my encounter with the thief I was sent to the Big Wharf to buy firewood. My senses were suddenly alerted by a suspicious movement somewhere in the crowd. As I fixed my eyes in its direction I spotted a man trying to slink unobtrusively into the background out of sight. At once I recognised him as the man who had tricked me over the lamp glass. I hung on to him like a baby monkey clinging to its mother, meanwhile shouting at the top of my voice: "Tif! Tif!" Soon a crowd surrounded us and a policeman came along. As soon as the policeman saw him he shook his head. "You again?" he asked. "What's it this time?" A thief so well known by the police does not waste his energy protesting his innocence. He did not even try to deny my story and after a few harsh words from the law, he handed over my money to me.

But my trips to Freetown were not only spent in catching thieves and avoiding trouble. The Europeans had built a community outside of low-lying Freetown in a vain attempt to avoid catching malaria. It was known as Hill Station and was an airy, pleasant place on the hills outside Freetown where the Europeans isolated themselves in wooden houses built on stilts. When I arrived in Freetown this little community had been set up for some time. One of the things I most enjoyed whenever I had some spare time was to watch the arrival of the white-hatted administrative officers at the railway station by the cotton tree. This railway line had been specially built from Hill Station to central Freetown to convey the European officials to and from their work. It was reputed to be the steepest non-funicular railway in existence, and as I was so interesed in trains and hoped one day to be an engine driver, this particular line held great fascination for me. From the train the passengers were carried to their offices in hammocks.

My life was made much easier when the Smith family decided to move away from Kissy village to a house in Upper Kissy Road in Freetown. There was no more hurrying back and forth between village and town and I was able to spend more time with my classmates at my new school. This was Bethel School in Easton Street where Mr. McCormack, who was to become a well known name in education, led us through the mysteries of Longman's Arithmetic, Nesfield's English Grammar and Prout's Hygiene.

During my time in Kissy and in Freetown, my father was always checking how I was getting on. He would pay us visits now and again and look me over to see how I was faring. I had known long ago at Moyamba, right at the start, that he was bent on making me 'sabi-book', as was my mother, although she wanted me to learn the Muslim book (the Koran), she herself being a Muslim; and she used to call me — and I still have memories of her voice — "Moi Siaka", which means Siaka the Muslim man.

When I returned home to my family for Christmas 1915, my school report showed that I was an average pupil and most of my family were impressed by the fact that I had reached Standard 4. But my father had higher ideals and asked me if I was really working hard enough. I replied that I was doing my best. "Perhaps it is the fault of the school, then", he said, as if unwilling to admit that his son was not a genius! And so he made immediate arrangements for me to enter the Albert Academy in Freetown when the next term began on January 21st, 1916. The Albert Academy was actually two years younger than myself. It had been founded by the Evangelical United Brethren, who saw the need for a fee paying school offering a high standard of education to youngsters from the provinces. Some of the leading Creole families in the Colony, such as the Metzgers, who believed in integration with the up-country people,

THE NOW DEFUNCT FREETOWN RAILWAY STATION IN WATER STREET AS IT WAS IN MY SCHOOL DAYS (ABOVE) AND (BELOW). THE HILL RAILWAY STATION SERVING AN EXCLUSIVELY WHITE RESIDENTIAL AREA BUILT ON TOP OF A MOUNTAIN OVERLOOKING THE CITY, SUPPOSEDLY TO PROTECT EUROPEANS FROM MOSQUITOES. IN THE EVENT THE MOSQUITOES EASILY PENETRATED THIS WHITE ENCLAVE, BUT THE BLACKS WERE KEPT AT BAY, EXCEPT ON APPROVED BUSINESS. THE LINE, LINKING HILL STATION WITH CENTRAL FREETOWN, WAS CLOSED IN 1929 AND THE TRACK WAS PULLED UP TWO YEARS LATER.

MY OLD SCHOOL, THE ALBERT ACADEMY, AS IT WAS WHEN I ENROLLED AS A
STANDARD FOUR STUDENT (ABOVE) AND AS IT IS TODAY (BELOW).

FREETOWN IN THE DAYS OF MY CHILDHOOD: A FASHIONABLE WEDDING AT COLLEGE CHAPEL, RAWDON STREET, IN 1915 (ABOVE) AND A CROWD WEARING EUROPEAN SUITS TO WATCH THE OPENING OF THE NEW POST OFFICE.

FOURAH BAY COLLEGE: PART OF THE NEW COMPLEX (ABOVE) AND THE BUILDING WHICH I KNEW AS A CHILD (INSET). BELOW, A GROUP OF STUDENTS AND TUTORS WITH THE BISHOP AND ACTING PRINCIPAL DENTON IN 1911. SWEATING IN THREE-PIECE SUITS, HIGH STARCHED COLLARS AND GOWNS WAS THE PRICE ONE HAD TO PAY FOR A HIGHER EUROPEAN-TYPE EDUCATION IN TROPICAL AFRICA

also sent their sons there rather than to the more fashionable fee-paying schools in Freetown. I felt very privileged to be going to such an exalted place of learning, and when I think now of how high the fees were I can only feel amazement at my father's determination to keep me there. It must have been a great sacrifice to him.

The two years that I had already spent in Kissy and Freetown had done something to rub off the rough edges of the country boy that I had brought with me to the big city. But it was only really when I attended the Albert Academy that I realised the real meaning of the word 'cosmopolitan'! There I was thrown in with Temne, Kono, Limba and Koranka boys — and boys from other Sierra Leonean tribes that I scarcely knew anything about. There were also students from Liberia, Nigeria and Ghana. The social and tribal mix was tremendous, but strangely enough, unlike adults, we boys always settled our differences amicably and with good humour. We often teased each other about our different accents and dialects, but it was always good fun and no one ever took offence. I learnt that it was not how people say something, but what they say that really counts, and this was a valuable lesson for me.

I see now that if tribal and racial integration is to be successful then it should start at the cradle, as it did with me. And although loyalty is a fine quality, unqualified tribal loyalty can be a destructive force, within the framework of a free, multi-tribal country. Some people have never been able to grasp the difficulty of swallowing such loyalty; only a few years ago a tribe's very survival would have depended on the drumming up of a strong tribal feeling. Then suddenly, almost overnight, individuals were being told that this loyalty was wrong and what should be encouraged *now* was African nationalism — all very confusing... And of course tradition dies hard and for many the ties of tribalism still seem greater than anything else. Often the bonds of tribalism lead to nepotism — something I have always disliked — and many an African leader has been vexed by this problem when filling key posts in his government. If he appears to favour one tribe more than another then he is heading for trouble. It is a wise and courageous man who picks his men according to their merit, and not because of their family allegiances. Africans must learn to accept their fellows for their own sakes if unity is to prosper in our continent.

Among the unifying factors which my friends and I at the Albert Academy had, and which kept us all together despite our ethnic mix, was hunger. It seemed that we could never get enough to satisfy our appetites, and for years it was as if I had a permanent aching hole in my stomach that needed constant filling. There were a number of mango trees in the school compound which, during the season, provided us with breakfast, for the school did not serve an early morning meal. Some of us would be under the mango trees as early as 2 or 3 in the morning to pick up ripe mangoes which had fallen from the trees or partly eaten mangoes which had been dislodged by bats. These latter were named 'batmot'; we started eating the fruit where the bats had left off. The day the mango harvest finished was a very sad one for it meant that we had nothing to eat until the first meal was served at 11 a.m. Then we had to wait until 5 o'clock for the next meal — but even then my stomach was still rumbling for more food.

I shall never forget the way meals were served to us for the procedure caused me so much heartache. We would assemble in the dining hall, our ravenous appetites tantalised by the delicious smell of the cooking. The senior boys at each end of the table dished out the food while we, the youngsters, sat on benches at each side of the table eagerly awaiting our serving. But any hope we entertained of filling our bellies was soon shattered when, time and again, we witnessed the meagre portions allotted to us. The senior boy who served the rice used to sprinkle a little of it on a plate and then spread it out to create an impression of plenty. When it was passed to his colleague to add the stew, he would put on the plate a mere spoonful of it which was sometimes little more than a practically meatless bone in a drop of gravy or a small sliver of fish stranded on a grain or two of rice. It amounted to so little that the whole helping could be swallowed in one gulp. The agony and resentment we felt were fanned to extremes when we watched how the seniors served themselves and each other. Their plates were stacked high with both rice and stew.

It was torture to watch those big louts stuffing themselves with what seemed exaggerated relish while my own stomach was still so empty. But unlike Oliver Twist in Charles Dickens' famous book, not one of us dared to ask for more, nor to voice our bitterness in the mildest of terms, for they were far bigger than we were — *and* better nourished — and we feared reprisals. I do not think anything in adult life can ever compare with the torment of intimidation and humiliation quietly suffered by juniors in a boys' school who are completely at the mercy of the seniors. This painful transitional period, the half-way house between boyhood and manhood, can sometimes change the whole character of a sensitive boy, and the change is not always for the best.

But I was really very lucky because I had an uncle, Momo Kallon, who was a soldier and was stationed in Wilberforce barracks on the outskirts of Freetown. Every Saturday I visited him and his wife, and a good meal was always assured! So once a week I would eat my fill, with no senior boys nearby to cheat me out of my share. It was a wonderful sensation to feel as if I could eat no more, and as if this wasn't enough my kind aunt and uncle would always give me threepence to take back to school with me. With this money I would buy cupfuls of groundnuts at a halfpenny a time to tide me over the long hungry mornings of the school week.

This constant quest for food reached a fever pitch with an incident in which some of my friends were involved. Some boys stole vegetables from a nearby farm which belonged to the family of the late Pa Luke, once a foreman in the Public Works department. For some time the boys had been sneaking out at night and stealing cassava — and so far they had got away undetected. But their luck ran out one Sunday morning when we returned from church having received the sacrament. Three of the boys went on ahead to the farm, and while they were busily digging up the cassava the Limba watchman caught them and insisted on taking them to his master. When the principal of the Academy, Professor D. E. Weidler, was told of their escapades he said "Take them along by all means, and don't spare the rod! Fancy stealing just after receiving the Holy Sacrament. What *are* boys coming to these days?" But the daughters of Pa Luke took pity on them and told the watchman to let them go. The boys were delighted at having got off so easily. But the next morning Dr. Weidler gave each offender a dozen strokes of the best!

About fifty per cent of the boys at the Albert Academy were called Mission Boys. Their parents could not afford the full fees, but as the boys were hard-working, well-behaved and showed promise, the school authorities felt they deserved help. The only difference between the Mission Boys and the rest of us was that in order to earn the supplementary money required for their fees, they worked for so many hours a day in the carpenter's and printer's shops. This meant that during some periods of the day they were working while we were studying. In spite of this advantage we had over them, it was nearly always the Mission Boys who came top of the class. The practical curriculum which was good for all of us, helped them in particular.

I was not long at the Albert Academy before I noticed that the different tribes have different idiosyncracies of pronunciation. We found that the newly arrived Temne boys could not pronounce the letter 'J'. For example, they would say: *Kottoh Yames yam di koonoo a wan yomp* which means in Engligh *Big brother James, bring the canoe alongside, I want to jump.* The proper rendering in Krio, of course, would be *Kottoh James, jam di kanoe a wan jompe.* We used to nearly split our sides with laughter. And then when it came to the Mendes, the pronunciation of the letter 'R' was anathema to them. Instead of saying *rope* they would say *lope.* Pronunciation of the word *shun* or the suffix *-tion* was always given as *sun*, for example, *salvasun* instead of *salvation.* Every tribe had its own bugbear. The Limbas put an 'F' wherever they found an 'H' and an 'H' wherever they found an 'F', thus *foo-foo* became *hoo-hoo* and *hog* became *fog*, whereas *feel* became *heel.* We mocked one another a lot.

I was later to realise that this same thing occurred even in the international field and I have met people of a big nation who, when they wanted to say *rice* say *lice.* So it is the same the world over.

Another incident of Academy days that stands out very clearly in my memory was the big influenza epidemic which fell on the city in 1918. One or two boys died in the school. As for myself, I lay down for a whole week just sleeping. I really do not know whether I should call it sleeping, it was more a sort of trance and I imagined myself walking through a very wide field for about seven days. When I was able to get up on a Saturday morning, I haltingly dragged myself along the streets of the city to Regent Road and on to Fourah Bay Road to visit my sister. I didn't come across a single human being on the streets. All I heard was the sound of hammering in the back yards where coffins were being made. We were lucky in the Albert Academy to have the ministrations of one of our bishops (I think he was called Bishop Howard). He carried a small stove about in the dormitories where he boiled or steamed a mixture and made us cover our heads with our country cloths and inhale the vapour from the receptacle on the stove. This did wonders in clearing our nostrils right up into our heads. One of the symptoms of the epidemic, as I remember it, was that one's nose got clogged up, then the head and the chest until eventually one succumbed.

My parents almost died of shock and worry when an itinerant unemployed man from Freetown, passing through Moyamba, called at our house and told my father, that almost all the childen in the secondary schools in Freetown had succumbed to the plague. My mother even said that she had dreamt about this and had actually seen a ghost. Fortunately, after a few days real news reached them that I was still alive.

I often recall with amusement what happened that Saturday

morning when I left the Albert Academy for Fourah Bay Road after recovering from my bout of influenza. When I arrived at my sister's, I found that she and the whole family with whom she was staying had just been laid low by the disease. At the same time I found that they had just finished preparing the usual Saturday foo-foo meal with the accompanying plasas — two big potfuls of it. Having been in bed for a whole week with scarcely anthing to eat, you can imagine the effect all this food had on me. I sympathised with the family most heartily and then paid full attention to the meal. My sister lay down watching me while I voraciously helped myself. Now and again I would stop, drink a cup of water and sympathise with her. We were told at the time that it was a visiting man-of-war which had brought the plague to Freetown from the Far East.

The subjects that I studied at the Albert Academy were not as many as young people are required to study today, but were the basics, that is, reading, writing, arithmetic, composition, history, geography and a bit of Latin. I mention this matter because I have noticed in the case of one or two students whom I try to help along, lists for books in about fourteen subjects. I notice pupils in Standard 6 or Form 1 buying books on economics and other higher subjects. I do not profess to know how the principals or school boards draw up their book lists, but I should imagine that it would be better to get a good grounding in the basics before tackling the higher forms of learning.

Perhaps I should use this occasion to emphasise a point which has been very sore with me for a long time, and that is the burden of the cost of books which parents have to bear. I feel quite certain that something can be done, and must be done, to relieve these parents. It is an unnecessary burden which they are called upon to shoulder while a few people enrich themselves in the process. That is why, as President of Sierra Leone, I gave my support to a project designed to expand and modernise the Government Printing Press. The new equipment includes machines to rule and make exercise books and, as a result, we are now producing at least a very large proportion of the stationery used in our schools, saving foreign currency for the country and reducing the expenses of parents. We now also produce some text books.

Not so long ago I met one of our students recently returned from Russia and we were discussing the subject he had been studying. The pamphlet which he showed me on the subject was a cyclostyled one; in other words, cyclostyled copies had been made from the original text, and that is what he said his class used. Copyright laws do not make it possible for us to do that here, but I certainly know that the price parents have to meet could be halved, if not quartered, if both the writing and production of more text books took place in Sierra Leone. Somebody has gone so far as to say that our boys and girls here pay more for their books than the undergraduates in Oxford; and here there are only a very few libraries, whereas in Oxford or Cambridge there are libraries everywhere to help students.

On Thursday nights after school we used to go to prayer meetings in the E.U.B. Church in Regent Road. On Sunday evenings, too, we would attend the same church and we would enjoy the march along Regent Road. We certainly had some big men in school in those days because as we marched along the street we would hear some of the children shout: "Look dem big pa way day go school".

But after school hours most of my time was taken up playing football. I was very keen and became pretty good at the game, for I was eventually picked for the school team to play regular matches against other secondary schools and Fourah Bay College. When I first started playing I was so small that the sleeves of my jersey covered my hands. This had its advantages for if I happened to handle the ball the referee rarely noticed it! I remember, too, a football match we played against the Grammar School at the recreation grounds when one of our players, Kamara, a big hefty chap, charged a lean youth from the Grammar School and threw him violently to the ground. His uncle who was standing on the lines went and picked up the boy from the ground and said to him: "Cah we go home yah; mek den Mende pa ya nor kill you for me".

I might have grown equally fond of cricket had I not been put off the game by an accident that happened to me. I was playing long-stop for a very fast bowler. To help stop the ball and to protect myself from injury, I had a piece of board which I held over my forehead as soon as the ball had passed the batsman. On this occasion I mis-timed the ball and lowered the board just as it reached me. The result was a severe crack on my forehead which nearly knocked me unconscious. I decided there and then that this was not my sort of game and have never touched a cricket bat since.

One little amusement was to go 'pump riding'. There were huge pieces of flat stone in the bed of a little brook. So we used to go along and sit down and propel ourselves along the surface of the rock, heading downstream. It took quite a bit of dexterity to avoid danger but boys never think of things like that. We enjoyed it very much indeed.

Foreign troops who were stationed at Kortright, near where Fourah Bay College now stands, used to provide us with a lot of fun. Some West Indian soldiers who used to wear long trousers and boots, would often roll past our school blind drunk helping to test our powers of mimicry as we tried to imitate their 'Bajan' accent. I remember once that four white soldiers got very tight and lost their way home. In their confusion they ended up in our school and accidentally entered one of the dormitories. Some of the boys, woken up by the noise, thought the soldiers where ghosts. A dreadful noise broke out as frightened schoolboys and drunken soldiers encountered each other, and eventually the police had to be brought in to escort the men out of the building.

The four terms corresponded to the four quarters of the year, with a short break after the first and third terms and a fortnight's break in the middle of the year. In December we had a long holiday of one month, so that all the boys could get home at least once a year to see their families. I can remember feeling like a tremendous man of the world whenever I met my old friends in Moyamba.

When we were about to go home, we, the freshers, were always supplied by some of the senior boys with a sheet of long English words for which we paid a considerable price out of our meagre pocket money. These were the words which we would use up-country to show the boys left behind that we had come from Freetown and had had some education. We would dress up in the morning and sit in a chair after having eaten a lot of cassava, and then begin to shout out a lot of big English words. Young boys would collect around us, presenting a scene that resembled the old Greek orators lecturing. One such sentence for which I paid a penny (which was big money in those days) read something like this: "Agitate the tintinabulary summons", meaning: Ring the bell". Or: "The conflagration extended its devastating career", meaning in ordinary English: "The fire spread". The principal heard about some of these exploits of ours and on our return to school he would line up those found guilty and give them six strokes each. But we had satisfied ourselves and achieved our objective. The poor boys back home had a lot of specious regard for us, so we did not mind the punishment!

December was the official end of the school year, and it was then that graduation day was celebrated. For six years I had watched each generation of boys go onto the platform to receive their certificates. For some reason it seemed as if I would never walk that path, mount the few steps and be handed that important bit of paper: it seemed such a distant attainment. But of course one day the time came for me to graduate from the Albert Academy. It came to me as quite a shock. I had become used to the protective walls of my school. I felt young and foolish and hardly able to cope with the demands of the real world. I kept asking myself anxiously: was I really equipped to leave school and earn my own living? Had I really learnt enough? Would I disgrace my family and teachers by the inadequacy of my knowledge?

My graduation day, my last day in the Albert Academy, was to be on December 1st, 1922. Apart from my school fees, which were difficult enough for my father to find, I had to have special graduation clothes made and extra money for the festivities. In order to find the necessary money, my father had to send one of his wives, Mammie Nancy, to Freetown for a whole month to sell cupfuls of rice; and goodness knows what sacrifices he and the other members of my family must have made besides. Nevertheless I know that, when I stood up to give my oration, it must have been a very satisfying moment for my parents who had both come down to Freetown. For my father it represented the answer to a prayer, the reward for years of hard work and self denial. For as long as I live I shall never cease to be grateful to him for the opportunities he made possible for me by the sheer sweat of his labour and his great faith in me.

Knowing what importance my parents put on this very special day I could not help but feel nervous. Each graduating pupil was required to deliver an oration, and I had taken a lot of trouble in the preparation of my speech. The chairman of the occasion was the Governor of Sierra Leone, who had only recently been appointed. His name was Sir Alexander Slater and he was a strong critic of secondary schools in Freetown. He believed that these schools neglected to train their pupils to use their hands and that they put too strong an emphasis on subjects like Latin and Greek. But our Freetown schools were very proud of their high standard of scholarship and learning and resented his suggestion that priority should be given to an industrial or manual education. Many Africans interpreted this to mean their activities should be limited to agricultural or general labouring, so that they would be kept forever as the labourers rather than the leaders of their own country. Not surprisingly, Sir Alexander was not a popular figure.

The subject of my oration was 'The Awakening of Africa', and well I remember my final rousing sentences. I urged my fellow students to strive onwards — "Never look back until, like Caesar of old, you will be able to say 'Veni, Vidi, Vici' — 'I came, I saw, I conquered!'" As I sat

53

down, exhilarated as young men often are at their first taste of public speaking, I hoped that my parents were thinking to themselves that their sacrifice had all been worth while, and that I had made good use of my education.

The ceremony ended with the singing of our school song:

The golden glow of December's Day
Rests o'er the verdant hills,
And the sunlight falls with mellow ray
On fields and laughing rills.
But ere its last beams fade away
Beyond the mountains high,
Our lips must bravely say
The parting words — Goodbye.

Kind friends and parents gathered here
Our gratitude is yours
For all your care and sympathy
Which endlessly endures.
We trust the future may perfect
The works your hands have wrought,
And may they bring good gifts to you
These years that swiftly fly.

When the graduation ceremony had finally ended my parents prepared a big dish of food which I shared with some of my friends. It was a very happy meal, all of us elated with the excitement of the busy day. We ate and ate until there was nothing left, and it seemed appropriate that after those first days of hunger when our tummies rumbled from dawn until dusk our school days should end on this note of plenty.

CHAPTER THREE

My First Job

When I left the Albert Academy I was full of ambition. At that time it was my hope that I would be able to continue my studies at the Lebanon Valley College in the United States of America. Of course, I knew that it was out of the question to expect my father to support me — he had already done all he could for me, and I was more than grateful — and so I was determined to work my passage to America and pay for college and living expenses as best I could by taking odd jobs. But the more I thought about it the more I realised that it would be selfish, and perhaps a little self indulgent, of me to further my studies. I was seventeen years old and I had just finished the finest education as it was possible to have in those days in Sierra Leone. My father had worked and saved and made sacrifices so that I could go to the Academy and I considered that it was now my duty to find employment as soon as I could so that I in my turn could make some contribution towards the education of other members of my family. Although I decided that this was the best path for me I still hoped that one day a chance for higher education would come my way. This hope was eventually rewarded in 1947 when I became a student at Ruskin College, Oxford.

I never cease to be amazed by the lengths that some Africans in the past have gone to in order to educate themselves, and when I look around at students today I sometimes wonder whether they fully realise how very lucky they are now. It saddens me that so many of them take for granted the incredible opportunities open to them. Many seem to see a university degree as the rule rather than the exception: it is no longer their privilege to attend a college but a right. I am always amazed by the letters I receive from scholarship students complaining that the very generous grants that they receive are not sufficient. They seem to think that cars, television sets and the very latest fashions form part of their proper dues. Yet I am not so old and unsympathetic that I am unable to identify myself with today's youth; had I been born half a century later I would probably be reacting in just the same way. There is nothing that youth does today that youth did not do in the past and I think the older generation should remember this and be tolerant. I know that when it is the turn of our young to shoulder the responsibilities of families, jobs, even of State, they will prove more than equal to the task.

My father probably had all the misgivings about me that we now have about our own children — after all, it is only natural that parents should want only the best for their offspring. Because he had been a soldier himself, he was always very anxious to see me in a uniform. He was certainly right to think that there can be no better training for a young man than a spell in the armed forces. The discipline and routine of service life, a kindling of respect for law and order and a sense of responsibility are valuable lessons for any young man. During the formative years of adolescence and early manhood there can be no better way of instilling a purpose in life. However, before arrangements could be made for me to enlist in the Army, my father learnt that there was a vacancy in the Police Force for a Sub-Inspector, and he urged me to apply. "Of course, you can't expect to be made a Sub-Inspector straight away, son," he said, but added optimistically "However, with your education it shouldn't be too long before you rise in the ranks."

I reported to the headquarters of the Sierra Leone Police Force in Freetown in January, 1923. I must say that I did this more out of duty to my father than for my own pleasure, and certainly life in the police force at first was very different from what I had expected. I had just reached the top of the ladder at the Academy, and now I found myself as a junior all over again. The bottom rung is always rather a depressing place to be, but it is something that must be put up with and got through. Indeed, if I was to have any hopes of getting beyond this first position to more dizzy heights, I had to establish a firm foothold and prove my worth. I'm afraid, though, that it is all too easy to be wise after the event; at the time I was young and in a hurry and itching to get on. As I stood in line with thirty or so other raw recruits to wait inspection I had already in my mind a picture of Sub-Inspector S. P. Stevens — complete with highly polished Sam Brown and baton. It was this vision that I kept firmly at the front of my mind that kept me going during the exacting drill and fatigue duty that all junior policemen have to go through. After a while, however, my aching feet and general weariness overruled this splendid vision, and I had to face up to the day to day realities of my new life.

The Police Commissioner, Major C. Hampden King, was the best possible kind of tough guy — a disciplinarian of the old school. After our swearing in, he gave our group a talking to in his West Indian drawl. He told us, among other things, 'If you take anthing like bribes or dashes or mass-mass while you are in the Police Force, you will be going to gaol as sure as God made Moses! You get me ?" I can still hear his voice say it. It was a sound admonition. And I'm afraid that quite a few policemen did tend to land up in gaol in those days.

The Police Force in those days was considered to be a place for illiterates and very few young men of secondary school calibre thought about it as a career. This was not so much because they were unattracted to the Force as such, but the truth was that those educated men who joined met with a lack of co-operation from the old hands that verged on hostility. Their lives were made miserable and their jobs difficult to do because of this obstructive attitude on the part of the illiterate element who would go to any length to safeguard their own positions even if this had a detrimental effect on the general efficiency of the Force. In my own case these old hands nearly succeeded in driving me out of the Police Force in those early days, and it was only the dread I had of disobeying my father that made me carry on.

Our course of training was extremely rigorous and started at 6.30 a.m. with drill practice. At 8.15 a.m. we had fatigue duty for an hour where we had to clean up the officers' compounds and their kit and generally be at their beck and call. We would then have an hour of instruction in the duties of a policeman which would be followed until 11.30 by more drill. Until 2 o'clock in the afternoon we would have a much needed break which would be followed by two hours of lessons in police duties. It was a tiring regime, and by 4 p.m. I was usually feeling pretty exhausted.

When I first joined the police there were no barracks and we stayed in various places in the city. This arrangement obviously had its difficulties, especially in the event of an emergency when the Force had to be gathered together very quickly. Commissioner King arranged for all policemen to move into King Tom Barracks which were situated a couple of miles from the centre of Freetown. This would have been at the end of 1923 — and the move was not as welcome as might have been anticipated. The barracks occupied an area of land originally purchased by the British Captain Thompson in May 1787 for the settlement of the first batch of freed slaves. Nearly 150 years later conditions there were not very much improved. The barracks had been left to rot since they had been last occupied by the artillery five years earlier. The buildings were in very poor shape, and had actually been condemned by the sanitary authority. Nevertheless, we were ordered to move in and make the best of it. It was not until June, 1929, that the promised improvements were finally made and the place became fit for human habitation.

To report for duty we had to march from King Tom to the Central Police Station one hour before we were due there. The journey took about half an hour, we rested for 15 minutes, fell in and had General Orders read to us and our beats allocated and then marched to our posts. After the eight-hour spell of duty our day's work was over unless we had been selected for reserve duty, which meant reporting back to the station at 7 p.m. and sleeping there 'on call'.

My first assignment when I joined the Force was dog-catching. This meant that I had to go out two or three days at a time with two illiterate senior men to catch stray dogs in the city of Freetown. Being the junior I was ordered to carry the empty sack. It was a horrible business. Many of the dogs were in an appalling condition through neglect and were more often than not semi-wild and vicious to handle. We had to aim to catch about three or four strays a trip, tie them in a bag and carry them back to headquarters where they were locked up in a box which was fitted to the exhuast pipe of an old ambulance truck. The engine of the truck was started and the dogs were suffocated by the poisonous fumes from the exhaust. I suppose that if such a method of destroying life were used these days the police would find themselves in court, but at least gassing was preferable to the method they had employed up to the previous year, of drowning the poor beasts.

I remember once in Kissy Street we had caught four dogs in our bag and, as the weight was very heavy, the policeman who was helping me to carry the load decided that we should put it down and rest for a while. As soon as we did so, pandemonium broke out among the dogs trapped inside the bag and before we could do anything about it they had succeeded in getting loose. Understandably they were in an ugly mood and as we tried to recapture them they began to attack us from all sides. An excited crowd quickly gathered to watch, applaud and shout advice. To take part in such an embarrassing spectacle, even as an insignificant recruit, was humiliating enough, but the last straw for me was when a girl friend of mine from Harford School in Moyamba, who happened to be passing by at the time, suddenly recognised me. With a look of utter astonishment on her face, she said: "But I thought you were a police officer. What on earth are you doing chasing all those dogs?"

We captured 422 dogs that year of which only 33 were lucky enough to be claimed by their owners. When I left the Force in 1930, although I was no longer employed as a dog-catcher thank goodness, 3,360 dogs were bagged of which 3,140 had to be destroyed. In 1925 a new dog pound was built near King Jimmy, a part of Freetown, and a cart was provided to convey the animals instead of the abominable sack I had had to use, and the following year the Police Force employed two labourers to catch dogs which relieved us of this most distasteful duty.

An even more unpleasant memory I have was when I was asked to guard a corpse that had been washed up until arrangements could be made for the authorities to deal with the matter the following morning. The body was that of a lighterman who had accidentially fallen into the sea two days earlier. I was terrified at the prospect of keeping it company until the morning. I had never seen a corpse before and the thought of death had rarely entered my head. To make matters worse two days of being in the water made the body a gruesome sight. I tried to hide my fear when I asked the duty officer if I was to be alone with the body. "Unless you can get your grandmother to hold your hand!" he bawled at me.

There were no electric lights then and the Government Wharf was lit by two kerosene lamps which shed an eerie greenish glimmer on objects within their limited range, making them take on weird shapes. This played havoc with my imagination and at times throughout that endless night not only the covered mound of human remains, but many other objects that surrounded me seemed to move when I blinked my eyes and just at the moment when I stopped staring at them. It was one of the longest nights I can remember, but like most terrible night-time fears, in the morning it did not seem nearly so terrifying.

I was very lucky because promotion came fairly rapidly for me. Within a year I passed from full corporal with two stripes to acting sergeant with three stripes. At the end of my second year I was made first class sergeant which earned me £7.15s. (Le15.50) a month.

The strength of the Sierra Leone Police Force in 1923 was about 300 men. By far the most numerous tribe in the higher ranks were the Mendes, 78 per cent of whom were literate. Of the Limbas, the third largest tribe in the country, there were only 15 and only three of us were literate. There were three divisions in the Force — A, B and C, each doing eight hours duty a day. I was drafted into B Division and sent out on the beat, patrolling the streets in eight-hourly shifts. The most dangerous of the beats in Freetown were numbers 5 and 9 which comprised the areas around Soldier Fort and Hill Streets. These were frequented by night marauders and the police were often involved in unpleasant incidents.

To walk the streets for an eight-hour stretch could be a very tiring and soul-destroying exercise. To begin with it took a heavy toll on your feet. Police boots, until you got used to them and wore them in, could cause awful suffering. They were as heavy as lead. The uppers were thick and inflexible, the soles were studded and a thick steel plate was fixed to the heels for added protection. I remember the time I was on the beat in Kissy Road during the first few weeks of my patrol duty. My boots were giving me such pain that I took refuge under what is now known as Over-Bridge near Eastern Police Station, removed my boots and rested my throbbing feet for a while. When I tried to get my boots back on it seemed a physical impossibility, so swollen had my feet become, and for the next hour or so I was hobbling like a cripple.

The uniform, too, could cause discomfort. During the dry season we wore khaki drill tunics and shorts but as soon as the rainy season came we changed into a uniform made of thick serge material. We were forced to wear the serge uniform throughout the whole of the rainy season, even on those days when, because it did not rain, the heat and humidity were intolerable. On such occasions merely strolling casually along one's beat had the effect on the body of having just run a marathon. Nobody ever thought of complaining or offering suggestions for improvement. No doubt it would have been considered sacrilege to tamper with tradition.

When rain threatened, those on traffic duty used to wear a large rainproof coat over their uniforn. I had lost a lot of weight that year of 1924 partly from the physical exercise demanded by the Force, partly from succumbing to a type of influenza that swept through our unhealthy barracks known as 'coryza', and partly from chasing a girl I rather fancied! The result was that my raincoat hung from me in folds. One day I was on traffic duty at the Cotton Tree when a tornado suddenly got up. The whirling gale whipped round my legs and inflated my loose coat, lifting me bodily off the ground and then flinging me down onto the road. Mercifully there was little traffic about otherwise the consequences might have been disastrous.

Although my feet and body gained nothing but discomfort from my period on the beat, my powers of observation were sharpened acutely and I had plenty of opportunity to witness the incredible variety of human beings that made up our population. In a single hour life in almost all its forms used to parade past me: those bent with age and the young mother suckling her baby, the cheerfully robust and the ailing, the affluent and the beggar, the black, the brown and the white skinned, gorgeously clothed or semi-nude. They all seemed unaware of one another and absorbed in their own affairs. There were not many motor vehicles in those days. For those interested in statistics there were 129 cars, 58 lorries and 121 motor cycles in 1924.

This was all to the good, for people crossed from one side of the road to the other so lost in thought that it never occurred to them to look to see if anything was coming. From what I see of the pedestrians in Freetown today, regardless of the hundreds of cars that speed nose to tail daily through the streets, they still have this dangerous habit of wandering about the busy roads like automatons, their senses apparently quite deadened to the blasting of horns and the screeching of brakes.

It is not unnatural for every policeman to see himself as a budding Sherlock Holmes, someone who is capable of sniffing out clues where others thought detection impossible. And of course it is the ambition of every policeman to make some worthy contribution to criminal detection that will find a place in police history. At the beginning of 1924 a European's house was broken into at Hill Station and £30 worth of property was stolen. This was certainly not an unusual occurrence for there were plenty of thieves in Freetown at that time. But in this case the policeman who arrived on the scene took back to headquarters a piece of glass from a window pane that the thief had broken in order to enter the house. When it was examined by the Finger Print Branch they found on it the prints of a notorious burglar called Baimbah who, until then, had always proved too clever to leave incriminating evidence behind him. He was arrested and brought before the Chief Justice who remarked that it was the first case he had dealt with during the whole of his experience in Sierra Leone in which thieves had been traced by means of finger prints. It was one day when I felt very proud to belong to the Sierra Leone Police Force.

Larceny has usually been one of the most common crimes and this was never more true than during my days as a policeman. Robbery has always been a problem in almost every country in the world. Punishments have been handed out with varying degrees of severity in an attempt to try and deter would be criminals and prevent people from offending again. In England they once hanged children for stealing, but at the opposite end of the scale prisons are now getting more comfortable so that a stay inside one hardly seems like a punishment. Some countries have resorted to cutting off hands and ears or publicly executing thieves in an a desperate attempt to curb crime. And yet people everywhere continue to steal.

It seems to me that this will continue as long as there are corrupt elements in our society, not just at the bottom but at the top of the social ladder. It is at the top where the greatest and most damaging forms of crime take place. The person who pilfers a crust of bread because he has no means of coming by food legally is hardly in that category, and it was often my sad duty to arrest people for whom stealing was the only possible means of sustaining life. A policeman's job is a varied one, and another task I had to face was coping with the excited crowds, traffic jams and accidents that came with the state visits of 1925.

In January, the President of Liberia and Mrs. King spent three days in the country and in April, although the Prince of Wales spent only one and a half days in Freetown, so many visitors arrived to welcome him that the whole Police Force was on duty the entire time he was there. His programme was so full that there were not enough of us, even with the assistance of the army, to man beforehand each and every reception planned for him, and this necessitated lorry loads of us being rushed from one locality to another ten minutes or so in advance of the royal party. By the time evening came most of us were having a job to keep awake.

I was then a sergeant and was put in charge of a group of policemen who were to keep order at Government House where a dinner and dance was being held in the Prince's honour. In posting my men for duty that night I detailed No. 248 Lewis to stand in the passageway between the dance hall and the pantry. As the stewards passed to and from the dance hall with glasses of various drinks, Lewis grabbed the leftovers and drank them off. By the time the dance had finished and I had rounded up my force Lewis was no longer at his post but under a mango tree on Government Avenue drunk and incapable, and stripped of his uniform by street urchins. In the morning we marched him to the Orderly Room.

Major Hampden King, our Commissioner, came from Barbados. As I have already mentioned, he was a very strict disciplinarian and frequently reminded us of our shortcomings. "It requires stirling qualities to make a good and reliable policeman", he used to say in a way that made me feel hopelessly inadequate. Lewis was not the only one to feel uneasy in the Orderly Room that morning as we awaited the expected storm of rage to issue from the Commissioner, for as the sergeant in charge I was more than likely to be the main target for his criticism.

However, something seemed to have happened to him as he took his seat before us. For several minutes he sat with his head resting in his hands. Maybe he, too, was worn out from the previous twenty-four hours duty; or perhaps, in view of the fact that the Governor had awarded 'full marks' to him and the Police Force for their share in making HRH's visit such a wonderful occasion, he felt sympathetic and even kindly disposed towards the poor wretch who had entered deeper into the spirit of the event than regulations allowed. At any rate his usual no-nonsense approach was quite lacking. With what seemed to be a great effort, he raised lead-filled eyelids and looked at Lewis over the tops of his spectacles. "248 Lewis," he said in his slow West Indian drawl, "I take it you thought the Governnor had made a mistake in not inviting you to the banquet last night..." The rest of the sentence was drowned in a thunderous roar of laughter that rocked the Orderly Room. "Order!" he yelled, glaring icily at each one of us in turn. "You can go!" he snapped, flapping his hand as if to hurry us on our way. It was the first and only time ever that he allowed a man to get away with drunkenness.

I did a spell as Station Sergeant in charge of the Central Police Station and was later transferred to Government Wharf as Harbour Sergeant. I have vivid recollections of days when the English and German mail boats docked. Half the population of Freetown flocked to the port to collect blocks of ice, fruit and vegetables, German lager and other produce from the cold storage of the ships, to meet friends arriving or to bid farewell to those departing. There was no ice manufacturing plant in the city in those days, so to be able to have a cold drink once in a while was a great luxury. Young boys used to gather on the quay just for the thrill of touching the ice and wondering at the marvel of it, for they had never seen anything like it before.

Nevertheless, it was not all fun at the quayside. Often steamers had to be boarded and searched for contraband and stowaways, and we would carry out this thankless task surrounded by a surly and uncooperative crew. Assistance had to be given to boats in distress and bodies had to be rescued from the sea, sometimes alive but more often dead and usually in a sickening state of decomposition. There were fights nearly every day between dock workers, as often as not worsened by a drop too much to drink. Our duties were not helped by the small slow moving rowing boats that we had to use. It was not until 1930 that these were scrapped and a motor launch from the Port and Marine Department was put at our disposal.

I was among those who underwent a three months' course in musketry at Wilberforce Army Barracks and qualified as Sergeant Musketry

Instructor. This instruction in the use of small arms was first introduced into the Police Force in 1925 after we had been re-armed with modern rifles. The course consisted of two grouping practices, one each at 50 and 100 yards; two application practices, kneeling and standing at 50 yards, and one application practice at 100 yards prone position.

I was in a slightly difficult position for many of the sergeants whom I instructed were old enough to have been my father. Such a situation can often lead to problems, particularly as there was some resentment between the badly educated, often illiterate members of the police force and men like myself who had received some schooling. I found the way round this potentially difficult set-up was to treat every one with respect and to always be tolerant and willing to listen to their points of view. On the rare occasions which I did have to discipline one of them I would always take the offender to one side and speak to him alone. I certainly did not wish to embarrass anyone in front of their colleagues. I think the care and trouble I took in my handling of these men was repaid as they were a very co-operative bunch, and this taught me the importance of success in human relationships.

The 1920's were difficult years. So many people had drifted into Freetown looking for jobs that did not exist that a large percentage of the population was unemployed and desperate. Those who had jobs found it almost impossible to live on what they earned on account of the relatively high price of commodities and the large number of mouths they had to feed. Trade unionism as such did not exist in Sierra Leone in those days and although there were various workers' unions, such as the Carpenters' Defensive Union which had been formed in 1895, they were not yet effective as negotiating bodies. In fact Government took a very tough line against them whenever they showed active signs of airing their grievances. The railway had long been a source of trouble. Economically it was disastrous and those who worked on it were dissatisfied with their conditions of service. On two occasions in 1919 the daily-paid workers on the railway had gone on strike because of the delay by Government in paying their War Bonus and the following year, in the hope of strengthening their bargaining power, they formed the Railway Workers' Union.

The Creoles had always considered their position to be a very strong one in Freetown but cracks were beginning to appear in this facade. The emergence of an educated elite in the Protectorate who showed signs of taking an active interest in the way their country was being run was a nail in the coffin of Creole leadership. This prompted the frightened

Creoles to form a Sierra Leone branch of the National Congress of British West Africa, which sought to bring about closer relationships between them and the Europeans. But nothing could halt the march of progress that had begun in the hinterland and was rapidly growing in strength. There was a general feeling of discontent in Freetown, and indeed in the rest of the country, and I can remember feeling at the time that trouble was definitely brewing. The slowly gathering storm finally broke when the Railway Workers' Union led a strike for improved conditions of service. It was the most violent strike ever experienced in Sierra Leone between the two world wars.

Disgruntled workers, irresponsible youths, layabouts and criminals ran amok in gangs; ransacking, pillaging, plundering and assaulting, forcing stores to barricade their frontages and innocent civilians to lock themselves indoors. Every single policeman was employed on strike duties and this made it necessary to appoint additional temporary staff to strengthen the Force and to patrol at night in those areas of town from which the regular police had had to be withdrawn. We took on three inspectors, four sub-inspectors and 160 special constables, both European and African, who proved themselves very well.

The thing that horrified me most about those hectic weeks was the ease with which a normally disciplined and rational being could turn hooligan; a law abiding citizen could turn thief and vandal, and a civilized man could turn primitive savage. Even members of the Police Force were not immune to the raging fever of destruction. One of our constables was convicted and sentenced to two years imprisonment with hard labour for conspiracy to blow up a railway engine.

While all this terrible violence was going on around me and the leaders of the country were involved in complicated political wrangling, I can remember thinking to myself "Thank God I'm only a simple policeman". I often laugh at this now when I think of what I have been through since then!

By 1929 I had worked my way through the lower ranks of the Police Force conscientiously and diligently, and, according to my reports, satisfactorily. When a vacancy occurred for sub-inspector, I quite naturally believed that I had a very good chance of being selected. The vacancy was gazetted and I applied, and then swotted up such subjects as police duties and common law in preparation for the examination I expected to take.

To my astonishment, about a week before the date on which applications had to be submitted, the whole procedure of selection was changed and a man outside the Police Force altogether was appointed to fill the vacancy. It seemed that people with influence in the city had made the necessary contacts on his behalf and pulled the all-important strings. What chance had I, a lone man from Limba country with no connections in high places, against such opposition? I was bitterly disappointed and disillusioned and decided to leave the Force.

The Commissioner of Police, who must have had a reasonably high opinion of my work and character, took the trouble of sending a senior officer to Moyamba to see my father to enlist his help in trying to persuade me to remain in the Force.

It was with reluctance, and only because of my father's encouragement to do so, that I agreed to stay on in the Police Force. I was then posted to Bonthe where I was seconded to the old Court Messenger Force as Staff Sergeant-Major. The Court Messenger Force was a semi-military body which was responsible for the maintenance of law and order in the Protectorate, for until 1952 the Police Force operated only in the Colony. It was really the personal security force of the District Commissioners who usually recruited its members itself. A Court Messenger's duties far exceeded those of a policeman, for in addition to police and detective work he acted as interpreter and intermediary between the Governor in Freetown and the Chiefs. I found the morale in this Force much higher than that in the police and I would have been happy to have remained a Court Messenger indefinitely. But it was not to be. My secondment lasted only six months because the original appointee returned and was reinstated.

I was then transferred back to Police Headquarters in Freetown more discouraged and pessimistic than ever about my chances of advancement. If promotion depended on my influential contacts rather than on merit, then the most I could hope for was a long service medal as the oldest entrenched First-Class Sergeant in police history. At 25, the thought appalled me and I hastily resigned from the Force before the moss of stagnation had a chance to start growing under my steel-plated boot soles.

Although I did not find the opening I was hoping for and which no doubt would have tempted me to make my career in the Police Force, the seven years I spent as a policeman were not wasted, for I learnt a great deal that has helped me in later years. I learnt to overcome my shyness and to associate freely with people from all walks of life, to listen to their views and to accept the fact that although those views might differ greatly from my own, they could well be the right ones. I

THE ONLY PICTURE OF ME (FOURTH FROM LEFT) AS A POLICE SERGEANT. IN THE CENTRE IS THE LATE SUB-INSPECTOR BRANDON. AT THE TWO EXTREMES ARE SERGEANT SANDAH (LEFT) AND WATER POLICEMAN SANDAH (RIGHT). AT THE RIGHT OF SUB-INSPECTOR BRANDON IS A GHANAIAN MEMBER OF OUR FORCE.

learnt that tolerance and good humour when dealing with the public can more easily win their co-operation and assistance. I learnt the value of regular exercise in keeping fit. I also learnt how to remain calm in the face of accidents and other emergencies, not to get over-excited and not to take people's words for gospel. This last lesson I find of particular value in my present position.

A few years ago, world recession and the sharp fall in the value of our main exports, caused us some financial difficulties. The International Monetary Fund (IMF) offered to assist us, but requested in the first place that we should devalue our currency by a fairly appreciable extent. This would have greatly increased the cost of living which, in a country like ours, is largely determined by the cost of imports, such as fuel and even some essential foodstuffs. Naturally, I was reluctant to support measures which would have had such an adverse effect on the lives of the vast majority of our people. On the other hand, I felt that a devaluation would hardly stimulate our exports, or make them more competitive, as it would have done in the case of an industrialised country. As regards our diamond exports, the only beneficiaries of a devaluation would have been the international brokers, enabling them to buy our gem stones at a lower price in terms of hard currency without necessarily stimulating the world market by reducing prices to the end consumer.

But the highly paid IMF officials had a standard recipe for balance of payments problems and were diligently doing the job they had been hired to do. Their zeal reminded me of an incident in my early police days. We had just caught a notorious thief who tried to escape and, as one of my colleagues began to rough him up to teach him a lesson, he shouted, "take it easy officers; if it wasn't for the likes of me you would be out of a job".

I did not feel it would be appropriate to tell the story to the IMF officials with whom I was discussing financial problems, but the thief's reflection which flashed through my mind at the time certainly helped me control my annoyance and take a more philosophical view of the situation. Instead of flatly rejecting the recommendations of the IMF experts, I expressed appreciation for their efforts together with the hope that a less drastic solution might be found. Eventually we agreed on a token devaluation, more stringent financial controls and the pegging of our currency to the SDR unit, rather than to the fluctuating Sterling.

When holding high office one is liable to hear a lot of advice, observations and gossip. The main job one has is to know how to sift whatever information comes in; how to recognise the wheat from the chaff, and — most important if you are a diplomat or a politician — how to dispose of the chaff discreetly so as not to give offence and lose a valued supporter!

When I look back now over my very varied career I realise just how valuable my years as a policeman were. The jobs I have had often strike me as being perhaps rather unconventional preparation for the post of President. European statesmen seem to spend years locked away in ivory towers learning the arts of diplomacy and leadership. I too have learnt the lessons of leadership, but not from textbooks. These lessons came my way as I tramped the beat of a policeman patrolling a city: for it was this way that I got to know my people, got to know what they wanted, got to know their problems. And so although I never got on in the Force in the way I had hoped for, no one could ever say my time was wasted. It was a period of my life that I now look back to with gratitude and affection.

CHAPTER FOUR

Surviving the Depression

A policeman lives and works at the interface between the people and the impersonal authority. In a way, no job makes a better preparation for the responsibilities of government. I have always been glad, whenever I have had to make policy decisions or initiate legislation, that my work in the Force taught me to observe the effects of the law on ordinary men and women and see how it touched their needs and concerns. The policeman may be one of the humblest agents of the Executive but he can also be, for that very reason, among the wisest. Fortunately, even after I left the Force, I stayed in jobs that kept me in touch with my people.

My serious political initiation came only after a solid basis of life experience was laid, gradually broadening and diversifying along varying but always popular lines. The process was often tough and painful at the time — especially in the 'thirties, the years of world depression, when no rewards came easily — but I can see in retrospect that it helped give me enough maturity to see and do my duty, first as a trade unionist, then as a politician, but always as a representative of the people to whom I belonged, when the right time came.

After leaving the Police Force I was surprised to find how difficult it was to fit myself into civilian life. This was no fault of mine, for I was keen to take any sort of job that offered prospects, but unless there was a need for security men, most employers were somehow reluctant to place an ex-policeman among their staff. For several months I drifted about doing odd jobs hoping for something good to turn up and feeling more and more despondent when it failed to do so.

If the future looked bleak for me, it certainly didn't for Sierra Leone whose financial prospects positively sparkled when a diamond was discovered in 1930 by the Geological Department in the Gbobora stream in Kono in the South-Eastern Province. It was the first of a rich deposit that was to be found scattered over some 480 square miles in the draining system of the Sewa River. From that moment onwards the diamond area of Sierra Leone became the Mecca of all those believers in get-rich-quick miracles. The country was inundated — and still is — with fortune hunters from far and wide, illicit diamond diggers and dealers, smugglers and others, robbing the Government of thousands of pounds of revenue per annum.

No matter how frequently raids are made to clear the area of strangers and illegal immigrants, however tight the security may appear to be, the racketeers persist, for police officers and security guards themselves, indeed even European employees of the mining company, have been found time and again unable to resist the tempation of stealing gems or conspiring with others to do so.

In view of the feelings of alienation and despondency I was going through when the first diamond was found in Kono, it is a wonder that I, too, was not prompted to join the diamond rush eastwards or the panners for gold along the river Makong where, since 1926, hopefuls defied fatigue and fever in their quest for a sizeable nugget. Somehow the idea of chasing rainbows has never appealed to me. It was always drilled into me both by my high principled father and at school, that there is precious little worth having in this life if you have not earned it the hard way. My feet were firmly planted on the ground, I expected to get my daily bread from the grindstone.

In 1930, the year when Sierra Leone was suddenly dazzled by the glitter of diamonds, other prospective mineral wealth also opened up new vistas to young men anxious to embark on a new career. Haematite iron ore had already been discovered in two large hills near Marampa known as Massaboin and Gafal, 52 miles from the sea in the Port Loko district. Subsequent exploration confirmed that the deposits were promising but there was uncertainty as to whether the quantity and quality of the ore would justify development. It took a canny go-ahead Scot, James Campbell, to find out.

James Campbell, a member of the Northern Mercantile & Investment Corporation Ltd., of London, was a mining expert. Having satisfied himself that the deposits at Marampa justified development — and this in spite of the world depression of the early 1930's — his company, in conjunction with the experienced mining company of William Baird & Company, formed the Sierra Leone Development Company Ltd., (DELCO), in 1930.

Armed with the necessary mining rights from Government under the Concessions Ordinance, Campbell administered the kiss of life to the two comatose giants of Marampa. Before mining operations could begin, however, a 52-mile railway track had to be constructed to convey the heavy iron ore from its source near the small town of Lunsar to a loading port that it was planned to build at Pepel on the Rokel River where charting of the river had shown that ships of up to 100,000 tons could safely negotiate the channel.

The launching of the Marampa project quickened the heart-beat not only of the Colonial administration, the mining company concerned, investors, gamblers and all those who anticipated vast profits from the exercise, but also of one unemployed ex-policeman nearing the end of his reserves of hope, optimism and daily bread.

"I hear they're starting work on that Marampa-Pepel railway project at last", a friend happened to mention casually to me one day in October, 1930. I could not have moved faster had he suddenly gone berserk and chased me with a cutlass. There was no time for explanations. Here at last was the chance I had been waiting and hoping for and there was not a minute to lose. I set out forthwith for Sahr Marank, which literally means *stone like an elephant* in the Temne language and juts out of a creek almost exactly half-way between the Marampa iron ore deposits and Pepel. It had suddenly become a booming settlement as a result of the company's decision to use it as its main base of operation with work on the future railway progressing simultaneously from Sahr Marank eastwards towards Marampa in one direction and towards the sea in the other.

As soon as I arrived in Sahr Marank, I presented myself as a prospective employee in whatever capacity they could find for me. I gave details of my education and experience to the man in charge of recruitment.

"Assistant clerk and telephone operator," he said, pointing to the door through which I must pass. "And make sure you arrive on time and do your job efficiently. We don't carry passengers here. Next one!" Without another word he turned his attention to the next man in the queue.

There is, I was soon to discover, no nonsense in working for a contracting firm. Time was money. Every second had to be accounted for and any employee who failed to pull his weight was sacked at once. There was no room for sentiment between employer and employee any more than there would be between a government and a contracting firm if the company fell behind schedule or did a shoddy construction job. There was no bargaining. You accepted the money offered and in return you were expected to do a good day's work. If you were above average there was no extra reward; if you were average you kept your job; if you were below standard you were very soon shown the door. Tough maybe, yet it is the only way to get a job done efficiently and, what is more, most men respect such treatment, for there is no doubt that a disciplined and orderly man is a happier, more productive and more progressive man.

Excuses are sometimes put forward that the average African worker is incapable of sustained hard labour because the diet he can afford to live on is way below the nutritional value he needs for expending such energy. This is certainly true to a degree, but as I see it, and from my own experience as an underfed worker at one time and another, the answer lies not so much in physical exhaustion through lack of calories, but in physical inertia induced by mental lethargy which is brought about by the uncaring and discouraging attitude shown by those in charge. However hungry and underfed a worker may be, if he knows that his very livelihood depends on digging a hole, he will dig that hole in record time and still have enough reserve of energy to collect his reward.

Nothing so demeans men's dignity as the vicious spiral of dole and unemployment. Nothing is so enfeebling as a meaningless job which poses no challenge to a man. And nothing in the world of employment is so corrupting as excessive security, which destroys incentive and discourages effort.

In most of Africa today, a large public sector bears the brunt of the demands development makes on our emerging economies. Creating positive morale in the public sector work-force has therefore been a problem we have all had to face and it has not always been easy to combine high productivity with compassionate employment and welfare policies. Back in the 'thirties, although I had no experience myself as a government employee, many of my friends worked in various branches of the administration and were the butt of many ribald remarks about their cushy jobs, their regular increments and their come-a-day go-a-day attitude that over the years extinguished any spark of enthusiasm they once had.

It was the great difference in the attitude of government employees and that of the workers in DELCO towards their work that struck me so forcibly when I first joined the Marampa Railway Construction, as the project was commonly called. Most of us were lean and hungry, some were visibly undernourished, yet there was no question of easing up on the job however idly-inclined or feeble we felt, for always uppermost in our minds was the fear of being sacked. It was tough in the extreme and many of us grumbled and criticised and kicked against authority when authority was out of earshot, as all workers do at times, but it made life simpler and the job more secure if we disciplined ourselves to give maximum co-operation, to do our best to see that the construction · machine of which we were an integral part ran smoothly on carefully oiled wheels.

Discipline from the employer's point of view was particularly necessary in the early 1930's, especially in the Protectorate where labourers, whether local or otherwise, lived in close proximity with the peasant population who were suffering such economic hardship that the bitterness and unrest that emanated from them could so easily have an adverse effect on the company's labour force. There was still much resentment over payment of the Hut Tax. Coupled with this, there was growing discontent over the disparity of treatment of the Protectorate people vis-a-viz those of the Colony, and the fact that what few imported goods there were during that period of world depression rarely reached those in greatest need of them, the masses of the hinterland.

It was clear to all of us at Marampa, employers and employees alike, that the peasants were in the mood for rebellion, though we did not view the matter in the same light. Whilst the company officials feared the repercussions such a rebellion might have among the workers on the project, we sympathised with the people, hoped for action and wished them every success. A bloody upheaval seemed near in February, 1931, when a Muslim visionary from French Guinea began interesting himself in politics rather than religion.

Haidara Contorfilli, as he was called, had for past year been rather flamboyantly evangelising the people in the Kambia District. He claimed he had been ordained by God "to prophesy about the prophecy of Mohammed". Kambia was just north of Port Loko District where we were working on the Marampa project and we heard many reports from time to time of his preaching. We found much of it amusing — the ravings of a religious fanatic, hysteria inspiring hilarity. Haidara claimed to have supernatural powers, to be able to change the sun into the moon, among other wonders, and he had an aversion to spinsterhood. "Give all unmarried women to husbands however the case may be", he urged.

I personally never met Haidara, but those who had mostly agreed that he had extraordinary magnetism and spoke with great conviction.

PANNING FOR DIAMONDS IN THE EARLY DAYS OF THE DIAMOND RUSH AND (FACING PAGE)....

THE GIANT SEPARATOR (ABOVE) INSTALLED BY THE NATIONAL DIAMOND MINING COMPANY IN 1973 (BELOW) THE HIGH-LIFT METHOD, INVOLVING DIVERS, NOW USED BY SMALLER OPERATORS ON THE SEWA RIVER.

It was not difficult to understand how such a man, at such a time, could inspire and give hope to, and offer the necessary leadership to, an unenlightened community bent on improving their wretched living conditions at any cost. As the Colonial Secretary of the day later assessed the position in the Sierra Leone Weekly News of February 21st, 1931: "The people must have complained to him of the hardness of the time due to the considerable fall in price of kernels and other staple products and their difficulty or inability to pay the tax... Some of the people readily believed and rejoiced that at last someone had come to rid them from the burden of taxation and acclaimed him an Angel of God."

Nobody, not even the Provincial Commissioner in Kambia nor the Colonial Government, which declared him "illiterate and comparatively ignorant", took Haidara seriously. Not, that is, until February 10th, 1931. On that date he addressed a letter to his followers in Kambia urging them to revolt. "God sends his messengers without guns or swords, staffs or daggers," he declared. "But he gives them something which is more than a gun or sword. I have the name of God with me; you should look at what is in the air, so you should not fear the European be he French or English, as the four corners of the earth are guarded by the Prophet Mohammed." He told them that both their local Paramount Chief and the Government had fallen and that he had cursed everybody in the Government. "I am also telling you not to pay your House Tax to any Paramount Chief." He did not seem to be any too confident, however, about the reliability of the invisible and invincible arms to be provided by God to his messengers, for he distributed among his followers a generous supply of machetes and guns which must have been smuggled into the country.

It was obvious now, even to the British, that Haidara was intent on challenging authority and a platoon of 34 men of the Royal African Frontier Force was despatched forthwith to put a stop to his rebellious uprising. The Colonial Secretary later explained to the Legislative Council Government's action in so doing: "The Government is tolerant enough of empty, though foolish, talk, and was tolerant towards Haidara himself until it became clear that he was bullying the more ignorant people in the name of religion and openly preaching sedition and defiance of authority. But no Government worthy of the name would tolerate activities such as he adopted latterly, or would fail in its duty of taking strong measures against those who preach sedition, whether orally or by the written word."

The army and the rebels came face to face on February 16th at Bubuya in the Northern Province. Among those killed in the brief but bloody encounter were Haidara himself and the British force commander.

As far as we on the Marampa Construction were concerned, the failure of the Haidara-led peasants to redress their grievances, sad as it was, showed clearly once more the futility of action by loose groups of people lacking organisation and level-headed leadership against all-powerful authority. We recognised that for the time being, until we organised ourselves into a trade union and were able effectively to fight for our rights and insist on fair play and fair pay through negotiations, the company must continue to have the first, last and only word. There was no alternative, things being the way they were. If we did not like their terms there was always a queue of job-hungry men only too ready to accept them.

At the peak of the Marampa Construction project there were about 5,000 men employed, including about 50 Europeans. It was possibly the last port and railway in Africa to be constructed entirely by hand labour with picks, shovels and head pans. Many of the Europeans were Scots who displayed the most incredible stamina in very trying circumstances. They were tough, energetic and diligent and they expected the rest of us on the site to be the same. There was no doubt that the example they set did much to spur on the whole project team.

I remember in particular the company's medical officer, Dr. A. A. McKelvie, a truly dedicated man who became so attached to Sahr Marank that after returning to Britain he wanted his ashes to be scattered over the site where he had spent so much of his energy. When he died and was cremated some years later, his relatives honoured his will sending to Sahr Marank the urn containing his ashes.

I found the broad brogue of some of them quite incomprehensible at first, likewise some of the English accents I heard, and I used to be amused at the badinage between the Scots and 'those Sasenachs', as they called their brothers south of the border, for I saw in it tribalism in its more sophisticated form, treated in the same light-hearted fashion as we had done as boys at the Albert Academy.

The Europeans lived on the work site which was at Sahr Marank near the Port Loko Creek Bridge. We, the African workers, stayed in Port Loko, three or four miles away, and had to trek to and from Sahr Marank each day. It was a strenuous schedule. Clocking-in time was 7 a.m. prompt; if we were as much as five minutes late we were sent home for the day and lost that day's pay. Work finished at 5 p.m., and by the time we had returned to our lodgings and had consumed our evening meal, we were usually too exhausted to do anything but go to bed and conserve our energy for the next day's work.

Still, I somehow found time to teach myself touch-typing and shorthand. There was a typewriter in my office which was seldom used and I thought it would be a good idea to acquire a new and useful skill. Somebody recommended a book in a 'teach yourself' series and I sent for it. As soon as it arrived I began to spend every minute of my spare time memorising the position of letters on a standard keyboard, as reproduced in the book, and practising the art of operating them with all ten fingers. Shorthand too became both a hobby and a challenge and I even wondered at times why people bothered to write in long hand what could so easily be recorded with just a few strokes of the pen.

I really enjoyed learning the techniques described in my book and what others thought was hard work I regarded as a sort of entertainment while the more conventional types of entertainment in which they indulged I tended to regard as a waste of time.

Then, when I felt I had mastered the skills of typing and writing shorthand, I began to teach them to several clerks in the office. I have often wondered what exactly prompted me to do this. I had never had the slightest ambition to be a teacher, and though I was conscientious where my job was concerned, I am sure that it was not the interests of DELCO that I had primarily at heart when I undertook to increase the work potential of their junior employees. I think, in retrospect, that it came as a natural reaction to me to help my fellow men share what little education I could impart to them when my own education had been so precious to me. After all, if you are starving and a bowl of food is put before you, you cannot greedily stuff yourself while others, equally hungry, look on.

The railway project was divided into two main sections, one stretching from Sahr Marank Bridge to Marampa, a distance of roughly 26 miles, and the other extending 26 miles in the opposite direction from Sahr Marank Bridge to Pepel; an engineer and an assistant were responsible for each section. In addition there were secondary sections, three on the Pepel site and two on the other. There were also two major bridges under construction, one at Sahr Marank, which I personally witnessed in all stages of development, and the other at Sankin Creek, about 5 miles from Pepel. The track gauge of the railway, a single trace, was 3ft. 6in., and when the line was completed and in regular use, four or five trains each carrying around 1,800 tons of iron ore, were hauled to Pepel each day by coal-fired steam locomotives of around 130 tons in weight. Unlike the national railway which proved such a drain on our economy that it was eventually phased out, the Marampa-Pepel railway has given valuable and efficient service throughout the 35-odd years of its active life.

While we were at Sahr Marank I used to go to Port Loko to collect mail about five miles up-river. We used a small boat with an outboard engine. Once on our way to Port Loko we saw an alligator lying on a huge stone on the side of the river with flies swarming all over its mouth. Not knowing anything about alligators, the launch skipper and I thought the creature was dead and decided to collect it, skin it and sell the hide. The skipper slowed the engine and steered for the rock where the alligator was basking in the sun. As soon as we got near the creature it gave a sudden jump which nearly capsized the boat. It was not dead at all, but very much alive, taking an afternoon nap and preparing to make a meal of the flies. It had very stale breath and I was told that when it opened its mouth the flies, thinking it was dead, congregated there; then, with one foul swoop, the alligator would snap its jaws and crunch as many flies as it could get. It was an unpleasant experience.

The Marampa Construction project came to an end in mid-1933 when the railway line from Marampa to Pepel was completed, and work on the iron ore mines was due to start later that year. We, the workers, expected to be immediately absorbed into the mining project, as the same company was to be in charge of operations, so we were very much taken aback when the whole lot of us were paid off. Luckily I hung around in the vicinity for a month or so in anticipation of re-employment, and before long DELCO began recruiting, taking on one or two of us at a time.

I was offered the job of telephone operator at 2/- (20c.) a day. I objected strongly to this offer as I was earning 5/- (50c.) a day when I left the Marampa Construction. It was then explained to me that the reason why the firm had not absorbed us immediately into the mining project was because had they done so, they calculated that we would have expected to receive the same pay that we had been getting on the railway project. How canny can a Scot get?

It is, of course, only in retrospect that an ex-employee can appreciate the tight shoe-string that DELCO had to operate on. Even after the mine became fully operative the margin of profits was very slim, for so many hands had to be employed both in the construction of the railway and port and in mining operations on account of the labour being entirely manual. In the early years iron ore was being delivered to Europe, chiefly the United Kingdom and Germany, for around 15/- (Le1.50) per ton. Out of that the company had to reimburse itself for the cost of mining, railway freight, loading the ship and ocean freight charges which were then about 8/- (80c.) per ton. At the same time, however, the question of the company's profit or loss concerned me less than the rough deal I considered had been given me. I was most reluctant to accept such a drop in salary when it meant doing the same job for the same company after two years of satisfactory service. But the alternative was to return to Freetown and join the ranks of the unemployed, which was even less attractive. So I signed on.

Work on this new mine was almost like the beginning of the construction work at Sahr Marank in 1930. We were living in Lunsar, about 2 miles from the works on the iron ore hill, Massaboin, and had to be on duty when the siren sounded at 7 a.m. The hill was inhabited by baboons which very often crossed our path. These large apes can be very dangerous if they are in a bad mood, if they are taken unawares or protecting their young. When blasting operations began at the mine they gradually dispersed and took refuge in other parts of the hill, which made our daily trek less hazardous.

Although I was employed as telephone operator and private secretary to the general manager, I soon found that when you are working on a newly opened mine under hardy Scots you can be called upon to do all sorts of jobs far removed from the one for which you were hired.

One day it was announced that the Governor, Sir Arnold Hodson, was going to visit the mine. All hands were mobilized into making the site as smart as possible in honour of this august personage. I was plucked from my switchboard, given twenty labourers and told to supervise the construction of a small road. After we had finished building the road, I noticed that it was a bit wet in places. Anxious to make a smart job of it, I looked around for some means of correcting this defect and my eyes alighted on a pile of sand conveniently heaped nearby. It was ideal for what I had in mind and I told the labourers to shovel it onto the wet spots to soak up the moisture. Our general manager, a Scot six and a half feet tall, arrived to inspect the road. Instead of admiring our handiwork he went into a fit of rage. "What the blazes d'ye mean by scatterrring that valuable sand all over the damned place? Did ye no' ken that it was brrrought up here at great cost for a special job?" This unexpected censure was humiliating enough, but when I was told that I would have to refund the cost of the sand my dejection sunk to unfathomable depths.

Not all my odd jobs on the Marampa mine project had such unhappy endings, I am glad to say. When the engine parts arrived from overseas and had been assembled, and the railway was about to be put into operation, the question arose as to who would take on the job of station master. The difficulty was that the engine drivers were all European and the management were most reluctant to appoint an African as station master because it meant he would have to give instructions to the drivers. Such a reversal of roles in the established white master-black servant relationship would *never* do! However, after much discussion it was found that there was simply no choice in the matter. The post would have to be filled by an African. Whether I appeared to the management to be the least likely to take advantage of my exalted position, or whether my passion for railway engines radiated so strongly from my person that they were attracted to me as if by a magnet, I never knew. But the fact is I was offered the job and so became the first station master — of any race — on the Marampa-Pepel railway.

The railway worked on a system of its own and there was only one station master. The system was called 'no signalman token'. After Marampa, there were three stops before Pepel. A loaded train on leaving Marampa was given a token or key by the station master after shunting processes had been completed. With this token on the engine, the train went into the main line at each stop, or loop, as it was called. It could not get out of the loop without certain operations. If it tried to do so it would be derailed. On arriving in the loop, say the first loop, for example, the driver would go into the token box and deposit the token with which he had travelled from, say, Marampa. If the forward section of the line was clear, the station master at Marampa would give the driver permission to withdraw the token for that section. The driver would then turn a nut on the instrument linked up to that section and he would be able to extract the token.

If the forward section was engaged, he would not be able to extract the token for that section. If the forward section was clear and he had been able to extract his token, he would then walk along the railway to a point before the engine and with the token he would operate a lever which opened the way for the train to move out of the loop. He would then go back to his engine and drive the train out of the loop. When the last truck cleared the lever which he had operated, the lever would again be reversed and locked. Upon being locked the points would then be set for the siding (not the main line). The driver could then take his train to the next loop. It was a bit of a slow process, but since it was a freight train, there was no special hurry and, under the system, accidents such as trains coming into collision, just could not happen. Of course trains did come off the rails now and again, but that was not due to anything like traffic collisions.

As station master I sometimes worked until eleven at night, then came back about three or four in the morning. During slack, or slacker periods, I also taught myself the Morse code then used to transmit messages and telegrams between Marampa, Pepel and Freetown. This was a slow and cumbersome system which, unlike the telephone introduced some years later, required trained operators. However, as station master, I felt that I should not have to rely entirely on the operators and that I should be able to cope in an emergency. Again, a 'teach yourself' book helped achieve my purpose and eventually I became so familiar with Morse that I began to teach it to trainee operators at the station. The messages we used to send were many and varied and were not confined to tonnages and shipments. "Arriving yours about 8.30 a.m. tomorrow," the cashier at Sahn Marank advised his counterpart in Pepel, adding: "If you will invite me to breakfast I shall be pleased to accept."

All this kept me so busy in my station master job that some nights I never went home. At the peak period we ran as many as seven trains a day. When the trains arrived at Pepel the wagons were emptied by mechanical process, one at a time, onto conveyor belts which moved the ore to a stockpile at the port. Underneath the stockpile there were valves which, when operated, dropped the ore through a regulated opening onto other conveyor belts which travelled out to the loading installations and loaded the ore into steamers. By this process huge ships of 40,000 or 50,000 tons could be loaded in a few hours.

The ore mined at Marampa was obtained by open cast methods and consisted of big pieces of rock which were blasted into smaller pieces. These were sorted, loaded into mine tubs and dropped into railway wagons to be hauled to Pepel for shipment. The first ship to be loaded at Pepel in September, 1933, was the *S.S. Hindpool* of 5,000 tons, which carried lump ore to Glasgow. In contrast, when I visited Pepel in 1972, I saw berthed there a vessel of 100,000 tons which took not more than eight or nine hours to load — I then heard that 2½ milion tons of concentrates, that is, treated fine powder ore, were exported in 1971.

This powder ore, which was found underneath the capping of red ore, had an iron content too low to warrant shipping in its natural condition and was therefore passed through a special mill which produced from it a concentrated product of around 66 per cent iron content.

Marampa was then one of the most up-to-date iron ore mines in the world. Accommodation was provided for both European and African employees; there were hospital, educational and canteen facilities, a club and welfare centre, a swimming pool, tennis court, cricket pitch and other recreational opportunities. Above all the management was actively concerned with the prevention of accidents. In the early stages of the mining there were a lot of accidents caused mostly by the weakness of an endless rope gravity haulage system. Loaded tubs being hauled by this contrivance en route to the railway wagons or the washing and screening plant would sometimes cut loose and come hurtling down to the loading platforms at terrific speed, more often than not killing or maiming a number of workers who were unable to get out of the way in time. To the management these were 'regrettable' accidents calling for a stereotype expression of official condolences, coupled with a minimal monetary grant to the bereaved families.

Unable to conceive the possibility of safety devices, such as those which were to be generally introduced in the mining industry some 20 years later, the workers came to accept these tragedies as inevitable occupational hazards, the price one occasionally had to pay for the privilege of a meagre but regular wage. To the survivors, "one" was naturally somebody else and, human nature being eternally optimistic, few were those who took seriously the risk of losing their own lives. To the families of the victims, however, it was a different story. Wives, children, brothers and sisters, could hardly control their grief when news of a fatal accident affecting a husband, a father, or a close relative reached them. They would rush to the mine from far and near, the muscles of their legs apparently stimulated by sorrow and despair. Still oblivious to fatigue, hunger or thirst, some eventually broke down as they approached the body of the deceased.

The immensity of the shock brought about by the loss of a dear parent came home to me once again in those days when I too was struck by a personal tragedy. Late on Good Friday 1941 the shattering news reached me that my father was critically ill in Moyamba. My step mother had arrived a few days earlier in Lunsar to spend a holiday with me. We instantly decided to go home as soon as possible and took the road to Moyamba early on the following day. Naturally, we had to rely on our feet and stamina to reach our destination in time to see the old man alive. We walked throughout Saturday and Sunday, stopping only from time to time for a drink of water, a bite of food, and to cross the Rokel River by canoe. When we arrived at Moyamba on Sunday evening, Easter Sunday, my father was already in a coma and died before the end of the day.

I had been deeply saddened when I lost my dear mother the very year I joined the Police Force and home had never been quite the same without her there. The loss of my father, however, was a very real tragedy to me. It was he who kept alive the flame of endeavour within me, who inspired me and gave me hope, who never allowed me to despair when things did not work out as well as I had hoped they would. To please him and earn his pride was the focal point of every venture and his death seemed to rob me of that purpose. Unlike my mother whose body was returned to her homeland for burial, my father's body, lying on the left side according to Limba custom, was laid to rest in Moyamba, his adopted home where he had spent so many years of his life and where he was an active member of the United Methodist Church.

Towards the end of my career at Marampa, I was eventually able to make some practical use of the initiatives I had taken in learning typing, shorthand and other office techniques. World War II was now raging in Euorpe, North Africa and the Far East and our European employees were naturally most interested in its progress. One of them was assigned the task of monitoring BBC news broadcasts — that is tuning in to the BBC on short waves — and typing out a news sheet for distribution within the company, a sort of miniature newspaper which became the only source of information for the expatriate Britons isolated in a small mining town in West Africa to supply iron ore for the Allied war effort. As fate would have it, the European 'editor' of our newspaper became ill and, as I was presumably the only other man in the company able to write shorthand, I was given the job of producing the news bulletin. This involved transferring me from the railway station to the main office with the grade of senior clerk and a salary of £200 per annum which made me one of the company's highest paid African employees. It also enabled me to follow current world events in much greater detail than I would have done as a station master and thus to develop an interest in, and understanding of, foreign affairs. This background knowledge proved of some use when I began to take an active part in politics and government.

Apart from one or two serious strikes that took place during the life of the Marampa iron ore mines, the project did continue to run

IRON ORE MINING AT MARAMPA: THE COMPLETION OF THE RAILWAY AND GIANT CONVEYOR SYSTEMS (ABOVE) PUT HUNDREDS OUT OF WORK. BELOW, A BULK CARRIER LOADING ORE AT PEPEL.

on the solid no-nonsense lines that its Scottish founders laid. Unfortunately, neither this conservative approach to industrial relations nor the devotion, sacrifices and hard work of employees, both African and European, could make up for the failure of management, over the years, to re-invest in the mine a sufficient proportion of their profits in order to modernise production and make it more competitive. By 1976, the slump in the world iron ore market, coupled with the exhaustion of the richest and most accessible deposits, brought about the closure of the whole operation, putting out of action a sizeable infrastructure, including a port and railway, and making redundant thousands of Sierra Leonean workers in a country already suffering from unemployment. As a result, Lunsar, which owed much of its development to the operation of the Marampa mine, became almost a ghost city, though the Government did what it could to mitigate the situation.

At about the same time, some 200 miles away, in Western Liberia, a similar fate struck the town of Bomi Hill where, in less than 25 years, an American company managed to remove to the United States a mile-high mountain of iron ore, leaving in its place a huge crater surrounded by a mass of abandoned installations and infrastructure and an army of unemployed workers.

In a way these experiences are typical of old-fashioned capitalist enterprise in colonies and underdeveloped countries. The quest for quick profits brings about a sudden inflow of capital together with the dislocation of traditional patterns and profound changes in the social and physical environment. Boom towns appear almost overnight, their bright lights and the prospect of a regular money income, however meagre, attracting tens of thousands of farmers who leave their villages to swell the ranks of the urban proletariat. Then, when the richest pickings have been exhausted, or market conditions change, the investors just leave the country without much concern for the social, economic and political havoc they may leave behind, and the human suffering their activities may have caused. The villagers who took the one-way road to wage-earning will have spent much of their working lives in the employment of the company. Few, if any, will ever return to their farms to grow the food so badly needed by their families and their fellow countrymen at large.

Lest these remarks should be interpreted as a general condemnation of foreign investments in developing countries, I should make it clear in the first place that my reflections on this subject refer mainly to the exploitation of finite or wasting assets, particularly in such areas as mining and forestry and, to a smaller extent, fishing. In the second place, I am glad to observe a new, progressive tendency on the part of responsible investors to take a longer-term view of their association with the country in which they operate and to adopt policies designed to safeguard not only the environment and the welfare of the people whose lives have been directly and irreversibly affected by the investment, but also the future interests of their own shareholders.

In forestry, it is now common practice to expect concessionaires to replant trees at least at the rate at which they take them away. Some have even shown sufficient foresight to replenish the forest with species which would provide the raw material for the development of local industries, such as Indian Malina trees used for making paper pulp.

In the mineral sector, while some companies still make a quick get-away after skimming the cream of a deposit and amortizing their initial investment many times over, other companies re-invest part of their profits in the country, either in modern equipment designed to make viable the exploitation of poorer quality ores, or in other areas such as industry and agriculture. At the same time they also train their employees to make a living in a variety of occupations unconnected with mining.

Thus, in the neighbouring country of Liberia, the largest of the iron ore mining concerns, after exhausting the direct shipment ore (ore which can be fed directly into furnaces) has invested millions in plant to beneficiate and pelletize the lower grade ores. The same company has also embarked on a 'spin off' programme of local agricultural development and the re-training of workers in anticipation of the day when they will have to find alternative means of livelihood.

At Marampa it was perhaps our good fortune that DELCO decided to wind up their operations long before exhausting the potential of the deposits. This has given us the chance to negotiate new agreements with more forward looking investors who would take full advantage of modern technology and would also show more consideration for the future of their employees.

Naturally, the re-opening of the Marampa mine would also constitute a useful source of revenue for the Government. A heavy hunk of iron ore is not an easy or desirable commodity to hide on one's person and smuggle out of the country, and unless you hoard a ton or two of it, even if you could find a ready buyer, the price offered would never compensate for the trouble taken in amassing it. So every ton of iron ore mined is revenue for the mining company and the Government of Sierra Leone.

This is not true of the more valuable revenue-earner on the opposite side of the country, the diamond mining area of Kono, where it is estimated that the money lost to the country through illicit diamond digging and smuggling has run into millions of pounds. Small-scale mining started in Kono in 1933; two years later a private expatriate firm, the Sierra Leone Selection Trust, obtained exclusive prospecting and mining rights for virtually the whole of Sierra Leone. In spite of their rigid security measures, it was found to be impossible to stem the flow of humanity hell-bent on discovering a priceless gem in the dirt and gravel of a river bed.

Not only the unemployed and foreigners joined the ranks of fortune hunters, but people in steady jobs such as teachers and clerks resigned their positions of security to gamble with their fate. Farmers left their crops unattended to join the stampede, which resulted in an acute shortage of rice and other vital foodstuffs, causing prices to rise beyond the reach of most of the workers. Living conditions in the mining area were appalling: too many people, too few houses, no sanitation and little food. In this squalor the fight for survival and the lust for diamonds became a cut-throat business. Forty-five murders were recorded in the area in 1954 and in one case a mob of gangsters killed and disembowelled a man to possess a diamond he had swallowed for safe-keeping.

I had recently been made the first Minister of Lands, Mines and Labour at this time, so I was acutely concerned with the explosive state of affairs in the Kono district. I realised that it would be incredibly difficult, if not impossible, to rid the area of illicit diggers and the only answer as I saw it was to organise them on an official basis by issuing licences to diggers. If this were done, those with licences would be only too keen to fence off their allotted area against illicit diggers, and if it were also arranged for them to sell through a government buying organisation which gave as good a price as could be had across the Liberian border, this would discourage smuggling and guarantee revenue for the country that at that time was being lost altogether. I believed that unless prompt action were taken by the Government to allow the people of the country substantial participation in the mining of diamonds, the whole situation would get out of hand and we would be faced with epidemics, riots and bloodshed of a most serious nature. I was even more convinced that this was the only course to take on my return from a visit I made to the diamond mines in the Gold Coast.

The Sierra Leone Selection Trust did not take kindly to the idea of licensed diggers and the negotiations entered into on the subject between that company and the Government in January, 1955, ended in stalemate. Talks were resumed in London on June 27th and I was a member of the delegation, led by the Chief Minister, Dr. Margai, which travelled to England to take part in these discussions. Agreement was reached in principle, but trouble arose over the amount of compensation to be paid to S.L.S.T., who were asking the unreasonable figure of £10,000,000. Dr. Margai returned to Sierra Leone and left me and his brother, Albert, to battle on. I spent almost three months in London before the company finally agreed to accept £1,570,000. They were tedious weeks indeed for one way and another Albert Margai and I failed to manage on the per diem allowances made to us and more often than not we could not even aford the bus fare from the Regent Palace Hotel in Piccadilly where we were staying to the Colonial Office in Victoria, and had to walk. I worked hard both physically and mentally to save the country nearly nine million pounds and felt very nettled when complaints were registered on my return that the sum agreed was too high!

The agreement made with S.L.S.T. in 1955 reduced their exclusive rights to an area of 450 square miles in the Kono district and in Lower Bambara Chiefdom and Kenema districts. All rights in the rest of the country were surrendered to the Government and a scheme for licenced digging in those government controlled areas was set in motion and was known as the Alluvial Diamond Mining Scheme. The first licence, at a cost of £9 a year or £5 for a half year, was issued in Lubu Chiefdom, Bo District on February 6th, 1956, and by the end of March, 1,500 licences had been granted. In addition the licenced diggers were required to pay rent of 4/- a week to the Tribal Authorities.

Similarly Government arranged to buy diamonds from the licenced diggers. On February 7th I opened the main buying offices at Bo and soon after the opening ceremony diamonds were bought to the value of around £2,000. Later that month a second office was opened in Kenema. Valuers also trekked through the bush to contact diggers in the outlying districts and bought stones on the spot. In addition the scheme provided for licenced dealers to cover the vast mining area. A dealer's licence cost £25 but it could be issued to a man of any nationality or race, unlike the digger's licence which was issued to Sierra Leoneans only.

The majority of diamonds found in Sierra Leone are of gem quality and average between two and three carats. But in January of 1945 one of the largest alluvial diamonds in the world was discovered in the Woyie River in Kono weighing 770 carats. Called the Woyie River, it was sold for Le500,000 (£250,000). On February 14th, 1972, the third largest gem diamond ever found was recovered in the Company's Separator House at Yengema from concentrates sent in by No. 11 Heavy Media Plant. It weighed 969.1 carats, nearly half a pound, and measured roughly 2½" by 1½", slightly larger than a hen's egg. I named it 'The Star of Sierra Leone', and it was recently sold for several million dollars. It was most fortunate that this diamond was found legally in the Company's Separator House. If it had been found by independent miners, passed to illicit dealers and smuggled out of the country, not only would Sierra Leone be a lot poorer financially, but the credit due to her for this record find would have been lost.

Both iron ore and diamonds are wasting assets and for many years the audited profits of neither DELCO nor SLST were published, so that Sierra Leone derived tax only from what the two exploiting companies declared to us as profits on their yearly output. It has always been my view, and I have made no secret of it, that any country blessed with mineral deposits or any other form of potential wealth should have a controlling interest in the management as well as at least an equal share in the income earned. When I became Prime Minister in 1968 I at once sought to clarify my Government's policy with regard to the mining companies by addressing the Sierra Leone Chamber of Mines as follows:

"I have asked to meet you because I understand that there is some apprehension in the Mining Industry and its ancillaries in regard to the policies of the new Government in so far as these policies will affect the industry.

"On behalf of my Government, I should like to say that we have no plans to change the operational policy of the mines now or in the immediate future. No one realises more than we do, the vital part which the Mining Industry plays in the economy of Sierra Leone and it is not our intention to do anything which will jeopardise the life of the 'goose that lays the golden eggs'. What we think any responsible new Government would do and what the people of this country expect us to do, is to examine closely every aspect of the industry so as to make certain that this country is getting the maximum financial benefits out of the mining operations, bearing in mind that the life of the mines is limited and taking into consideration the country's serious financial situation, not to mention the need for money for development. For example, we intend to find out if we cannot share with the mining companies the financial benefits which should accrue to them as a result of devaluation. We intend to find out whether the eight year tax holiday which one of your companies is to enjoy conforms with the general principles of mining agreements in other parts of the world. We should also like to find out the precise basis for the calculation of the profits of which 50-60 per cent are supposed to be reserved for our benefit by some of the mining companies."

Although there was at that time a Sierra Leonean on the Board of the Sierra Leone Selection Trust, and our Government netted around 70 per cent of the company's profits through the Diamond Industries Profit Tax and Income Tax, I was not satisfied, upon examination, that the country was getting the maximum financial benefit from the Mining Industry and that, indeed, it never would unless and until it became a major shareholder in the enterprise. In December, 1970, therefore, my Government acquired 51 per cent of the SLST shares and the company was renamed the National Diamond Mining Company of Sierra Leone Limited (DIMINCO). It was recently pointed out to me that since the formation of DIMINCO an increasing number of large diamonds are being found in the Separator House in Yengema. Part of this may be due to my Government's action in driving from the mining area all so-called 'strangers', that is, those found guilty of not being in possession of non-citizen Registration Certificates, of entering Sierra Leone without travel documents and of being in the diamond protected areas without Residential Permits.

At the Separator House the threat from thieving is the most dangerous because the diamonds are easily selected there within a short time. It is one thing to steal at the plant sites and from the dumps where one has to do a lot of washing of gravel before getting the diamonds, and another thing to steal from the Separator House where gems, cleaned and sorted, are more or less offered on a plate.

This alone proves how important it is for us to participate in the mining of our mineral resources and I strongly feel that any future agreement between our Government and a company wishing to re-open the Marampa mine will have to provide for the operation to be conducted on a partnership basis between us. Such partnership agreements should have been drawn up, financed and put into effect at the time of Sierra Leone's independence in 1961, when the country officially came of age and was allowed to control its own affairs. Without such active participation, neither the exploiting companies nor the exploited country concerned can respect one another and operate the mines so that the maximum productivity is achieved for the benefit of both partners. My Government is going all out to get the indigenous people involved in our economic development, for it is shameful to have to admit that today, over 20 years after gaining our political independence, something like 70 to 80 per cent of the economic activity of the country is in the hands of foreigners. Of course we realise that we cannot legislate people into business. There has to be training and a certain amount of aptitude, and a willingness for sustained hard work. We realise, too, that there is a great need for outside capital and technical know-how, both of which we wish to encourage in every possible way. It is vital that we concentrate on our economic development, for I strongly believe that it is this which puts flesh and blood on the skeleton of political development.

CHAPTER FIVE

My First Step in Politics

How did I become an African nationalist? I was just a shy provincial boy in a hicktown job. But it was that little world of Marampa that, in a curiously roundabout way, launched me into politics. Almost without intending it, certainly without planning it, I accepted a role in the great work of liberation of my country and a part in shaping her political future. But it all began modestly, on a small and very human scale, in the circumstances I encountered or, perhaps more accurately, that encountered and gradually impelled me, in the course of my life in the mining community.

I did not take either of the conventional roads to political awareness that many of my contemporaries followed. I had not yet had enough education to make an intellectual. I was never the typical angry young ideologue. I had none of the fervour of new ideas brought back from Europe or America by the globe-trotting college men who were beginning to filter back to Sierra Leone from university training abroad. Nor had I been through the horrible purgation of active war service. Plenty of our boys saw the world from the blunt end of a rifle, fighting to keep the British Empire going: they learned nationalism in a tougher and more thorough school than the budding student revolutionaries. They had seen the myth of white supremacy, with its mask off on the Burma battlefield, or its pants down in behind-the-lines brothels. Many of them had lost limbs or blood or good looks but they had all gained insights into the realities of Sierra Leone's colonial predicament and could no longer be fooled.

I had not seen the world but I had seen suffering and I had felt the suffering of others. In some ways, I think my faint impulse towards some sort of political consciousness began with that kind of compassionate reflex. It is a common experience with sensitive boys touched by the effects of rapidly broadening experience.

It was, for example, only because of the simple promptings of humanity that I had wanted the peasant rebels to succeed — certainly not out of any enthusiasm for Haidara's politics which, I thought, verged on the insane. I was only beginning to perceive the links between suffering and oppression, but I wanted to see the wretched peasant masses somehow find the power within them to rise up and achieve a better life for themselves. Despite my sympathy for the rebels, however, my preference, by temperament and training, was for more practical responses to hardship. In my immediate surroundings, in the plight of my fellow workers in the mining industry, I found my first real chance to put whatever talents I had to use.

There was a touch of youthful idealism — almost of fanaticism for a good cause — about the campaigning I began for the mineworkers. But it was not ideologically inspired. It was constant contact with the grinding deprivation the workers went through that set and kept me going. My future political life was built on solid, deeply-dug foundations of years of trade unionism down the mines and in the bush. My trade union years were a sort of political pre-incarnation.

To this day I am glad to have travelled the trade union road to political involvement. It meant a re-opening of my experience of the grass roots of Sierra Leone. It taught me how popular organisations work. It encouraged me to see myself always as the servant of collective interests greater than my own. In the old days, my mining friends in the union often came to say 'thank you' for little victories wrung with great effort over wages and working conditions. I have a much bigger 'thank you' to say to them for all that they did — albeit unwittingly — for me.

If the battle against hardship in the mines was about fifty per cent of my political initiation, the rest came from my sense of being an African. It is hard for anyone outside the continent to understand what being an African means to me and to millions of my brothers. It means being the heir to a stifled civilisation. It means being half-deprived of identity. It means having nothing to show and everything to prove. It means being a victim of rape and robbery and slavery. It means a slow stirring from shock — the numbing, sometimes crippling shock, of a culture controverted by generations of colonialism and racialism. It means having to struggle for every dignity and human right. It means having to face apparently insuperable problems, apparently impossible odds.

I cannot conceal the fact — though it is undiplomatic to admit it — that the injustices and racialism of the colonial regime in Sierra Leone helped to make me an African nationalist. I do not say this in any spirit of hostility to the British I knew in the old days, many of whom I admired, even loved. They were doing a difficult job which they had chosen as a nation but not in every case as individuals. They were locked into a system of values and prejudices they had acquired from backgrounds and circumstances which were an inescapable part of history. I apportion no blame. But I want to try to express what it was like to be an African and a worker in those times. I want the younger generation of Sierra Leoneans to understand it. I want the friends of Sierra Leone in Britain and the whole western world to try to understand at least some small part of what it was like. Then they will begin to understand the history of my country, and in particular my own political awakening and that of hundreds, thousands, millions of my countrymen.

Even as a child at school I was dimly aware of the controversies that raged over the curriculum. I gradually came to realise as I got older that this was a consequence of the basic colonial dilemma — the clash of interests and aspirations between the imperial master-class and the subject race. The educational system in which I grew up was not run primarily for the benefit of the boys and girls — though, of course, it did us a lot of good and I am deeply grateful for it. It existed to help make colonial government work.

From school onwards, every frame of life in which I found myself supplemented and stimulated my awareness of the inadequacies of colonialism. The feeling, for example, came through the experience of winning ill-begrudged promotion to a managerial job at Marampa, or being bawled out by a basically well-meaning Scot. The sneer of cold command came all too easily to thin European lips. When men are typecast as master and subject, irrespective of merit, the affection of superiority becomes a habit for those in the dominant role. The illusion of superiority fostered in the remote luxury of Hill Station was not hard to mistake for reality. Equally inevitably, I reacted against a set-up that condemned my country to exploitation and my race to contempt. We acknowledged the achievements of the British but wanted the chance to achieve things for ourselves. We did not hate our colonial rulers but could have loved them better in their own country. Starting in the 'thirties, growing to intensity in the 'forties, I felt an insistent yearning for liberation.

But first there were immediate problems of misery and deprivation in the minefields to confront. Conditions for the miners in those early days at Marampa were terrible. They worked strenuously for six days a week at a wage of 9d. (7½c.) a day plus two cups of rice and a pinch of salt. They were little better than slaves. They soon developed the weary attitude of hopelessness. They cultivated a resignation born of despair, spirits crushed, bellies empty. The only way they could ever improve their lot was concerted action — industrial action: downing tools and paralysing mining operations, so that the management would be forced to listen to their grievances.

There was not much in the line of labour regulations in those days. The Trade Union Ordinance had not been enacted, so no trade unions could operate. When conditions got too pressing and we dared to make a bit of a noise, the manager sent for the District Officer at Port Loko and he came along with his court messengers and put the fear of God into us. I remember one morning while we were in the workers' compound in the labour camp, a court messenger collected about four of as at 6 o'clock and took us to the office where we met the manager and the District Commissioner. The District Commissioner said to us: "Look here, I have heard that there is going to be a strike in the mine and that you are the ringleaders. Well I want to warn you that if there is any trouble here, you will be in for it." This went on almost every quarter.

Each man pulled for himself and it was only when things got extremely bad that they managed to get together to register their resentment. They organised strikes — in 1932, for instance, when they held out for twelve days — but in most cases if the mine owners were not able to quell the disturbance on their own, the Government despatched police, court messengers and in one case, even soldiers, to intimidate the strikers and establish law and order. The strikers got simply no redress whatever.

I was physically and emotionally close to these desperate men. I had a better paid job, but as an employee of the mining company I was in a position to sympathise. I felt the same insecurity, the same anxiety, the same loneliness and economic impotence. I was joined to them by the friendship that comes from daily contact, mutual knowledge and, at least partly, a shared lot.

My feelings for the miners were such that I just could not stand by and do nothing, even if by helping them I jeopardised my own position, for I knew that I would invite fire from three directions: from the colonial government, from DELCO and from the Paramount Chief of Lunsar. The Government at that time did not recognise trade unionism in the country and quashed it whenever it looked like taking a hold. As far as DELCO was concerned, it adopted a policy of guarded acceptance of trade unions. While it would certainly have preferred to settle disputes through an elected committee of the workers rather than have to face an angry confused rabble whenever there was discontent, it was most anxious to avoid the Paramount Chief's displeasure.

The Paramount Chief looked on a trade union of mineworkers, representing as they did almost every tribe in the country including the Creoles, as a sort of plot by outsiders to undermine his position. The company had visions of wage rates getting out of hand by demands from a union. The Paramount Chief regarded a trade union as a foreign body in a tribal community threatening to give 'strangers' in the district an alarming corporate voice and usurp his authority over his own people. It was the very last thing he wanted and I recognised from the beginning that it was from him that I would have the greatest trouble.

Moreover, as it was later revealed, the newly installed Paramount Chief of Lunsar in Port Loko District, Bai Koblo Pathbana II, was receiving from the company a 'subsidy', known as lease-rent, of £15,000 a year, a great deal of money at the time — money which could have gone some way towards improving the lot of the workers. Since the mine happened to be within his Chiefdom, the subsidy could be regarded as a sort of royalty paid to the local Tribal Authority though, as a mining royalty, it was obviously most inadequate.

Ostensibly, one third of the subsidy was intended for the administration of the Chiefdom, one third as rental or compensation to the actual owners of the land used by the company, and the remaining third for the Paramount Chief himself. However, the distribution of the funds was left to the discretion of the Chief who, according to all available evidence, kept virtually all the money for his own use. In return he was expected to give his full support to the company and the colonial administration in their efforts to maintain 'law and order', that is to suppress any attempt by the workers to fight for their rights and better conditions.

Nevertheless, knowing conditions in the mines and in the area, as I did, when I became Minister of Lands, Mines and Labour in 1952, I negotiated with the Colonial Office in London for the lease-rent to be increased by a relatively small amount and for the increase to be backdated by three years. This after obtaining firm assurances that the two thirds of the payment, earmarked respectively for the administration of the Chiefdom and as compensation for the actual owners of the land, would be used for the purpose for which they were intended.

To appreciate the importance attached by the Company, and indirectly by the Colonial Office, to the services of the Paramount Chief it may be noted that I had little difficulty in obtaining satisfaction on the lease-rent increase and backdating issue while our requests for minor concessions for the workers met almost invariably with the strongest resistance. Invested with the traditional gown of absolute authority, armed with substantial funds which he could dispense at his discretion, and enjoying the confidence and active support of the colonial government, as represented by the Local District Commissioner, Bai Koblo soon became the most powerful and influential African in the area — a most redoubtable opponent whom only a foolhardy fighter would want to challenge in open combat. Later, Bai Koblo's influence was extended almost to the national scene when he married Madam Ella Gulama, daughter of the legendary Paramount Chief Julius Gulama (later a Paramount Chief in her own right) in my home District of Moyamba.

All this made it necessary to pick my steps very carefully at the start so as not to draw attention to myself. I, therefore, began by gathering the men together in small groups, listening to their grievances and showing them that the solution lay in their own hands by coming together as one man and speaking with one voice. Only then, I assured them, would they discover the strength of their negotiating power. Other leaders soon came forward to sow and nurture the seed of trade unionism among all categories of workers in the country, all at great personal risk to themselves, among them the late J. Akinola Wright who was co-founder with me of the United Mine Workers' Union.

In 1935 the mine workers of Marampa, now organised and with an elected spokesman, came out *en masse* in a protest strike against low rates of pay and long working hours, indecent treatment meted out to them, poor medical facilities and compulsory overtime hours. As a result of this strike, and one that followed at Pepel a short time later, the mines' management was moved at last to a grudging response. They set up a grievance machinery to examine workers' complaints, though nothing much else was achieved. However, the very fact that the employers were prepared to listen at all to the men's complaints showed clearly that they recognised their potential bargaining strength now that they had organised themselves into a union, which was no mean feat.

In 1937 the Marampa Mine Workers' Union applied to the Government for registration but as the much hoped for Trade Union Ordinance had not yet been enacted, their application was turned down. It took the horrors and hazards of war to make Sierra Leone safe for trade unions.

At the outbreak of World War II, Freetown, of course, became an essential port in the planning of naval operations; and the mining industry among others, became an extremely important part of the war economy. This naturally threw many areas of the country into unprecedented industrial and commercial activity which in turn created a situation where the need for trade unions became suddenly and increasingly obvious. Thus what we were called upon to do was not only to enter into this new organisational field with all the natural hazards that this entailed, but to do it in a social and economic situation which itself had been transformed almost overnight. This was a double handicap which nearly overwhelmed us, and in retrospect I marvel that we survived at all for the first few years.

The enactment of the Trade Union Ordinance, which was based on that in force in the United Kingdom, led to a rush of activity, and organisations were registered in all the main industries which at that time amounted to about half a dozen. Registration itself was a simple matter and in a comparatively short space of time there were about twenty unions in existence trying as well as they knew how to get established in a situation where there was no machinery for collective bargaining. None of us knew about either collective bargaining or statutory wage-fixing. None of us had any experience. As we saw it, we would in due course win recognition from the employers simply through the strength and militancy of our respective memberships, from which time our policies would be determined by the degree of co-operation which would develop between us. So we sat down and wrote letters to all the employers in sight. The most that could be said for the progress we made at this time was that sometimes our letters were acknowledged. But in spite of the legalisation of trade unions it became obvious that the employers had little intention of entering into anything like a permanent relationship with us.

In retrospect it is difficult to blame them entirely for adopting this attitude. While we were under the mistaken impression that no procedures existed which would enable us to represent our members, the employers clung to the primitive system of industrial relations which had operated for generations, a system in which the Government was itself the sheet-anchor. The fact is that the Government was by far the biggest employer in the country and it had always determined the wages and salaries of its own workers by order; other employers were expected and advised to fall into line in due course. This was a most elastic arrangement for them and its operation was, of course, simplicity itself, but it left no function at all for the trade unions, as we gradually came to realise.

Oddly enough, I do not think either the Government or the employers were consciously practising any deceit in this matter. I believe they honestly thought that at the outset, that is, for some years to come, the newly registered unions could not expect, because of their lack of experience, to enter into any arrangement with them which called for more than occasional consultation within the framework of the existing system.

The Marampa Mine Workers' Union was among the first to be registered in 1939 — a glimpsed flicker of light like a lamp in the deepest shaft. Hopelessness was suddenly dispelled. There was no question any longer of managements ignoring unpalatable facts. The flame quickly spread bringing hope and encouragement to depressed workers throughout the country. Steadily we union leaders plodded on, building up membership, solidarity and funds. It was necessary to educate the large mass of illiterate membership concerning the principles of trade unionism, which was no small task, but more difficult still was the effort involved in exacting dues from the workers who could ill afford to contribute a cent from their meagre pay packets. Even when we eventually managed to get their wages raised to around 2/- a day plus a pound of rice a week, it was as much as I could do to raise as little as one shilling (10c) a month from them. It was also difficult to keep track of members for, particularly at planting and harvest time, there was a substantial turnover of labour. Many workers, too, as elsewhere in the world, wanted the benefits of being a trade union member but without subscribing if they could avoid it. Eventually the Marampa Construction Company agreed to introduce the check-off system, that is, deducting union dues from wage packets.

Perhaps the most disappointing experience I had during this period was not so much with employers as with the slow progress of our members to understand the new situation which had come about. As I was to learn later in Britain, unions can gain experience with difficulty; to attract financial support during the early days of a union is an almost impossible task. This was my main problem and that of my colleagues in the other unions. Furthermore in the mines our problem was made much worse by the nature of the labour force. Many, if not most of the labourers were young men who came from outside the district with a cash target in mind and they returned to their homes when this had been achieved.

There were times when I felt I was beginning to get to know them. I remember one cheery young chap with a laugh that would split a pit prop, whose compulsive happiness not even the hardship of the mines could erode. I liked him for his indomitable spirit and unshakeable morale. There was another young lad with a real gift for language; though I have forgotten his many stories, the fluid sound of his voice remains in my memory. I recall a third, very young, very likeable but very callow man, who could never overcome a kind of superstitious unease which he felt about the union, saying he would never get a benefit from his membership before he died. But just as I began to grow to love them, they would be off like slurry from a tip. Sometimes I felt deeply lonely.

There was also another serious problem to overcome. When I came later to read about the work of Sidney and Beatrice Webb on British trade unions, I was struck by their definition of these organisations, which they describe in the main as "a continuing association of workmen for the improvement of their wages and conditions of employment". The key term in this is 'continuing association'. This is the essential feature of any successful organisation. Yet it is an extremely difficult concept to explain to men who come from non-industrialised and simple communities when they engage in employment. To them money is given only for tangible benefits like food and clothing. Taxation, they often feel, is just extortion and the idea of paying regularly to an organisation for unspecified benefits which may or may not come their way in the future, is often far too sophisticated a notion for them to grasp in the uncertain circumstances in which they live their lives.

It was understandable, therefore, that quite often it would happen that prior to a wage claim, the union would receive plenty of financial support from the workers, but as soon as our efforts were crowned with success, the contributions would fall off very considerably. This was not evasion. As far as the men were concerned, they felt that they had discharged their responsibilities in financing the union to secure the benefits obtained, much as they would pay a lawyer for any services rendered but not retain him indefinitely.

I do not know to what extent this attitude has been, or still is, shown in Western countries, with respect to either trade unions or any other kind of necessary social organisation, but I feel sure in my own mind that there are few countries where the need for a clearer understanding by ordinary people of the concept of 'a continuing association' is not being wrongly described as apathy. We are too quick to assume that men are born with social insights which can in fact only be appreciated by them after long and patient instruction. It is for this reason that I strongly advocate an increasing interest in the possibilities open to us for still further improvements in our approach to adult education.

Our union finances remained unstable for a long time and we were not alone in having to cope with this problem; other unions also had to deal with it. In those days, employers were not disposed to help us in any way believing, wrongly I think, that trade unions are more amenable when they are weak. In fact we knew that we could have done them a great deal of damage had we so wished, but we refrained from such irresponsible action. What they did not realise was that it would have cost us nothing to have brought about a strike because we had no funds for strike benefit. Nor, on the other hand, did we have sufficient money to mount a national conference for the avoidance of strike situations which were building up on their own account without any encouragement from us.

In those early years of our trade union development there were no models we could turn to for guidance in what was then Colonial Africa. Nigeria, Ghana and The Gambia had nothing to offer us and we had no reason to look to the east and central parts of the continent. Our efforts at establishing unions, however much they may have fallen short of perfection, had certainly met with enough success to focus attention on them by the Colonial Office, which no doubt prompted Ernest Bevin, then Minister of Labour in the British Coalition Government, to promote the idea that if trade unionism was to be established in the then Colonies, those who were anxious to develop it should be given some practical assistance. This resulted in advisers being appointed in most of the territories, and the man who was appointed to Sierra Leone, Edgar Parry, arrived here in the middle of 1942.

Personally I was not wildly enthusiastic about European Government officials at the time because during the organising of the mine workers at Marampa I had met with unwarranted opposition from one of them which, increasing as it did the reluctance of the mine owners to accept our union for the purposes for which it had been established, did nothing to improve my feelings towards a government which claimed to be anxious to promote trade unionism. But I saw no reason to allow animosity to stifle common sense, and decided I could lose nothing by talking to Parry.

"The trade union organisation in this country is very poor," he said with brutal frankness. "If you intend to follow the course that has been taken by the British movement it will be some years before you can hope to make any impact on the industrial scene." I and other union leaders asked him to enlarge on the British practice. "First of all," he said, "you must secure a respectable membership and, with the power that this will give you, to gain recognition from the employers. Even this will take a fair amount of time."

Parry went on to give an account of the negotiating machinery in current use and a description of the statutory wage-fixing methods adopted in those instances where the unions were unable to negotiate from a position of strength. As he saw it, there was clearly an immediate need in Sierra Leone for some proper and permanent system of determining wages and conditions of employment throughout the country. Whether or not workers were illiterate, socially backward or not yet fully aware of the assistance that trade unionism could give them, was irrelevant to this need.

As the unions could not at that early stage of their development demand such a system from the employers, it would be necessary for the Government to establish by legislation an adequate number of bodies through which wages and conditions would be negotiated, fixed and settled. Furthermore, the unions should be given as much represen-tation on these bodies as if they were in fact fully representative of the people engaged in the industries concerned. He felt that there was no place for gradualism in the matter of trade union recognition in the situation with which we had to deal.

"To the best of my knowledge," he declared, "no government has ever taken such a bold step before, but I cannot recommend such a proposal unless you yourselves will agree to certain conditions, the main one being that you will be willing to amalgamate your existing organisations to the point where there is only one union for each industry and thus ensure that the workers will only speak with one voice. A single union," he added, "would also be able to provide sufficient funds to give a modest salary to one full-time official and thus ensure his independence."

This was logical. Initially there were four separate mine workers' unions — Marampa, Pepel, Yengema and Hangha — and as each one grew in strength, the impossible position into which they were put by having all their officials employed in the mines and by each mining union working independently, became more and more apparent. In 1943, therefore, the Marampa and Pepel unions were amalgamated and I was asked by the men to become the union's first full-time official. I readily accepted the men's offer despite the fact that it involved leaving a fairly secure and relatively well paid job for one providing the prospect of constant harassment by the colonial and tribal authorities, as well as a smaller and uncertain income.

However, when I handed in my resignation, DELCO was not aware of my plans and of the offer made to me by the union. The company appeared to be so delighted to get rid of one whom they regarded as a troublemaker that they gave me a gratuity of £200 to enable me to return to my home town of Moyamba where, they thought, I would buy a house with the money and live happily ever after, minding my own business, while they continued to exploit our workers unhindered by a union organiser.

When they heard that I had settled down in Lunsar instead of Moyamba they immediately called in Bai Koblo, then Paramount Chief designate, instructing him to see to it that I leave the area forthwith. At the time, Bai Koblo was still undertaking the mandatory two-month period of initiation during which he was forbidden by tribal custom to leave the bush. Disregarding tradition at the beck and call of his new masters, he hurried to the company's headquarters to receive his orders and then summoned me. When he realised that neither persuasion nor threats would make me leave Lunsar, he complained bitterly to the District Commissioner that I was making trouble in his Chiefdom and urged him to get me removed from the town.

The District Commissioner, a Mr. O'Dwyer, must have known that his task would not be an easy one and that the Marampa workers would do everything possible to keep me in Lunsar. As I entered his office, summoned by a Court Messenger, I felt that he was determined to secure an initial advantage by humiliating and intimidating me. "Stevens", he snapped. I immediately interrupted him as politely as I could: "Mr. Stevens, Sir, if you please", I retorted, stressing the first word. He was taken somewhat aback but went on to accuse me of using illegal methods of organising the union. He then more or less ordered me to leave the District, hinting that if I refused to do so he could have me put in jail. However, he suggested that he was merely carrying out the wishes of the Paramount Chief who wanted me out of his Chiefdom. I reminded the District Commissioner, again very politely, that I was a native of Sierra Leone and had the right to live where I liked in my own country. "Please tell the Paramount Chief", I said, "that I will not budge and that he cannot get me out." I then added co-operatively,

"Certainly I will leave, Sir, provided, of course, you serve me with an order to do so."

A couple of days later, nearly 4,000 Marampa mineworkers came down to Lunsar to make it clear to all concerned that they too had a say in the matter. I had to use all my influence and powers of persuasion to get them to go back quietly and avoid a showdown. But both the Paramount Chief and the District Commissioner undoubtedly got the message.

Some time before there had already been a terrible strike in Marampa which lasted three weeks or more and resulted in much riotous behaviour including arson. In spite of the accusations levelled at me, as leader of the Marampa Mine Workers' Union, of aiding and abetting and my name being brought up in the Executive Council in connection with the affair, the union did not sponsor the strike at all. Our main occupation was to counsel patience, constitutional representation and other peaceful means of negotiation since, apart from anything else, it was obvious that not much could be done along the line of strikes without the workers being well organised. An official enquiry into the strike was instigated, which cleared me and the union of any blame but found fault with the mines' manager who was sent home.

Following my encounter with the District Commissioner I also despatched a telegram to Parry in Freetown, putting forward the facts of the case. He found nothing illegal or rebellious about my activities, especially since I had been cleared by the Commission of Enquiry into the Marampa riots, and, in his position now as Acting Commissioner for Labour, he ruled that in future no trade union man or industrial dispute should be interfered with unless there were riots. Subsequently, I had more friendly meetings with District Commissioner O'Dwyer and never harboured a grudge against him. He had been doing his job in what he believed was the interest of the British Empire and of the Allied war efforts while I was doing mine in the interest of our workers. I understand that after returning to Britain he lost his sight, but not his courage, and became a blind physiotherapist or manipulative practitioner.

In 1945, we amalgamated with the Yengema union to form the United Mine Workers' Union, the headquarters of which were established in Freetown, away from the mining areas, and I was asked to become its first full-time secretary-general.

So it was that with a sigh of relief from many quarters, I left Lunsar for Freetown. With the amalgamation of the three mine workers' unions, the establishment of a headquarters in the capital and the services of a full-time secretary, the apparently ineffective representations which had been registered all along by the individual unions over the years, were pressed home in earnest. We showered our complaints on both employers and Government, submitting memoranda, resolutions and reports in profusion. Arthur Creech Jones, a life-long British trade-unionist and former National Secretary of the powerful Transport and General Workers' Union who had just become Under-Secretary of State for the Colonies in the first post-war Labour government, sent a succession of teams to investigate our complaints. Meanwhile, even as the war was drawing to an end, we achieved some concessions for our Marampa workers, including a six-day week, as against the seven-day week worked hitherto, and a reduction of the expected output per man from 50 tons per week to a flexible norm ranging from 32 to 42 tons.

The first major wage negotiating exercise was the preparation of a wages schedule for all daily paid workers. Prior to this, artisans' and semi-skilled workers' rates of pay were subject to the whims of the foreman-in-charge; this, I held, was a most unsatisfactory and unfair state of affairs. The agreed wage schedule formed the basis for all future wage negotiating and resulted ultimately in a Wages Board being appointed. In addition to wage rates the Board fixed holidays with pay, sick pay, overtime rates and so on. Wage increases were from now on always a fixed amount to every worker which thus reduced the differential between the labourer and skilled or semi-skilled workmen.

Along with other mine workers, I was nominated a member of the Wages Board on which the employers were equally represented. There were in addition three independent members one of whom was the chairman. From a voting point of view, it was vital to us, the workers' representatives in particular, that the three independent members of the Wages Board could be relied upon to remain independent and to understand the issues which came before them. Some of those who opposed the setting up of the Board did so on the grounds that people could not be found locally whose qualifications were suitable and whose detachment could be sufficiently assured to fill such positions.

As it turned out, it would have been difficult to have found three more able men. The chairman was Father Mackey, then Acting Bishop of the Roman Catholic Church in Sierra Leone, who brought a balanced social conscience to our proceedings along with great weight and authority. The other two members were, to the surprise of many, both Africans. The elder of the two was J. Akinola-Wright, a Sierra Leonean who had retired from a senior post in the Nigerian Civil Service, and the younger was Robert Gardiner, a Ghanaian who was until recently the Secretary-General of the Economic Commission for Africa, but who was at that time teaching at Fourah Bay College. All three men were held in high regard and contributed a great deal to the work of the Board.

I well remember the day the Wages Board was inaugurated in the Legislative Council Chamber which was housed in the old Secretariat building. The business was purely ceremonial with a goodwill speech by the Colonial Secretary, an acknowledgement by the Chairman and suitable statements by the leaders of the two sides. I listened intently to Father Mackey's address, as did others, for it was in complete contrast to the conventional words of good wishes expressed by the Colonial Secretary. There was nothing antagonistic about it; it just sounded strange. One part in particular, which creased the brows of us representing the wage-earners and caused the employers to smile and nod in agreement, is still fresh in my memory: "... a man may not work for an inadequate remuneration," the Father read. "The remuneration must be enough to support the wage-earner in reasonable and frugal comfort".

It was only later that I learnt that he had read to us from the Encyclical Letter of Pope Leo XIII, published as far back as 1891, the 'Rerum Novarum' otherwise known as The Workers' Charter. This famous and sombre statement is one of the most valued declarations made by the Church on social and industrial policies and could not have been uttered on a more suitable occasion.

It was a big step forward and a great day when we, the representatives of the workers, faced representatives of the employers on equal terms and when, we were able to fix a wage of 2/- (20c) for the mine worker for an 8-hour day with time and a half for overtime, double time for Sundays and holidays and twelve days annual leave.

A mines manager once said to me: "You ought to be very glad of the help the Labour Department is giving you." So I replied: "The Labour Department, especially in its present set-up, has helped you far more than it has helped us. If it had not been for their persistent effort in counselling patience and tact, for their honest attempt to understand the men's point of view and for their explaining government's attitude in matters of industrial disputes, I must tell you that industrial relations in the mining industry would have deteriorated to such an extent that it would have required the urgent attention not only of the local government, but perhaps also the Government of the United Kingdom.

In the eyes of the average native worker," I continued, "Government and the mining employers, both being European, will stick together. When labour unrest develops, instead of Government trying to understand the workers' point of view and meeting their demands even to a minor degree, they rush in policemen, court messengers and soldiers to intimidate and suppress them. Realising that Government, their last resort, has failed them, the workers resort to other means to ward off oppression and injustice."

I was indeed proud of the improvements achieved in the working conditions for the mine workers, but I was far from satisfied. There was still no security of employment, benefits, treatment of industrial diseases, adequate medical attention or recreational facilities; and compensation for injuries was scandalous. For fatal accidents, for which the highest amount of compensation was awarded, the amount was reckoned at 30 months' earnings on the basis of a 26-day month. At the time this worked out to be about £52 (Le104). Fifty-two pounds for a whole human life!

It was with my appointment to the Wages Board that I entered for the first time what could be called any sort of public life in the capital. I had, of course, done a considerable amount of work for my union, but this was outside the Colony area. Now, however, I was leader of a group nominated by the Government to serve on an official body whose objects could not have been nearer to my heart. It seemed now as if we might make some progress.

There we were, the employers, the union and the independent members, along with a small secretariat, all set to run an organisation of which not a single one of us had any previous experience. Yet anyone who cares to study the full records of the Board from its beginnings will find that it has conducted its affairs with competence right from the outset. And I think it will be found that the same is true of all the other bodies that were subsequently established. Positive and constructive achievements make news, yet here we all were doing things, important things, just as effectively as they were doing them in Britain at that time.

Here, for the first time, we were part of the decision-making body ourselves and I was anxious to learn about the procedures by which such organisations operated and to watch the methods and style of men experienced in the use of power and persuasion. I saw how much our independent members resorted to the latter and how, when they had to make use of power, they always seemed to behave as if they did not realise it was at their disposal. I have always had a great admiration for men who possess strength but use it modestly. I cannot recall when our independent members made use of their votes on later occasions because thier powers of persuasion were so effective that it was seldom necessary to take a poll. This was a valuable lesson for me; and so was the need to observe the procedures of the Board.

When we made any sort of claim we had to adduce evidence, and now that we were fully recognised by the employers, we had to learn to be as businesslike as they were in our dealings with them. Like many people, I have a strong dislike of red tape; on the other hand I have long realised there are certain formalities to be observed if your relationships with others are to bring about mutual improvements.

In due course not only the mining industry but all the principal industries were operating inside the framework of some wage-fixing or negotiating body for which provision was made in the legislation. The unusual feature of this legislation was that whenever an agreement was negotiated, its terms were not merely confined to the parties to the agreement. All employers of the groups of workers specified were obliged to pay the same wages and to provide the same conditions of employment. This meant that in effect almost everyone working for anyone anywhere was entitled to a legally enforceable minimum wage. The Act under which this was done has now been replaced by a more comprehensive measure, but its main provisions have been retained because they have been so useful to us. I am very glad indeed to see that the present generation of workers have become as accustomed as British workers to see their wages and conditions of employment flow from agreements made between their own representatives and the employers.

I see in this a social achievement of a sort which augurs well for our future throughout our society. In the long run our success will depend upon our capacity to adapt ourselves to constructive change and to rid ourselves of the inhibitions which stultify our efforts. Ordinary people have participated in the establishment of social organisations in which they have transformed their own lot. They have taken themselves out of feudal conditions into the world of the most modern industrial societies in a very short period of time. Although it is a fact that only comparatively small numbers of people have been involved in this transformation, this takes nothing away from its significance. In 1971 we enacted an Industrial Relations Bill which is very comprehensive indeed but it only came on to the Statute Book *after* the fullest consultation with people affected by it, and they are as responsible for its successful operation as is the Government. I have no doubt that they will live up to their responsibilities. The record of the trade unions has not been unblemished. Events have taken place which we would all like to forget. Nevertheless, I believe that over the years during which the changes I have written about have happened, it has been proved that Africans are as socially adaptable as any people in the world.

I have referred above only to the relationships between employers and workers. There has also been another development which is no less important for society. During the Second World War, because of the general illiteracy among workers, they were obliged to turn to men to lead them who, by and large, belonged to the lettered class. These leaders strove as well as they could to improve the working lives of their members but it was inevitable as time went by that the difficulties they faced almost daily led them to depend increasingly upon their own personal judgements rather than upon the collective views of the membership which itself floated up and down unpredictably.

I know that we often found ourselves in defensive positions where we had to make decisions which, according to the rules, should have been taken by an executive committee or even the full membership. Some of us, I suppose, became so accustomed to this state of affairs that we began to accept it as a natural way of doing the job. Whether or not this was a healthy development I was too close to the situation to decide. What I do know, however, is that at the present time the officers of our unions are not given the latitude which was accorded us. It is now by no means unusual for union leadership to be subjected to criticism and it is not relevant to the point I wish to make whether this is justified or not. I only wish to record that such a change has come about. The members of mass movements can sometimes be cruelly critical of their leaders but on the other hand, what a great step forward it is that they have learnt to criticise at all.

I have read somewhere that the three great legal relationships in life are husband and wife, parents and children and master and servant, or, as we would say today employer and employee. With us, this last one is going to become an increasingly important relationship since I can foresee that greater and greater numbers of our people will be coming into paid employment. In addition to this group we must also take into account those who, while not employers or employees in the strictest sense of these terms, are, or will become, associated with production and development boards and the like in various forms of co-operative enterprises where power must be delegated to individuals or small groups. No developing country can avoid changes of this kind and I think we should consider some of the problems they will present us with.

The truth is that we are sometimes so bemused by the great variety of political theories which are offered to us that we tend to overlook the fact that the basic master and servant relationship has not yet been abolished under any political system in the world. It remains even in those countries where the most modest standards of living are sought. Mass production brought about by modern or at least suitable technology, is accepted everywhere as an aim of policy, and with it the need for organisation and — we must face it — the direction of the many by the few. This is an inescapable condition of living in the modern world and I do not think that sufficient attention has been paid to the consequences of this fact.

The simple question we have to answer is how a high degree of individuality can be maintained in communities where centrally controlled organisations must be increased in order to provide our growing material needs. Now the elitists are in no doubt about the matter. We should let things run their natural course and allow them to play their directional role for which they are so obviously well equipped. Nor are they greatly concerned whether the prevailing political philosophy of the country is capitalist, socialist or anything between or beyond these two, so long as they are given the powers of direction.

So far as I can discover, much more thought has gone into promulgating the unproved doctrine that we should hand over our affairs to 'good' elites than to practical proposals whereby the majority of those working or co-operating in an industry can themselves effectively manage and control these well intentioned leaders. Almost every time I raise this matter there are shrugs and smiling references to Yugoslavia. As I understand it, the great heresy of which that country is guilty is that the workers there have the power to appoint their own managers and that it is in their interest to choose good men since any improvement in the productivity of their undertaking is reflected in their own incomes. I am in no position to judge whether this is a good or a bad practice. What does impress me, however, is that Yugoslavia has struggled against very powerful forces to keep it.

It seems to me utterly unacceptable that once we admit, as I most certainly do, that some men are more gifted than the rest of us, we are expected to concede that because of this the only logical conclusion we can reach is that we should hand over all effective power to this minority. I can see no logic in this argument, nor can I see why we cannot examine alternative proposals which will make our industrial leaders much more responsible to the people they are called upon to manage. It may be that there are inherent difficulties in our situation which would make it impossible to adopt any known practices. However, we cannot afford to neglect the experience which has been accumulated by those who have tried to solve the problem.

Nevertheless, I have a strong feeling that, in the end, we in the African states, and especially in this region, will have to find our own ways of safeguarding the individuality of the ordinary man inside industry. I have great admiration for the technology of the West but their conflicting ideologies about the creation and distribution of wealth and power do not commend themselves to me. We are often told that the most harmful social disease they suffer from is 'alienation' which, as I understand it, means that the highly specialised and fragmentary nature of modern industry divorces a man from the social purposes of his work and leaves him an unthinking drudge without real interest in either his employment or his society. It is argued that he becomes merely a link in the production chain.

This picture might well be overdrawn but as far as we are concerned, I think there is enough truth in it to make us consider very seriously what steps we should take to prevent the emergence of this social disability here. Even the enemies of Africans pay tribute to the spontaneity and love of life which we show in abundance. Indeed some speak patronisingly of the childlike nature of the African. It occurs to me that there has been no time in the social history of the world when the childlike approach was more called for. If we are childlike in sociological terms, very well; children are not only willing to learn, they are also frankly curious and uncommitted. We will need all these qualities if we are to find out how to make use of the productive organisations we require without dehumanising our people in the process. For my part, I would aim higher and consider to what extent work, education and even pleasure can be brought together into a social framework where each of them is compatible with the others.

CHAPTER SIX

My Political Apprenticeship

Through the Wages Board, my union work took me straight into the political world and the national arena. I came to understand politics as an essentially practical discipline. I learned not to see economics in isolation, but in a broad context of nicely balanced political interests. I became an initiate in the mysteries of confrontation and negotiation, diplomacy and compromise. I got a bird's eye view of the late colonial political world; I could see the divisions, the difficulties and the options. But the Wages Board, although much of what it did was effectively political, was not an explicitly political organ; nor did it cover the whole range of politics — particularly of mass politics and the politics of national and African liberation, in which I was becoming increasingly interested, increasingly involved. The British Empire was puffing and wheezing its way to decrepitude like an old man running after his hat. Its frayed bunting was caught by the first winds of change. I found myself in the eye of the wind.

In Sierra Leonean terms, this meant being part of Protectorate politics. The neglected majority of Sierra Leoneans in the hinterland of the country were beginning to kick, not just against British mastery but also against the relatively over-privileged status of the coastal Colony area. Tribal antagonism was always just below the surface, and sometimes it broke through to make fissures in Protectorate unity; there was a quasi-tribal element in much of the resentment felt — most of it for no good reason — between the various communities of up-country men. But the crucial issues among Sierra Leoneans were between Colony and Protectorate; issues of how the balance of resource allocation was to be reconstructed to give the Protectorate a fair deal; how political representation was to be divided between Colony and Protectorate in the coming sub-colonial phase of Sierra Leonean history; how power was to be wielded between the two historic communities as independence approached.

My background had made me completely objective where tribalism was concerned. It also gave me a sense of belonging in both Colony and Protectorate. I sympathised with Protectorate aspirations not just out of regional chauvinism, though I was conscious of being an up-countryman by parentage and birth, but out of a straightforward sense of justice, fortified by political pragmatism. It was a plain fact that the Colony was over-represented in such institutions as the British allowed us. It was a plain fact that the Colony had got the lion's share of the meagre development the country had enjoyed under British rule. It was equally palpable — at least to most of us in the 'thirties and 'forties — that the future of Sierra Leone lay with *all* Sierra Leoneans. And the people of the Protectorate formed the vast majority. They simply had to be brought into the political process if we were to confront the British in unity and get the chance to build a democratic and developed society in the future. I had got to know the Creoles' special sense of identity pretty intimately as a small boy. I had come to terms with all the little difficulties of living among them and now felt as much at home in Freetown as in Gbonjeima or Moyamba. It had been tough work adjusting to the diversity of backgrounds I had been exposed to as a child but it gave me a tremendous depth of perspective in beholding my homeland. I think I was lucky to be a member of a fairly small group in the first generation of my countrymen really to feel what it was like to be a Sierra Leonean in the fullest sense; not primarily or solely a Creole or a Protectorate man or the member of a tribe. I used whatever influence I had with friends in Freetown or up-country to make them see Sierra Leone as a national entity. And I found there were many Creoles who saw and welcomed the practical necessity of sharing their destiny with the rest of us.

Even so, with so many conflicting tendencies at work, even the most far-sighted of us knew that national unity would take a long time to construct. The real work went on underneath the institutional super-structure that was gradually taking shape, at a moral and pyschological level, but it is only possible to chart the progress of the institutional revolution. I had a part in the first stage of this: the erection of the Protectorate Assembly. Like the Trade Union Ordinance, this was conceded by the British in response to popular pressure, not out of altruism but out of the necessity imposed by war. In 1944, Governor Sir Hubert Stevenson drew the attention of the Legislative Council to the disproportionately high representation of the Colony vis-a-vis the Protectorate. Everyone was well aware of this already, of course, but it was a convention of colonial government that the Governor's initiatives were always invested with a spurious air of novelty. The following year an attempt was made to rectify the situation first by the creation of a District Council in each of the 13 districts in the Protectorate, and secondly by the establishment of a Protectorate Assembly of 42 seats which was to advise the Colonial Government on all Protectorate affairs.

The District Councils comprised two representatives from each chiefdom in the district, one of whom had to be the Paramount Chief and the other a member of the chiefdom appointed by the Tribal Authorities over which, of course, the chiefs wielded great influence. The 42 seats in the Protectorate Assembly were allocated as follows: 26 for the representatives of the 13 District Councils (which, in fact, were all held by chiefs), 10 for official members (British Colonial officials headed by the Governor) and six nominated unofficial members, four of whom were to be African. As Secretary General of the Marampa Mine Workers' Union I was nominated to one of these unofficial seats to represent the workers, or, in official jargon, "representing interests not represented on District Councils".

As can be imagined, the four small voices of the unofficial African members, the only people in the whole Assembly who truly represented the interests of the under-privileged masses, stood a pretty slim chance of making themselves heard or of achieving anything that was not in the interests of the Colonial officials and the 26 elected chiefly members who supported them. The establishment of the Protectorate Assembly certainly brought the different tribal chiefs together, which was an achievement for the Colonial Government and roundly applauded by the chiefs themselves, but the Assembly as constituted was far from being the representative body that we had been agitating for. In creating it the Colonial Administration had failed to take into account the changed relationship that had developed since the war between the new educated element and the chiefs. No longer did the Protectorate people automatically accept the chiefs as their spokesmen.

With education and the spread of progressive ideas, many of us recognised the handicap of relying on what boiled down to yes-men of the Colonial regime acting on our behalf. The time had come when those of us who understood the true needs and aspirations of the masses, who lived and worked in close contact with them — who, indeed, were of their number but who were educated enough to negotiate terms on their behalf — should do so directly and have the courage to present their case as it existed, without any apologies, embellishments or side-tracking, however much it displeased the authorities to hear it.

Our persistent agitation for more realistic representation naturally angered the Paramount Chiefs who were understandably jealous of their traditional rights as unquestioned rulers in their provinces. That a group of men should emerge among their subjects whose progressive ideas threatened to undermine their authority was dangerous enough. That those men sought to voice such ideas personally, as representatives of the people in the Assembly, rather than let the Paramount Chiefs speak for them in the customary manner, struck at the very roots of traditional chieftaincy and was something totally unacceptable to them.

Chieftaincy has played and must continue to play an important role in African life, for it is part of our tradition and the very basis of our society. In the past it was the chiefs who kept law and order among their subjects, who administered justice, meted out punishment and established a code of behaviour. The Colonialists did as little as possible to interfere with the status of those chiefs who showed a willingness to co-operate with them. They respected them and handled them with kid gloves, for it was very much in the interest of peaceful and effective government to have them as allies. The chiefs could be relied upon to carry out government policy, for they knew that however little their traditional authority may have seemed, on the face of it, to have been affected by the advent of the Colonial Government, that Government would not hesitate to remove any chief who worked against it. So it paid both the chiefs and the Colonialists to rub along together, and the Colonial Government was as disturbed as the Paramount Chiefs when the educated minority threatened to change the old order of things.

But for the war, no doubt this young and progressive element would have been put smartly in its place, but the time had come when the Colonialists could no longer afford to turn a deaf ear to reason, from wherever it came, and when the chiefs, if they hoped to survive at all as rulers, would have to adjust themselves to a changing society.

Unfortunately for the chiefs, the backing they had relied upon for so long from the Colonial Administration was showing definite signs of sagging. They knew they stood a poor chance of holding out alone. For a time they tried, desperately hard, and the gap that resulted between them and the educated element became so wide that at one time it seemed that reconciliation was out of the question. Eventually, of course, they had to come to terms with reality. With the awakening of political consciousness among the masses and at a time when the tendency was to kick against authority in general, to have obstinately clung to an out-dated system would not only have exposed the sterility of chieftaincy, but have invited disrespect and even ridicule from the people.

On the other hand, to combine their great knowledge of traditional matters and the innate wisdom passed down to them from their ancestors, with the modern-type wisdom, acquired through improved educational facilities, of specialists in technological, scientific, economic and political spheres who seek to develop a nation, is to enrich our heritage, to enhance progress and to make for national stability. So long as chieftaincy operates as an arm of the national government, projecting that government's policy and undertaking at local level the settling of disputes, advice on problems and the general promotion of peace and harmony among the people in its provinces, it cannot fail but provide a most valuable and welcome service to Sierra Leone.

As far as the youth of today is concerned, there is a tendency the world over to reduce everybody to one level, to knock the pedestals from under the feet of traditionally respected and revered personalities and to regard as passé and archaic a preference for old-established and well-tried principles. I hope this is a passing phase; if not it is a tragedy. To belittle those in positions of authority, be they parents, teachers, chiefs or Heads of State, is to belittle one's own self to a degree where one's very soul is relegated to the gutter. Fortunately for Africa this anti-social trend has not as yet gained much ground among our youth and I am sure that the traditions of chieftaincy that played no small part in our children's formative years have done much to preserve our sense of value and respect for our elders.

We, the youth of yesterday, had no intention of belittling or undermining the chiefs of the Protectorate when we insisted on a more realistic representation of the people. We were most anxious to work in harmony with them, but we could not afford to humour them at the expense of progress. It was in an effort to shorten the gap that had developed between us, to work for a united and progressive society of chiefs and people in the Protectorate and, at the same time, to continue to agitate for fairer representation, that I helped to found the Sierra Leone Organisation Society (S.O.S.) in 1946. That same year saw the revival of the Protectorate Educational Progressive Union (P.E.P.U.) which had become inactive several years after it was first formed in 1929. The aim of the P.E.P.U., which was founded and financed by chiefs, was to spread education in, and generally work for the progress of, the Protectorate. These two organisations having similar aims and embracing both the educated element and the chiefs of the Protectorate, did much to draw the two together.

Membership of the Protectorate Assembly had made me a politician 'and no bones about it'. As with the Wages Board, it was from the jetty of trades unionism that I had been launched on the ocean of national politics. It was a new and heady experience to have a whiff of direct responsibility for the long-term future of my country. I could not let that opportunity slip. No man with any guts or gumption could. My participation in S.O.S. was an attempt to make something of my chance, to create an organisation that could formulate long-term objectives and campaign effectively for them. It was more than a lobby, it was a pressure group. It was more than a pressure group, it was a proto-party.

In the S.O.S. we lost no opportunity to keep the British Government *au fait* with Protectorate affairs. We pointed out that the common people of the Protectorate, as taxpayers, should be entitled to even more representation than the natural rulers of the country and that we objected to the monopoly of representation which the chiefs held in the Protectorate Assembly and elsewhere. We proposed that in the reconstituted Legislative Council which was being contemplated, each Province should be allowed to elect at least two persons from among the progressive and literate element to represent their interests in that decision-making body, and that these elected members should automatically become members of the Protectorate Assembly. As a result of our agitation, some concession was granted us when in October, 1950, the representation of the educated elite in the Protectorate Assembly was increased to six seats.

With the people of the Protectorate now asserting themselves and demanding more and more say in national affairs, it was clear that revision of the existing constitution was necessary in order to meet the requirements of the situation. Proposals for this revised constitution were formulated by the Governor, Sir Hubert Stevenson, and published in October, 1947. These provided for a total of 24 seats in the Legislative Council, 14 of which were to be held by Africans, to be composed of eight official and 16 unofficial members with an African majority of fourteen against two within the unofficial majority.

Of the 14 Africans, four were to be elected directly by voters and represent Colony constituencies, nine were to be chosen from among the elected District Council members of the Protectorate Assembly and one from among the African nominated members of the Assembly. In view of the fact that the Paramount Chiefs dominated the Protectorate Assembly which was to nominate the nine Protectorate members to the Legislative Council, it was pretty certain that those nine seats would be filled by chiefs or their reliable conservative supporters.

If only the Colony elite could have swallowed their pride, animosity and suspicion, if only the Paramount Chiefs could have overcome their eagerness to please the Colonial Government, in short, if only both parties had put the interests of the country before their own personal concerns, what an opportunity was afforded them, through the proposed unofficial African majority, to work as a united front for our early political independence. But alas, the carrot that was so temptingly proffered rotted before their very eyes, for neither was brave enough to grab it himself, humble enough to assist the other in reaching for it, nor far-sighted enough to recognise the mutual benefit assured them if they approached it hand in hand and shared the eating of it. However good the proposals looked on paper, therefore, the position would be little changed in practice and the Colonial officials, faithfully supported by the Paramount Chiefs, would still reign supreme in the new Legislative Assembly.

But in spite of this, most of the people in the Protectorate welcomed the proposals, for they saw in them at least a step in the right direction. It was better to have a more proportionate representation by our own people, even if this was not yet by direct franchise, than to suffer the humilitation, frustration and injustice of our affairs being handled by those in the Colony whose only interest in us seemed to be in delaying for as long as possible the day when our people would claim their rightful heritage and take their places in the political, professional and administrative arenas which had for so long been denied them. The new progressives in the Protectorate, of course, would never be content until universal adult suffrage was introduced into all parts of the country and members of the Legislature truly represented the common people; but in the meantime our main concern was to see that the precious bit of ground we were likely to win if the proposals were enacted did not grow moss or disappear from beneath our feet altogether. However slow our progress had to be, however formidable and trying the odds set against us, we were confident of our ultimate success, for we were determined, uncompromising and, above all, patient.

I felt I was not only a politician, but a pretty practical one. My apprenticeship in the Protectorate Assembly had brought me fairly fast to the threshold of political maturity. Looking back on those days, though I often felt frustrated with impotence before the bland and impassive Colonial regime, I think it was a good thing, from one point of view of my political training, to have so much responsibility and so little power. Power without responsibility corrupts. Responsibility without power educates. I bore a heavy load of duty as a union chief and a popular representative. Whenever my busy schedule gave me time to think about it, I felt inadequate. The more aware I was of learning fast, the more I sensed that I still had a long way to go.

OUR TRADE UNION LEADERS WITH THEIR BRITISH ADVISER EDGAR PARRY AND HIS WIFE IN THE CENTRE. NEXT TO PARRY IS AKINOLA WRIGHT, CO-FOUNDER WITH ME OF THE UNITED MINEWORKERS' UNION. TOMMY YELLOW, SECRETARY OF THE SEAMEN'S AND WATERFRONT WORKERS UNION, IS ON MRS PARRY'S LEFT WHILE MARCUS GRANT, LEADER OF THE ARTISANS AND ALLIED WORKERS UNION, IS THE LAST SEATED ON THE RIGHT. THIRD SEATED FROM THE LEFT IS O. WALKER, THEN A MEMBER OF THE T.U.C. I AM STANDING IN THE LAST ROW, THIRD FROM THE LEFT.

CHAPTER SEVEN

A Study Period in Oxford and London

Shortly after the publication of the 1947 Constitutional Proposals, I was absent from Sierra Leone for 18 months or more. Edgar Parry, the British Labour Adviser, who had taken a great interest in my trade union activities, suggested that I might try for a British Council scholarship to study industrial relations at Ruskin College in Oxford, and later undergo a six months' training course run by the Trades Union Congress in Clapham, which involved attending union meetings, working in union branch offices and visiting mines. Naturally I was delighted with the chance this would give me of increasing my knowledge and generally broadening my outlook so that I would be better equipped to deal with the political work in which I was becoming increasingly involved. Fortunately I was awarded this scholarship and late in 1947 I set sail from Freetown for Liverpool.

As the ship sailed northwards and the blue seas and warm sunny days gradually gave way to strong north-easterly gales and black skies, I began to doubt the wisdom of my journey into foreign parts. I was apprehensive about how I would get on with my fellow students. In Africa almost all white people looked down on Africans, keeping themselves aloof from us and going about in our midst with an Arch-angelic air of superiority. In the workshop, in the office, no matter where, whenever issues cropped up in which an African was pitched against a European, the conclusion was a foregone one: the European could never be wrong. Like the Pope, he was believed to be infallible.

Europeans who did try to befriend us did so at their own peril. Such fraternisers were regarded by their compatriots as having let the side down. At the very least they could expect to be ostracised and have their names taken off the membership list of The Club, but the more usual treatment was an abrupt departure, a one-way ticket home for what was called 'leave prior to retirement'. In the mind of the average colonial European, socialism was not for export, colonial affairs were not party politics. Socialists, trade unionists, conservatives, no matter what banner they travelled under, they were all the same in their dealings with us.

So one can imagine the trend of my thoughts when on entering Ruskin College in January, 1948, I found myself one of two West Africans amongst a host of European men and women.

Ruskin College was founded in 1899 to provide working men and women with opportunities for full-time education and was the first residential college for adult education to be established in Britain. I lived in an extension of the College called The Rookery, a beautiful old house in Headington, parts of which dated back to Tudor times, which had only that year been purchased by Ruskin to accommodate forty students.

I must admit that I was greeted on arrival in a most friendly and welcoming manner both by my fellow students and the members of the staff, but in view of my experience of Europeans in Africa, I doubted their sincerity. Politely but stiffly I acknowledged their handshakes, then lit my pipe and blew out a cloud of smoke, partly to cool my nerves and partly to establish a screen behind which I could take stock of my colleagues without appearing to stare at them. They were a lively lot and although they were as strange to one another as they were to me, I noticed that they were already on first-name terms. Before I knew it I found myself the centre of a group of white faces, all eager to introduce themselves and to learn my christian name. Within minutes the warmth that emanated from them began to penetrate my smoke screen and melt my defensive shield, and to my great surprise I felt the tension within me relax as I naturally responded to the atmosphere of cordiality and helpfulness that is found only among genuine friends. Effortlessly they drew me out of my self-imposed isolation and treated me as one of themselves.

My all too brief sojourn in Ruskin College was one of the happiest periods of my life. From the Principal, with his rich, sonorous voice, his ready availability at all times and his willingness to help, right through the whole staff, all were so tactful and gracious, and never once was there any suspicion of condescension in their attitude towards me as an African. The student body — Englishmen, Scotsmen, Welshmen, Irishmen and Americans — the whole lot were wonderful companions. Communists and fellow travellers seized every opportunity to discuss the grand millennium when the workers would rule the world. Socialists were always advocating hastening slowly, and so on. They taught me how not to go to bed before one in the morning, how to hurry for a second helping at table, how to make do with little and how to develop a taste for kippers which I sprinkled with cayenne pepper and cooked over a gas ring.

The only occasion when I nearly came to blows was with a Scotsman who shared my room and who insisted on the window being kept wide open each night whatever the weather. As soon as he opened it I got out of bed and closed it. Grumbling, he got up and opened it again, then I, my temper visibly rising, slammed it shut. One night after this had been going on for some time we met in the middle of the floor like two fighting cocks, each one waiting for the other to show his spurs. Suddenly the stupidity of the whole thing hit me and I withdrew. I realised that the cold icy air was as vital to that hardy Scot as the African sun was to me and I was, after all, a guest in his country.

That winter of 1947 was the coldest the British could remember. I shall never forget my horror one morning when I gripped the chrome handlebars of my bicycle with my gloveless hands and found they had stuck!

It was not only among the students and staff at Ruskin that I met this spontaneous acceptance and kindliness. The country was suffering acutely from post-war depression with the accent on queues and ration books. Food was scarce and both housewives and shopkeepers were harassed by the problem of making a little go a long way. My meat ration, the butcher told me, was two pounds a month. "I'll take two pounds of beef," I told him as I counted out my money. He stared at me with astonishment, "Well, as yer like," he said, shrugging his shoulders, "but don't come back next week, mind, and expect to get any more. That there's yer month's ration, mate." I stewed the whole lot and ate it. The following Saturday I again tagged on the end of the queue. "'Ere you!" he called, catching sight of my black face, "I reckon I told yer..." I looked at him innocently and hungrily, smiled and winked, but kept my place in the queue. When my turn came he disappeared behind the scenes and returned a few minutes later with a newspaper bundle which he put in my hands. "Just this once, then," he said. "But remember, mate — no more till next month. Yer'll get me wrong, yer will."

The whole time I was in England I was regularly served with two pounds of beef a week. I could well have understood it if I, so obviously a stranger, had been put in my place both by the butcher and the queue of housewives, but never once was I treated with anything but good humoured tolerance.

The fishmonger was equally kind. Being hard up much of the time I sought fish heads, chicken necks and gizzards, and bits and pieces that often end up in the refuse bin because for some reason the Europeans were revolted by some of these most nutritious and delicious parts of fish and poultry. "Mr. Jackson," I used to call as I poked my head hopefully round the door. "Can I get a salmon's head?" He growled, "What — you again?", throwing a damp squelchy parcel in my direction. If he hadn't a fish head he would always find something else; he never sent me away empty handed.

I met with only one rebuff on account of my colour during my stay in England. It happened in Derby where I had gone to attend a Trades Council Conference. A room had been booked for me in one of the hotels there but when I checked in, first the receptionist, then the manager, after one look at me, flatly denied that a reservation had been made for me. The booking, they said as an afterthought, was for 'Stevenson', and it was quite obvious that they resented the fact that a man with a name like Stevens should have a black skin.

As I found out later the hotel was not even fully booked at the time. Although it appeared to be a case of blatant racial discrimination, I did not want to make a fuss about it; but my hosts — the Conference organisers — took strong exception to the attitude of the hotel keeper and went as far as to report the incident to the Secretary of State for Colonies, the Rt. Hon. Arthur Creech Jones, who expressed his regrets. Of course, this was long before the passage of legislation banning racial discrimination in Britain and no legal action could, therefore, have been taken.

Perhaps I was lucky, for, apart from that incident, I found myself readily accepted by almost everyone. Few, except children, even gave me a second glance. "Have you been down a mine, please?" one shy little spokesman of an inquisitive group of youngsters asked me one day.

The family with whom I lodged in Balham when I attended the trade union course at Clapham could not have been nicer and done more to make me feel at home. How loath I used to be to get out of my warm bed and be slapped hard by the sudden impact of the biting cold morning air. If I lingered too long, however, I would hear my landlady's agitated voice calling from the bottom of the stairs: "Shaki, your breakfast is spoiling". This was as effective as a cannon shot for getting me moving.

I was so dumbfounded at the warmth and friendship I found among the Europeans in Britain that it was impossible to connect them with the same breed that were inflicted upon us in Africa. I asked myself time and again: how is it that the Europeans here are so different from the great majority of those who go out to us in the colonies? What changed them so? How can they ever really know us and understand our feelings when they are so 'far away' from us?

Such behavioural change is, of course, typical of an unchecked and unchallenged elite. I remember on one occasion raising this question of elitism when I was at Ruskin, but to my surprise I was not encouraged to pursue it. "Surely that's hardly a subject of much importance to anyone concerned with trade unions or the labour movement," I was told. Although I accepted this view at the time, I have since become very much concerned with the subject, for in many of the books which I come across dealing with the new African countries I often see references to the elites or new ruling classes which, it is claimed, have emerged in them. I myself have used the term several times in this book when referring to the privileged few among us who, through opportunities of education or environment, were the first to be given a say in the government of our country. Elsewhere, however, the references to these elites are generally brief but they seldom fail to leave the impression that an elite group is a dubious thing for an African to belong to.

For my part, I am sorry that no African writer I have read has dealt with this subject in any depth, because it is one of very great importance to us. So much so that no matter how inadequate they may be, I feel I must offer some of my own views on it. I do not wish to speculate about the nature of those who could be described as our own particular elites at this stage, but I can have no reason to think that they are markedly different from those we find elsewhere in Africa, or indeed in the West.

The meaning of the term 'elite' seems to be variable so I shall take it here to refer to the few governing the many in all the organisations found in society. Naturally this doctrine raises many questions, such as, how they come into existence, how they maintain themselves in power and above all, how can they be controlled.

The few things I have read about elites have been about those in the West where the subject is receiving more and more attention. Although I did not study it too closely, the book that interested me most on this topic was one entitled *The Managerial Revolution* by an American named James Burnham, who argues that no matter how much ordinary people try to keep power in their own hands, an elite will grow up from among them, tend to take away that power and largely nullify their ambitions. Although socialists dedicate themselves to social economic change, the real revolution would come from elite managers in industry and commerce who, by applying their expertise, would take power away from the capitalist owners of the big enterprises and themselves determine their policies. This would eventually spread to all areas of activity throughout the community and a managerial society would be established. According to Burnham, who, I must point out, was writing during the last war, the same development is taking place in countries which have already established socialism and we must therefore look forward to living in a world completely and consciously dominated by elites of one sort or another.

However much one may dislike the way that Burnham develops his argument, his main theme that the few govern the many and should do so, cannot be ignored. There is no doubt that, whether they have heard of him or not, he has many supporters and it would be foolish to suppose that intelligent and educated Africans are not among them. And this poses a very special problem for us who are in the earlier stages of development.

There can be little doubt that the vast majority of people, both in Africa and throughout the Western world, accept without question the fact that the few govern the many and, moreover, that the governing few like it that way for no other reason than to secure for themselves the enjoyment of privilege, power and wealth. There is however a sizeable minority who, whilst acknowledging this to be a fact of life, do not necessarily agree with it but feel that no great improvement can be brought about in their own lives unless they accept it, believing that their prosperity comes in the wake of the successful few and that there is no other way of achieving it. This is the minority which exercises so much influence at general elections.

It is noticeable, and natural, that ordinary people only see elitism where it makes its greatest impact upon them, but they do not see its ramifications. They know that the thing exists and they tend to leave it at that unless they feel compelled to fight it because of an attack upon some vital interest. They will certainly not have learnt anything about elitism in any education they may have received, and it is understandable that they develop an attitude of helplessness towards it when it discloses itself to them as they take on the responsibilities of adult life. The charge of apathy which is so often hurled at them by political activists is not as justified as many of them imagine. The so-called indifference of many voters does not, in my opinion, always stem from a lack of interest in how they are governed. On the contrary, it all too often arises from the firmly held conviction that whichever party they choose to support, they will still not be freed from the pressures which they believe their rulers and managers bring to bear upon them. Even when they are nurtured in ignorance and are driven solely by their instincts, the behaviour of large numbers of people is seldom as irrational as it appears at first sight. But it is not convenient for elites to recognise this because it is essential for their purposes to project the notion that the motives of most human beings are not often guided by reason, and that without their leadership catastrophe would engulf us all. Having gained general acceptance of this notion they then proceed to create an even more powerful myth, namely, that we are under an obligation to submit ourselves to them on the grounds that what is so clearly of such benefit to our society is morally desirable, and therefore our laws should be based on it.

It seems to me that any theory of society which is formulated by a minority and which makes that minority the principal beneficiaries of its own proposals is suspect from the outset. It might also be added that generally those who voice this suspicion are soon made to realise that they are to be counted among the greatest enemies of the community. The last thing the 'few' are ready to concede in practice is that there should be open competition among elites.

One of the greatest weaknesses of elitist theory would appear to be the sweeping nature of its basic doctrine. While I agree that the influence of a self-conscious 'few' can only too readily be seen in the affairs of organisations all over the world, it by no means follows that this tendency will necessarily continue at either its present, or on an increased, scale. If it were really the case that all the highly intelligent men and women who are to be found in the ranks of the rulers, managers and leaders of the hundreds of institutions — including universities — which go to make up the modern state were engaged exclusively in the acquisition of power, wealth and privilege, then the battle for improving and transforming the shape of any society would be lost before it could be joined. But it is here, I think, that the theory, and its practice, falls down. Even among this comparatively small group it seems obvious to me that the universal belief that all men are not alike is equally true. It is far from being the case that all intelligent men are devoted only to their own advancement.

Furthermore, it is important to remember that the ruling classes are not composed exclusively of the most gifted men. Prominent, if not dominant, among them are those who owe their positions entirely to the accident of birth and favourable laws of inheritance. In noting this I should also like to offer a quite different observation which many may think is naive. It is that my life has been greatly influenced by the fact that the very greatest thinkers and artists do not seem to have troubled themselves overmuch about power and wealth, and while it is true that many of them gained fame during their lifetime, many died without any recognition at all. Unfortunately, the mere modelling of one's behaviour on such great men is not sufficient if one is to deal effectively with elite groups in whatever country they appear. Checks and balances must be applied to those who speak for us and act in our name and the particular manner in which this should be done is for each country to determine for itself, always bearing in mind that those rising from the grassroots to apply the checks on our behalf will constitute a budding elite.

It is often overlooked or suppressed by elitists that the main opponents of their outlook have been men and women who themselves originated from social classes which do not normally take a progressive view of society. It is, however, a fact that in the West the contributions of middle and upper class people to the liberalisation of the community have been of the greatest importance, and the less developed the country the more important these contributions have shown themselves to be.

Unfortunately it appears to be the case that, all over the world, ordinary people have not reached a sufficiently high standard of education to be able, unaided, to bring about the social reforms they are most in need of. Even in the most advanced countries working class leaders have not emerged in anything like the numbers that are necessary if they are to succeed in playing their rightful part throughout their communities. It is true that trade unions have become effective within their chosen sphere, but outside this area the field is on the whole dominated by people of the middle or upper classes. This is not to say that working class people do not desire reform; indeed they do, but they are not skilful in either formulating or promoting it and it is here that progressively minded people from other social groups are most fitted to help them. Self-regarding elite types are not normally found in this kind of work. Thus it can be seen that even outside the field of trade unionism the harshness of those in executive authority is moderated very considerably by the activities of people who are equally competent and, above all, equally coherent.

It is here that we in a developing country, such as ours is, are seriously handicapped, mostly for reasons which, in my opinion, are part of the colonial legacy. I was recently asked by Lord Fenner Brockway what I considered to be the disadvantages left by the old colonial regime. Without hesitation I replied that the most harmful feature about colonialism is that it induces passivity. Because of the inordinately long period of colonial domination which was imposed on the former Colonies, the initiative for independent and thoughtful action in the handling of our affairs was lacking in our mentality when the time came for us to take control. We had been brought up to look to the colonial masters for everything and had developed a couldn't-careless attitude to matters affecting our own country. If we discovered somebody making away with government property or idling his time at work, we did not see anything wrong in it because we felt anything was justifiable as long as it was against the direct interests of the Colonial masters. Thus, at independence we had the formidable task of decolonialising our mentality and our outlook to problems of national interest. In other words, we had to re-educate ourselves in our approach to the problems of our country and of the world at large.

People whose only role is the acceptance of direction lose both interest and initiative, and this applies not only to the great mass of the population; it also has a serious effect on those who, had they been in a free society, would have played, as others elsewhere have done, a full part in the life of the country and sought to improve it. But it was characteristic of colonial government and of the commercial and industrial undertakings which tended to follow its lead, that it felt that everything except the most innocuous activities came within its purview. Because of this our better educated classes became inhibited about putting their hand to anything that could in the vaguest sense be described as potentially political. That is why the majority of our political and trade union leaders did not seek employment with the usual organisations. So it came about that anyone who wished either to reform or to protest became a professional, although the term generally applied to him was 'agitator'.

As I see the position in Sierra Leone, we are now in a situation where although groups of leaders have necessarily and speedily come into existence since the mid-fifties, because of the comparatively short period of time that has elapsed since then, we have not witnessed as yet the emergence of corresponding groups who could act really effectively as 'counter-elites', that is, informed people who have a keenly developed awareness of the public good, who are prepared not only to draw attention to the abuse of power but also to promote more enlarged concepts of general welfare, without seeking advantages for themselves.

I have already offered what I believe to be logical reasons for the apparent absence of this type of citizen in the past, and I am not unmindful of the excellent work being done today by a growing number of individuals to ameliorate the conditions of their fellow countrymen. Nevertheless, the fact remains that much more organisational work needs to be done if their efforts are to be put to the best use and attention is to be focussed upon the most urgent of our social and economic needs. The number of men and women who are now in possession of higher education and professional qualifications has increased very rapidly over the past ten years or so, and I feel that too few of them have expressed their social consciousness in practical terms.

Perhaps much of this reluctance to engage in new areas of endeavour is due not only to induced apathy, but also to the mistaken impression that all social activity should stem from the Government. In view of our history this attitude is quite understandable; nevertheless it stands in dire need of correction. The total good that can flow to a people can never be provided by a government. Ideas for social and economic improvement are not engendered solely by official departments, as those of us who are familiar with the West very well know. In Britain, for instance, not only do non-governmental organisations inspire legislative and other reforms; they also concern themselves with their proper implementation if they are enacted by Parliament.

The idea of specialised groups working within groups is also found in Britain; one that springs to mind, which was well known to many of us, was the Colonial Section of the Fabian Society, itself an off-shoot of the Labour Party.

It must now be clear to us that, where we have not already done so, we must begin to envisage a structure in our society in which governing and controlling groups must continue to play an essential and permanent part. In this respect we will be no different from other countries. We can, however, unlike most of them, take realistic steps at the outset to consider how far the presence of these groups should lead us to build a society in which they will not dominate, but rather participate, in a community life in which other social groupings will also play a vital and integral part. I believe it is very important for us to recognise the need for this fully and openly.

It is well worth the trouble to study the conventional views of elite groups in advanced countries. Without exception they first lay down that entry to any of them can be based only on merit and, in the first instance, the criterion is generally intellectual. Then the would-be candidate must further prove himself by passing the relevant specialist examinations to secure full entry into the group, and the success he obtains at this stage can be of great help to him in the subsequent progress he can make inside. In some cases this success can be overvalued and sometimes lead to the rapid promotion of men who, although intellectually distinguished, find it difficult to understand the viewpoint of ordinary people.

However, as a general principle we can hardly quarrel with the idea that a man should offer some proof of his intelligence before he is accepted as a member of a ruling group. It only remains to discover whether entry to these groups is open to all so that the community can benefit from all of its members who are capable of directing its affairs. To this the answer is invariably in the affirmative, but closer investigations often reveal that there are pre-conditions for entry which are themselves thought by many to be socially divisive, but since these are not imposed by the groups, their affirmative answer can hardly be challenged.

In the light of all this it might well be asked what reasonable objections can be made against the claims of those who consider that they are best fitted to be in control of the most important organisations in the country. Although it is often put in more elegant language, the short answer to this question is that tests of cleverness bear no relation to moral worth, and in the modern world we are becoming increasingly aware of the fact that governments and commerce and industry are faced with moral issues which are in every way as real as those which are faced by individuals. While it is true that a man may be both clever and good, we have no reason to believe that there is a necessary link between the two qualities. The main charge against the elitists is that they tend to obscure this fact and to imply that the mere possession of intelligence is of itself indicative of moral responsibility. My reading of history does not confirm this.

The position then, as I see it, is that while it is essential for our well-being that we should elect and appoint competent men and women to conduct the affairs of the public organisations in our country, it is fair to neither us nor them to assume that they will always seek the best interests of the community. We must continue to accept the need for checks and balances not merely in the shape of regulations where these appear to be necessary, but also for creating more public awareness of the organisational life of the country. I urge this because no greater stimulus can be found for encouraging those in control of our affairs to give of their best than the continuing development of such activities.

Up to now I have discussed this subject mostly in terms of elites and, as I describe them, 'counter-elites'. There is, however, another very important element to take into account if we are to move ultimately into a fully self-conscious democratic state: the will of the majority of the people. It is hardly surprising that past elites have shown little inclination to take account of them, especially with regard to their potentialities in society. But it appears to be true of ruling groups everywhere that they find it difficult to convince themselves that ordinary people are ever able to initiate policies which really are for their own good, and they are equally reluctant to concede that their own particular sort of intelligence should be less able to see the essentials of a situation than the collective common sense of those who happen to be most affected by it.

One of the greatest deceptions practised on the mass of the people is to persuade them that if they have a choice of political parties from which to elect a government, they are living in a *fully* democratic community. This proposition is obviously specious if the leaders of the parties on offer are wedded to the concept of elite government, because they will never agree that every voter should be as influential as they are themselves in the determination of policy, and it is noticeable that their support for democracy tends to wane if the masses do not follow them blindly. What they look for are adherents, not for people who wish to participate in the process of governing.

I believe that the best proof that a party can offer to a people of its true democratic intentions is by heeding the natural similarities between men in society rather than their differences. I have never heard anyone advocate absolutely flat equality of treatment for everyone and for the foreseeable future I do not think I could give my mind to the notion. Nevertheless, we in our Party believe that every man and woman has a body, a mind and a soul, and each one of them is entitled, as far as we can provide them, to all the means that are necessary for the full development of these endowments. On the other hand, we shall tolerate no groups who regard themselves as supermen and require that they must be treated as if they were a different species from the rest of us.

Only if we can grasp the vital importance of this approach can we hope to combat the dangers of ruling groups which aim to take possession of our people and country. As I have pointed out, we must have men in positions of power throughout the whole of our society, and if we are sensible we will choose the most competent men from among those who, happily, are available to us. But let us see to it that we do not charge this group with responsibilities which we have no right to ask them to accept. By this I mean that if it is not made clear to our leaders in all walks of life that we hold men accountable for their actions, then we can have no justifiable complaint if they adopt policies which do not meet with our wishes.

Men who are under effective direction will tend to follow the instructions of those who control them, but if control is not applied to them, then they have no alternative but to devise both their own policies and the manner in which they are carried out. On the other hand, leaders are seldom unresponsive if those who appointed them maintain a continuing interest in their activities. We are too easily persuaded that all abuses of power stem from the malpractices of leaders when in fact their true origins arise from the abdication of control by those whom these leaders represent. Sometimes it is difficult to draw the line between interfering with the proper administration of an organisation and expressing legitimate concern about its progress. At our stage of development we should not be unduly worried if in seeking the latter, we find ourselves unwittingly guilty of the former.

Elitism is something which has always existed everywhere in the world in one form or another, and my observations are intended to make us recognise this fact. It would be extremely foolish of us to imagine that we can escape its dangers more easily than others have done unless we adopt a policy directed to this end. As I have indicated, I believe such a policy can be formulated in a manner flexible enough to serve the varying circumstances in which we will find ourselves in the future.

First, of course, must come the frank recognition of the problem itself; along with a refusal to accept the view, too prevalent in the world, that no remedy can be found for it. With this premise must come an acceptance of the need to encourage, and to fully organise, those among our educated people who wish to apply themselves increasingly to those programmes of social and economic welfare which are already part of our development. There is a great and immediate need for this. Secondly, there is the need to apply ourselves to the realisation of our aim for the education of our people, failing which elitism must prevail. There is an assumption behind Abraham Lincoln's famous statement about government *by* the people which is often overlooked. Without knowledge men cannot effectively govern themselves either as individuals or as communities, though knowledge can often be derived from experience and does not necessarily imply a formal education.

During this study period in England, I discovered a great deal about trade unionism which gave me heart. It was only then that I realised that difficulties are inherent in any attempt to establish workers' organisations in any country, whether it is 'developed' or not. I was astonished to learn that during the period of the early British trade union movement, the workers were no more responsive to disciplined membership than I had found my own to be. In many ways this was the chief and most encouraging lesson I learnt in England. Before this I had tended to despair of ever seeing a really closely knit and influential movement in Sierra Leone; but when I discovered that our faults were similar to those which had plagued the early leaders of the British unions, I took fresh heart. Not, I may say, because they too had sometimes been as ineffectual as our own, but because it showed that in conditions of ignorance the reactions of all men are much the same and that Sierra Leonean workers were not uniquely backward.

Looking back now it seems odd that some of the most valuable things I learnt at Oxford were in a sense only incidental to the main purpose of my stay there; which was to get a real understanding of the administration of modern trade unions and to get a good grasp of the British system of industrial relations. In fact when I left Sierra Leone we already had a system which was quite a creditable version of the British one. As regards trade union administration, it soon became clear to me that our organisations were far too small to be able to gain much benefit from British methods.

Nevertheless, I learnt a great deal at Oxford and also a great deal going about the country. For instance, I was particularly interested to find that the average worker in the United Kingdom was just as indifferent to the affairs of his union as I had found my own people to be. I discovered that it was not uncommon in a branch of perhaps three thousand members for the secretary to have to make special efforts to see that a dozen or so turned up for the monthly branch meeting to provide the necessary quorum. At first I was appalled by this as I had been in similar circumstances in Sierra Leone. Later I came to understand what I believe to be the real reason for this seeming indifference; the elite-creating tendency of large numbers of poorly educated men.

In any group, large or small, there are invariably a few members who take a continuing interest in any organisation for their mutual benefit. The general membership tend to regard these individuals as their natural leaders since they are better informed and more coherent than themselves and, furthermore, they are workers like themselves. Because of this, I believe they observe an unspoken compact. They feel that their own attendance at meetings is not necessary because they are convinced that if any new benefits can be assured, their natural front-line leaders will be at the meeting doing all that can be done to get it.

So, in their own minds, they are far from indifferent to the real purposes of their union, as is readily shown whenever it is thought expedient for them to show their massed strength. There are obvious dangers in this, but it is difficult to persuade the rank and file that this is so because they are quick to point out that unlike other elites, their leaders seek neither social nor financial gain in the course of their activities on their behalf. This is a powerful argument to rebut notwithstanding those instances where we know that this loyalty has been abused.

LIONEL ELVIN, THE PRINCIPAL OF RUSKIN COLLEGE DURING MY PERIOD OF STUDY IN OXFORD, WAS SUCCEEDED IN 1950 BY H.D. HUGHES (ABOVE), FORMERLY A LABOUR M.P., WHO RETAINED THE POST UNTIL 1979 AND THROUGH WHOM I MAINTAINED A CONTACT WITH THE COLLEGE FOR SOME YEARS.

RUSKIN COLLEGE, OXFORD, AS IT WAS IN MY DAY, AND STILL IS.

CHAPTER EIGHT

Constitutional Reforms and the 1951 Elections

On my return to Sierra Leone in 1949, Governor Stevenson's Constitutional Proposals had already been put before a Select Committee. This committee consisted of the Attorney General, all seven Unofficial Members of the Legislative Council, plus seven co-opted Extraordinary Members — three Creole and four Paramount Chiefs — and the Chief Commissioner of the Protectorate. The three co-opted Creole members resigned before the Committee got down to business because they believed that the presence of the Chief Commissioner would deter the Paramount Chiefs from speaking their minds. Perhaps they had a point in principle, though in practice the Paramount Chiefs had little to grumble about as far as the proposals were concerned. The Select Committee accepted the proposals with the additional recommendation that the representation of the Protectorate should be increased to fourteen and that of the Colony to seven. Their Report was unanimously approved by the unofficial members of the Legislative Council and the Secretary of State for the Colonies was accordingly advised.

However, things were far from being as harmonious and progressive as they might appear. The fact that agreement was reached by the Select Committee was certainly no small achievement in view of the strongly conflicting attitudes of the Protectorate and Colony towards the original proposals. The truth of the matter, however, as subsequent events exposed, was that the Select Committee had no real power to speak for the masses, neither for those in the Protectorate nor for the Creoles outside the Legislative Council. The bitterness and contention between the two elements reached a peak after the Committee's report had been agreed upon and had exposed the deep-rooted animosity of one against the other and of each against those who had represented them on the Committee. It was on top of such a foundation that the proposed Constitution was expected to thrive.

It was not to be wondered at that from the outset the Creoles viewed the new Constitutional Proposals with the deepest concern. They were so obsessed with the idea that they were superior, racially and intellectually, to the native population that they blinded themselves to political actuality and social change. Having studied their history one cannot blame them entirely for clutching at any straw on the fast flowing tide of events that would eventually engulf them. The root of their trouble was their inborn insecurity, the tragic outcome of feeling European, looking African and being at home with neither. Yet, however shattering it may be to one's morale to return home after years of living in bondage to find the ancestral doors slammed in your face, with proper adjustment and a lot of giving on the part of the stranger at the door, in less than a generation complete integration would have resulted. The colour of your skin does not of itself guarantee a welcome home by those who share the same pigmentation and similar problems.

When much of the African continent succeeded in freeing itself from the shackles of colonial rule, black-skinned people from many parts of the world took one-way tickets to Africa viewing the situation as a back-to-Africa homecoming. But to their chagrin they found they had less in common with their African brothers than they had with Europeans and Americans, in spite of their common ancestry, and it was only those who made a genuine attempt to live and think in the African manner who remained.

Acceptance of one human being by another is not a mere matter of common race, creed or nationality but a natural outcome of being on the same wavelength, of being able to communicate and understand and of showing mutual respect for one another. Human relationships succeed or fail according to the degree of adaptation of each toward the other. As far as communities are concerned, the adage 'when in Rome do as the Romans do', is sound advice. As the Creole community have had to learn the hard way, for a minority to integrate harmoniously with a large and established body, most of the adaptation has to come from that minority. Their great mistake was to attach themselves to another minority; and an alien and transient minority at that.

Things might not have been so difficult for the Creoles when the time came for them to accept realities if, when adopting British attitudes and using these as a yard-stick for correct behaviour, they had given more study to the way the British have of accepting the inevitable and surrendering to it with a reasonably good grace when to do otherwise would be to lose face. Unlike the colonialists, the Creoles proved themselves incapable of adjusting themselves to changing circumstances.

They had developed an *idée fixe* that the Protectorate African was a breed apart and should never be allowed to meddle in Colony affairs, that is to say, in the colonial administration. The colonial government, on the other hand, when it recognised the unmistakable signs of political awakening in the Protectorate, took steps, however cautiously and reluctantly, to grant our people a measure of participation; first in Protectorate affairs, then in the National Assembly. This process graduated upwards until the moment arrived when they could no longer decently delay handing over the reins of government to a constitutionally elected government of the people of Sierra Leone as a whole.

Most people are reluctant to surrender power, for there is no doubt that power *is* sweet to those who wield it. But, as many a fallen idol can testify, that sweetness can taste awfully bitter when a man's power declines if he is not prudent and courageous enough to face facts, accept the situation as it exists and bow down to defeat graciously. To cling on obstinately to what was *once* power when in reality that power has passed out of one's grasp, is the surest sign that a leader's days of usefulness to a people are over.

I remember well that the 1947 Constitutional Proposals, posing as they did a threat to Creole supremacy in the country's affairs, drove the Creole-dominated National Congress to desperate measures in an attempt to defend their position. Their first reaction to these proposals was made known late in 1947 when they demanded that three additional seats be allocated to the Colony, which would increase their representation to seven, and that literacy should be a prerequisite to membership of the Legislative Council. The Paramount Chiefs accepted the demand for three additional seats on condition that the Protectorate representation was increased by the same number; but to the second demand, which was obviously aimed at exacerbating the already tense relationship between the chiefs and educated Protectorate element, they vehemently objected.

A fair percentage of the chiefs in the Protectorate Assembly were illiterate, but this fact had been considered by the colonial government as of secondary importance to the usefulness of their presence as Members of the Assembly. Understandably, the Protectorate progressives welcomed anything that would thin out the number of chiefs in the Assembly and give them the chance they had been waiting for to fill their seats. In 1948, the progressives, through the S.O.S., urged the British Secretary of State to impose a literacy qualification on all those who aspired to election to the Legislative Council. Even some of the educated chiefs supported the literacy demand and at one time feelings ran so high on the subject that it seemed as if chieftaincy would become dangerously divided against itself.

Fortunately, before a point of no return had been reached, both the chiefs and the educated element of the Protectorate brought reason to bear and saw that by bickering among themselves they were merely falling for the bait profferred by those in the Colony who sought to convince the colonial government that the native population were not yet responsible enough to take part in the country's administration. Both commoners and chiefs alike realised that if they hoped to achieve their goal, they must stick together and remain resolute and uncompromising where Protectorate interests were concerned.

When the Creoles failed to disrupt the chiefs and people of the Protectorate over the literacy issue, they began to behave in a most irrational manner. They had nothing good to say about the 1947 proposals, but instead of utilizing their energy and intelligence in offering constructive alternative proposals or devising a plan whereby both Protectorate and Colony might come to terms and work together for the benefit of the nation, they wrote abortive petitions to the British Secretary of State, following them up with equally ineffective delegations. They stressed that, as British citizens, they had the right to be governed only by persons of the same status, not by 'foreigners', as they declared the British-protected Africans in the hinterland to be, which appeared to them to be what the new constitution had in mind for them.

In September, 1948, they petitioned the Secretary of State to reject the colonial government's 'plea that the illiterates should not be discouraged from entering the Legislative Council', and pointed out that 'from a constitutional point of view, a legislative council in the Colony with a majority of foreigners, as British protected persons are in the Commonwealth, is contrary to the whole conception of British citizenship. British citizens have the right that they shall be governed only by such persons as are of the same status as themselves. ...by the suggested set-up of Protectorate majority, persons who are not British subjects would be empowered to make legislation that may seriously affect the rights of British subjects. So long as Sierra Leone continues to be divided into Colony and Protectorate..., the people of the Protectorate cannot govern the people of the Colony even by a manipulation such as is proposed to be done by the new constitution.'

As far as the Protectorate people were concerned, they continued, through the S.O.S., to demand a more democratic form of election for their members to the Legislative Council. They protested to the Secretary of State that the government had never nominated 'the progressive and younger element outside the chiefs' class' to the Council, nor had any non-chief been included on the Select Committee to consider constitutional proposals affecting the great majority of the population.

In the Legislative Council the battle raged. The leader of the Creoles moved that, in the light of the widespread opposition to the proposals, further consideration should be given to them before they were enacted. Paramount Chief Bai Koblo threw in the suggestion that if the Colony and Protectorate were separated, the Protectorate people might reclaim the land inhabited by the Creoles which they had ceded to the British Crown. The Acting Colonial Secretary, in the aloof role of referee, blew the whistle by citing a pronouncement of the Governor that "the most important thing about a Constitution is not the precise detail of its form, but the spirit in which it is made to work". The Government, he added, did not propose to intervene in the matter.

A short while later a new Governor, Sir George Beresford-Stooke, arrived on the scene and made an attempt to set up a more representative committee to reconsider the Constitution, but he failed even to get agreement on the composition of such a committee. In May, 1950, therefore, he recommended to the Secretary of State that the 1948 proposals agreed by the Select Committee be implemented and it was announced that the new Constitution based on those proposals would come into force in 1951.

In June, 1950, the S.O.S., now despairing about agreement between the Colony and Protectorate ever being reached because each one wanted majority rule, endeared themselves to their Paramount Chiefs by urging the British government to implement the proposals forthwith "so as to enable the people of the Protectorate to have a say in the management of their affairs and thus end the shameful and undemocratic policy of taxation without representation."

Dr. Bankole-Bright, leader of the newly formed Colony party — the National Council of the Colony of Sierra Leone (N.C.) — wrote in the *Weekly News* in August:

" The Protectorate ...came into being after the butchering and massacre of some of our fathers and grandfathers ...and their blood streamed in the streets of Mendi land because they were described as 'black English men' showing the 'white English men' the country. Yes, their blood streamed with the blood of English men and only fifty years after this treacherous and villainous act Loyal Sierra Leone is asked by the British Government to vacate her seats in their British Legislature (this is what it tantamounts to) for the descendants of the murderers of our ancestors."

Now that all hope of altering the proposals to their advantage was lost, instead of accepting the fact like intelligent people, the N.C. launched a bitter smear campaign against Protectorate leaders and became more and more obstructive in their desperate attempt to check, at all costs, encroachment by Protectorate Africans on what they considered to be their beat. The negative and totally unrealistic attitude they were adopting was becoming intolerable and getting none of us anywhere. Even the colonial government was losing patience and sympathy with them and in 1950 it warned them that "deadlock or no deadlock ...we cannot afford to stand still any longer. We must go forward..."

As far as the Protectorate leadership were concerned, though we were confident that given enough time the Creoles would play themselves out, as the months of obstructionist tactics and vilification dragged on it became clear that if nothing was done to check this, it could go on interminably. In September, 1950, therefore, Dr. Milton Margai, voicing the feelings of the majority of the people of the Protectorate, declared in the Protectorate Assembly that steps would be taken to seek the immediate enactment of the 1947 Constitutional Reforms as originally proposed.

Margai blamed the Creoles, "a handful of foreigners", who had been given shelter by our forefathers, for the fact that Sierra Leone was still saddled with an archaic constitution because, he said, they had "no will to co-operate with us and imagine themselves to be our superiors because they are aping the Western mode of living and have never breathed the true spirit of independence." Moreover, they did not impress the Protectorate people as being sincere in their actions towards them. Feelings had run so high, he said, that no useful purpose could be served by sitting with them in a committee at that time, but after everybody had calmed down they would all be in a better frame of mind to remodel what they had accepted.

"If the 30,000 non-natives in the Colony should attempt a boycott," Dr. Margai declared, "I can most definitely assure the Government that all of the seats on the Colony side would be occupied by our countrymen. We mean to push ahead and we are in no way prepared to allow a handful of foreigners to impede our progress."

The delaying tactics of the Creoles and the effect these were beginning to have on the Protectorate did much to unify the Chiefs and progressives of the Protectorate. In an attempt, no doubt, to strengthen this delicate entente, the Governor took the opportunity to impress upon the Chiefs the importance of a close relationship between themselves and the educated element. The month following Dr. Margai's heated outburst, the Governor addressed the Protectorate Assembly on the subject of the forthcoming Constitution which, he said, would represent a big step forward in the history of Sierra Leone.

" If it is to achieve its purpose," he declared, "it will be essential to adapt traditional customs and practices to modern requirements. Traditionally, the old men were the repositories of wisdom. They still are, but the younger men, thanks to education, also have their wisdom. It is essential that these younger men should be given an adequate opportunity to take part in government, whether in District Councils or elsewhere. If they are not given this opportunity, the result will be a feeling of frustration amongst them; and instead of the combination of old and younger wisdom being used for the progress of Sierra Leone, both may be wasted in mutual antagonisms. To achieve the best results will call for patience on both sides. Patience by the older men for the novel ideas of the younger, who may seem to want to change everything in a hurry; patience by the younger men for the ideas of the older who may seem reluctant to change anything at all. By patience and combination it will however be possible to obtain the best of both wisdoms and the result will be ...the orderly progress desired by all."

With the prospect of the coming elections, the Protectorate leaders decided that the time had come to form a political party. In April, 1951, therefore, the S.O.S. and P.E.P.U. joined forces to form the Sierra Leone People's Party (S.L.P.P.). I was about the only foundation member of this party who could claim neither royal blood nor big business associations. I was an entirely self-made man from the labouring masses — if I can use the term 'self-made' for one who lived from hand to mouth as I did at that time — and I never pretended to be otherwise. Dr. Milton Margai, who, because of his seniority and the general respect he commanded through his years of medical service in the Protectorate and his chiefly connections, was our natural choice as leader.

Even though the S.L.P.P. was formed as a political party to fight the 1951 elections, it was not by any means a national party in the true sense of the word, for there was little incentive to enrol mass membership at that time when, as far as the Protectorate people were concerned, they had no vote in the elections anyhow. The aim of the party was to contest the seven Colony seats and to supplant, in as gentle a way as possible, the Paramount Chiefs in the Legislative Council with the more representative non-chiefs among us. To curry favour with them in the hope that they would bring pressure to bear in the Districts to elect our party candidate in place of their own nomination, we included in our manifesto the promise that we would review the inadequate salaries of Paramount Chiefs and insist that all enquiries affecting Paramount Chiefs must be presided over by a Supreme Court judge as opposed to an administrative official.

The previous year, when all hope of preventing the 1947 proposals from being enacted was lost, Dr. Bankole-Bright had reformed his Sierra Leone National Congress into an almost exclusively Creole party called the National Council of the Colony of Sierra Leone (N.C.S.L.), the main aim of which was to prevent Protectorate encroachment on Creole preserves. Its manifesto took more the form of an aggrieved protest than a party programme. "We object to foreigners prepondering in our Legislature," it wailed.

In May, 1951, just before the last meeting of the Legislative Council prior to the elections, a member of the N.C.S.L., Mr. Metcalf A. Cole, wrote to the Governor resigning his seat in the Legislative Council; as he felt his position in it had now become quite untenable. The proposed reconstitution of the Legislative Council, he declared, was "altogether inimical to the progress and development of the Colony and Protectorate of Sierra Leone," and was calculated to thwart the legitimate claims and aspirations of the people to self-government. The people he represented, he said, could no longer enjoy that 'freedom from fear' in which, for many decades now, they had lived. He was perfectly certain, he concluded, that the whole scheme was worse by far than "the present outmoded constitution under which Sierra Leone is now governed."

The Governor, in accepting with regret the member's resignation, endeavoured to correct many impressions that he had formed regarding the position of the Colony vis-a-vis the Protectorate under the proposed constitution. Among other things he said he was unable to understand the statement made by Mr. Cole that the people could no longer enjoy the 'freedom from fear' that they had enjoyed for so long. If it referred to the fact that the Protectorate would have a majority in Council and would, therefore, ignore or reject Colony interests, he said he did not believe that this would be the case as the leaders of the Protectorate had steadfastly proclaimed their desire to work in the closest co-operation with the Colony people for their common good, and he considered it was quite clear that they meant what they said. It was his view, he declared, that the Colony people had before them great opportunities to use their political experience and wisdom to bring about the closest and warmest association with the Protectorate which would only be for the ultimate and lasting benefit of the country. "A state of affairs in which Colony and Protectorate are perpetually separated," he said, "will hamper every kind of development and will delay the achievement of self-government."

This prompted an even longer letter from Mr. Cole who recorded in detail the views that he had steadfastly maintained throughout the discussions on the new constitution. Finally he reiterated the well-voiced view of other anti-Protectorate Africans: that British subjects in the Colony of Sierra Leone had the right that they should be governed *only* by such persons as were of the same political status as themselves. "This right of self-determination is now in peril," he said. "It is in grave danger of annihilation, by reason of the new Constitution, whereby British Protected persons are not only to sit in Council, but to carry the majority vote over British subjects in the Colony."

This correspondence between Mr. Cole and the Governor was, with Mr. Cole's permission, published in full in the *Weekly Bulletin* of June 19th and 26th, 1951.

I have mentioned this member's resignation and the reasons for it only to give yet another example of the defeatist and obstructionist attitude of some of the Colony politicians. Rather than give the experiment a try, even if only for the anticipated pleasure of saying "I told you so" when it failed, rather than offer their greater knowledge and experience to those of us who were late starters and, by working hand-in-hand with us, benefit not only themselves but the country as a whole, they preferred to dig trenches around their illusory strongholds and isolate themselves; believing, perhaps, that if they shut their eyes and plugged their ears long enough, the nasty bogey that haunted their dreams and imaginations would one day cease to exist. It is difficult to imagine such intelligent and educated men, men who had so much to contribute, and from whom we of the Protectorate had so much to learn, so obstinately refusing to accept the realities of a situation when there was everything to be gained by all of us simply by co-operation.

The Legislative Council elections took place on three different days. On October 23rd, the two elections to the Protectorate Assembly were held. This was followed on November 8th by the twelve District Council elections; and the Colony elections took place on November 16th. As far as I was concerned, of course, October 23rd, 1951, was the most important of the three dates, for I had been nominated by the Governor from among the African members of the Protectorate Assembly as a candidate to stand election to the Legislative Council and had the honour of being the first person to be elected to that newly constituted body.

That historic meeting of the Protectorate Assembly remains most vividly in my mind. There were two boxes of different colours marked 'For' and 'Against' with my photograph and name attached. These were locked and sealed by three independent witnesses and carried into the polling booth which had been specially erected. The Clerk of the Assembly read the formal notice of my nomination which was proposed by Dr. Milton Margai and seconded by Paramount Chief Fabunde Gberl. The Chief Commissioner presiding over the Assembly then invited the proposer to speak on his resolution for a period of five minutes.

" We have been called upon to elect a member from this august body to the Legislative Council," Dr. Margai declared. "As this is the highest body in the Protectorate we must do our best to select the best men from it, men who are really our countrymen and will be able to stand and really do credit to us in the Legislative Council. I have been boasting to our Colony brothers that the Protectorate has got the men, so I feel I will not be doing my duty to myself and my country if I fail to produce the best man there is. The man I have in mind is Mr. Siaka Probyn Stevens."

Dr. Margai went on to give an account of my qualifications for the candidacy, pointing out that I had been a member of the Protectorate

Assembly since its inception, more or less a permanent member of its Standing Committee, a nominee by the Governor to the City Council, a member of a number of Government committees, spokesman for the mine workers and General Secretary of the Sierra Leone Trade Union Congress, "which is an organisation with the highest number of literates in the country and which is a body recognised by Government for dealing with labour matters." He concluded by saying: "My dear countrymen, let us show today our unity and solidarity in registering our votes in the box with the photograph of Mr. Stevens."

The Chief Commissioner's announcement that the resolution had been carried by 23 votes to four was met with loud applause and my heart swelled with pride as fellow members crowded round to congratulate me.

"Your Honour, Members of the Assembly," I said. "I rise to thank you from the bottom of my heart for the honour which you have conferred upon me and for the confidence which you have placed in me. I pray that God may give me wisdom and understanding to shoulder the heavy responsibilities which lie on me in the days ahead. I thank you very much indeed."

Unlike the requirement in the Colony that all voters had to speak, read and write English, all members of the twelve District Councils were eligible to vote whether or not they could read and write in English. Of the twelve members elected to the Legislative Council by the Districts on November 8th, only four were not Paramount Chiefs, in spite of our persuasive manifesto, and three of these were S.L.P.P. candidates. In the seven electoral districts in the Colony, where voting took place a week later, the S.L.P.P. contested five seats and won two of them. With the elections over, the new Constitution came into force on November 19th.

Although the new Legislative Council provided for an unofficial majority, neither of the two contesting parties, the S.L.P.P. or the N.C., actually gained a majority of seats in the election. It was because of this that the Governor advocated a coalition because he felt that the co-operation of the two groups in the Executive Council would better serve the interests of the country. I was one of a group of S.L.P.P. representatives who went to Government House to make clear to the Governor our stand on the matter. We pointed out that we were in the majority in the Legislative Council and were thus entitled to claim full unofficial representation in the Executive Council. We had, we declared, no intention of joining forces with the National Council even if this meant that all the Executive Council seats were given to N.C. representatives.

On the face of it, this would appear to be an example of the very thing I and others condemned regarding members of the N.C., namely, refusal to co-operate. But the point had been reached by this time when any faith we of the Protectorate might once have had in Colony intentions towards us was utterly lost. Co-operation to them meant the chance to get a big foot in the door and then grab the key to it. To have joined forces with the N.C., when we had at last gained a majority of seats and when their declared policy was to keep us 'foreigners' from carrying weight in *their* Legislature, would have lost us what precious little say we had won for ourselves in our country's affairs. To co-operate with the N.C. at that time would have been on their terms only, which would boil down to surrendering the rights of the vast majority of our people to further the selfish interests of an ambitious few.

At the private meeting held a few days later with members of the S.L.P.P. and the N.C. it became obvious that the rift between the two was now so wide that any further attempts to bridge it would be futile. The N.C. leadership was so adamantly opposed to Protectorate participation in the central government that they would accept no compromises. It therefore rested with Dr. Margai, as leader of the majority party in the Legislative Council, to name his chosen lieutenants as unofficial members of the Executive Council. The five 'ministers' he selected for his 'cabinet' were his brother, Albert Margai, Chief Bai Farima Tass, two Creoles, A. G. Randle and M. S. Mustapha, and myself. He chose the two pro-S.L.P.P. Creoles from the Colony because, as he explained it, "we would have made a vital mistake if we had decided to rest just on our majority and select only Protectorate people."

My official appointment as an 'Appointed Member' of the Executive Council, the highest authority in the land, was made on December 3rd, 1951. It is difficult, even now, to express exactly how this affected me. I was naturally supremely elated and proud of the honour bestowed upon me at the time, but these were very temporary emotions. The feeling uppermost in my mind was one of humility, of embarrassment almost, at being picked for such high office. With serious doubts as to my ability to perform efficiently what was expected of me, I decided it was a time to take stock of myself.

I believe it is very necessary to do this at a time when life is bestowing its blessings on you rather than during a black period of failure when, with head in hands and in a mood of despair, you ask yourself: "Where did I go wrong?" By that time, even if you are truthful enough to admit the error of your ways, it is too late to make amends. The honour shown me by my appointment to the Executive Council brought the fact sharply home to me that I was in that position not because I was somebody's blue-eyed boy or because I had bribed or cajoled my way there, but only because I had established myself as the voice and champion of the workers. Never, I said to myself, must I allow myself to get so far removed from those who depend on me that I cannot hear their voice, that they cannot reach me or dare not approach me. Swollen pride in those in high positions, like a pot-belly, can so easily cause them to lose sight of the solid earth beneath their feet; a very unhealthy and dangerous state to be in.

To protect those who had put their trust in me and to whom I was obliged, I wanted my views to be made known not only in the Executive Council but also in the Legislative one where some Creole elements could be expected to make a last attempt to reduce our newly acquired influence in the affairs of the country as a whole. The reconstituted Legislative Council was not in session as yet, but the decision of the N.C. leadership to oppose any form of majority administration for Sierra Leone was a foregone conclusion.

When the Council eventually met in the third week of January, it became clear that not only the hope of national unity would have to be abandoned, for the time being, but that every effort would have to be made to save the territorial integrity of Sierra Leone. Indeed, we heard that if the rabid Creole politicians lost all hope of controlling the whole country, they would attempt, in the last resort, to sever the Colony from the Protectorate.

On January 22nd, 1952, the *Weekly Bulletin* reported:

" After an adjournment lasting seven weeks, the reconstituted Legislative Council in its First Session, resumed its sitting at the Legislative Council Chamber on Friday morning presided over by His Excellency the Governor. ...For the first time in the history of the Legislative Council, members of a political party (the Sierra Leone People's Party) sat on the Government side of the House with ex-officio members."

The resentment of those on the other side of the House at the presence in that august assembly of Protectorate Members continued to smoulder. Then, on July 29th, 1952, the Leader of the Opposition, Dr. Bankole-Bright, could no longer contain the fire that raged within him. He had, he declared, served as a Member of the Legislative Council for fifteen years and had "come to the conclusion seriously that I have never met a council or a government with such a bundle of confusionism as the Council of this Government that exists today. ...Here is a government attempting to hand over British subjects for 160 years to a foreign Protectorate State to be governed contrary to British principles and justice ...trying to merge the Colony into a foreign or Protected State without first developing the spirit of partnership ... trying to bring a cleavage betwixt the friendliness of the two peoples ...Here is a government that has created the greatest difficulty and the greatest illegal and unconstitutional reform by creating a party system within the Legislature ...that has illegally and unconstitutionally created an Executive Council composed of foreign elements to legislate for British subjects." If the British forsook them, he said, they would rather seek justice elsewhere than "be put under the control of an illiterate mass of people who have not yet grasped the principles of legislature ..." He then put the following motion before the House:

" That this Sierra Leone Government stands impeached by the Creole element of this Colony through their representatives in the Legislative Council who are members of the National Council of the Colony of Sierra Leone in that it has by its action brought into existance a cleavage between the people of this Colony and Protectorate by abrogating the ethical principles governing British Law and Order in attempting by legislation to create unconstitutionally an Executive and Legislative Council controlled by a majority of Protectorate people who are not British subjects, inimical to the interests of the Colony and contrary to the fundamental principles laid down in the acquisition of this Colony in 1788 as a result of which there is now existing strained relationship between the Sierra Leone Government and the people of this ancient and loyal Colony.

"Furthermore, that in consequence of the present existing relationship this Colony through its National Council's representatives now *asks* for its independence to control its own affairs which will be in keeping with the proclamation of Her late Majesty Queen Victoria in 1865 as the result of the findings of a Select Committee of the House of Commons dated the 3rd day of March, 1865."

There was an angry buzz of indignation from Members on the Government benches who were quite naturally incensed by many of the remarks made concernig the Protectorate during Bankole-Bright's lengthy speech. The Acting Colonial Secretary described it as an electioneering speech which in his view became in parts somewhat insulting to many Members of his side of the House. He appealed to Members to approach the matter from the point of view of the motion alone and not from the introductory speech. "It takes two to make strained relations, just as it takes two to make a quarrel," he remarked, and wondered whether, when considering the demand from the Creole element for an independent legislature in the Colony, the majority of non-Creoles in the Colony had been consulted; the number of Creoles in Freetown and the Colony were 28,050 as against 87,584 non-Creoles.

"How can they survive without the Protectorate?" asked one member. "According to native law and custom no one has the right to sell land, and I feel therefore that the mover of the motion has no claim on the land in which he requires independence." Another voiced the opinion that it was not against the Government but against the integrity and personality of the people of the Protectorate that the motion was aimed. "Who grew the rice that saved the Creoles from starvation during the war? The hard-working people of the Protectorate! Where were the Creoles when Hitler was bombing the world, when the Sories, Limbas, Konos, Korankos, Mendes and Sherbros gave their life blood to save them and give them freedom?" Another declared: "There are certain people who have been accustomed to be in authority; they do not want to see others come up. ...There are some people on the other side of the House who come here merely to earn some money ...Surely such persons have not the interest of the country at heart."

The motion was lost by 22 votes to three with one abstention.

THE EXECUTIVE COUNCIL OF SIERRA LEONE IN 1957. ITS AFRICAN MEMBERS INCLUDED (FIRST ROW L. TO R.) PARAMOUNT CHIEF BAI FARIMA TASS II, MILTON MARGAI AND MYSELF. STANDING BEHIND WERE M.S. MUSTAPHA, A.G. RANDLE AND ALBERT MARGAI. THE GOVERNOR, SIR MAURICE DORMAN, IS IN THE CENTRE.

THE P.N.P. GROUP AFTER OUR MEETING WITH LENNOX-BOYD, THE BRITISH COLONIAL SECRETARY IN 1957. I AM THE FOURTH IN THE BACK ROW WITH ALBERT MARGAI ON MY LEFT.

FOUR OF THE FIRST SIX AFRICAN GOVERNMENT MINISTERS IN SIERRA LEONE: MILTON MARGAI (TOP LEFT), ALBERT MARGAI (TOP RIGHT), MYSELF (BOTTOM LEFT), AND M.S. MUSTAPHA (BOTTOM RIGHT).

CHAPTER NINE

The Minister's Desk

The British may have had plenty of defects as an imperial race but you had to admire their sense of reality. At the end of the day, when the dismantlement of empire became inevitable, they surrendered power with good grace and made thorough, if belated, transitional arrangements. In the early 'fifties it was our own follies and divisions that impeded progress, first to self-government, then to independence. I remember them as years of pride and exhilaration; when I became one of the first Sierra Leoneans to hold ministerial office in my country.

I feared the new challenges and responsibilities, but my relish and my excitement and my hope were all stronger than my fear. What blighted my life and brought anguish to my heart was the way so many of my fellow countrymen faltered in that critical time. Some feared independence; some valued their sectional interests above those of the country as a whole. Some gave themselves up to personal ambition as though the liberation of our homeland was of interest to them only for what they could get out of it. Others simply did not understand what was going on and let their minor, short-term aims take precedence over the pursuit of the real prize.

We went through terrible troubles and torments in Sierra Leone in those years — including some of the worst strikes and civil commotions the country has ever seen. I and the other new ministers were all inexperienced men trying to cope with thousands of strange and new perplexities in circumstances that often seemed little short of dreadful. But as I struggled from day to day to discharge my duty, with all the clutter of a minister's desk, and answer with urgency the immediate and sometimes desperate demands of the people, I tried all the time to treasure experience against the day when independence would multiply my difficulties and opportunities. I strove never to lose sight of the great goal of freedom for my people.

At the end of March, 1952, the Governor announced that as a

further step towards the development of fully responsible democratic government in the country, unofficial members of the Executive Council would assume a special interest in groups of government departments which, it was hoped, would eventually form the basis of ministries. Although our duties were purely administrative and all policy making was still in the hands of the British, it was at least a step in the right direction; the planting of the seed of our political power.

The departmental groups first allotted to me were Posts and Telegraphs, Co-operation and Fisheries; later, in August, I was given instead Surveys and Lands, Mines and Geological Survey. According to the *Weekly Bulletin*, the official organ of the Public Relations Office, I made history on the 17th June when I 'officially and ceremonially' opened a modern telephone exchange at Bo, declaring communications to be the life-blood of progress and making four test calls to Freetown.

My colleagues and I were perfectly happy to undergo this period of understudying provided it was a temporary measure, for a thorough mastery of the workings of the main government departments was essential before we could feel confident enough to assume responsibility for the formulation of policies. One cannot create anything of substance and durability unless a solid and reliable foundation is first laid. Envious opposition members taunted and ridiculed us during our apprenticeship, referring to us as 'baby ministers', unseasoned politicians', 'ministers in training', and 'men who have not the remotest idea how the Central Government is administered'. There was no disguising the sourness of the grapes. The bitterness they felt about the presence of Protectorate men in both the Legislative Council and the Executive Council was intensified by the fact that we had proved ourselves to be far from the ignorant, irresponsible and incompetent people they had made us out to be; nor had we given any evidence of avenging ourselves for the years of neglect and shoddy treatment we had suffered. What we sought was equality of education, progress and development for all Sierra Leoneans, both those in the Protectorate and those in the Colony, preferably with the co-operation of the Colony representatives in the Legislative Council, but if that co-operation was not forthcoming, then we were prepared to ride rough shod over them in order to see justice done.

In December we felt the time had come to assume further responsibility for the subjects with which we had been charged. It was a year since we had been appointed to the Executive Council and we had undergone six months' probation for ministerial appointments during which time, as Milton Margai put it, "we had digested nearly everything that was given us". On December 16th, therefore, our leader moved in the Legislative Council that: "This Council considers that the time has come for assumption of Portfolios by Members of the Executive Council." Dr. Margai urged that in order to do this, all that was necessary was a slight alteration in the Instrument. He was against scrapping the existing Constitution and adopting another at that time because it had taken four years "of arguments and counter-arguments to make a start and now when the country is gradually pursuing a great development programme in order to improve our economic position, to just stop and plunge the country again into a constitutional struggle, I am of the opinion that it is not to our best interests". The main cry of the teeming masses, he said, "is not for a new Constitution but for us to make a great attempt to raise their standard of living, thus eradicating hunger, poverty, disease and ignorance." By the proposed slight alteration in the Instrument, he declared, the Government would have all it needed to carry out its programme.

Dr. Margai mentioned the fact that arguments might be advanced by some members that those members who formed the present Executive Council were incapable of carrying out such important government functions. "I can declare categorically," he said, "that after twelve months of close study of the members I have with me in the Executive Council, I am confident that they are all quite capable to carry out the duties; and not only that, but if Your Excellency wants some more members I can assure Your Excellency that I shall have no difficulty in producing them from our ranks."

His speech on the motion met with resounding and prolonged applause from all members apart from the few die-hard anti-Protectorates in the National Council whose leader, Dr. Bankole-Bright, rose to his feet and declared that he would have been able to accept the motion without any difficulty if the members of the Executive Council had been members belonging to the Colony who had a high educational standard and 150 years of association with the British people and their customs.

"I go further," he declared, "and say I would have been pleased to support this motion if there had been a coalition of both the Colony and Protectorate whereby one will be able to learn from the other. But when it comes to the question of relegating the duties of ministerial posts to members of the present Executive Council, composed mostly of our Protectorate people, I say without the slightest doubt that they are not qualified to do so." He went on to say: "When you visualise the type of men who have been controlling the departments of this country, when you look at their educational standard, when you look at their experience, I ask is it reasonable to assume that men — some of whom, I say with no degree of insult, have only been second and third grade clerks in government service — of this type should be brought now to control men with such experience:"

It was not, Dr. Bankole-Bright declared, a matter for trial and he wanted no experiment. It was a matter of forming a government for the first time with the eyes of the world upon us. "I say, Sir," he said, "It is whimsical to think of the type of men in the Executive Council who are being called upon to control the present Heads of Departments. But apart from this intellectuality," he went on, "there are other qualities necessary for the post of Ministers. You have got to consider that you have to put in that position men of integrity;... men who are inspired, men who should take an interest in treating cautiously the people they have got to deal with." Finally he admitted that the principle embodied in the motion was good and they on their side would like to see it implemented, but they wanted it done the proper way. "I say, Sir, the manner in which the motion is brought here is irregular," he said. "It aims at making a structural alteration to the Constitution which has not got the mandate of the electorate and therefore we shall vote against the motion."

This speech by the leader of the National Council illustrated clearly how the deep-rooted intolerance of the Creoles towards the Protectorate people predominated their thought and action, blinding them to all else but attack; like a red rag to a bull. After a lengthy diatribe, aimed to show our incompetence, he finally ended up by agreeing with the substance of the motion except for the fact that it was *ultra vires* the Constitution. How much more responsible would his speech have been, and how much more sympathetic support would he have won from both sides of the House, had he opened his remarks with this point and confined his speech to this one objection, rather than use the occasion to air his personal bitterness and grievances.

In the brief speech I made in support of the motion, I reminded Dr. Bankole-Bright that almost all constitutions in the world were experiments, that it was only by experimenting that people were able to see errors and correct them. With regard to his observation that the Ministers, when created, would control Heads of Departments, I said: "With due deference to the colossal knowledge of parliamentary procedure of the Honourable Member for Freetown Central, I would say that my idea of a Minister is not to control a Head of Department but to work in collaboration with him. I would also like the Honourable Member to know that in some circumstances a civil servant with some experience carries far greater influence than a Minister."

Whatever was said about the motion, I declared, it did represent a step forward in our constitutional advancement, which is what we wanted. We had, at the moment, an unofficial majority in the Executive Council but blame was sometimes attached to us for certain happenings in the Government over which we had no control. "What we are trying to do now," I said, "or what is envisaged, is that we should have a firm grip over the departments so that we may exercise the responsibilities which we feel sure members on the other side would like us to exercise. Whatever the Honourable Member on the other side thinks about our educational qualifications, or about our integrity, the fact remains that we, as officials on this side, represent the vast majority of the electorate of the whole of Sierra Leone. In other words, we are the representatives of the people who pay the bulk of the taxes here by which the Government is run, we have a right to be placed here and we have a right to decide what is going on in this country."

I cannot describe — certainly, the mere words of my speech cannot convey — what I was feeling inwardly that day. I had no illusions about ministerial status ushering in some kind of political nirvana; on the contrary, I was probably more wary of British intentions than turned out, in the event, to be justified. Certainly, I was aware of a long hard road ahead to full independence. Mingled with my eagerness for ministerial office was a strong measure of apprehension, which I hardly dared confess even to myself, that I might not prove equal to the job. But underlying all these feelings, I had a deep conviction that the day's business was of transcendent importance to Sierra Leone.

I knew, at a level of conviction deeper than reason, that it was an important step for Sierra Leone to have Black ministers in power, for native Africans to exercise responsibility for policy in our own country for the first time in 150 years. At the same time my emotions felt somehow clogged with resentment of the opposition's pettiness of heart and smallness of vision. I was hopeful for my country and yet troubled for her for I could see that the strength of the divisions that rent her would weaken our government and delay our national destiny. But I cannot claim to have seen half the trouble that lay ahead or even a fraction of the time and toil it would cost to build the national unity and sense of identity which Sierra Leoneans enjoy today.

The motion was carried by 22 votes to 4 with one abstention and in April of the following year, the newly appointed Governor, Mr. Robert de Zouche Hall, announced to the Legislative Council that, on the advice of the Secretary of State for the Colonies, Her Majesty had been pleased to alter Her Royal Instructions so as to provide that the Unofficial Members of the Executive Council should be Ministers.

"I am pleased to inform Honourable Members of this Council," the Governor declared, "that, in accordance with the discretion vested in me by Her Majesty's Royal Instruction, I have charged the following Ministers with responsibility as follows:-

Dr. M. A. S. Margai	- Health, Agriculture, Animal Husbandry and Forests.
Mr. A. M. Margai	- Education, Local Government and Social Welfare.
Mr. M. S. Mustapha	- Public Works, Railway and Road Transport, Port and Marine, Civil Aviation, Meterology.
Mr. A. G. Randle	- Commerce and Industry, Co-operation, Posts and Telegraphs and Fisheries.
Mr. S. P. Stevens	- Surveys and Lands, Mines, Labour and Geological Survey."

At his own request, Paramount Chief Bai Farima Tass II, the sixth Unofficial Member of the Executive Council, was made Minister without Portfolio because he felt his chiefly duties would not permit him the necessary time to devote to government affairs.

Never before had the words 'responsible for' had greater significance for me. It is one thing to prepare one's self for a position and quite another finally to occupy that position. It was with a sense of bewilderment and inadequacy that I first sat myself down at my desk in the Ministry and forced myself to accept the fact that I was now the hub around which a sizeable section of the country's day-to-day business revolved, the smooth running of which depended ultimately on the correctness of my assessment of a situation and the decision I made on what action had to be taken. Certainly I had the expert advice of my ministerial secretary and the heads of each department, but the final decision, duly noted and signed by myself on the minute sheet, was my responsibility and mine alone. Much depended on the relationship I established with these advisers. It was not in my nature to flaunt power and I have always been a ready listener to people's views and ideas for I find that they nearly always include some useful contribution, however, small, among otherwise mundane topics that can set one's mind to work to produce a fresh approach or a more knowledgeable grasp of a subject. From the outset, therefore, I encouraged all members of my staff to consult me whenever they felt the need to do so and emphasised to them the importance of team work to the successful running of the Ministry, or any other institution.

It was not an easy matter either for me, the first African Minister, to dominate the expatriate staff of the Ministry of Lands, Mines and Labour, or for the Europeans to have to take orders from an African, particularly, perhaps, when he was a man from the 'backward' Protectorate who was less academically endowed than themselves. But I feel that my genuine eagerness to listen to their opinions and advice and, because I found that advice to be more often than not sound, the fact that I generally acted on it did much to save face all round by establishing among us a feeling of equality rather than of master and servant. And, however freely these men expressed their views to me or registered their disagreement on my decision, I never detected a lack of respect for my position.

An impartial and efficient civil service is essential for the successful performance of one's ministerial duties. A good civil servant, whatever his own political views may be, must prepare himself to serve loyally a Minister of any party, whether he be true blue conservative or red hot communist. Nevertheless, it is not unusual, human nature being what it is, for a civil servant to delay a matter that conflicts with his own ideology and rush through one of which he is in favour. A Minister must be ever alert to this kind of obstructionism and deal firmly with those who indulge in it, for it is on him that the axe will fall for incompetence, not with the civil servant.

I found that the harder I worked, the harder and more conscientiously the whole staff worked, and I realised that the way I behaved and the competence I showed in the performance of my work would be quickly noted and would reflect themselves on the whole Ministry staff. I was now a public figure and whether I survived as such or not depended on the image I presented to that public. Keeping in touch with the people is, of course, a Minister's primary duty. However efficient he may be at his office desk, it is the success of his relationship with his constituents that is the determining factor in his political career, for he depends on their votes to keep his seat in the Legislature. Few days passed without delegations seeking an interview with me and it was rare that a night at home was undisturbed by some man, woman or group of people anxious to off-load their problems onto my broad shoulders. Even if people did not monopolise my evenings, there was always a mass of paperwork to be studied either in preparation for Executive Council meetings or a backlog of documents and files from the office.

"Bo mercy pan you, you no go lef papers? You no go play with den pikin?" my wife complained time and again, exasperated by my nightly absorption with papers and my neglect of our young children with whom I had once regularly played games before they went to bed.

I think perhaps the most irksome duties expected of me as a Minister were those that were supposed to be relaxing and pleasurable, namely, cocktail parties and formal dinner parties held in honour of some visiting celebrity. Unless the conversation was inspiring or witty, I found that my mind wandered off on to some problem that awaited me on my desk, on suitable material for a forthcoming speech or on palaver in my constituency. It was disconcerting at such times suddenly to find myself accosted by a well-meaning person intent on being sociable who sought my opinion on such trivia as unseasonable weather, the latest women's fashions or some idle gossip.

It is bad enough for anybody's image to appear detached or disinterested, to excuse one's self — however politely — and retreat to a dark corner, or to yawn; but in a politician's case, such behaviour can lose him valuable votes. It was not that I was unable to throw off the cares of the Ministry and enter into the spirit of the party; indeed I have always enjoyed convivial company and can act with as much gay abandon as anybody. But the small amount of interesting and worthwhile conversation that one finds at cocktail parties is so outweighed by the predominance of inane chatter that unless one is in the mood for hilarity alone, I feel such functions are unnecessarily time consuming and serve no useful purpose.

Likewise, State banquets and high-level receptions, by their very formality, can force one to become so painfully restrained that one fears to let one's hair down at all lest in an unguarded moment a word slips out that has not been carefully enough weighed, is picked up by an alert reporter, given banner headline treatment and made political capital of by opposition elements. Many a political career has suffered as a result of a casual remark let slip in the wrong ear.

My newly acquired status brought with it a sudden surge of popularity from the most unexpected quarters. The crowds of my own people who haunted me night and day, I understood, for I was now the butt of their complaints and the dispenser of their remedies. This was part of my job. But I was quite overwhelmed by the number of expatriates who, seemingly unaware of my existence over the years, found an urgent need to befriend me, and of the number of foreign visitors whose 'musts' on their itinerary included a visit to me and, if possible, a photograph of themselves taken with me as if I were an historical monument.

Many of those who came to see me bore gifts. The giving of gifts to those in power, such as our chiefs, is not new to Africa. Nor, deplorable as it may be, is bribery, traditionally known as 'shake hand' because a person who seeks a favour has something concealed in his right hand which he passes to the one from whom he hopes to obtain the favour when he shakes hand with him. However, in most cases neither the gift offered freely nor the amount involved in a 'shake hand' were of much value and rarely exceeded four or five pounds.

It was, therefore, quite a shattering revelation to me to find that many foreigners who visited me practised our 'shake hand' with a vengeance, offering what to my mind represented a positive fortune. On the first occasion when this happened to me, my emotions passed from blank amazement, through embarrassment, humiliation and revulsion to indignation, but I was unable to do anything except stand there speechless and listen to a spate of well rehearsed and self-assured sales patter. When I was finally left alone to collect my thoughts and decide what action I had to take, all I could think about was how on earth anybody could afford to give away so much money.

It was only when I had been in office a while that I discovered that almost without exception, companies and business enterprises the world over who seek the award of a contract make in their estimates a generous allowance for contingencies which covers not only unforeseen expenses such as increases in the cost price of materials, but also an amount of money which it is intended to offer as an *ex gratia* payment to those responsible if the contract is won. Consciences are spuriously mollified by admitting the money is there to be used for that purpose and if you do not have it somebody else will. The practice would be differently received in most quarters if the money were offered overtly only *after* the award of a contract and paid not into individual's pockets, but into the national coffers, or party funds or put to some collectively useful purpose. As things stand, the individual who accepts the bribe is well and truly compromised by the briber.

The reason I treat the subject here is to enlighten up-and-coming African politicians in particular about some of the temptations that will strew their path. They are especially vulnerable to such offers because of the relative poverty from which most of them rise and the pressure of their obligations, once they become 'Big Men', to African society with its extended family commitments. Their comparative ignorance of the sharp practices of some foreigners can make them easily duped *ingenues* in the remorseless world of international wheeler-dealing.

Most men in public positions the world over need money, but the need is far more acute for those who have only just left the bread-line. As far as an African is concerned, once he is elevated to a position of authority he is expected to support a horde of hangers-on, remote members of his family many of whom he never before knew existed. He must hand out largesse, educate not only his own children but those of family members, entertain more lavishly and more frequently than before and dress himself and his family in clothes befitting his status. It is all part and parcel of his new position. Money slips through his fingers like quicksilver and he can never have enough of it to satisfy his dependants. When it can be had so easily, when all that is required of him in return is his influence in tipping the scales in the award of a contract or manoeuvering some other proposition in favour of the donor, the temptation is enormous and it seems foolish to him to refuse such an offer. Fresh in his memory, too, is the hardship he suffered on the way up the ladder, the years of poverty and near starvation he endured and the longed-for education he could never afford, and perhaps also the stench and dampness of a prison cell. With plenty of money in the bank at least his own children would be spared such deprivation.

Yet, as I have stressed elsewhere, it is at this point, when a man appeases his nagging conscience with the words: "Just this once can't do any harm", that the rot begins to set in and rapidly spreads. Much wants more, consciences no longer prick and the acceptance of bribes becomes a habit. Not only Ministers and those at the top are vulnerable, but departmental heads, secretaries, anybody, in fact, who has the remotest chance of using his influence; and before long the whole country is entangled in a suffocating web of corruption. The sooner we take firm and decisive steps to eradicate this scourge the healthier will our society become.

During my three-and-a-half years or so in office as Sierra Leone's first Minister of Lands, Mines and Labour, I had plenty of practice in riding storms, particularly as regards the Departments of Mines and Labour. The root of the trouble in the mid-1950's really lay with the diamond rush which, between 1952 and 1954 had swelled the population in the Kono, Kenema and Bo districts from 5,000 to 30,000, and by 1956 the number had increased to as many as 75,000 persons. As I have already explained in the chapter dealing with the mines, this posed a formidable problem socially, economically and politically and took precedence over all else as far as I, the Minister responsible, was concerned. But for several weeks my attention was diverted to trade union disputes in Freetown and to the serious rioting that followed in their wake.

The migration of fortune-hunters from agriculture to the diamond mines, plus a bad harvest in 1954, were responsible for a shortage of the staple food of the workers — palm oil and rice — the prices of which soared beyond the reach of many people. The Government attempted to ameliorate the hardship by importing a quantity of both products and controlling the selling price in the market, but this only temporarily appeased the masses. Trade Union representatives were daily at my office complaining that Government, far from controlling the rise in the cost of living, had added fuel to the flames by increasing the salaries of civil servants. They were in an angry mood and seemed to expect me, as the Minister responsible, to perform a miracle which would glut the market with produce and fill the people's pockets with the wherewithal to buy it. The fact that I could not do so made it seem to them, or so I sensed, that I was not doing my job very well, that I had forgotten what it was like to be one of the toiling masses, or that I just did not care.

As a simple trade unionist my position would have been different, but as a Minister of the Government I could not interfere with the working of the machinery of the Joint Industrial Councils which had been set up seven years before as free and voluntary bargaining organisations under constitutions by workers' and employers' representatives on behalf of the interests they represented. In this particular case, after a deal of negotiating, the representatives of the two main unions concerned, namely, the Artisans and Allied Workers' Union and the Transport and General Workers' Union, decreased their wage claim from 2/6d. (25c) to 1/6d. (15c), while the employers raised their offer from 2d. (2c) to 4d. (4c) for the Colony and 3d. (3c) for other areas.

When neither side would budge from these figures, the employers moved that the matter should go to arbitration, but the workers were against this and a deadlock resulted. The constitutions of the Joint Industrial Councils provided that where such a deadlock was reached, the matter should be referred to the Governor for arbitration under the Trades Disputes ordinance. However, before steps were taken to approach the Governor on the matter, the workers' representatives on both Joint Industrial Councils held two public meetings after which they served a 14-day strike notice on almost all the major employers of labour in the country.

I did my utmost to persuade the General Secretaries of the two unions to re-open negotiations and advised them that Government had already taken steps towards constructing a revised cost of living index based on a survey by an impartial expert; but they refused to consider further negotiations. On January 27th, 1955, I summoned a fully representative meeting of the Joint Industrial Council Chamber to go over the issues involved and to state the line Government proposed to follow in the matter. I pointed out that in the present situation it appeared as if the workers were not honouring their side of the bargain.

"I wonder what would be the reaction of the workers' side if the boot had been on the other foot?" I said. "I think the workers' side would agree," I continued, "that a great part of the structure of society is based on people honouring agreements which they have freely and voluntarily entered into. This is true in the industrial field no less than in other aspects of life. To use a piece of industrial relations machinery when it suits one's purpose and to discard it when one thinks it convenient to do so, would spell chaos for industry and I feel sure that if this had been our record in the past, we would not up to now maintain the high reputation we enjoy in the field of industrial relations."

I pointed out to them that whatever other issues might be involved, Government felt that while the Joint Industrial Councils' machinery was in existence, the parties which had come together in the setting up of the machinery had a clear and honourable duty to use it to its fullest extent for the settlement of all differences.

In the sort of democracy by which we were governed, I declared, the workers were free to withhold their service and the employers were free to institute lock-outs, generally speaking, but I warned that attention should be paid to certain public safeguards laid down by law and by the unions themselves, such as in regard to vital services, and drew attention to the strike notice served on the Electricity Department which, I pointed out, was contrary to the law. I mentioned other stipulations contained in union rules which, it seemed to Government, had not received the serious attention they deserved, and finally appealed most strongly on behalf of Government to the workers' side to reconsider the whole matter dispassionately and see whether they could not find accommodation for their demands within the boundaries of their self-created machinery.

As a result of this meeting, the two General Secretaries of the unions wrote the following day to the Commissioner of Labour withdrawing the strike notice and asking for a resumption of negotiations, which took place on January 31st. At this meeting the trade unions reduced their demand by 3d. to 1/3d. (13c) and the employers asked for an adjournment to consider it. At a further meeting on February 2nd, the employers raised their offer to 6d. (5c), which was unacceptable to the workers and the meeting adjourned without agreement.

I immediately called for an informal meeting, in my house, of those primarily concerned and made a fresh appeal to the trade unions to use the established machinery. Two days later the workers reduced their demand to 10d. (8½c), but the employers stuck out for 6d., promising that if the new cost of living survey that was due to be produced by an expert so warranted it, they would re-open negotiations. The workers would have none of it and on February 5th a second strike notice was issued which was this time referred to as a 'General Strike'. In the notice it was explained that the action they had resolved to take was not done maliciously 'with a view to break contract of service with Departments of any description', nor was it intended to deprive the inhabitants of the Colony and Protectorate of Sierra Leone, but was born of extreme circumstances over which they had no control. The strike was to commence on February 9th, 1955.

The Sierra Leone Council of Labour, the supreme body of the trade union movement in the country, had not been consulted. When it met on February 10th, the Council declared that it viewed the situation with disfavour and felt that although there were reasonable grounds for the claims of the workers concerned, much good could have been derived if persistent effort were continued through the prescribed channels instead of resorting to strike action with all its repercussions. It appealed to the unions concerned to call off the strike immediately.

"In making this appeal," it declared, "the Council of Labour has in mind the fact that of all the British Colonial territories, the trade union movement in Sierra Leone has always enjoyed the enviable position of having the highest reputation in the field of industrial relations, and boasts of a negotiating machinery which conforms very closely to that which obtains in the United Kingdom."

The strike continued for five days, ending on Monday, February 14th. Two days after the start of the strike rioting began. Unruly mobs flooded the streets of Freetown, stoning, looting and assaulting, aiming their attack in particular at those wearing collars and ties, the symbol of the civil service, the privileged elite who had been given a pay rise. Underground high voltage cables were cut and the water supply to the main power station was cut off in an attempt to sabotage the electricity supply; all telephone, telegraph and rail communications with the Protectorate were severed, as well as telephone communications in Freetown; the entire rediffusion service was put out of action; the city water suply was severely interrupted and road blocks were placed in strategic parts of the city.

On February 11th, the second day of the strike, Dr. Bankole-Bright decided to address a meeting of the strikers at the Queen Elizabeth II playing field. In an emotional speech he encouraged the strikers and offered them the support of his National Council; he attacked the Government in general and certain Ministers in particular, and whilst he did not actually advocate violence in so many words, he expressed the view that any possible breakdown of sanitary and electricity services were of no interest to hungry men. Whatever his real intentions, the fact remains that it was after this speech that violence increased in volume and ferocity and was responsible for the deaths of seventeen civilians and one policeman and the injuries of over a hundred others.

In the Shaw Report which was commissioned to enquire into the Freetown strike and riots, Dr. Bankole-Bright was reported to have considered it a 'strange coincidence' that his speech should have been followed by such an outbreak of violence. "This is as may be," said the Commissioners; "we have already seen that prior preparation by way of sabotage to certain services had already taken place, and while the speech was being delivered the construction of road blocks was being actively proceeded with. In our view the speech was unwise. It was clear on the evidence that Dr. Bankole-Bright had not informed himself of the issues involved in the industrial dispute. A person in his position and with his long political experience would have been well advised not to commit himself publicly to encouraging men to strike. We do not think, however, that it was his intention to incite violence; and, indeed, there is no evidence that his speech had that effect."

Maybe not, but I contend that but for his attack on the Government and certain Ministers, the strikers would not have thought of venting their spleen on myself and two other Ministers. At 4 p.m. on the same day that Bankole-Bright delivered his speech, an angry crowd gathered before my house, 33 Fort Street, stoned the windows and then forced their way into my compound where petrified members of my family had gathered together a pile of personal belongings prior to taking refuge in a neighbour's house. Jeering and abusing them, they helped themselves to whatever they could lay their hands on and then proceeded to give the same treatment to the houses of the Minister of Works & Transport, Sanusi Mustapha, and the Minister of Education, Albert Margai.

Later that year riots of an even more serious nature broke out in the Northern province when the people rebelled against the Paramount Chiefs. The Governor, Sir Maurice Dorman, described the rebellion as being "apart from the uprising in Kenya, the most serious incident of the people taking the law into their own hands in Africa during the present century".

The S.L.P.P. was closely bound up with the Paramount Chiefs for it was through their backing that the party came into power and through their Native Authorities that law and order in the Protectorate was principally maintained. The majority of people still regarded the chiefs as their leaders and advisers, but a disrupting influence was beginning to penetrate their ranks, born partly from objections to the payment of taxes and the high cost of living in general, and partly from the spread of dissatisfaction from the overcrowded diamond mines. The lawlessness in the diamond mining area was bordering on anarchy. Ruthless gangs raided the S.L.S.T. and licensed diggers' areas and fought any resistance, even at times when the police attempted to intervene. When the rainy season got under way and flooding made digging too difficult, thousands trekked home taking with them their disrespect for law and order and their disillusionment at not having made a quick fortune. This served to exacerbate the already existing discontentment in many parts of the north.

In addition, with the building of road and rail communications many people who had previously been cut off from outside influence were beginning to broaden their outlook. Travelling to other parts of the country, they began to seriously question the authority of the chief, in particular his right to levy taxes to provide for his personal requirements, to expect as a right gifts and obeisance, and to demand that they labour for him. More and more was demanded of the poor wretched taxpayers whose collector, the village headman, now paid over the money to the Native Administration without the District Commissioner being present.

In 1955, District Councils were empowered to levy a rate called a 'precept', which ranged then from 9/- (90c) to 16/- (Le1.60) but was due to be increased by about 5/- (50c) the following year. The people were already paying a substantial Hut Tax of around 10/- (Le1) and this additional burden to be imposed upon them was just about the last straw. In Port Loko, the people were incensed when their Paramount Chief proposed, in November, 1955, to levy an extra 5/- on all taxpayers in his chiefdom to build himself a new house. When objections were raised, he agreed to give up the levy, but only on the condition that free labour was provided instead.

This and similar demands on the people by their chiefs triggered off rebellions against chiefs and Tribal Authorities in almost every chiefdom in the Port Loko and Kambia Districts. Chiefs either fled or were chased out of their houses and many were forced to live in 'voluntary' exile. Their property was ruthlessly destroyed and everything they possessed rendered worthless. When the riots died down in mid-March, 1956, it was estimated that £750,000 worth of damage had been done to property; almost all of which belonged to chiefs and Tribal Authorities. At least 23 people were killed and three policemen who disappeared were presumed murdered.

A commission, chaired by Sir Herbert Cox, Q.C., was set up to investigate the rebellion which it described as 'a civil war rather than a disturbance', and which expressed shock at the degree of demoralisation it found among the people in their customary institutions. It condemned the behaviour of the chiefs and cited instances of greed, extortion and corruption by them and by all those involved in native administrations. It found that most people, whilst objecting to illegal extra taxes, licence fees and fines extorted from them by the chiefs, still respected the office of Chief, if not the holder of that office.

Much of the trouble, the commission found, stemmed from laxity of administrative control over the chiefs and Tribal Authorities and it recommended that the Tribal Authorities should be replaced by smaller more representative bodies, that central government supervision of local authorities be tightened up and that taxpayers in the Protectorate should no longer have to pay tax through the village headman or section chief, but should pay direct to the Chiefdom Treasury.

Although the Cox Commission recommended otherwise, the Government did eventually pay substantial sums in compensation to a number of chiefs who suffered losses at the hands of the rioters. Later that year, three independent Commissioners, Sir Harold Willan, Sir David Edwards and Mr. Justice P. Storr, were appointed by Government to inquire into the conduct of 20 chiefs referred to in the Cox Report. Eleven chiefs were found guilty of conduct subversive of good government and five were asked to resign, among them Paramount Chief Bai Farima Tass II, Minister without portfolio and a Member of the Executive Council, and Paramount Chief Alikali Modu III, the representative of Port Loko District in the Legislative Council, who both resigned from their seats on the Councils and from their chieftaincies. Four chiefs and sub-chiefs were deposed, one suspended indefinitely from all powers and functions and one suspended for a period.

Whilst chieftaincy was not my direct responsibility much blame for the rebellion against it was attached to the undermining of respect for law and order following on the diamond rush which very deeply concerned me both as a Minister and as a member of the S.L.P.P. Even though the agreement with S.L.S.T., which I had worked so hard to bring about, released certain diamond-bearing areas to licensed diggers, the inhabitants of the Kono District were dissatisfied with the terms of the agreement for they felt they should have a larger share of the benefits from the mining in their district than that allowed under the agreement. They complained, with some justification, that they had more diamonds in their area than elsewhere in the country but the least chance to dig them. They blamed the S.L.P.P. Government not only for this, but also for the lack of amenities, such as water supply, roads and schools, which they felt were due to them on account of their large contribution to the national revenue. To give substance to their grievances, they formed the Kono Progressive Movement (K.P.M), the first effective radical party of the people to arise in opposition to the S.L.P.P.

In the 1960 local election campaign the K.P.M. mobilised support from the masses with such vote-catchers as: *'To Save Your Diamonds — to Revive and Protect Your Trade — for the Prosperity, Peace and Progress of Your Country and for Freedom and Plenty — Vote Solidly in the Great Freedom Pot and FREE SIERRA LEONE PEOPLE FROM IMPERIALIST EXPLOITATION."* This paid off handsomely by winning from them 24 of the 30 seats in the District Council.

In August, 1957, when I was no longer in office, illicit miners operating on land reserved for the S.L.S.T. organised an attack on the S.L.S.T. plant at Yengema in protest against the company's strenuous pleas to government to have them removed and, some say, to grab a share of the company's production of diamonds which they felt were rightly theirs. I was in London at the time undergoing a medical check-up, but because of my close association with the mines, I was asked by some sections of the Press to give my views on what were the main causes of the troubles in Kono.

"The trouble is," I said, "the people in Kono have little or no diamondiferous land in which to mine. The breaking of the monopoly agreement and the introduction of licensed mining did not mean much to the individual Kono man or woman. Rightly or wrongly they felt that the best lands were in the S.L.S.T. areas and that the areas allocated to them were worthless. Although the cause of the recent outburst is no justification for violence and lawlessness, I think it is necessary to get at the underlying causes of the trouble so as to prevent any recurrence. "Apparently, early this year," I went on, "some person or persons attached to the Mines Department made a blunder of the first magnitude. In trying to cut boundaries for licensed mining from non-S.L.S.T. lands, persons who were responsible encroached upon S.L.S.T. areas. Seventy or eighty licences were issued and alluvial mining began. The Company was quick to notice the encroachment and a first-class row ensued. This blunder was most regrettable because it simply fanned afresh the dissatisfaction which already existed about allocation of lands between the Company and licensed mining. The Government was in a dilemma. It was pledged to protect the Company from such infringement and apparently one of its own servants had been responsible for the infringement."

I went on to say that I felt that the Kono people, in my opinion, could have got more and better lands if they had not been misrepresented at the talks in London in 1955 when the Leader of our Delegation stated that the chiefs and people of Kono had no desire for licensed mining in their country and that they preferred that all diamond mining in Kono should be done by the S.L.S.T. Neither Albert Margai nor I shared this view and I disagreed violently with the Chief Minister, Dr. Margai. In the end we had to compromise and the compromise was that the exclusive Prospecting Areas should be divided between the company and licensed mining roughly on a fifty-fifty basis.

Although in the intervening years I have had immensely more power and responsibility in a series of jobs in my country's service, I still recall my first spell as a Minister with excitement and even a little of the same awe I felt when I sat for the first time at the Minister's desk. This is not just a matter of nostalgia with which an old man thinks back to the time of his greatest vigour. There was a real sense of pioneering about that phase of my life which has been echoed in many of my more recent endeavours but never, perhaps, so perfectly recaptured. And though I even then had plenty of experience of life's ups and downs, and plenty of foreboding about my country's future, I had not suffered the disillusionment and deep trial of ideals that awaited me in subsequent years. Even the threats to my security and my family in the crisis of 1955 left no really ineradicable scars on my idealism. Later, even after I had overcome the embitterment of the struggles of the late 'fifties and 'sixties for unity and democracy in my country, somehow the savour of politics was never quite the same again. Like the mangoes we used to pluck as small boys from the trees in the schoolyard, politics when I was first a Minister still tasted clean and fresh and wholesome. I still find political life rewarding and get a renewed thrill of pleasure from every small success accomplished and every day of duty done. But I miss that taste.

CHAPTER TEN

Into the Wilderness

As the life of our Government wore on, my apprehension increased. There was no drive or resolution in Milton Margai's leadership. Instead of being forced nearer by dynamism, the prospects of independence seemed to fade in a haze of temporising and indecision. The Party, too, was a source of profound anxiety for me. I could sense its loss of direction, of destiny. I had taken part in its formation and fought in its cause because I thought it would be an effective democratic organ for the representation of my people. Instead, it had so far been little more than a vehicle for the sectionalism and elitism of a small controlling clique. There seemed to be no will at the top to turn the S.L.P.P. into a popular party with a mass organisation. It was barely a party at all, I began to feel, in any normally accepted sense. Even Milton Margai himself seemed confused at what exactly he was leader of when, in opposing a motion in the Legislative Council concerning the composition of the Executive Council on January 31st, 1952, he referred to it as "the group I was dealing with — call it a party, a small community or merely a number of people..." I almost sweated with embarrassment.

There was no effective central party organisation or control of local units and although the S.L.P.P. boasted a paid-up membership of between 7,000 and 10,000 persons, there was little evidence of this. When the Party held its second ever national convention in 1956, for instance, only 70 delegates turned up. There was little discipline within the party, an almost complete lack of interest in party affairs by Legislative members and little contact between them and their constituents. Rivalry was rife among party members and many of them used the party purely for personal promotion, putting self before party interests. In the 1957 elections, for example, an S.L.P.P. supporter, backed by a prominent party leader, opposed the official party candidate in one of the Colony constituencies, while in the Protectorate at least 35 out of 43 candidates who ran as independents only joined forces with the S.L.P.P. when the election results were known and the party won a resounding victory. The party leadership connived on this unprincipled politicking by adopting candidates *after* their election, simply because they had been successful at the polls! The S.L.P.P., in short, practised the politics of the cock-eyed.

The Sierra Leone *Daily Mail* of January 13th, 1956, in an editorial headed 'Almost Dead', assessed the position thus:

" Interest in things political in this country is almost nil. Once a political party has been formed for one reason or the other, usually to afford a handful of people a chance to run for immediately pending elections, and that object has been achieved, then there is very little heard of and from that party until election time comes around again..."

The trouble stemmed from the fact that Milton Margai, perhaps because of his blood ties and long association with chiefs, had always preferred to work almost exclusively through the Paramount Chiefs and District Councils to gain support of the people, rather than the method normally adopted by politicans of approaching the people direct and rallying their support, popularizing the party and its aims and encouraging them to participate in the running of it.

Paramount Chiefs had been an integral part of the S.L.P.P. since its inception and without their support the party would no doubt have ceased to exist long ago. I had nothing against the chiefs. Indeed, I acknowledged time and again their usefulness and the need we had of their support and participation in the country's affairs. But I saw that the time had come when the mass of the people had to be personally involved in the nation's affairs, when they had to think for themselves, to form their own judgements independently of chiefly influence. It was time for the people to be allowed a free hand in choosing their representatives in the Legislature.

I, and several of the party members, wanted to see more action and it was becoming increasingly obvious to us that Dr. Margai was not the man to produce it. His approach towards constitutional reform and independence had become, to my mind, too cautious and apologetic. He positively fawned on the British. It was well known, for instance, that he looked to the Governor for the last word, that the Governor had more influence over him than his own Ministers and party men. He lacked the vital spark with which to light, and keep alight, the people's torch of freedom as well as the militancy of those African nationalist leaders who succeeded in bulldozing their way to victory through the most formidable of colonialist barriers because they had first secured the full backing of the masses.

The leader of a subject people is expected by those people to be uncompromising in demanding restitution of their rights, not humbly grateful for the occasional payment on account. A political broadcast Milton Margai made during the 1957 election campaign typifies his complacency at the leisurely pace things were going. "We," he said, referring to the S.L.P.P. leaders, "were the first Ministers ever in Sierra Leone. We were pioneers. The evidence of how well we have done our jobs is seen in the readiness with which Her Majesty's Government has agreed for us to take another step towards self-government." Despite his great diplomatic and intellectual gifts, his political vision had alarmingly blind spots. He was never able to see democracy from the inside or feel it in his guts, like those of us with popular roots. Perhaps, his way up had just been too easy.

The further step towards self-government to which he referred was the adoption of the 1956 constitutional reforms under which a House of Representatives would replace the Legislative Council and would consist of 57 members, including four ex-officio members and two nominated members to represent special interests. Of the 51 elected members, 12 were to be Paramount Chiefs, 14 members elected from the Colony area, 24 members elected from the Protectorate (two from each of the twelve districts), and one member elected from the Bo urban area.

The educated Protectorate men had never ceased to agitate for a system of direct elections on a broad franchise and this had eventually prompted the Government in June, 1954, to set up a Commission for Electoral Reform under the chairmanship of Bryan Keith-Lucas of Nuffield College, Oxford. The Commission found that there was little serious opposition towards universal franchise from those they interviewed, apart from a few illiterate chiefs, one of them on the grounds that a taxpayer franchise would mean all men were equal. A Protectorate man, M. J. Kamanda-Bongay of Bo, voiced the opinions of the majority of us when he expressed astonishment that in 1954 the question of whether or not universal adult suffrage should be introduced into the country should be the subject of a commission of enquiry.

The Commission recommended a two-stage progression towards universal franchise. The first stage was to be in time for the 1956

District Council elections. This provided for a taxpayer franchise in the Protectorate which was to include women who paid taxes, were literate or owned property. As far as the Colony was concerned, it recommended an income franchise to include all men and women of 21 or over, literate or otherwise, who either occupied premises rated at £2 annually or who had a yearly income of £60, and who had resided in the area for the previous six months. The second stage, which was to be introduced in time for the 1957 general elections, was to be universal franchise. The Commission recommended in addition that Paramount Chiefs, to spare them the indignity of possibly losing a seat to a non-chief in an open contest, be given separate representation in the Legislature and that the non-chief members from each chiefdom on the District Council be elected directly rather than appointed by their Tribal Authority. All these proposals were accepted by the Government.

The Legislative Council should have been dissolved in October, 1956, but its life was extended by an Order-in-Council first to January 30th and again to April 8th, owing to delays in preparing lists of voters for the elections. Many members expressed dissatisfaction at the postponement of the holding of the elections and I declared that as far as members of the Government were concerned, we were no longer willing to remain in power without a fresh mandate.

In his speech proroguing the Legislative Council, the Governor, Sir Maurice Dorman, referring to the parts played by the six African Ministers who had, he said, faced responsibilities with resolution and good sense, declared: "Some will not agree with what they have said or done, others will — but whatever may be our differences none would say now that Sierra Leone was not capable of ministerial government."

The country was divided into 35 electoral districts and the date set for the election was finally fixed for May 3rd, 1957, for all but seven outlying districts which were to go to the polls on May 8th. For the first time direct elections to the central Legislature were to be held in the Protectorate and as far as we of the Protectorate were concerned, we considered it a great achievement after the years spent agitating for it.

A number of parties contested the seats. Apart from the S.L.P.P. and the National Council, there was the United Progressive Party (U.P.P.) formed in 1954 by Cyril Rogers-Wright; the Labour Party; the Kono Progressive Movement and Edward Blyden III's Sierra Leone Independence Movement which, with the N.C. and the Labour Party, failed to gain a single seat. A number of candidates irrespective of their party allegiance, stood as independents. There was, of course, much speculation and a fair measure of bitterness over the selection of party candidates.

It was now that I first crossed swords with Banja Tejan-Sie, though I did not appreciate the importance of the encounter at the time. He was then S.L.P.P. Vice-President, but, after a hard fight with me, lost the official party nomination for Port Loko East. He responded by promptly resigning the vice-presidency and standing against me as an independent. I did not realise how rankled he already felt, but the fact that I won the seat was something I believe he never quite forgave me for, not even when, some years later as Prime Minister, I recommended him for the highest appointment in the land, that of Governor-General. I suppose I should have been prepared for the hostility he subsequently showed, but although I do not think I am ingenuous about human nature, I have never really learnt to understand a harboured grudge. Sierra Leone politics in those days was like a small dance floor, where the same people kept bumping into one another. It was my rule not to mind, and I was too ready to suppose that other people felt the same way.

Electioneering campaigns were most costly affairs in those days, for every candidate, whether nominated by a party or standing as an independent, had personally to finance his own. I journeyed extensively in my constituency stopping wherever I saw people to talk to and, physically exhausted, my eyes inflamed and stinging from the dust off the roads, and my voice hoarse and rasping, I urged them to opt for my party whose voting symbol was the palm tree.

" Vote for the S.L.P.P.!" I exhorted them. "Vote for the S.L.P.P. and be sure of independence by 1962; The S.L.P.P. does not make idle promises. When we say we will bring independence to Sierra Leone by 1962, we know what we are talking about. 'Ah-ha' you may say, 'S.L.I.M. promises it *next* year and the U.P.P. by *1960*.' My friends, I say to you in all seriousness — don't mind them. I tell you such rash promises are unrealistic, irresponsible, mere vote-catchers. Don't be bamboozled by them!

"Vote for the S.L.P.P., the only party that will deliver the goods on time and as promised; the party that will abolish the posts of Chief Secretary and Chief Commissioner of the Protectorate; the party that will appoint a Deputy Governor who will be responsible for Defence & External Affairs; the party that will bring to all of school age free education by 1960 — do you hear me? — FREE EDUCATION BY 1960!

"Vote for the party that promises that within the next five years it will develop Fourah Bay into a full university college with honours degree courses; the party that will undertake a five-year plan of road building, that intends to spend five million pounds on providing all trunk roads with bridges and tarred surfaces; a party, my friends, that will uphold the authority of the chiefs and concern itself with their welfare. The S.L.P.P. is the only party with the welfare of the chiefs and people genuinely at heart. Vote for the Palm Tree! VOTE FOR THE S.L.P.P.!"

Even as I uttered the slogans I was choking back inward doubts.

We won a landslide victory. Out of the 39 popularly elected seats, S.L.P.P. official candidates won 25, the independents, all of whom declared for the S.L.P.P. immediately after the elections, won 8, the U.P.P. won 5 and the K.P.M. only 1 seat. With the support of the Paramount Chiefs who had been elected by the District Councils, the S.L.P.P. had a total membership of 45 out of the 51 elected members of the new House of Representatives.

It seemed that there were some in high places who had been somewhat concerned about the outcome of the election in Port Loko East where I stood as the official party candidate. Firstly, there was the Governor who had arranged to have specially relayed to him an up-to-the-minute blow by blow account of the voting in that constituency. For a while he must have got as far as easing the wire that secured the cork on the champagne bottle, for it looked as if my opponent Tejan-Sie was all but at the winning post; but when the votes were recorded in the last station in the Sando Magbolonto chieftaincy, the pendulum swung very much in my favour and gave me a comfortable victory.

It was widely rumoured that Tejan-Sie was fancied in certain quarters as a successor to Dr. Margai as Prime Minister after independence, when Dr. Margai would become Governor-General, and was being quietly eased into an advantageous position. Fate, however, dictated otherwise.

The second person with a deeply furrowed brow that day was the Paramount Chief of the district, Bai Koblo Pathbana II, whose *bete noire* I was from my trade union days in Marampa. He had sworn to God that no Limba man would ever represent his constituency. We have crossed a few times on the dance floor of politics since then. And we seem to have established an understanding, for I am not aware that he has any objections to serving as a Minister of State under a Limba President! Our *entente* teaches an invaluable political lesson: politics is in large measure the art of conciliation and co-operation. If charity does not prevent you from developing inflexible enmities, then sheer commonsense should.

In spite of those who may have wished it otherwise, I won the seat for Port Loko East and looked forward to taking an active part in achieving political independence for Sierra Leone in the shortest possible time. Naturally I not only hoped for, but anticipated a ministerial appointment, for at such a crucial stage in our history it was only to be expected that all of us who had had experience in government — and there were few enough of us in all conscience — would be called upon to serve our country.

Now that the S.L.P.P. were firmly in the saddle, Albert Margai, myself and a number of others in the party were more convinced than ever that Milton Margai was no longer active enough to force the pace we would have to maintain if independence was to be achieved in the foreseeable future. Something had to be done about it, and quickly, and unpleasant as the prospect was, we saw it as our duty to the nation to force him to resign from the leadership in favour of a younger man. Albert proposed that I should take over as the new parliamentary leader, but I refused. I felt that Albert was the natural choice as successor to his brother. With his youth and energy and his insistence on self-government at once with no half measures or compromises, he was, to my mind, just the sort of revitalising shot in the arm that the country needed at that time to rid it of its lethargy. He had also polled the highest number of votes of any candidate in the election. I promised him my full support and at the parliamentary caucus on May 19th he won the leadership from his brother by 22 votes to 21.

I had not been home very long that night, and it was getting very late, when Albert suddenly arrived. He told me that, after the meeting, members of the Margai family had gone to see him and, condemning his action as shameful and disrespectful, prevailed upon him to step down in favour of his older brother. Family pressure in Africa is, of course, a very real force and the last thing a man would want to be accused of is bringing dishonour upon his kith and kin. Albert had finally agreed to step down, he said, but only on condition that Milton consulted him on all matters of policy.

My wife, who had just been rejoicing with me over the new leadership, was shocked and distressed at this latest development. "Albert," she said, choking back tears, "you have ruined us."

To have openly opposed the party leadership and engineered a take-over that had failed, was certainly not the happiest of positions to be in, particularly for one with hopes of a portfolio, but I looked upon it more as a temporary set-back than ruin. I had done what I did because I sincerely believed it was in the best interests of the party and Sierra Leone. Never at any time was it my intention that anybody, least of all Dr. Margai, should interpret my action as an attack against his person. I had the greatest respect and affection for him both as a man and as the leader of the Protectorate people in particular. But he had reached the point when he was unable to drive any more without his foot being planted permanently on the brake and his eye constantly on the look-out for the white policeman's signals to halt or advance with caution. It grieved me, therefore, that Dr. Margai and some of his supporters were unable or unwilling to accept what I had done in the spirit in which it was meant. No doubt it was to punish me and to put me firmly in my place that no portfolio was offered to me.

Albert Margai, who had held the portfolio of Local Government, Education and Welfare in the previous government, was offered that of Works and Housing. This he rejected and at a meeting in the Wilberforce Memorial Hall on May 26th, he gave his reasons for so doing. First, he said, the selection of portfolios had been wrongly done; secondly, the portfolios had not been offered to the S.L.P.P.'s best people; and thirdly, he alleged that there had been too much interference by the Governor in the allocation of portfolios. He concluded by saying that he now found it difficult to accept any offer of compromise which fell short of Dr. Margai relinquishing the leadership of the Parliamentary Committee of the party. He did not at that point, however, resign from the party but sat on the back benches.

With Albert out of the Cabinet, the only man among the new Ministers who had previously held a Ministerial post was Sanusi Mustapha.

Albert Margai was not alone in criticising the selection of Ministers in the new Cabinet. There was a general feeling that personal animosities and vendettas had been allowed to sway justice, reason and good government. One citizen, in a letter to the Editor of *West Africa* which was published on June 15th, 1957, expressed the views of many others when he remarked:

"Except for a few unexpected Ministerial appointments, there can be no very serious objection to most of the personalities. But the actual allocations cannot be defended. With perhaps one exception, the Ministry of Education, and with some reservations, one or two others, one wonders whether a revision is not necessary.

"... The new cabinet therefore looks remarkable not so much for what it includes as for what it excludes. The treatment given to Mr. Siaka Stevens can be explained, perhaps understood and yet hardly pardoned. While one has some sympathy for a Chief Minister who prefers more amenable colleagues, one cannot completely overlook, without a sense of uneasiness, such a cavalier rejection of talent and experience, especially at a time when the supply of both qualities in Sierra Leone seems to fall short of the demand. This is far from asserting that any man is indispensable in the country; it is merely stating what perhaps has already been obvious to keen observers that some men have at least proved themselves dependable and as such they cannot be ignored.

"Had Mr. A. M. Margai been as over-ambitious as some of his critics have tried to make him; had he been more interested in himself than in his party and in his country, probably the present situation would have been completely avoided. But if he had miscalculated, if he had tried to play too much of the statesman and far less of the politician, his prestige has been in no way diminished. ..."

I did not make things any easier for myself by instituting legal action against Dr. Margai, claiming that he was not the accredited leader of the parliamentary party. Even though I later withdrew the charge, it was an added blot on my party record that I could well have done without.

Certainly I was disappointed at being passed over, but I had no hard feelings and was quite prepared to do whatever I could from my position on the back benches to ginger things up and expedite independence. However, after two months I knew that my position had become impossible. To have continued to support a party in whose leadership I had lost confidence was sheer hypocrisy which I have never been able to stomach. I came to the conclusion that the time had arrived when it would be better for me to be outside rather than inside the party since I no longer shared the political outlook of the leadership of that party on fundamental issues. In July, therefore, I resigned from the S.L.P.P. At the time it seemed a heartsearching dilemma and a bitter decision. But there were so many more acrid and agonising experiences ahead of me that I now look back on it with detachment.

Shortly after this the Governor sent for me and offered me some job overseas, but I preferred to remain and work for the interests of those whom I represented in the House and of the nation as a whole. There was no doubt that I was regarded as a potential trouble-maker, a tiresome man to have around, especially now that I was outside the control of the party in power. The last thing the British and Dr. Margai wanted was a spanner thrown into the delicate machinery of negotiations they had set up for the eventual transfer of power. Nobody could question my wholehearted desire for political independence, but I was not so desperate for it or obliging that I would agree to accept it willy-nilly on any terms, especially if such terms made a mockery of that independence. As far as I was concerned, it must be outright self-government with no conditions or strings attached, or nothing at all.

To my amazement, a few weeks later an action was brought against me by two petitioners, both of Lunsar in the Port Loko District, accusing me of using undue influence and bribery during the general election in May. I engaged one Otto During to defend me but just before the trial he fell ill and left my affairs in the hands of his young nephew Ken During. The judge, Mr. Justice E. Fashole Luke, who was to become later Speaker of the House of Representatives, was so harsh and aggressive towards my poor defence lawyer that he reduced him to tears.

My counsel maintained throughout that the petitioners had failed to prove their case and that there was not a shred of evidence to show that some of the voters were prevented from voting or that they voted in an irregular manner as a result of my conduct. Counsel for the petitioners prayed the court to disregard my denial of the allegations, saying that I and my agents had, among other things, made use of the words 'Government' and 'Governor's candidate' during the campaign and displayed a Government publication which bore drawings of palm trees. The palm tree, incidently, was the symbol of the S.L.P.P. which I was quite entitled to display. The hearing lasted nearly two weeks. Judgement against me was a foregone conclusion. The election in Port Loko was declared void.

I was not alone in losing my seat. Election petitions were filed against several other anti-Milton Margai members of the House with the intention of filling them with more malleable material. The country was scandalised.

A letter from a Sierra Leonean, published in *West Africa* on September 14th, 1957, voiced the views of many of his countrymen. Whilst expressing disapproval of the use of bribery, intimidation and corruption of any kind and welcoming measures taken to discourage it, he stressed his concern at the rate members of the House were losing their seats.

" Bribery," he wrote, "is one of the main charges against ejected members. Bribery, in a society where an elaborate 'gift system' is still recognised as part of the special convention, can often be difficult to discern. A gift of £4 from a prospective candidate, before or during an election, to a village chief or elder may appear to a court as a bribe when it may in fact be nothing worse than the traditional 'shake hand'. It is, of course, true that a candidate will by so doing make himself more acceptable. But what if a defeated candidate, to a less successful extent, also indulges in a practice of this kind. The motive for offering a gift as opposed to the mere fact of giving must be taken into account if a gift is to be distinguished from a bribe. The real difficulty is where to draw the line.

"The effect of these ejections on an electorate which has just for the first time been enfranchised may be unfortunate. It may make the right to choose his representative appear to the average elector in Sierra Leone to be a farce. In short, too rigid an adherence to the letter of the law in such matters as disputed elections in Sierra Leone may well create more anomalies than it is intended to remove."

There were some, of course, who thought differently. Such as another Sierra Leonean who, replying to the above letter through the columns of *West Africa* a month later, found it deplorable that so many candidates had lost their seats because of bribery and corrupt practices, and was glad that there were people who had the courage to expose such practices. There was no difficulty, he said, in drawing the line between bribery and 'shake hand' since they were one and the same thing.

" 'Shake hand' is naked bribery," he declared. "It is given with the intention to produce results in favour of the giver. 'Shake hand' is a cancer which *must* be destroyed in our (Sierra Leone or African) society or it will destroy us."

He was not one of those, he said, who believed that every tradition of ours, good or bad, had to be preserved.

But I hardly felt touched by the controversy. My own conscience was clear. I knew very well, however, why so many people were disturbed by what had happened. As far as they were concerned the issue was not whether the 'shake hand' practice was right or wrong. The question they asked was why a mere handful of people had been accused of a practice in which so many others were known to indulge; and was it a mere coincidence that those who had been singled out for punishment happened to have recently fallen from grace? It was also noted, of course, that this traditional practice had never before given rise to legal proceedings. That it should suddenly be regarded as serious enough to justify the attention of the Supreme Court was beyond most people's comprehension.

When I arrived home that evening after losing my seat in the House, I found my wife in floods of tears. "We are finished! We are ruined!" she moaned. "Nonsense!" I rebuked her sharply. "Do you think I was born a parliamentarian? Do you think a seat in the House is the be-all and end-all of life?" I went to bed and slept sounder than I had done for many a night. In the morning my wife remarked on the fact. "I can't understand you," she said. "How can you sleep as peacefully as a baby, as if you hadn't a care in the world, when you have just lost an election that has cost you well over two thousand pounds?" I replied, "What is past is past. The only benefit you can hope to gain from the past is experience. You cannot try to recreate the past: one must live with it, you get nowhere regretting or mourning it. We can only look to the future and that is what we are going to do now... Where's my breakfast?"

It was apparently not sufficient that I should lose my seat as the representative of Port Loko East. The fear that I might win another seat through a bye-election became very real for my detractors when I declared my intention of standing as independent candidate in Freetown West II where a seat had recently been declared vacant.

I had hardly had time to launch my campaign when further legal action was brought against me. At Dr. Margai's instigation, Paramount Chief Bai Koblo Pathbana II and Kandeh Bureh, Minister of Works and Housing, charged me with election offences. This was a very serious charge, a death knell indeed as far as a politician was concerned, because if found guilty one stood to be struck off the list of voters for seven years.

The trial took place in Port Loko Magistrate's Court which sat only once a month. It dragged on for nine or ten months which meant that I had to travel from Freetown to Port Loko and back every month. The presiding magistrate, who was no doubt getting as bored with the business as I was and recognised it for what it was, a trumped up charge, eventually confided in me with disgust that he was under great pressure to convict me regardless of the proof or otherwise of my guilt. He could find no evidence to support the charges and, when further adjournment of the case became too obviously a face-saver for my powerful accusers, he cleared me of them.

In the meantime, having lost the Freetown West II seat to a U.P.P. candidate, I took on the job of public relations officer for DELCO with the idea of eventually becoming their Resident Director in Freetown. But my heart was still very much in politics and I had from time to time long discussions with Albert Margai and several others who were discontented with the S.L.P.P., about forming a party of our own.

In December, 1957, constitutional talks took place in London between the Sierra Leone and British Governments with a view to removing all official members except the Governor from the Executive Council. Albert Margai, who to date had received little enough from his older brother as compensation for loss of the parliamentary leadership, was included in the delegation to London. Albert was not alone in believing that he would be amply rewarded when, with the removal of the European official who held the nation's purse strings, he would be offered the portfolio of Finance. To his chagrin, when on August 14th, 1958, the appointments to the new Executive Council were announced, it was Sanusi Mustapha, not he, who took over the position of Minister of Finance.

There was only one thing now left for Albert to do, namely, to leave the S.L.P.P. as I had done. Having decided this we set about forming a new party to be called the People's National Party with Albert as Leader and myself as General Secretary and an executive of 13 members. On September 2nd, 1958, Albert Margai, Chairman of the S.L.P.P., S. T. Navo, one-time party Chief Whip, and A. J. Massally, Deputy Speaker of the House, announced their resignations from the S.L.P.P. The next day, September 3rd, we issued the following statement:

" In view of the fact that the people of Sierra Leone are evidently disappointed in the political, social and economic state of the nation, the People's National Party has come to the conclusion that there is an urgent need for a new political party not committed to protecting the interests of sectional groups to the detriment of the whole country, and being of the opinion that the party in power has failed to adopt a nationalist policy which will assert the rights and protect the interests and freedom of all Sierra Leoneans, is resolved to produce a nationalist front that will lead the country to immediate political independence and economic stability.

"This point of view is reinforced by: the absence of any apparent sign that the country is moving towards independence; the failure of the Government to manage the country's finance which has resulted in unemployment and trade recession and threatens to mortgage our resources and Independence; the glaring mishandling of the mineral policy to the detriment of the country and its people which has resulted in discriminatory laws, jeopardising the freedom of the people and curtailing their natural rights."

This last item referred to motions introduced and lost by A. J. Massally and Albert Margai in the House of Representatives on the day they had resigned from the S.L.P.P. and were sitting as independents, and when the House sat until after 9 p.m. With regard to Government Orders restricting the entry of 'strangers' into certain diamond areas of Kono, Mr. Massally had alleged that the Government had delegated to the Tribal Authorities the duty of defining the word 'stranger', which he considered to be *ultra vires*, inconsistent with the laws and the land and discriminatory, and he had urged the House to annul the Orders. The S.L.P.P., he said, were advocating a policy of unity in the country but were in fact restricting the movement of non-native Kono people.

Criticising Government's diamond policy, Albert Margai had said this was responsible for the present financial crisis and should be revised along lines that would augment the revenue of the country and also directly benefit the people. He had declared that it was because of such policies that "he refused to enter the Parliamentary group" and that he had not been 'thrown out' as some had alleged.

Now that I was Secretary-General of the P.N.P. and likely to be fully occupied with party affairs, I did not want my political activities in any way to be a source of embarrassment to DELCO, a company with which I had had such good relations for so many years; so I forthwith resigned my post as their public relations officer.

The first thing we did was to issue the following notice in the local press:

THE PEOPLE'S NATIONAL PARTY
P.N.P.

Motto: *Forward Together*

A New Political party has been formed:

THE PEOPLE'S NATIONAL PARTY

This is the Party to save Sierra Leone from Constitutional Stagnation and Economic Chaos.

An Inaugural Meeting of the Party will be held

**at the Wilberforce Memorial Hall
on Friday 12th September at 8 p.m.**

Speakers will include:

Hon. A. M. Margai, Hon. H. I. Kamara, Gershon Collier, Esq., Hon. S. T. Navo, M. S. Turay, Esq. M.B.E., Berthan-Macaulay, Esq., Hon. A. J. Massally, Siaka Stevens, Esq.

Party Headquarters,
61 Westmorland Street,
Freetown.   A. M. MARGAI, M. S. TURAY
Tel: F 2525   for Working Committee P.N.P.

The P.N.P. made an immediate appeal to the younger element of the S.L.P.P., to the up-and-coming professionals and to the skilled and semi-skilled workers both in Freetown and in the Provinces; to men and women, who, in fact, because of the lack of direct contact between the S.L.P.P. leaders and the masses, had up to now been mere outsiders looking hungrily in. For the first time the ordinary citizens felt an effort was being made to allow them a say in the country's affairs, and the crowds who flooded the Wilberforce Hall whenever we held meetings and the enthusiasm with which they participated, was proof of the need for such a people's party that truly involved the people.

That the P.N.P. caused concern among the S.L.P.P. members was the talk of the town and if we achieved nothing else by our presence, at least we lit a fuse beneath their armchairs in Freetown which sent them scuttling round the countryside to take a look at how the other half, the forgotten electorate to whom they owed their comfortable positions, lived.

" It is observed," wrote a man from Bo to the Editor of the *Daily Mail* on September 24th, "that since the creation of the People's National Party, Ministers of the party in power are making frequent visits to their constituencies. As for me, I never thought that members of the S.L.P.P. would ever take the course to speak to one of the poorest labourers who assisted them in the elections, as I feel they have no time for the poorer classes. ...It was only when it was rumoured that the P.N.P. was touring the provinces that members of the S.L.P.P. for the very first time after the elections had the courtesy to run to the provinces to meet their electors."

The initial membership fee of the P.N.P. was 6d. (5c) with an additional 6d. annual subscription. Under its constitution the supreme government of the party lay in the hands of the National Annual Convention whose function it was to formulate policy, draw up a programme of the party for the following year and to elect all national party officers.

The P.N.P. was against tribalism. It strongly maintained that chieftaincy had and would continue to have a most important place in our national development for a very long time to come, but it held that in order to enhance their dignity and respect, chiefs should clearly stay out of politics.

With regard to expatriates in government service, the P.N.P. pledged itself to bring about Africanisation in all branches of the service as soon as trained Africans were forthcoming, for it was only right and just that trained Africans should be given first preference in their own country.

At a later date, I went further to explain our stand on expatriate employment. I agreed that because of the skills they possessed, we had need of expatriates at that time, but I stressed the fact that the Sierra Leonean must be master in his own house and be given the opportunity of deciding the number, quality and calibre of the people who came to us. What was more important, we must be allowed to negotiate with such outsiders, on a basis of equality, concerning the conditions under which their services would be made available to us. It was P.N.P. policy to invite and give every encouragement to expatriates who had a specific contribution to make but it would offer no place for the know-all type of paternalistic expatriate.

Only one month after we had launched the P.N.P., Ahmed Sekou Toure, leader of the Parti Démocratique Guinéen in neighbouring Guinea, put into practice what he had long been preaching: "Freedom with poverty is better than riches with slavery". With daring and aplomb he led his people to cry with one massive voice 'NON!' to living any longer under a French constitution. To us of the P.N.P., with our avowed intent of achieving 'immediate independence', this act of Sekou Toure was a tremendous morale booster. In mid-October a delegation of us went to Conakry to congratulate the new President and the Guinean people. The S.L.P.P. made no such move and Albert Margai made it very clear to Sekou Toure that we did not represent the Sierra Leone Government.

" We have come here to congratulate you and your people not as representatives of the Sierra Leone Government," he said, "but as representatives of the People's National Party, a party which is thinking along the same lines as you have been. Nevertheless I can assure you that the sentiment we shall express to you tonight would be the sentiment that would have been expressed if all the people of Sierra Leone were with us..."

One could not help but admire this young man who, at the age of 36, found himself overnight the head of an independent African State. He stood quite alone for not a single leader in the other French West African territories supported him. It was a formidable task and he had no illusions about the risk he had taken and the toughness of the road ahead of him. His gaiety as we celebrated the occasion suddenly vanished and his eyes hardened as he explained the position as he sincerely believed it to be. The proposed new constitution, he said, did not offer genuinely equal partnership to Africans. "Full independence is the only basis on which Africa can go into partnership with France or any other country," he declared, and it was to preserve African integrity and dignity that he had chosen to go it alone. It was indeed an unenviable burden to be saddled with but there was little doubt in my mind that he would prove to be perfectly capable of shouldering it, and as we left him I had the feeling that Africans everywhere had reason to be very proud of him.

The secret behind Sekou Toure's successful 'masterstroke' was, of course, a disciplined and organised national party. It brought it home to me once again how many precious years we had wasted in Sierra Leone bickering among ourselves over issues which, in the final analysis, had little or no bearing on the thing we all craved for: political independence. The truth was that so very few Sierra Leoneans showed much real concern for anyone but themselves, their immediate families and their tribes. We seemed unable to think of ourselves as a nation in the real sense of the word, as integral parts of the great whole.

Hard as I worked to spread the P.N.P. throughout the country, the position one year after our formation was that apart from the headquarters in Freetown, we had only three organising secretaries to cover the whole of Sierra Leone. And their job was a most discouraging and difficult one. The chiefs, solidly behind the S.L.P.P., were a force to be reckoned with, for they were liable to penalise those of their flock who strayed from their chosen political fold. Even those, therefore, who sympathised with the P.N.P. dared not come out openly in support of it for fear of reprisals. It was therefore not surprising, though admittedly disappointing when, in the 1959 District Council elections, we won only 29 of the total of 309 seats, and only 10 per cent of the total vote in the Freetown Council elections.

Whilst the P.N.P. continued to agitate for immediate independence to be preceded by a further general election so that the people could decide at the polls which political party they wished to lead them to that 'desired haven', the recently knighted Milton Margai, on a visit to London to receive his accolade from the Queen, was still not going to be rushed. He hoped, he told the British press, that before the present term of office of the S.L.P.P. ended in 1962, negotiations would have begun with the Colonial Office for Sierra Leone's independence and that the point would have been reached where he would be able to go to the country in a general election and ask the people whether they wanted independence on the terms that by then would have become clear. "We are not," he said, "in a hurry to push matters at this stage, nor do we envy any other Colony who may be ahead of us; we prefer them to carry on while we follow later." *West Africa*'s comment at the time was: "That seems reasonable enough and there should be no obstacle to such a time-table provided that the chronic state of disorder in the Kono area is dealt with before this... "

A third of the total police force had been moved into the Kono area in an effort to restore some sort of order and to protect S.L.S.T.'s property from being attacked by gangs. Nightly raids were being made on the company's richest diamond producing areas by illicit diggers in gangs of 40 and upwards, which unless checked would result in an appreciable loss of national revenue. But apart from the loss monetarily, such gangsterism and Government's failure to control it was hardly likely to enhance Sierra Leone's image abroad and attract foreign investment.

New legislation was hastily introduced in February to increase the powers of the police so that they could more speedily remove all but Kono people from the diamondiferous areas, whether they be Sierra Leoneans, Guineans, Lebanese, Europeans or whatever. In addition, Government took power to remove and exclude from the area anyone it considered likely to endanger peace, order and good government. This last measure was to be used only in carefully considered cases and an independent committee was to be established to hear any objections to such removal orders. Terms of imprisonment would be meted out to all those who infringed the 'strangers' laws, or who illegally possessed, prospected, mined, dealt in and exported diamonds.

The following month I went to London on behalf of the P.N.P. to register with Members of Parliament and officials of the Colonial Office our complaints against this legislation. Whilst the P.N.P. fully agreed that under the mining agreement with S.L.S.T., which I personally had helped to bring about, the Government had to provide adequate protection for the Company, it found fault with the new legislation on three counts: firstly, although it was said to be an emergency measure, no time limit had been set; secondly, Konos could now be treated as 'strangers' in their own country and were liable to local deportation and, thirdly, the Chief Justice could now, in certain circumstances, alter or increase the sentence of a magistrate, but was not required to give his decision in open court.

"What is the position of anybody sentenced in this way if he wishes to appeal," I asked, "since normally he would appeal to the Chief Justice himself? And," I added, "doesn't the provision show lack of confidence in magistrates?"

The P.N.P. also felt that the legislation had been passed with unnecessary haste without allowing either the Opposition or Government back benchers time to consider it properly and produce reasonable amendments. It believed it was being unfairly operated and that people who had lived for a long time in the Kono area were now refused permits and were losing their property without compensation.

In June, 1959, the Colonial Secretary, Mr. Lennox-Boyd, visited Freetown to hold preliminary discussions with members of the Government and party leaders on the independence issue. His visit was not without excitement for at one point, while he was closeted with Ministers in Government House, the huge crowd that had gathered outside the gates grew hourly more impatient. Loudspeakers started chanting party slogans, one against the other, and inevitably this prompted the people to rally round those they supported and abuse those they didn't. Before long fighting broke out and stones were thrown wildly, some breaking windows of Government House. By the time order was restored by means of a riot squad and tear gas, four policemen had been injured and eight demonstrators were arrested and charged with disorderly behaviour. The visit, however, ended happily with the announcement that the Colonial Secretary was agreeable for discussion on further changes in the Constitution to take place in the early part of 1960.

Even our Premier, it seemed, had been aroused by the freshening wind of change and was geared for action. "We have been sleeping in this country," he told the welcoming crowd on his return from a visit to Liberia that December, "and as a result of what we have seen in Liberia there is going to be a change."

I felt sure that this was a genuinely auspicious note. The persecution I had been through — though nothing, of course, compared with what was still to come — had been traumatic and dispiriting. But it was forgotten in the electrified atmosphere of 1959. The scent of independence galvanised me. I felt alert and valiant. And I was ready to rejoice at the chance of a renewed role in the dearest quest of my life. My excursion into the political wilderness seemed to have renewed my strength.

CHAPTER ELEVEN

Freedom behind Bars

There is an old Chinese story I rather like about a peasant who lost his only horse. His neighbours said, "Your only horse has disappeared. Bad luck!" the peasant replied, "Bad luck? Good luck? Who knows?" The next day the horse returned, bringing twenty wild horses with him into the peasant's compound. The neighbours said, "You have gained twenty new horses. Good luck!" The peasant replied, "Good luck? Bad luck? Who knows?" Then the peasant's only son broke a leg training the horses. The neighbours said, "Your only son has broken a leg and the harvest is at hand. Bad luck!" The peasant replied, "Bad luck? Good luck? Who knows?" Within a few days the recruiting sergeants arrived and conscripted all the young men of the village except the boy with the broken leg. The neighbours said, "Your son has escaped conscription while ours are all gone. Good luck!" The peasant replied, "Good luck? Bad luck? Who knows?"

The story can be made to go on *ad infinitum*, of course. But it shows — even in a shortened version — that we should accept misfortune with an open mind. Most of us seem to go through life learning from misfortune. But at the time, the advantages of disaster are hard to appreciate. The lessons of ill luck are difficult to assimilate. When we do notice them, we react with surprise. It seemed to me an odd paradox, for instance, that I should have learnt some of my deepest and truest lessons about freedom when I was behind bars as a political prisoner. There I discovered that freedom is a state of mind — something a man can create inside himself, whatever the circumstances. Even in prison — especially in prison, I felt free inside. Nobody could take my inner freedom away, whatever they tried to do to me. Knowledge of the essentially inward nature of freedom is humbling for politicians, who can only affect external conditions of freedom. The things we strive for — national liberation, democracy, civil and human rights, constitutional guarantees of liberty — all help to create the right environment, but the deepest barriers against freedom lie embedded in men's heads and hearts, where the strength to overcome them can also be found.

But I do not want to make myself out to be a hero. My imprisonment was irksome and might have been demoralising. But it was a mild affair compared with the sufferings of prisoners, especially prisoners of conscience, in some less enlightened parts of the world. I was relatively well looked after by my gaolers. And because of the inner resources on which I was able to draw, I never suffered the hopelessness which is the worst affliction of the prisoner — far worse, it seems to me than any merely physical deprivation. The circumstances which brought me to gaol are a matter of historical record. The Constitutional Conference was scheduled to take place in London in April, 1960. There was no doubt in anybody's mind that it was the will of every thinking Sierra Leonean, irrespective of party allegiance, that independence should be achieved at the earliest possible moment. As the old Creole proverb said, "We all na wan konko". But let there be no mistake about it: our unity of purpose was punctured by political divisions. There were politicians in the leadership of the community who privately attached more importance to leading the race than winning it. Their desire for the privilege of leading the country through the gateway to freedom and ruling it from then on clouded their concern to achieve the fairest and fastest settlement. Considered from one angle, the Constitutional Conference was a carve-up. I refused to accept it, I resisted it. And because the people gave me their support I came to pose a threat to it. And so I landed up in prison.

The party leaders at that time, both in and out of the House of Representatives, were many and their support uncertain until a fair and proper general election, that is, one man one vote cast without influence or duress from Paramount Chiefs and Tribal Authorities, should determine it. In the House there were fourteen Opposition members against thirty S.L.P.P., divided as follows: P.N.P. five, U.P.P. four, Independents three, and the Sierra Leone Progressive Independence Movement (S.L.P.I.M.), which was a strange merger of the Kono based K.P.M. and the Creole S.L.I.M., two. In view of the fact that none of them was capable of forming an alternative government, the Speaker held that there was no official Opposition, no official Opposition Leader and nobody, therefore, entitled to draw the salary pertaining to that office. When the two S.L.P.I.M. members allied themselves to the P.N.P., Albert Margai was still unable to convince the Speaker that with seven seats, that is, half the total of the Opposition members in the

House, he qualified as the Leader of the Opposition, for members transferred their allegiance from one party to another so frequently that in the Speaker's opinion, the position of the Opposition at any one time was too fluid to depend upon. Only recently, for example, a split in the U.P.P. leadership had led to a minority group of that party forming the Independent Progressive People's Party (I.P.P.) and sitting separately in the House.

One thing the Opposition parties had in common was a desire to reduce the strength of the S.L.P.P. in the House, and with this objective in view, they urged for the removal of the Paramount Chiefs to an upper house. Beyond this, their entrenched personal animosities, grudges and grievances one against the other separated them on many issues that but for their pride they would have agreed on. Once, during the City Council mayoral elections, the P.N.P. and the U.P.P. came close enough together to invite speculation about a possible merger. Denying the rumour and defending the P.N.P. actions, Albert Margai declared that the P.N.P. remained a distinct entity from the U.P.P. He went on to explain that "we only joined them to fight for a common cause — the election of a black mayor". A European had previously held the office.

Outside the House the National Council was still as conservative and anti-Protectorate as ever in spite of the death of its founder, and the Settlers' Group, formed by the more militant Creoles, after having challenged the legality of the 1951 Constitution, were busy campaigning for the Colony to become a separate and independent state. To add to the confusion of a would-be electorate, Wallace-Johnson established another party called the Radical Democratic Party which, when it sagged for lack of support, he eventually merged with the P.N.P.

Although we had been spared the violence and bloodshed that preceded the granting of independence to many African states, we certainly created difficulties for ourselves in other respects for no other country on record can surely have thought up so many different approaches to a common goal.

Early in 1960, secret discussions took place between the S.L.P.P. Government of Sierra Leone and the British Government during which the draft of the new constitutional proposals were examined.

Meanwhile we of the P.N.P. produced a 'constitutional manifesto' which put forward the party's policies for the forthcoming constitutional conference in London. Independence, we said, must be the main aim of the conference but we renewed our call for a general election. "Following the precedence in other parts of West Africa," the manifesto declared, "it is obvious that a prerequisite to independence is a general election which will give the entire country an opportunity to decide on the party and the terms and conditions under which the country will move to independence".

Owing to irregularities that had recently taken place in local government elections and in the appointment of information agents, to say nothing of the pressure brought to bear by the Government on Paramount Chiefs and Tribal Authorities to induce the people to support the S.L.P.P. Government, we advocated that an independent Electoral Commission should be appointed to investigate and supervise such an election.

The P.N.P. advocated the establishment of a House of Representatives "all of whose members shall be directly elected by popular vote on the principle of universal adult suffrage," and an Upper Chamber "comprising Paramount Chiefs and Nominated Members drawn from specialised sections of the community". It strongly believed and emphatically affirmed "that the Judiciary should be independent of political control" and advocated that the judges should be appointed until retirement and be removed only by a two-thirds majority; and it strongly recommended also that safeguards be written into the constitution to protect the interest of political parties other than the government party contesting future elections and to protect minority rights.

In order to acquaint Opposition Members with the Constitutional Proposals and to endeavour to iron out major differences of opinion quietly in Freetown before proceeding to London where the eyes of the world would be upon us, Sir Milton invited representatives of all parties in the country to a round-table conference. I expressed to him the vital need of our delegation to have expert advisers to guide us in the conference and he assured me that these had been provided for. Another thing that worried me was information I had that a defence agreement had been concluded between the British and Sierra Leonean Governments and this was going to be signed at the Conference; the Premier said this was not the case.

With regard to the holding of a general election before independence, which the P.N.P., the U.P.P. and several other parties had persistently agitated for, I took it that this was a foregone conclusion for Milton Margai himself had only recently, in London, publicly stated that there would be a pre-independence general election for the people to decide for independence or not. In addition to the Premier's statement on the issue, general elections had been a prerequisite for the granting of independence by the British in the case of other African countries, even in Ghana where Nkrumah's Convention People's Party was not only unquestionably truly representative of the people, but had been in office only two years at the time, whereas the S.L.P.P. Government would be four years old in 1961, when we anticipated independence, with only one year to run.

There was no doubt in my mind, therefore, that our Premier would stick to his word and the British Government to their precedent, and an election would be held shortly after the London Conference. Although 1961 had been set by us as a dead-line for independence, the date we had in mind and were working towards was December 7th, 1960.

All of us at the round-table conference in Freetown agreed that the main point at issue was the transfer of power by Britain to Sierra Leone and that, as all other views that divided us politically were so small in comparison, we would bury our hatchets for the time being and proceed to the London talks as one united body bent on achieving independence.

This all-party coalition, formed on March 25th, 1960, was called the United National Front (U.N.F.) and was led by Sir Milton Margai. When some of us pressed for further details of this coalition we were told that its main purpose was to present a united delegation at the London Conference and that further details concerning it would be worked out later and communicated to us. I was never given any such details and because of the pressure on us for quick general approval on the formation of the United Front, it was not even possible for us to consult our supporters before taking action.

When we arrived for the first session of the talks at Lancaster House in London, I noticed that whereas the Secretary of State, Mr. Ian MacLeod, had eight advisers, we had none at all. Even the Governor of Sierra Leone and the legal draughtsmen we had brought with us sat with the British delegation on the opposite side of the table from us. As soon as I saw this one-sided affair, I reminded the Premier, *sotto voce*, about his assurance to me in Freetown that provision had been made for expert advisers to attend us. In a loud voice so that the whole Conference could hear, he declared: "We are dealing with old and trusted friends, so we have no need for expert advisers."

I was angry and humiliated, but above all confused. Even for the diamond negotiations the Sierra Leone delegation had the advice of a firm of reputable accountants and lawyers. Yet now, when the affairs of the whole country were to be discussed, when the future of our nation hung on the outcome of our negotiations, we had not a single expert on constitutional law and defence matters to advise us. We were expected to pit our own wits against those of the Colonial Office experts.

The Colonial Office then presented a paper on interim constitutional changes which they said had to be tried out for at least a year before independence. This puzzled me. I pointed out that our Premier and his colleagues, during their preliminary talks in Freetown, had agreed that the date of independence should be December 7th, 1960. If the proposed interim constitutional changes were enforced, then this would mean delaying independence until at least April, 1961. Surprisingly this did not seem to worry the Sierra Leone delegation at all; they had nothing to say in support of my argument and accepted the Colonial Office proposal.

I referred to this matter again in the paper I submitted to the Conference, pointing out that:

"Since it is agreed by all sides that Sierra Leone, by her past performance, has always shown a sense of responsibility in constitutional matters, I see no reason whatsoever why we could not now skip the interim phase and go right on to independence and in asking H. M. Government for this advancement, we would be asking no more than the U.K. Goverment is now prepared to give to Somalia which only a few years ago did not even have a legislature.   If the rest of the Sierra Leone delegation agrees, I propose that we negotiate on the basis of complete independence by December 7th, 1960, that we leave out the Interim Constitutional Changes, the acceptance of which can only stand in the way of our achieving independence for Sierra Leone by the declared time.

"It must not be forgotten that independence for Sierra Leone is a thing which most people not only at home, but elsewhere, feel is long overdue and anything which is likely to stand in the way of the country gaining independence this year should be avoided, if there is not to be public discontent."

The next anomaly was in regard to expatriates. In the preliminary talks in Freetown it had been agreed that compensation would be paid to expatriates at independence but nothing was discussed about staggering that compensation. I was therefore astonished when the U.K. delegation produced a paper for our approval which stated that compensation was to be paid to expatriates by instalments with interest over a period of about eight years; and I was even more astounded when, defending themselves against one or two stalwarts who voiced objections, they stated that Sierra Leone had asked for this in order to encourage Europeans to stay. Never at any time had such a thing even been mooted during our preliminary conference in Freetown. Such an arrangement would make a nonsense of Africanisation, for the key positions in Sierra Leone would remain in the hands of expatriates for the next eight years or so. In the paper I submitted I stated that I had nothing against expatriates but that it was clear to me that full compensation had to be paid at the time of independence and fresh contracts entered into with those who elected to stay on thereafter.

In spite of Milton Margai's assurance to me regarding a defence agreement, it was clear that vital and far-reaching agreements on defence matters had been arrived at between the Governments of Britain and Sierra Leone, without the knowledge of and prior consultation with the people of Sierra Leone. The British Admiralty would retain and operate, in peace and in war, the existing naval fuelling base, the Boom Defence Depot at King Tom and the restricted use of Freetown anchorage. As a non-Government member of the delegation I was not supposed to know all this, let alone give my views on it. I had been told that I was only expected to discuss and endorse the general principles brought up at the Conference, that the details were a matter for the two Governments. How could I sit there and remain mute on matters that were of the greatest concern to me and my countrymen whose representatives at the Conference appeared to have been gagged?

I made it clear to the Conference that I was not personally opposed to any United Kingdom proposals for defence arrangements on independence as such, but what concerned me was whether a Government which had spent over half of its normal life would be a proper body to consider and ratify such a vital matter which was likely to have far-reaching repercussions. "My view on this issue is," I said, "that any Government or Legislature which is to give a decision on the issue should be a Government of the people's most recent choice, and the full details of all that is involved should have been thoroughly explained to the whole country, if it is not to appear that Sierra Leone is to get independence with strings attached."

This matter, to my mind, was of such a serious nature that it was more essential than ever that a general election should be held before the transfer of power, so that the people would have a chance to accept or reject a Government that proposed to offer a part of Sierra Leone to a foreign power as virtually a war base. It was obvious that agreement between the two governments had already been reached and the signing of the pact would be a mere formality provided the existing Sierra Leone Government remained in power long enough to guide the agreement safely through the Legislature after independence and get it ratified. It was in the interests of both parties concerned that the S.L.P.P. Government should cling on to the reins of government at all costs. The last thing either of them wanted was a general election.

There could have been no shadow of doubt in the minds of all attending the Conference that I could not possibly associate myself with the decisions taken at the Conference. I had raised objections both verbally and otherwise and made my stand abundantly clear at the conclusion of the paper I submitted, stating:

" Lest it should be thought that I am actuated by personal interests in making these and other suggestions, I may say that it would be the easiest thing in the world for me to do. To come here and fall in with other views and keep quiet on vital issues on the understanding that my interests would be well looked after on our return home. ...I have very strong feelings on the points which I am bringing before this Conference and I am quite ready and willing to sacrifice my personal interests for them."

Even though my own party members, as well as others I knew to be in sympathy with my views expressed, did not speak out in support of me, I still felt sure that when the time came to sign the final agreement such men would find it impossible to go against their consciences and sell out for their personal gain. On the final day, when the press and television teams were admitted to the Conference room to record the signing of the historic document, I still believed that Albert Margai and others would withhold their signatures. But one by one they dutifully signed their names, smiling as they saw before them not a constitutional agreement regarding their country, but a ministerial portfolio, a plum government post, a reward for being a good boy. Of course that had been part of the bargain: Milton Margai had insisted on leading the U.N.F. and becoming the first Prime Minister of an Independent Sierra Leone, and had promised the Opposition party leaders admission to the Government immediately after the Constitutional Conference in return for their unqualified support at the Conference.

I pushed the paper away from me in disgust and refused to sign, declaring my reasons for doing so.

There were several who criticised my behaviour, among them two of my colleagues in the P.N.P. Gershon Collier, a member of the P.N.P. Executive who attended the Conference, wrote in his book *Sierra Leone — Experiment in Democracy in an African Nation*:

"It was left to Siaka Stevens... to provide the only discordant note at an otherwise very peaceful and unemotional gathering... He himself had taken the most active part in all the discussions and negotiations that had preceded the establishment of the United National Front. ...When Stevens left Freetown for the London talks, we all naturally assumed that he was going to support the general position as he had not up to that time given any hint of dissentient opinion. ...Siaka Stevens stoutly announced, when it came to his turn, that he would not sign. He then proceeded to enumerate his reasons, the details of which he had circulated to the press beforehand. These reasons were not in any way new. They were in fact the same matters of P.N.P. policy that had been conceded by the P.N.P. when agreement was reached on the formation of a national coalition."

"There were those, however, who believed that Siaka Stevens found the courage to assume his posture because he was fully aware that he stood little chance of personally deriving much advantage from the arrangements of the United National Front. The plum of a cabinet portfolio, as he might well have seen it, was beyond his grasp and he was not, at the time, a member of the Legislature..."

Certainly when I left for London I was fully prepared to support the general position had the assurances I had been given been honoured; but I found out all too soon that I had been duped, that the promises made by the Premier in Freetown were utterly worthless. I lost any confidence in him and became highly suspicious of his all too ready acceptance of anything the British Government offered. *Why* did we have no advisers? *Why* the evasiveness over the defence agreement when it was as good as a *fait accompli*? *Why* the staggered compensation for expatriates when this would mean an excessive burden on the limited exchequer and a block to Africanisation? *Why* the change of heart over the pre-independence general elections? *Why*, in fact, should an exception be made by the British in the case of Sierra Leone when a general election was not only timely but the country was crying out for one? As Collier so rightly remarked, the reasons I gave for not signing the final document were not new; they were matters I felt strongly about and had fought for all my political life. To have sat dumbly at their demise without protesting would have been completely out of character and I would be branded for ever more as insincere and an opportunist.

Albert Margai, leader of my party, who did all right for himself in the new U.N.F. as Minister of Natural Resourses, found it 'significant' that I first adopted an objecting attitude soon after the Conference decided that there would be no general election before independence. "It is not unlikely in my opinion," he is reported to have said in the *Daily Mail* of May 26th, 1960, "that Mr. Stevens would have signed the report if there was a possibility of his becoming a Member of the House before independence."

Of course I would have liked a seat in the House. Any politician would, at any time. But in my case, never at the cost of my principles and convictions, of exposing myself as a hypocrite. I have a temperamental aversion to jumping on band wagons. Certainly, I could never join one for selfish ends at the cost of the nation.

Before leaving London I had printed 10,000 copies of a pamphlet entitled *Why I did not Sign the Conference Papers* which I brought back to Freetown with me and distributed to people all over the country. I was boiling over with indignation, dictating straight from the shoulder without roughing out a draft, almost without pausing for thought. I gave my reasons in plain down-to-earth language. "If you do not agree with me, I bow," I concluded. "If you agree with me, then you must use every possible constitutional means to protest — by letters to the press, by peaceful demonstrations, etc. We must get UNCONDITIONAL INDEPENDENCE. Sierra Leone belongs to all of us, we have the right to know when we are being committed. The British Government has given us the 'goat' of Independence but they are holding the 'rope'. We must press for the rope..."

I arrived home by air about a fortnight before the rest of the delegation as they travelled by sea. I held my peace for two weeks after their return so as to give them a chance to tell the people what took place at the Constitutional Conference, but when nothing happened I myself called a series of meetings, starting with a mass meeting at the Recreation Grounds in Freetown on June 19th, explaining the whole position from the preliminary round-table talks to the conclusion of the London Conference and the stand I took.

There was a massive response to the call I made for a general election before independence and I soon realised that if we were to succeed in forcing this issue, organisation was essential. On July 9th, seventeen of us met at the house of Alhaji Gibril Sesay in the East End of Freetown and a decision was taken to form a mass movement to be known as the Elections Before Independence Movement. At a mass meeting of the Movement at the Queen Elizabeth II Playing Field on July 17th, a resolution was passed by over fifteen thousand people from all walks of life, calling on the British Government to take immediate steps to bring about a general election before independence in accordance with the practice adopted in most other formerly dependent territories.

I think most supporters of the E.B.I.M. shared my vision of the Movement as the nucleus of a political party. There was no other meaningful opposition to the United Front, despite the nationwide clamour against the incumbent regime and the shameless manipulation of the independence settlement. The need for a party embodying our opposition to the Margai Government was glaringly obvious. But we felt restrained by caution and a lingering desire for national unity. I discussed the situation endlessly with my close comrades — men like S. I. Koroma, now first Vice-President; C. A. Kamara-Taylor, now second Vice-President; and S. A. T. Koroma and S. A. Fofana, who later were to become members of my cabinet. We all came from modest backgrounds and had trade union or co-operative affiliations. We all had the popular roots and organisational and managerial experience that convinced us that a genuinely popular mass political party was a possibility in Sierra Leone. We knew that we could create such a party as the S.L.P.P. had never been and never even tried to be — a party of the people.

At the Queen Elizabeth II Playing Fields three months later, on October 17th, the Elections Before Independence Movement was declared a fully fledged political party to be called the All People's Congress (A.P.C.) with the red rising sun as its symbol. It was the first party to be led entirely by northerners who were nearly all commoners with the interests of the working class close to their hearts. Our main objective at that time was to bring about a general election as soon as possible, but we declared ourselves to be dedicated to creating in Sierra Leone "a welfare state based upon a socialist pattern of society in which all citizens, regardless of class, tribe, colour or creed, shall have equal opportunity and where there shall be no exploitation of man by man, tribe by tribe or class by class".

A few weeks after the formation of the A.P.C., on November 1st, 1960, we won by sizeable majorities of 707 and 314 votes, two of the three contested seats in the Freetown City Council elections, and lost the third seat by only 27 votes. For such a young party to gain such a victory in the most articulate part of the country was a true indication of the lack of confidence which the people had in the coalition government, and we lost no time in capitalising on the fact. Encouraged by our success, we travelled throughout the country, undaunted by the hostile attitude of many of the Paramount Chiefs and the threats made against us by the now somewhat desperate S.L.P.P. supporters. One thing soon became abundantly clear: if a general election were held, the A.P.C. had a very good chance of winning it. The Government realised this, too, for no longer did they regard us as a mere embarrassment and inconvenience. Our activities were carefully noted, reported upon and exaggerated; an intolerant and aggressive attitude was adopted towards us and we were subjected to all forms of victimisation. Before many weeks had passed many arrests were made of both leaders and supporters of the A.P.C. Far from intimidating us, however, this treatment encouraged us, for it assured us of the very real threat we posed as an opposition party. Only a man with his back to the wall who is unsure of his survival will resort to such desperate tactics.

In February, 1961, I went to London to put the demands of the A.P.C. for elections before independence before the British Government. With reference to the Colonial Office argument that the London Constitutional Conference had agreed, with one exception, that there should be no elections before independence, I submitted a paper expressing surprise that the British Government should have seen fit to take directions on such a vital matter from a Conference consisting overwhelmingly of Ministers of the Government and Paramount Chiefs who, to all intents and purposes, were also servants of the Government. To us, I said, it looked very much like an accused person being asked to sit in judgement over his own case.

A Labour Member of Parliament, Mr. Robert Edwards, drew the attention of Members of the House of Commons to the 'state of unrest' that existed in Sierra Leone which was due to become independent on April 27th, and to remark that he had received a resolution from the Sierra Leone Council of Labour, a non-political body, threatening passive resistance. The Colonial Secretary admitted that a campaign had recently developed under the auspices of the All People's Congress in favour of a general election before independence, which had resulted in a number of arrests, and that certain leading members of the A.P.C. had been charged with offences, but he added that these events in no way implied a general state of unrest or any change in the general support of the country for independence, and that the charges were made against the party members in accordance with the ordinary processes of the law.

On March 16th, 1961, I was served with warrant no. 612 by the Metropolitan Police, E Division of Bow Street Police Station charged as follows:

" On warrant granted at Freetown, Sierra Leone, on 6th March 1961, endorsed by K. J. P. Barraclough, Esq., Magistrate at Bow Street Metropolitan Magistrates' Court on 16th March, 1961, [You] stand charged with the offences of (1) libel, (2) Sedition, (3) Conspiracy."

The application for my extradition was heard on March 23rd, but adjourned on condition I returned to Sierra Leone. My counsel gave an undertaking that I would return to Freetown to answer the charges levelled against me and I was remanded until April 1st on my own bail of £500. I agreed for a senior police officer to accompany me to Freetown and to hold my passport until my arrival there.

By now the Coalition Government had labelled the A.P.C. a terrorist organisation and professed to believe that it was financed by an outside power for the purpose of further subversive activities in Sierra Leone. Three leading members had been charged with incitement, tried by a judge alone, convicted and sentenced to a term in prison. Soon after my return to Sierra Leone, I.T.A. Wallace-Johnson, C.A. Kamara-Taylor and myself were charged with sedition, criminal libel, conspiracy and incitement. A few days later the entire executive of the party were charged to show cause why we should not be bound over to keep the peace and to be of good behaviour. The atmosphere was very tense and there were odd outbreaks of violence among the less responsible and less tolerant among all parties concerned. Some of my supporters broke up a meeting of Mendes on the grounds that independence was a national issue and not a tribal one. This prompted the Mendes to form the United Front Volunteers, an army of about 1,300 civilians bent on defending the country against the A.P.C. 'terrorists'.

One did not need the gift of clairvoyance to foretell events. "We must prepare ourselves to meet any situation," I warned the Executive of the A.P.C. at the conclusion of an emergency meeting I had called. "Return to your homes and wait. Do not try to resist arrest when the time comes. Our defeat is not a dishonourable one; it is a very temporary one, a mere set-back. There is no reason for any of us to feel humiliated, downhearted or embittered."

A day or two later, on April 18th, a state of emergency was proclaimed and the entire Executive of the A.P.C. were detained. Later other supporters of the party in various parts of the country were rounded up, making the total number of those arrested 43.

It was my first taste of prison life. The Superintendent in charge of the Central Prison in Pademba Road, Thomas Decker, admitted me efficiently and with seeming detachment, but not unkindly and not, I felt, unsympathetically. He indicated to Wallace-Johnson and myself that we should follow him across the courtyard. Instead of being led to one of the four block of 72 cells, which I had expected, he branched right towards the hospital and directed us up the stone stairway to the main ward. Opposite the entrance to the ward was a single solid cubicle measuring about 10ft x 12ft which was probably normally used by the medical officer or the duty nurses. There were windows in three of the walls and two beds in the room, mine along the wall opposite the door and Wallace-Johnson's at right-angles to it, against another wall. The door was closed upon us and we balefully took stock. Wallace-Johnson, who had had experience of this sort of thing during World War II, gave a grunt of approval. It was not quite up to Ritz standard, he confessed, but infinitely superior to a straw mat on the floor of a small cell which he had shared with several others.

We were certainly given preferential treatment. Thanks both to the Medical Officer, who recommended that our diet be supplemented by such foods as butter, bacon and salad, and also to Decker who made sure we got these extras and other perks besides, our confinement was not so irksome as it might otherwise have been.

On April 26th, the eve of Independence, the Prime Minister sent me a bottle of brandy. Whether this was to celebrate the nation's freedom with or to drown my sorrows in for the loss of my own freedom, I knew not, but it was a thoughtful gesture and made me think of Edmund Burk's recommendation of magnanimity in politics as being "not seldom the truest wisdom". I promised myself that if ever the wheel of fortune brought me to a position of power again, I would try to show a deeper kind of magnanimity. I resolved on reconciliation and decided that I would never punish a man merely for hostility towards me, only enmity to my country. I do not believe in turning adversaries into enemies. I do not believe that political dissent can ever of itself be a crime. And ever since my own taste of prison I have tried to tolerate and absorb all shades of opinion in Sierra Leonean politics, including those which have differed from my own views and as far as possible to bring them into the political process. Of course there are always some who out of pride or principle or perversity refuse to join in peaceful poltical evolution. When they prefer self-exile, conspiracy or terrorism and refuse to be reconciled despite all the opportunities democracy affords, there is little one can do. But to victimise opponents who are willing to work within democractic constraints to express and canvas views of their own is always wrong.

I was fortunate to be well treated in gaol. But not well enough to make me wish the same experience on anybody else! Still, I got a lot out of it. The comradeship of an old campaigner like Wallace-Johnson was reward in itself for suffering the injustice and frustration of confinement. I always felt his adherence to the A.P.C. was a pretty impressive accolade for the party. I was proud to have the friendship and support of the man whose record as a friend of the people of Sierra Leone and a campaigner for unity and independence was unrivalled in length and consistency of service. He added an extra 'something' to the credentials of the A.P.C. All of us who were privileged to be his colleagues in the party prized his companionship. The A.P.C. was a fitting culmination to his lifetime's search for a political organisation that could express the unity of Sierra Leone and the needs of her people.

More generally, I got valuable experience of life and politics and knowledge of myself from prison. I got to know myself pretty well in the long hours and days and months of enforced inactivity. I had a chance to reflect — a sort of stocktaking of my life. I emerged not only with the conviction of inner freedom which enormously strengthened me for the struggles which were still ahead, but also with an unshakeable certainty that the A.P.C. had the right solutions for Sierra Leone. I seemed to *know* that, however long it took, the principles we stood for were sure to prevail.

THE SIERRA LEONE DELEGATION AT THE.....

A GROUP OF DELEGATES SELECTED BY SIR MILTON MARGAI ARRIVE AT LONDON AIRPORT TO AN OFFICIAL WELCOME. I HAD MADE MY OWN TRAVEL ARRANGEMENTS.

SIR MILTON MARGAI SPEAKS AT THE OPENING SESSION AND FAILS TO EXPRESS ANY RESERVATIONS ABOUT THE TERMS OF THE PROPOSED AGREEMENT.

....LONDON CONSTITUTIONAL CONFERENCE

A SECTION OF THE SIERRA LEONE DELEGATION AT THE CLOSING SESSION. I HAD OBJECTED TO SOME OF THE PROVISIONS IN THE PROPOSED AGREEMENT AND ALSO TO THE MANNER IN WHICH OUR DELEGATION CONDUCTED THE NEGOTIATIONS.

SIR MILTON MARGAI, THE PRIME MINISTER DESIGNATE, SIGNS THE HISTORIC REPORT COMMITTING SIERRA LEONE TO THE INDEPENDENCE TERMS WHICH I REFUSED TO ACCEPT.

OPPOSITION TO DR. MARGAI'S LONDON DEAL ASSUMES THE PROPORTIONS OF A MASS MOVEMENT - THE E.B.I.M. - WHICH ATTRACTS POPULAR SUPPORT THROUGHOUT THE COUNTRY (ABOVE) AND FROM WHICH THE A.P.C. PARTY WAS TO EMERGE AT A PACKED MEETING (BELOW) AT THE QUEEN ELIZABETH PLAYING FIELD IN OCTOBER 1960.

THE CEREMONY IN THE HOUSE OF REPRESENTATIVES AT WHICH THE DUKE OF KENT, ON BEHALF OF HIS COUSIN, QUEEN ELIZABETH, HANDED OVER TO SIR MILTON MARGAI THE FORMAL CONSTITUTIONAL DOCUMENT EFFECTING THE INDEPENDENCE OF SIERRA LEONE UNDER THE TERMS OF THE LONDON AGREEMENT (ABOVE); AND (BELOW) SIR MILTON EXPLAINS THE TERMS OF INDEPENDENCE TO A CROWD OF SUPPORTERS AND ONLOOKERS.

THE PATRIOT AND FIGHTER FOR SOCIAL JUSTICE WITH WHOM I HAD THE PRIVILEGE OF SHARING A (COMFORTABLE) CELL AT PADEMBA PRISON DURING THE INDEPEN-DENCE CELEBRATIONS PERIOD.

CHAPTER TWELVE

Leader of the Opposition

"I do not expect that detainees will be kept longer than is really necessary," declared the Prime Minister in the House of Representatives at the time of independence. "As soon as we are satisfied that the country is out of danger, we will let almost all of them out." Although the state of emergency was not lifted until August, 1961, the moment when we were apparently no longer considered to be a threat to the security of the State came on May 18th, when I and the last fifteen of my fellow detainees were released from Pademba Road prison.

I have never advocated violence and, even though I was in gaol, I did everything within my limited powers to reason with and discourage certain of my Party supporters who, angered and frustrated at the imprisonment of the party leaders, wanted to take matters into their own hands. Some of the more extreme elements did give vent to their feelings by threatening to blow up certain buildings and by encouraging a general strike; but in spite of the accusations against them, no such action actually took place.

As soon as I was released, I impressed on my Party members that even though our pre-independence demands had not been met, self-government was now a reality and for this alone we should be glad. Our energies had now to be directd towards making that independence work. There was, I declared, only one sure way to gain and hold political mastery over our rivals and that was through the ballot box. Our chance to do this would come the following year when a general election was due to be held. It was up to us to campaign for that election in an honest and responsible fashion for only by so doing could we hope to win the confidence of the masses.

So that there would be no doubt about my position and that of the A.P.C., I published a statement in which I declared: "Independence having become an accomplished fact and the Government having given the assurance of general elections in 1962, the A.P.C. calls upon all its members to maintain the Party policy line of (a) full respect for law and order, and (b) constitutional and lawful procedure in all matters. The A.P.C. has never stood, and will never stand, for violence, sabotage or unconstitutional action."

My taste of freedom was short-lived. A few weeks after my release I was re-arrested and charged with criminal libel and conspiracy in connection with the publication of a pamphlet two months before. On June 27th I was tried, convicted and sentenced to serve six months on each count to run concurrently.

Once again the prison gate locked behind me. Decker admitted me, numbered me 829/61 and led me, alone this time, to the cubicle in the hospital block which I had so recently vacated. Without Wallace-Johnson to chat with, the prospect of six months' confinement was dreary indeed and I began to contemplate the effect prison life must have on long-term convicts.

I still had reason to feel fortunate. I was again a privileged prisoner. I had a bed in a room to myself. I was on the special diet 'B' with extras. I had access to books, paper and pencil. Above all I had hope, for I had not been imprisoned without trial and I was optimistic about the appeal I had lodged. In short, I was in the pink compared with most prisoners. I was in a dark tunnel but could see my way out of it.

My ideas about prison life were still pretty rudimentary, despite my previous experience, and I was not sorry for the chance to develop them more fully. I began to see that the erosion of a convict's morale begins less with the restriction of his liberty than with the challenge prison poses to his own sense of identity. Prison degrades. It degrades, in bad cases, to the point of dehumanising. Even in my short spell in gaol I felt as if I was getting detached somehow from my individuality. It is like feeling a stranger to yourself. Once you are numbered like a head of cattle and squeezed or submerged in an ill-fitting regulation prison uniform, you become practically indistinguishable from the crowd of fellow-prisoners. The erosion of personality is frightening. It can reach a point when your alienation from society becomes alienation from yourself and assimilation into a crowd becomes destruction of identity.

It is too easy for the average citizen to feel indifference or contempt for the men on the wrong side of the prison walls. Of course, most convicts are criminals who deserve what is coming to them. They must pay the penalty for their crimes and their time behind bars has to be gruelling in their own interests as well as those of society. Justice demands satisfaction. Criminals need discipline. We have sixteen gaols in Sierra Leone and I am not about to turn any of them into a sort of ideal home for delinquents. I want them to be a deterrent to would-be criminals and a repellent to old lags. But believe me, when you have seen prison from the inside you come to realise what rehabilitation is all about. There is a need to reintegrate convicts as useful members of society, and there are opportunities to make prison life contribute to the process. When a man is serving his sentence there is nothing to be gained from making him feel sub-human.

On many occasions when I was a Member of Parliament I drew the attention of the House to the poor quality and inadequacy of prisoners' food and to their living conditions in general, and improvements have certainly been made in these and other fields over the years. But although material conditions are important, nothing can compensate a man for the forced lowering of his standards. It is in this direction, the treatment of and attitude towards prisoners by those who control them, that there is the greatest need for improvement. When I was in prison I sometimes felt there were parallels between the fate of unreformed prisoners and the plight of the under-achieving workers I had known in Marampa. Both groups were at least to some extent victims of the hostile authoritarianism to which they were exposed.

In any establishment it is the management which determines how efficiently objectives are met and which bears the responsibility for the well-being of the inmates. You can build the most modern prison building equipped with every facility for the healthy accommodation of prisoners, but unless you have staff of the right calibre and outlook, the convicts will be no better off than they ever were. So the first step towards ensuring that a prison does properly the job expected of it is to see that the Director or Governor of the prison is a strong disciplinarian but not lacking in tolerance and understanding of human failings; a man who is firm but approachable, who is not too stone-hearted to feel the warmth of compassion, nor too lenient to inflict the stiffest punishment when this is called for. Likewise, those under him, the warders, must be of tough no-nonsense men, but not bullies and tyrants; men who must aim to command respect by reason of their fair and just treatment, rather than earn for themselves the fear and hatred of those they oppress and intimidate. We need firmness allied with fairness. We want men who are tough but not hard, disciplinarians who are not draconian.

As far as prisoners are concerned, more care ought to be taken in grouping them according to their social background and intelligence and the jobs they are directed to do should be as nearly as possible commensurate with their qualifications and aptitude. It is far from uncommon for illiterate or semi-literate warders to take pleasure in humbling an educated prisoner, particularly if he is in the professional class, by making him do the most lowly and distasteful job possible. If such a man is sensitive, which is often the case, the effect on him of such treatment can be devastating. Similarly, to cloister together men whose intellects are poles apart can be torture to all of them and can only damage their mutual relations. Such disharmony can quickly spread throughout the prison. It is enough that a man is paying for his crime by being kept in captivity and isolated from his family and friends without the added burden of unnecessary tensions being forced upon him. Because he is a prisoner this does not mean that he is insensitive and incapable of emotion, nor does it entitle those who guard him to crush his spirit, to demean him and rob him of his self respect.

Above all, while a prison is a punishment centre, it is at the same time, or should be, very much an institution for correction and rehabilitation. There are far more civilized and effective ways of impressing on a prisoner the fact that crime does not pay, than hard labour on a bread and water diet. Through friendly lectures and discussion groups the subject of crime can be dealt with in such a way that many men will, through their own powers of reasoning and common sense, recognise the futility of anti-social behaviour and direct their minds towards a more honest and worthwhile future. Every possible attention should be paid to training men, both mentally and physically, to fit themselves into society again when their debt to that society has been paid. When a man's sentence has been served, no stigma should attach to him. If when released he is lumbered with an inferiority complex or a persecution mania, then the prison has failed in its job towards him in particular and towards society in general, and such a man may well turn again to crime if only as an entrée to the shelter of the prison walls.

Detention without trial is, of course, the most soul-destroying type of incarceration for there is no chance of fighting for your liberty. It is a matter of waiting indefinitely for the Government to have a change of heart towards you. Knowing from personal experience what this is like, it appalled me when, some years later, during my Prime Ministership, circumstances were such that it became necessary in the interest of national security to declare a state of emergency and detain without trial some of my own people, including former colleagues. It was the kind of decision I most detest. I can honestly say that I would rather lose my own position and even my own life to conspirators or rebels than deprive others of life or liberty on my sole responsibility. But I took on that duty when I accepted high office. I am bound to act solely in the public interest without counting the cost in personal agony. No one who has not had to do it can know what it is like. You have to make your decision in an aching, impenetrable void of loneliness. You torture yourself with doubt. You go on worrying even when it is too late to worry — to punish yourself, I suppose, for having had to make a decision you always half regret. It needs an exhausting effort of self-discipline to go through with it.

I have never found that level of self-discipline easy to achieve but somehow I have always managed to force myself to act. And, ironically, perhaps, I have been able to call on reserves of discipline I learnt from prison life. Sometimes, in a job like mine, you have to go through the whole painful process quickly, even instantaneously, to deal with a sudden terrible emergency which threatens the state. Then the agony is even more intense and is followed by a kind of inner soul-searching which you have to force yourself to get over. Thank God I have only had to exercise my ultimate constitutional power rarely and, especially in recent years, have found my country at peace, enjoying stability and democracy without incurring sudden dangers from within!

Disagree as one may with the practice of preventive detention, in developing African countries where it is becoming more and more the habit of ambitious, power-seeking elements to plot the overthrow of legally constituted governments, the question arises: what else can one do with these subversive factions?

The British Government had no qualms during the last war about incarcerating for the duration — and without trial — anybody suspected of treasonable intent or of activities aimed at hindering the war effort. No matter what excuses are made for this being merely a war-time measure, the future of Britain in 1939 was no more precarious than the future is today of independent African States which depend heavily on the stability of their governments in order to attract foreign investment vital for their economic development and their very survival. The alternative to taking this preventive action, namely, to sit by and watch helplessly as a few saboteurs and traitors take over power by force, plunge the country into bloodshed and chaos and arrest its progress, is not only unthinkable for any responsible government, but would prove to the world at large that the incumbent regime had no business to be in power at all because it was not, in fact, in control of the country's affairs.

It is a government's business to protect the interests of the nation that has elected it from being undermined by anybody from wherever they come, and to deal with the situation in the most effective way it can.

Until some of our politicians and would-be politicians graduate in the basics of democracy and parliamentary procedures and learn how to behave as responsible and constructive opposition members instead of opposing Government on all issues willy-nilly and plotting its downfall, measures must be taken to control their enthusiasm for room at the top until they have earned the right to be there. As far as my A.P.C. Government is concerned, preventive detention has been resorted to *not* with the intention of suppressing opposition parties, but because wisdom and common sense dictated that we should act to secure the peace of the country and the security of the citizens. There were times when we had to keep our wild horses securely corralled — but only while they were positively dangerous.

The British Colonial Government, which was still in ultimate control at the time of my imprisonment, took exactly the same precaution in the case of my party colleagues and me when, through the simple act of declaring a state of emergency, they were able to detain us in Pademba Road Prison to keep us out of the public eye throughout the whole of the independence celebrations. Detention without trial is not, therefore, an African innovation. Distasteful as it is, most will agree that it is certainly more desirable and infinitely more humane than some methods used, though rarely high-lighted, for dampening the fuses of firebrands in some other parts of the world.

I served only about fifteen days of my six months' sentence on this occasion, for I won my appeal and was released on July 12th. My spell in gaol was no cause for shame. Prison was a commonplace — almost a necessity — of African political life. There was a growing conviction in West Africa at the time that no politician could go far unless he was a prison graduate.

The general election was scheduled to take place on May 25th, 1962, and the election of Paramount Chief members two days earlier, on May 23rd.

By this time both the P.N.P. and the U.P.P. had merged with the S.L.P.P. This, on the face of it, was a formidable force to reckon with. But the S.L.P.P.'s weakness lay in the loose knit of its fabric, in its lack of control over its local units, its dependence on the support of the Paramount Chiefs and, above all, the rivalry between many of its leading members which caused much confusion and bitterness in the nomination of their candidates. Many members had entered the ranks of the S.L.P.P. via the United Front even though they had been ferocious partisans of the P.N.P., U.P.P. or whatever. Their fissile loyalties showed up clearly in the jockeying for positions.

By a conscious decision of Sir Milton Margai's, the S.L.P.P. sucked in all the flotsam and jetsam of Sierra Leone politics indiscriminatingly. There was no dialogue with the ill assorted *omnium gatherum* of newcomers, no attempt to adjust the party line or induce men to join by reasoned persuasion. The only incentive was the extensive patronage of the Government. I made a mental note of the chaotic course of this unwholesome spectacle. Later, when the A.P.C. was expanding and gradually absorbing more and more of the politically committed groups in the country, I was careful to see that we grew by persuasion and modified the Party organisation to maximise dialogue without weakening the Party. The unseemly example set by the S.L.P.P. in the 'sixties taught us the virtues of planned and principled expansion.

At the time of the 1962 election, we were as yet an unknown quantity as an opposition party, though we had already given no small indication of our potential strength in November, 1961, by winning four of the six contested seats in the Freetown Municipal Elections. We experienced some difficulty in putting up candidates in some of the constituencies because the opposition to our Party in various chiefdoms was such that not even our sympathisers dared to come out openly in support of us, let alone a man to campaign on an A.P.C. ticket. In spite of this handicap, we managed to contest 32 of the 62 seats, 15 of which were in the Northern Province, 11 in the Western Area and 6 in the Southern and Eastern Provinces. The S.L.P.P., despite the wrestling and wrangling of its members, succeeded in putting up official candidates in all but three constituencies.

The S.L.P.I.M. were strongly opposed to the S.L.P.P. whose government had failed consistently to develop Kono with the money it had got from the diamond mining in that area, and who were now using suppressive measures against opposition activity in Kono; they were equally critical of the pro-S.L.P.P. chiefs in Kono who had enriched themselves by leasing Kono farm land to strangers. So determined had they become to oust the S.L.P.P. that their leader, Paramount Chief Mbriwa, approached me suggesting an alliance between our parties to contest the four Kono seats. I was elated at the prospect. The A.P.C. aspired to be a nationwide force. The need for a political organisation which united Sierra Leoneans from all over the country was absolutely vital because of the depth of tribal divisions and the wickedness with which some politicians exploited them. Solidarity between the A.P.C. and the Kono party would stimulate the course of national unity.

Two weeks before election day this alliance was announced and it so worried the S.L.P.P. Government, that in the hope no doubt of disorganising and demoralising the S.L.P.I.M., it suspended Chief Mbriwa for what it described as 'general misbehaviour' and 'flouting the authority of the Government'. This action only served to strengthen the cause of the S.L.P.I.M. and to give extra impetus to its campaign. The result was that on election day S.L.P.I.M. won all four seats and two-thirds of the vote.

The S.L.P.P. was in an advantageous position in that being the party in power at the time, its members — in particular the Ministers — had the benefit of large financial support from commercial firms and the mining industry. Even if this money was not used for the party campaign in general, as many complained was the case, the lucky few whose pockets were so well lined were able to secure their seats pretty well by 'shake-hands' and gifts to the right people.

The financing of election campaigns is becoming more and more a determining factor in the outcome of an election and, as such, more and more to be deplored. The trouble is that few political parties the world over are, from membership fees and fund-raising rallies alone, able to bear the expense of election campaigns which seem to grow more elaborate as the years go by. The alternative, therefore, is for candidates to finance their own campaigns, which is unfair to those without private means, or for the resources of big business and the man-in-the-street to be ruthlessly tapped. Inevitably where the party in power has served the interests of entrepreneurs during its term of office, it can expect to be heavily financed in its campaign for re-election by industry and commerce. It is one thing for a company to contribute, say a loudspeaker van or other necessary equipment for conducting a successful campaign, but once sums of money are involved the electoral process is corrupted. Inequalities between candidates vitiate democracy. The rights of the people are in hock to the rich.

The A.P.C. was a radical party known to stand for a bettering of conditions for the workers. As such, we were naturally denied the financial backing of business concerns. Likewise, we were generally denied the support and votes of those who were under the thumb of Paramount Chiefs, most of whom were virtually servants of the government and could be easily manipulated by our opponents. Even though under the Electoral Provisions Act of 1962, chiefs were forbidden to interfere with any political meeting unless it was likely to lead to a breach of the peace or become disorderly, or to use threats or fetishes to influence electors, supporters of both the A.P.C. and the S.L.P.I.M. were constantly intimidated, harrassed and threatened by chiefs and their henchmen, which made the business of campaigning in those areas hazardous to say the least.

However, if we did lack money and chiefly blessing, we had a fund of sympathy and support from a wide cross-section of the people, not only from those in the Northern Province and the underprivileged in general, but also from many Creoles who, disillusioned by the U.P.P. allying itself to the S.L.P.P., sought means of checking the growth of a Mende dominated party. In the A.P.C. they and others saw a party that was the complete opposite of the S.L.P.P. which was dependent on the monied classes, the Paramount Chiefs and the personal charisma of its leader for its survival. The A.P.C. was a party of the people and for the people and composed for the most part of the younger and more active element; above all, it was the first party ever to pose a threat to the power of the chiefs over their people.

We won 16 of the 32 seats we contested and these, with the four seats won by the S.L.P.I.M., gave us only eight seats less than the total won by the S.L.P.P. of 28 out of 59 contested seats. It was encouraging to note that in proportion to the number of seats contested, the A.P.C. did better than the S.L.P.P., winning exactly half. Only 14 out of 47 Independent candidates were successful, and all of these declared support for the S.L.P.P. a few days after the election.

I now became the official Leader of the Opposition in the new House of Representatives of 74 members, the Speaker of which was my old rival of the previous elections, Banja Tejan-Sie.

Edward Stanley, Earl of Derby, addressing the British House of Commons in 1941 said: "When I first came into Parliament, Mr. Tierney, a great Whig authority, used always to say that the duty of an Opposition was very simple — it was, to oppose everything, and to propose nothing." Tierney quite obviously spoke such words with his tongue firmly in his cheek for no Opposition that adopted such a negative policy could hope to survive; but it would seem that many latter day politicians, particularly those in the younger African nations, who find themselves on the Opposition benches of their Legislature, have taken his statement very literally indeed, and oppose willy-nilly whatever the Government proposes. When they adopt this attitude they make no worthwhile contribution to the nation's business, have no hope of altering the tide of events on account of their minority vote and become merely ineffective representatives of a people who, for financial reasons alone, would be better off without them.

I prefer to think of an official Opposition not so much as a group of anti-Government Members of Parliament, but more as sentinels alert to the abuse of power, guardians of the nation's interests who take nothing as read but search assiduously for flaws in the Government machinery and in its activities, who draw attention to them and insist on them being corrected; men whose aim it is not to object to a Government proposal for no good reason, but rather to offer constructive criticism and alternative suggestions that they feel would better serve the needs of the people. It is important to remark here that it is not only the Opposition that mulishly opposes. Government members can be equally unprepared and unwilling to consider any suggestion, however helpfully it may be made, from the opposite side of the House.

As Leader of the Opposition I found much in the House to oppose, criticise and, at times, applaud and support. One of the first things I agitated for, though unsuccessfully, was the setting up by Government of a Commission of Inquiry into the disturbances in the Kambia District at the time of the recent general election campaign, when the A.P.C. candidate was arrested and detained by the Paramount Chiefs, his mother assaulted and many other supporters of our Party were injured in unwarranted attacks upon them and wrongly imprisoned.

"In the last sitting of the House," I said when tabling my motion, "an Honourable Minister mentioned that they on the Government side had sole responsibility for the Government of this country. I challenged that statement because I felt that not only the Hon.Members on the Opposition side here, but every true Sierra Leonean, has a share of responsibility in the government of the country, a responsibility for seeing that things go on in the country the right way, and it is a duty which we should not take lightly. It is my humble view that when there is persistent disturbance in any particular area, it is our duty to make proper enquiries so that we may be able once and for all to quell this disturbance in order that it does not rise to something out of proportion."

Owing to a backlog of cases in the lower courts of law, a Bill was introduced which provided for the appointment of lay magistrates with limited jurisdiction to help deal with the situation. This I strongly opposed for apart from anything else, I saw it as a retrogressive step. "When I was a boy going to school," I said, "one of the things that used to strike me very forcibly in those days was the difficulty we used to have with District Commissioners acting as magistrates in the former Protectorate area. When a District Commissioner sent for someone, a Court Messenger would go and say: 'The D.C. wants you.' The individual would be seized by force and 'befoe jacko cut yi' (before you can say Jack Robinson') you are in gaol. ...The late Shorunkeh Sawyer, the late Sir Ernest Boeku Betts and the late Otto During were all fighting to put an end to such powers in those days. Now that there are legal brains on the Government side who can appreciate the difficulties in such a situation, I hope they will be able to put an end to these District Commissioners serving as magistrates." We had, I said, legally trained men to dispense justice, but what we were proposing to do under this Bill was to take people out of the streets who had no legal training whatever, and make them magistrates. I considered it absolutely necessary that we had properly trained people for the job, even if it meant for the time being accepting as magistrates lawyers with less than the required minimum of practical experience.

On behalf of the Opposition members, I associated myself with the sentiments expressed by the Speaker on the occasion of the Prime Minister's 67th birthday. "I think it is true to say," I declared, "that Sir Milton Margai has rendered valuable service to Sierra Leone. And although politics are politics and we have our differences, yet from the democratic point of view, once an election has been won and the representatives of the community have been put in their proper positions, it is but proper that we should give acknowledgement of service and of faithfulness where it is due. I can assure the Prime Minister that even though we may criticise policies now and again, yet he can rest assured that we will tackle our job in a spirit of responsibility not only for him but also for the country as a whole."

Four days later I did find cause to criticise the Prime Minister over an answer he gave to a question of Sierra Leone's position with regard to the European Common Market. "We await Britain's final decision," he declared, "whether or not to join the European Economic Community. If Britain joins, Sierra Leone will become eligible for association, and in that event we will apply for associate membership alongside the French-speaking associated states whom I have consulted. If Britain does not join, we will seek special trade agreements with the Community."

A policy whereby we had to wait and see what Great Britain did before taking a decision ourselves was a policy that did not appeal to us on the Opposition side, I said. It was not a policy which a young nation like Sierra Leone should pursue and we felt a more positive line should be taken in such matters. The decision we arrived at should be ours alone and not dependent on what foreigners did. I stressed that the Common Market issue had vital political implications. Joining the Common Market would imply that we had joined the broad Western alliance.

"The reason for the Common Market," I declared, "is that certain nations in Europe find that they are losing their positions of influence and power and prestige and so they are trying to group themselves together ...in order that they may be able to tackle the new world problems ...and for economic *and political* purposes." It seemed to us that the Government's foreign policy of non-alignment was incompatible with joining the Common Market which excluded countries of the Eastern bloc. "Those that are not with us are against us," I said. "If we are in the West then we have the East against us."

We in Sierra Leone had to look after our own interests first and any decision taken had to reflect the point of view of Sierra Leone and not that of any other nation. I pointed out that if we based our decision on that taken by the United Kingdom, it would be derogatory to our independent status. On an issue like the Common Market in any case, we felt we should have an opportunity of expressing our views before Government took any decision on it.

The Charter of African Unity was signed in Addis Ababa on May 25th, 1963. Speaking on the motion to ratify this Charter on August 2nd that year, I said that it was with the utmost gratification that I rose to second the motion so ably moved by the Minister of External Affairs. "This is a matter in which we are totally, wholly, absolutely in agreement with the Government, and we hope that the foundations which are being built now will be able to stand the test of time, because in the world as it is today I do not think there is any place for small units."

I pointed out that the greatest nations of America and Russia were both composed of people of many national backgrounds living in many states. "It is but right and mere commonsense that we in our continent should get together and form some kind of organisation which will be able to negotiate and to deal with other parts of the world on a basis of equality and mutual respect because that is what really matters." I stressed that we of the Opposition were wholeheartedly in agreement with the Charter of African Unity.

There were sometimes most unpleasant issues to deal with that, hard as one tried to prevent it, were bound to tarnish the good name of our country. One such was the Director of Audit's report on the Accounts of Sierra Leone for the year 1960/61 which was so unsatisfactory that the Prime Minister was obliged to appoint a three-man Commission of Inquiry to investigate the matter. When the report of this Commission was completed serious irregularities were exposed involving individuals, among them Cabinet Ministers. The Government issued a statement on the Commission's report aimed at reducing the mountain of unsavoury facts disclosed to a mere molehill of misunderstanding, and sought the approval of the House on it. The Prime Minister, while admitting that he knew very little about accounts, said he had looked at them and found them quite clearly to be 'an exaggerated account of what took place during Independence ...with so many things and a lot of work to combat with". As far as financial arrangements were concerned, he assured the House that there had been no misappropriation of funds. The complaint, he said, was on procedural matters 'with one person saying that this ought to be done this way but with the rush and every other thing, it is done in a different way". Was that a crime, we wanted to know? It was he who had to decide whether a Minister had committed a crime or not, and if there had been fraudulent conversion, he would have let the matter go to court.

No matter what argument he put forward to defend the actions of those mentioned in the report, he was, to me at any rate, quite unconvincing, and reminded me, somewhat pathetically, of a mother hen making futile attempts to protect her brood of chicks against a swooping hawk. Reluctant as many of us were to have to discuss such a damaging report, to have failed to do so and to have accepted the Government White Paper without registering our objections to it would, as one member pointed out, amount to repudiating the Director of Audit, the Public Accounts Committee, which was constituted by members of both sides of the House, and the Commission of Inquiry composed as it was of men of honour.

"The stench rose to high heaven," I declared."It is our duty, it is our business, politics apart, to save the good name of this country. It is our business to put into action that little flame of honesty, of truth and of justice which ever burns within every one of us." What was revealed to us was, like the iceberg, only a mere eighth of the whole, I said. "Honourable Members, you know it; the public knows it; you know that the public knows it and the public knows that you know. Why fool ourselves?" I pointed out that the White Paper before us had been prepared by a group of Ministers including the Cabinet Ministers who were involved in the matter.

"This has not been the case," the Prime Minister interrupted. "I particularly asked them not to turn up at the meeting whilst we were discussing it." The public, I said, had no evidence of this whatsoever. "When a Minister is not on leave and is in a country, he is supposed to be doing his duty, because we pay him for that. ...We have every right to maintain that this Paper was prepared by and with the concurrence of the other Ministers who are involved in this matter. That is bound to be accepted; and we maintain with very great respect that a fundamental provision of ordinary justice has been violated and therefore, Sir, it follows that the Government's White Paper is of no standing and by virtue of ordinary justice, it is null and void." I then proceeded to deal, item by item, with the report of the Commission of Inquiry.

In conclusion I reminded Members of the House that this was not a matter of public politics and that when we voted thought should be given to the people outside. If those responsible had not acted in the correct manner we should be honourable enough to say so, because the money involved was not our individual money, but was owned by farmers and boatmen and others who paid taxes which we collected and they expected us to spend it rightly.

In a final attempt to impress upon Members where their responsibility lay, I quoted the following lines of Josiah Gilbert Holland (1819-1881) which had made a strong impression on me when I first read them:

"God give us men! A time like this demands
Strong minds, great hearts, true faith and ready hands;
Men whom the lust of office does not kill;
Men whom the spoils of office cannot buy;
Men who possess opinions and a will;
Men who have honour; men who will not lie;
Men who can stand before a demagogue
And damn his treacherous flatteries without winking;
Tall men, sun-crowned, who live above the fog
In public duty and in private thinking."

Inspiring words indeed, but they fell for the most part on deaf ears, for the motion was carried by 45 in favour, 16 against and 5 abstentions.

In supporting a Government motion in November, 1963, to approve and ratify the Khartoum Agreement of that year which established the African Development Bank, I took advantage of the occasion to stress the need for appointing only the most competent and experienced men and women to represent Sierra Leone on the international scene, regardless of their party allegiance.

"Up to now," I said, "the policy of this Government in the matter of representation on committees and organisations and other such bodies, has been that one has to be a member of the Government party or one has to be a member of the inner core P.N.P., or one has got to lick spittle or go down on one's knees, before one can represent the country on such bodies. I think the criterion should be that whatever a man may be, in whatever political camp he finds himself, if he is a competent person, then he should be put there to represent us, because people who are put on such bodies should be so qualified that they can demand the respect of people outside." I recalled that sometimes people had been sent abroad who could not even use a knife and fork, and that one representative of ours who was asked in East Africa what was the population of Sierra Leone replied: "one hundred thousand".

"We have a Prime Minister who has a lot of power and responsibility," I said, "but it is the duty of the members to tell him when things go wrong. You cannot have a Prime Minister without the support of the Honourable Members, therefore you should not be afraid of telling the Government what is the truth. Regarding our representation at the Development Bank, please pick a man who is suitable for the duties, because if you send an unsuitable person he will not only disgrace himself but he will disgrace the whole country."

The Prime Minister was, in the early months of 1964, showing signs of deterioration in his health and his absences from the House were becoming more frequent. In March, when I introduced an amendment to the Government's motion on the Speech from the Throne, a speech I criticised as being disappointing, lacking in substance, dynamism and inspiration, I raised the vital question as to whether the Head of Government was in a fit physical condition to carry the heavy responsibility of office any longer. I suggested that the medical opinion on this question appeared to be in the negative and that the responsibility for dealing with this situation rested squarely on the shoulders of each individual member of the Government and, indeed, of the whole House. Few people, apart from those of us closely associated with him, noticed his growing feebleness, for he had never been a robust looking man, and the nation was therefore shocked when, on the day following the third anniversary of our Independence, April 28th, he quietly died.

"Sir Milton Margai died in action," I said when paying tribute to him in the House the following day. "We shall not forget him and no history of Sierra Leone will be complete without a word about his continuous service. We shall miss him and we shall miss his tolerance." I found it most difficult to express myself on such an occasion. "He has helped us," I continued, "and has well directed our affairs. He achieved unity among us; during a time in our history, in fact, he was the only man who could give unity to our country, especially amongst the Paramount Chiefs."

Although there were many, including members of his own party, who did not always agree with Sir Milton's policy and openly opposed him, overriding such disagreement was the deep respect they had for him. As far as the masses were concerned, they revered him as the father of the nation and many of them voted for him because not to have done so would have seemed to them ungrateful and discourteous. Sentiment, as far as progress is concerned, can be a very costly and harmful indulgence. How much better it would have been for the nation, for instance, if Sir Milton had been persuaded to resign from the premiership at the time of Independence and been appointed our first Governor-General. During the three years of life that were left to him, he could have played a valuable and rewarding role as the elder statesman, guiding his successor and the younger politicians in the art of government, curbing their personal ambitions and generally keeping a fatherly eye on them. Instead he died in office, which was little short of disaster for Sierra Leone, for, in my opinion, it was this unfortunate occurrence, coupled with the fact that elections were not held prior to Independence, that was at the root of our later political upheaval.

Sir Milton's death brought to an end what I would describe as a prolonged post-Independence honeymoon. Too many people had got into the habit of resting on their oars or rowing so leisurely that an atmosphere of lethargy pervaded the place. With his departure from the scene, with the reins of government in the hands of younger, more energetic and more ambitious men, the country's affairs would undergo a radical change. This should be all to the good for it was high time that Sierra Leone moved at a brisker tempo if she wanted to avoid becoming a backwater in the eyes of the more rapidly developing African States and of the world in general. As an independent African State we had an important contribution to make towards the development and unity of our Continent, and we owed it to our sister States to keep pace with them.

At the same time, the success of any radical change in policy would greatly depend on the wisdom and appeal of the man at the helm. To try to introduce new ideas overnight to the then conservative and tradition-conscious Sierra Leonean community would have been pure shock tactics and strongly resented. However urgent the need for change, a new man, if he were politically astute, would take time and care to woo and convince, rather than offend by abruptly sweeping aside old standards and established customs.

As soon as the Prime Minister died, his Office was taken over by the Attorney-General, Berthan Macaulay, who the following day advised the Governor-General that as Sir Albert Margai was the man most likely to command the support of the majority of the Members of Parliament, he should appoint him as Prime Minister. The announcement of Albert's appointment was greeted with astonishment and incredulity, grief and anger by a large number of the people, for he was in many opinions the least fitted of anyone for such an appointment. Never once had he even been chosen to act as Prime Minister during Sir Milton's absence, as had M. S. Mustapha and J. Karefa-Smart. He was popular neither with the electorate nor with many members of his own party. Though I had backed him for the premiership once before, I knew his hour had passed. The setbacks he had suffered had embittered, even corrupted him. He was no longer the same man I had been comrades with before. I doubted whether his character was strong enough to withstand the corrosive effects of supreme power. I was afraid that the general distrust in which he was held was probably justified.

Though Albert's appointment may have been constitutionally in order, his ability to command the support of the majority of M.P.s was soon seriously debatable when, immediately after he took office, 35 Members of Parliament from both sides of the House, including three Ministers, petitioned the Governor-General complaining about the manner in which Albert's appointment was made. Rumour was rife that, confident of the backing of two of his supporters in positions of power, namely, the Attorney-General and Col. David Lansana, then in charge of the army, Albert had threatened to take over by force if he was not appointed legally. I would certainly think that pressure and persuasion were used on the Governor-General, if only on the grounds that Albert considered that by rights he should have been the S.L.P.P. leader for the past seven years, a fact few could really quarrel with. Many hearts cooled towards him since then, however, and the feeling was fairly general that his feet had grown too big to fit his dead brother's shoes. The fact that he had squeezed himself into them regardless only accentuated people's resentment.

Albert was flamboyant, boisterous and self-satisfied enough to ignore a sensitive atmosphere. Indeed, now that he was in power, I really believe that his cup was so full that it would never enter his head that some might begrudge his enjoyment of it. The first jolt to his over-confidence occurred a few months after he had taken office when the A.P.C. won an action against the Freetown City Council in the Supreme Court on the grounds that it was improperly constituted. The fact of the matter was that when a vacancy occurrred in the West Ward, the S.L.P.P. majority, rather than abide by the rules and allow the alderman to be elected from among the councillors for his ward, which would have meant the appointment of an A.P.C. man, elected one of their members from an East Ward seat. The Supreme Court ruled that it was up to the Council to remedy this illegality. This prompted Albert to dissolve the Council and announce that instead of the present system whereby an election was held each year for a third of the membership, the entire Council would be elected every third year. He increased the number of elective members from 12 to 18 and, with an extraordinary display of confidence, reduced the number of nominated members from 6 to 3. When the Council elections took place in October, to the dismay and astonishment of our rivals, the A.P.C. won 11 of the 18 seats, including 3 of the 6 in the East Ward which was an S.L.P.P. stronghold. With the 3 S.L.P.P. nominated members, we had a majority of 1.

"Shaki!" cried my elated supporters as they crowded around me. "This is your great chance to become Mayor of Freetown and give the Party a further two votes." As I was not a member of the Council I would have the Mayor's original and casting votes. I hesitated at first, for I did not want to undertake anything that might distract me from my time-absorbing work as Leader of the Opposition. But I saw in it not only an honour, but more a victory for my Party, an even bigger victory than at first it might appear, for we Northerners, the once 'untouchables' of the Protectorate, had now won the confidence and support of the somewhat sophisticated and critical Creole population of Freetown. Not to be ignored, too, was the salary I would earn of £1,000 per annum, money that could help us considerably in financing our next electioneering campaign.

So I agreed to become the 39th Mayor of Freetown, a post which I held for just over a year. Matchet's Diary in *West Africa* of November 21st, 1964, noted that I had the "the presence for the job" and was a "stickler for correct procedure"."He has started off well," the diarist stated, "by paying courtesy calls on the Governor General, the Prime Minister and other notables, and it is expected that, as Mayor, he would strive to be the representative of *all* citizens. But he would also strive to see that his party implemented its election promises." The diarist then quoted me as saying that "there's plenty to do, but I'm not going to make this a full-time job."

Looking back at the period during which I served the Freetwon City Council, first as a nominated member in 1948 and later as Mayor in 1964, I can say with some satisfaction that the Municipality made significant strides.

It was shortly before I became Mayor that the old Wilberforce Memorial Hall burnt down in a mysterious fire which broke out during the early hours of October 17, 1964. The Memorial Hall had housed the Town Clerk's office, the Mayor's Parlour, the City Engineer's Department, a branch of the City Treasury and the Archives. The Council had rented offices to accommodate its homeless departments, but these were scattered in different areas which made the administration more difficult.

One of my first tasks as Mayor was to search for a suitable building to house all the departments under one roof. After delicate negotiations, I succeeded in acquiring all the buildings in the compound of the old French Company for a modest sum which the Council was able to pay in two instalments.

During my tenure of office it was my policy for the Council to become more and more involved in primary education to which the less privileged children had virtually no access at that time. As Mayor, I succeeded in doubling the intake of pupils at the First Municipal Primary School, the old Grammar School, at the commencement of the school year. I am happy to see that the Freetown City Council now runs a number of primary schools attended by well over 10,000 pupils.

As a member of the Council, prior to my election as Mayor, I had already brought my trade union background and experience to municipal affairs. When I joined the Council its workers were unorganised and their conditions of service left much to be desired. The Mayor at the time, Dr Taylor-Cummings, was most cooperative and gave me every encouragement and assistance to introduce new salary structures and conditions of service for the staff. These were eventually adopted which improved conditions for our employees for the first time in over 15 years.

During my term as Mayor, I also sought out a number of Sierra Leonean engineers working in England. They were all anxious to return home and show that Africans were capable of carrying out the most exacting engineering jobs. On my return from England I kept pressing the central Government to give these Sierra Leonean engineers a chance. Eventually the Government responded. This was the beginning of what was to become known as Africanisation.

MAYOR OF FREETOWN - AT LONG LAST THE CHAIN OF ELECTED OFFICE RESTS ON MY SHOULDERS.

CHAPTER THIRTEEN

I become Prime Minister

There is a catch in my throat as I turn to begin this chapter. I write unwillingly, recalling emotions that were hard to cope with at the time. I have to face again in memory some of the most traumatic events of my own life and the history of my country. I find, almost suprisingly, that I can remember it all with the vividness of a nightmare. I remember the pressure in my fingertips as I clasped the book at my oath-taking as Prime Minister of Sierra Leone. I remember the punctured swell of happiness as into the glow of a glorious moment soldiers burst with guns levelled at my chest. I can still hear the indrawn hiss of disbelief of the friends and officials gathered round me for the ceremony. I can recall the smell of greased metal as I gazed, raging and helpless, down the barrels of the guns. I remember being overwhelmed by a sense of unreality from which I was only recalled by the sheer physical hunger of the long and lonely wait at gunpoint in the glum grandeur of State House.

The bizarre story of my first premiership begins in the aftermath of the Freetown City Council elections. Ironically, the victory of the A.P.C. rebounded against us, for it convinced Albert Margai that he was incapable of winning a democratic election by fair means. With the approach of the general election scheduled for 1967, he embarked on an elaborate programme of manipulation intended to procure a result favourable to his side, while also — and even more dangerously — hatching contingency plans in case of defeat. He never intended to take us on in a fair electoral contest — of that I am convinced. And he never intended to yield power even if his attempts at election-rigging failed. In the A.P.C. we were still a bunch of political innocents when faced with the levels of chicanery and deceit which Margai was actively preparing. We were naive enough to give him the benefit of the doubt. We knew there would be electoral malpractice and even some violence. We expected to cope. But that the Government was so thoroughly corrupt we barely imagined; that the election would end in a coup engineered by Margai we hardly dared conceive.

In his relations with his own party, in his disposal of government patronage, and in his initiation of new policies after the Freetown Council elections, Albert Margai betrayed his own desperation. It was apparent that he was prepared to risk national unity and solvency in an obsessive effort to cling to power. Part of his response to our gains was perfectly rational. He tried to copy the A.P.C. by giving his own party something like the same sort of nationwide grass-roots organisation as we were building up. But the S.L.P.P. simply did not lend itself to that type of reform. Its tradition was too elitist. It was too dependent on the chiefs. Most big men in the party liked the loose fit of its broadly woven fabric and refused to be constricted by a tighter organisational mesh. Within his party, all Margai could do to fortify his own position was to manoeuvre his old henchmen and ex-P.N.P. cronies into the central positions of command. They formed a little closed court, beleaguered and introspective. At its centre, Albert Margai sat, like a sultan in his seraglio or a dictator in his bunker, comforting himself with the approval of sycophants in growing remoteness from real events.

While stuffing his henchmen into the power-centres of politics, he was cramming every vacancy in the civil service and armed forces with fellow-tribesmen. Margai's retreat into a tribalism more divisive and a sectionalism more acute than any previously practised even by the S.L.P.P., was the worst thing that had happened to Sierra Leone since Independence. When we needed unity most, Margai set us at each other's throats. When we most needed to set tribalism aside, Margai exploited it with a frantic ruthlessness. When we were striving for equality, Margai made a cult of discrimination. There were two good reasons — good from his point of view — for this policy. By enlivening inter-tribal tensions he hoped to activate Mende sentiment in his own cause so that he could use it to keep power, however the election went. He also hoped that the in-built imbalance of the electoral system, which gave a disproportionate share of the Legislature to the Mende south, would favour him at the polls. He was wrong on both counts. Large numbers even of his own tribesmen rejected his divisive policies and voted for us. And the men he appointed to positions of stranglehold dominance over the institutions of the country fulfilled his expectations in part by opposing democracy. But when the crunch came, they too abandoned Margai and opted for radical solutions which he had not foreseen.

Most of his energy went into plotting the extermination of my Party. He travelled extensively in the Districts directing the Paramount Chiefs to encourage their people to support the S.L.P.P. and to oust the A.P.C. from their areas. With the idea of smoking out those chiefs who were secretly supporting the A.P.C., he announced in January, 1965, that Paramount Chiefs now had the right to take part openly in political campaigning. Woe betide those who now campaigned for a party other than the S.L.P.P. or who claimed as an excuse for not campaigning at all that they were 'above politics!'. But if he succeeded in coercing the chiefs into supporting him, he lost favour among the majority of the people under them. I think it is fair to say that most people were sickened by the measures taken by some chiefs to suppress us. We were branded as 'the northern man's party'.

Naturally the impetus for our success came from the north and east — the areas Margai had deliberately excluded and alienated, the neglected areas, the indignant, deprived areas. But we were striving to be a party of national unity. Our aim was to transcend tribal and regional barriers. Though the Sierra Leonean people had been suppressed for generations and many were ignorant and illiterate, they were not stupid. Most people could see through S.L.P.P. propaganda. Most could make critical judgements about the coercive measures Margai forced on the chiefs. The result played into our hands. The chiefs were discredited by the excesses to which they were driven. Their already tenuous hold over the people was weakened. The membership of our Party got an enormous boost. And the enhanced popularity of the A.P.C. was ultimately reflected in the polls.

Meanwhile Albert Margai was growing more reckless and unstable with every day that passed, with every speech he made. At Bonthe, for instance, in March, 1965, he uttered threats which — extraordinary as they seem by any reasonable standard — were becoming typical of him. A Member of Parliament has recalled his exact words: "I have all the power," he said, "I am standing here by the hill with my Bren gun and people hold machetes to come and fight me. I shall kill them baybayraybay" — meaning 'I shall kill scores of them' in Krio. The germ of derangement — of paranoia, of megalomania — is apparent in this sort of outburst. Margai was unable to cope mentally, it seems, with the failure of his government and the loss of popularity.

A few days later the Prime Minister warned Opposition members in Parliament that the 'time is ebbing fast' and that if we felt the sand sinking from under our feet he would beg his colleagues to accept us if we changed allegiance 'within a time limit'. He went on to say: "All this talk of 'general elections when we the Opposition will form the Government', that is all fantasy. The problem I have now about liquidating the A.P.C. on the political platform is easy; the facts are there. ...They know I am operating the machine, knocking the right key and giving the correct sound. I am saying it so that it may get into the ears of the A.P.C. The people are being misled that the A.P.C. has the following in this country. What following and where?"

Four of our Party members were serving one-year gaol sentences on trumped-up charges for riot and assault in connection with a bye-election. With the obvious aim of unseating them, the Prime Minister introduced a motion on May 4th, 1965, that Standing Order 77 — Absence of Members — be revoked and replaced by a new Order by which any member who, without good cause, was absent for a total of thirty days during an annual session of the House would lose his seat. A committee consisting of the Speaker "and such members as shall be nominated by each party on the basis of one representative for every fifteen or part thereof of its number in the House", would determine whether or not the excuse given for absence was reasonable.

"Mr. Speaker, Sir, I consider this motion as the beginning and end of parliamentary democracy in this country," I said the following day when the Report of the Standing Orders Committee on the subject was presented to the House for adoption. "...All of us on this side think that this motion is aimed primarily at our men who unfortunately find themselves in prison today. You can unseat them a dozen times, and a dozen times they will get back into Parliament. ...We consider the amendment a very dangerous piece of legislation. We feel, Sir, that Parliament or any Committee set up by Parliament would be taking a very grave step to deprive any section of the electorate of this country of the services of their representatives. ... Our main fear is that the Government might be trying to deprive the Opposition of some of its members. They say on the face of things that they welcome the Opposition, but they are taking steps which tend to drive the Opposition underground." I likened their claim to welcome Opposition to the relationship of a leopard with a dog. "Leave both at the back of the yard and you will will soon find one in the other's stomach. ...You love us and we love you too. But in spite of the wonderful relationship between us, let us remain at arm's length. The Opposition will always co-operate for the safety of the ship of state, and I think we are second to none in that. But when the ship of state is being driven into sand banks, we will drag you out and put you out in order that the ship may be controlled."

The motion was carried, of course, by 46 in favour and 10 against. We lost four members but gained one from the Government benches when J. Karefa-Smart left the S.L.P.P. and joined the A.P.C. Karefa-Smart was Albert's chief rival in the party. He had recently accepted a post at Columbia University in America which would have made it impossible for him to attend all sessions of the House and he would have inevitably lost his seat as a result under the new Rule. Some believed that it was, in fact, he who was the main target for Albert's weapon rather than the four Opposition members.

The Prime Minister's next move was to suppress any news about our activities by directing the Ministry of Information that no publicity should be given to the Opposition via the Sierra Leone Broadcasting Service. As the *Daily Mail* also gave less and less coverage to our activities and became more and more a propaganda medium for the S.L.P.P., our only means of putting our views across to the people was through our Party newspaper, *We Yone*, which I had launched in August, 1963.

The harder Albert Margai worked at crushing the A.P.C. the more damage he did to himself and his party. Opposition to him was particularly strong in the North where the people felt they had been given a raw deal. And with some justification, for the Cabinet was manned almost entirely by Southerners and Mendes, development funds were concentrated in the South and the collapse of the Produce Marketing Board meant that the farmers could not be paid for their crops in cash. While the impoverished people in the rural areas wondered where their next meal was coming from and dreamt longingly of tractors and badly needed farm implements, news reached them of the opulence and high living of party members and public officials in the capital, of blatant cases of bribery and corruption and the delivery to the Prime Minister, 'Albert Margai of Africa' as he was now styled, of a duty-free Cadillac. What country in the world would believe we needed a loan when our leaders indulged so lavishly and when a small country like ours could afford to take conference delegations of 32 members abroad at a cost of Le40,000?

Although Albert Margai was adept at political manipulation, he had no real talent for democratic politics. He only tampered with the top people. In Kono, for instance, he tried to regain a foothold by making peace with Tom Mbriwa, whom he reinstated as Paramount Chief and inveigled into joining the S.L.P.P. But Mbriwa's former supporters declined to follow this equivocal lead. The S.L.P.I.M. was finished as a major political force, but its heirs were the younger, more radical elements in the mining areas who formed a new party, the Democratic People's Congress, in close alliance with the A.P.C. We ran candidates on a joint ticket in the general election and swept the board in Kono. The anti-S.L.P.P. trend in the east was irreversible. Margai's electoral prospects were concentrated in the Southern heartlands he wooed so assiduously, enclosed by an arc of A.P.C. support stretching from Freetown through the Northern Province to Kono. Margai could not break out of the increasingly tight encirclement. He felt trapped.

By the end of 1965 he was reduced to trying desperate conjuring tricks. Apparently oblivious of the antagonism he was creating against himself, he opted for a bold stroke in an attempt to revitalise his fortunes and those of his party. But nothing could have been more ill-timed than the proposals for a one-party system of government which he introduced into Parliament in December, 1965. He made no secret of the fact that he was a great admirer of Kwame Nkrumah of Ghana and tended to ape the Nkrumah line. I.T.A. Wallace-Johnson, the A.P.C. member, pointed this out when he wrote in *Salneb* of July 17th, 1964 that "there are thousands of Nkrumahs all over Africa, and we make bold to say one has recently been produced in Sierra Leone in the person of the new Prime Minister, Albert Margai". However highly Nkrumah may have been regarded in Sierra Leone, few of our people relished the idea of a Ghana-type set-up here with Albert Margai running the show. Fortunately for those both in and out of Parliament who opposed these proposals, the overthrow of Nkrumah two months later somewhat dampened the fire of the authoritarian enthusiasts and before long the issue fizzled out.

One of the aims of the A.P.C. written into its constitution was "to consolidate our Independence by maintaining the complete unity of the nation under a unitary form of government". In spite of this, I spoke against Albert's proposals when they were debated in the House. I opposed the proposals not because I was against a one-party system of government as such, but primarily on account of the inordinate speed with which the Prime Minister was rushing through a matter of such importance to the State and because it was not made clear in his proposals what type of one-party system he had in mind. I pointed out that there were different kinds of one-party systems, such as those of Kenya, Tanzania and Ghana, and that it was important that the system proposed was clearly defined. It was dangerous to agree such an issue in principle, because before you knew it your hands would be tied behind your back. Secondly, I did not think that the Prime Minister's proposals were in the best interests of the people, taking into account the historical and cultural background of Sierra Leone; and, thirdly, at that particular stage of development I felt the establishment of a one-party form of government would be contrary to the entrenched clauses of the Constitution. In any case, I stressed vehemently that on such a vital issue, the people should be fully consulted before demonstrating their approval or disapproval freely and in secret through the ballot box. It had to be a *popular* decision.

A one-party state, if it is to function successfully as a type of democracy, has to evolve. It cannot be imposed as a short-term expedient to keep a particular set of politicians in power. When at last Sierra Leone did adopt unipartisanship in 1978, it was as the result of a long process of consultation among the people and between the parties, in the course of which the A.P.C. absorbed other political groups by reasoned persuasion and modified its own nature to accommodate enough breadth of dialogue to make the new system work. It was a far-reaching, even visionary step, designed to mobilise the entire political nation in the interests of the country, integrate all political talent in the national effort and channel political energy away from tribalism and sectionalism into national construction. I think it showed that a one-party constitution could fortify and enhance democracy, whereas in the 'sixties it would only have endangered or destroyed it. I am proud of the way the system has worked; without a formal 'Opposition', government has actually been opened up to a wider range of sources of ideas and influence than ever, through the A.P.C. grass roots organisation and Central Committee. The experience of the Margai blueprint for a one-party state in the 'sixties might well have deterred us forever from making this sort of constitutional experiment. But though I am glad we did not take the risk then, I am equally glad that we were not put off when circumstances changed and the time for a one-party constitution became propitious.

My feeling at the time Albert put forward his proposals for a one-party system was that Sierra Leone was not ready for such a radical change, nor was such a system then called for. My feelings were confirmed after consultation with the people and this prompted me to publish the following statement on behalf of the National Executive of the A.P.C. and of the Kono based D.P.C. in *We Yone* of January 8th, 1966:

" The Executives of the A.P.C. and the D.P.C. have found that Party members as well as non-Party members are totally opposed to the one-party system of government especially when they observe the happenings in other parts of West Africa where the system obtains.

"The Parties also feel that the introduction of the one-party system of government in the present form of the Constitution would be a violation of one of the entrenched clauses of the Constitution which guarantees the right of FREEDOM OF ASSOCIATION. The Parties feel that even if it is proposed that such an entrenched clause of the Constitution should be altered, then the electorate should be allowed to give their verdict on the proposal through the medium of the ballot box as laid down by the Constitution."

A sure indication of the effect Albert's proposals were having on the people was reflected in the way the voting went in the District Council elections held on May 27th, 1966. In spite of the hostility of the chiefs towards our Party, we made substantial gains, particularly in the North where we won 72 out of the 95 contested seats.

One would have thought that this would dampen Albert's ardour for a while, at least until after the general election, but early in 1967 he provoked widespread anger once again when he published his draft Republican Constitution. It was not that the people were against a republic in principle — indeed as we were one of the few independent African States still under a monarchial form of government, there was a general feeling among all sections of the community that the sooner we became a republic the better for African unity. But the people's attitude towards Margai personally was becoming distinctly wary, like that of a housewife towards a persistent slick-talking salesman when she wants the goods he offers but suspects they are flawed. Albert Margai's draft Republican Constitution in its original form gave him considerable power over the judiciary and in other clauses it increased his power in general. And why the rush? With the general elections due in a couple of month's time it seemed that he was trying to push things — first the one-party State proposals and now the Republican Constitution — unnecessarily and unreasonably fast. One could hardly blame the people for becoming suspicious of his motives; they viewed with caution any change in the Constitution or system of government that might be used by Albert for his personal advantage.

The member for Freetown West I, after the lengthy introduction of the Bill entitled "The Constitution of Sierra Leone" by the Prime Minister, spoke on behalf of my Party by stating that the A.P.C. considered it "most unfortunate that the draft Republican Constitution Bill, which must have taken the Government some considerable time to prepare, should have been thrust on the electorate of the country at such short notice". The details of the Bill had been published as late as December 22nd and Parliament did not sit until January 16th. It was therefore "impossible for the people's representatives in Parliament to discuss the details with their constituencies before appearing in Parliament to debate the Bill", he declared. "Apart from the above observation," the member went on, "a casual glance at the Bill reveals a situation in which the Prime Minister has near absolute powers, the President becoming a glorified Minister, and the powers of the Judiciary would be dangerously interfered with. In fact it is felt in many quarters that the present draft Republican Constitution is tantamount to a One-Party Government Constitution in disguise. In view of the foregoing considerations among other things," he said, "we on this side of the House, constituting the A.P.C. Opposition, are unable to participate in the present discussion on this important and far-reaching Bill, and reject it in its entirety."

Under the Independence Constitution, Sierra Leone's monarchical form of government could only be changed by the passing of the Republic Bill by a two-thirds majority, followed by the dissolution of Parliament, the holding of a general election and the passing of the Bill again by a two-thirds majority of the newly elected House. Under the same Constitution, the House had to be dissolved five years after its election, which meant that a general election had to be held at the latest by mid-1967. As the A.P.C. abstained from voting on the draft Republic Bill when it was first presented, it was carried by the necessary two-thirds majority of the House. As far as Albert Margai and his Republic were concerned, everything depended on him and his party winning the forthcoming elections.

His prospects, however, could not have been more gloomy. Discontent with the S.L.P.P. was now being voiced in all quarters. The support it once enjoyed from much of the Creole population of Freetown was lost. In the Kono District, the diamond mining area, the people still begrudged the fact that so little government money had been spent on local development when their diamonds contributed so largely to the national income, and the fact that such a large proportion of the profits from diamonds found its way into expatriate and non-Kono hands. The Northerners were solidly united in their opposition to a government that had almost totally neglected them. Over and above this, accusations of bribery, corruption and the mishandling of public funds had been so widely publicised that a commission of enquiry had been set up to investigate the truth of these allegations, and the leader of the S.L.P.P., the Prime Minister of the country, had been asked to appear before that commission. For some of Albert's one-time supporters who were not themselves involved in shady deals, and for those who were cautiously sitting on the fence, this was the final straw, the ultimate in national humilation and degradation.

The people were not against politicians or public officials having financial interests in business concerns as long as these were come by honestly and not at the cost of the nation; but anybody who aspires to leadership, who hopes to gain the respect of the nation, cannot while he is entrusted with the welfare of that nation, put his own or his party's interests before national interests. That is what prompted me to plead in Parliament that any member of the House who had outside financial interests should declare these and be prohibited from debating any matters in which he had vested interests. What irked and confused the Sierra Leoneans at this time was the way many of our leading politicians and officials were practising an extreme form of capitalism under the label of socialism. They were bleeding the country dry. It was worse than the white capitalism they so fervently condemned. In Parliament I compared the two, saying that white capitalists behaved like rats at night — when they bit your skin you did not feel the pain too much. But the black capitalists' bite was lethal. They took the lot, leaving nothing at all for you.

So unpopular had the S.L.P.P. and its leader become that, barring coercion, intimidation and fraudulent practises by them and their supporters, the A.P.C. could almost certainly have won an election hands down without even going to the trouble of issuing a manifesto and canvassing the electorate, even if for no other reason than that we were the only alternative to the party they so wanted to be rid of. So much ammunition was being gratuitously fed to us by the S.L.P.P. that we had no difficulty whatever, either on the platform or through our weekly newspaper *We Yone*, keeping up a lively attack against the Government under such banner headlines as: *'Throw the Rascals Out!'*. Our campaign was particularly successful because the Government-controlled *Daily Mail* refused to allow space in the paper to independent opponents of the one-party system and other highly controversial issues promoted by the S.L.P.P., with the result that many leading citizens contributed anti-government articles to *We Yone* and other opposition weeklies of the day, such as Cyril Rogers-Wright's *Shekpendeh* and Wallace-Johnson's *Think*, because they had no other means of airing their views. The embattled press carried a great deal of weight, especially among the Creoles. The lame and unconvincing defence put out by the *Daily Mail* and *Unity* only strengthened our cause. Even if the belated demands made by *Unity* for the censorship or banning of *We Yone* had been implemented, it would have made no difference at that stage; the damage had already been done to the S.L.P.P. cause. The people were already aware of the state the country was in.

Early in February, 1967, the date for the general election had still not been announced, but from the Prime Minister's symptoms of acute frenzy, it was obvious that an election was imminent. Late in January the Acting Chief Justice, C. O. E. Cole, who in May of the previous year had displeased the powers-that-be by granting an interim injunction to the A.P.C. leaders seeking to refrain the One-Party State Committee from meeting, was replaced by one of Albert's most trusted ex-P.N.P. colleagues, Gershon Collier. When the Bar Association challenged the legality of Collier's appointment, Albert's reaction was to appoint Collier to the substantive post of Chief Justice.

The Army Commander, Brigadier Lansana, a Mende and close friend of Albert Margai, could also be relied upon to support him to the hilt. But things were not all they might be in the army itself and a general atmosphere of dissatisfaction was felt among all ranks. Lansana was not popular as a commander. He had been greatly criticised for the methods he used in regard to promotions and in handling military affairs generally, for it was felt by many of his junior officers that he gave preference to the Southerners at the expense of the Northerners. Early in 1966 a Forces Council had been established to examine this matter but tension still existed between him and the Northern element of the army, one of whom was his second in command, Colonel John Bangura.

With the success of the recent military coups d'etat in Nigeria and Ghana to warn him of the unexpected role an army might play in a country's political affairs, it was no wonder that Albert Margai read the writing on the wall. Overt tribal antagonisms threatened to disrupt the army. Under the circumstances, how could he rely on the loyalty, support or non-alignment of such a divided force during the coming elections? There was obviously only one way as he saw it. In view of the fact that the plans he had made might need the full force of the army to put him back in power, he had to remove those officers who might make trouble for him, whose support could not be relied upon.

With senses now alert for improbity, certain A.P.C. bloodhounds unearthed secret information about what the Prime Minister planned to do and in *We Yone* of February 4th, 1967, we stole a march on him by publishing details he himself was planning to expose at a time to suit him, of an alleged army plot against him and Lansana. The Government press at once denied the truth of this allegation and accused the A.P.C. of using it as propaganda to intimidate and confuse the masses. Four days later, on February 8th, in the hope of pouring oil on the now tempestuous waters, Albert Margai announced in the House that his proposals for a 'democratic one-party system' had been dropped, and the committee appointed to examine them had been abolished. A few hours after this he announced on the radio that plans had in fact been discovered for a military coup and that those responsible had been incited by several of his leading opponents, including myself. Nine officers, including Bangura, were arrested. With the removal of these nine officers, who were either Northerners or Creoles, the army was left firmly and, as far as Albert was concerned, loyally in the control of Lansana and other Mende officers.

It soon became obvious from the preliminary hearings that were held in connection with the alleged military coup that it was going to be difficult, if not impossible, to prove the existence of such a plot, and although it was repeatedly announced that the nine officers were going to be brought to trial, they never were, which led many people to be convinced that the whole thing was a figment of S.L.P.P. imagination.

Although suspected anti-government elements had been weeded out from among the officers, dissatisfaction was rife elsewhere in the army. One day a group of army sergeants came to visit me at my residence. They were disillusioned and resentful. The injustice of the 'coup' affair rankled, and they pleaded with me to take counter-measures. They were professional soldiers. To them the obvious course was an armed attack — hitting back the only way they understood.

I could see that the mood of the people in general was becoming dangerous. Feelings ran high not only among the representatives of other ranks in the army who had come to enlist my support, but with Albert's ever-increasing number of opponents in every walk of life. The soldiers made no secret to me of their determination to be rid of him at the first opportunity. As leader of the Opposition I had it within my power to sway the country in one of two ways: I could have thrown in my lot with the forces of violence, or I could use every ounce of tact, patience and persuasion I could muster to cool the white-hot fever of impending revolt. But, in fact, I felt I had no choice in the matter; I have always been and will ever remain a non-violent man. I abhor brutality, terrorism and senseless bloodshed, and I have rarely yet found a situation that cannot be more effectively solved through tolerant discussion than by the sword or rifle.

A leader cannot hope successfully to govern a country either by force or by sticking rigidly to chapter and verse, for in each case he fails to take into account the all-important human dimension. His role is to guide and lead individual men and women, intelligent beings of varying moods and ideas, who have placed their trust in him and who expect to be consulted on any issue likely to jeopardise that trust or imperil the peaceful government of the nation. Whatever he may think to the contrary, in the final analysis neither the best police force in the world, nor the most efficient army, can maintain order without the co-operation of the people. Once a leader has won the co-operation of the public, any legislation put on the statute book can become effective. If the people understand that it is in their interest, they will abide by such law. Force may be necessary at times, but it should only be thought of as a very last resort, when all else has failed and when it is the only means left of restoring order.

As I saw it, in February, 1967, although the situation was explosive, the small measure of influence I could bring to bear was committed to peace. "Have patience," I urged the sergeants. "The general election is imminent, and believe me, we will overcome the S.L.P.P. — but through the legitimate means of the ballot box."

Quite obviously it was Albert's intention to 'discover' the army plot immediately before announcing an early election date so that the suspected plotters, before there was time to prove them innocent, could be safely held in custody pending investigations until after the election. At the same time he may have speculated on the general shock of such a disclosure winning him sympathy — and sympathetic votes — from a stunned electorate, provided the elections were held before the shock wore off. Even though things did not work out as he had planned, if he had been a shrewder politician and a subtler tactician, he might still have succeeded in hoodwinking enough people to tip the scales in his favour for as long as it mattered if he had acted on *We Yone's* exposé and advanced his schedule by four days. How much more convincing this would have appeared! As it was, the people were neither shocked nor sympathetic nor easily convinced; they were rather confused and suspicious and more than ever determined to vote him out of office.

As soon as the fruitless hearings in connection with the alleged plot had closed, and the public had been promised an early trial of the nine officers involved, it was announced that the general election would be held on March 17th for the sixty-six ordinary seats and on March 21st for the twelve Paramount Chiefs who were elected by traditional and district councillors. Until now it had always been the custom for the polling for the Paramount Chiefs' seats to take place before the ordinary constituency seats. It is not clear what advantage the S.L.P.P. hoped to gain by this reversal of policy, for whilst Paramount Chiefs were not under any obligation to do so, it was usual for them to give their support to the government of the day. I suppose Margai foresaw that he would fail to get a unanimous declaration from the chiefs in favour of the S.L.P.P. and that this in turn would harm his party's prospects at the popular polls. But whatever the reason for the move it seems to have been miscalculated. As events turned out, he might have procured a majority for the S.L.P.P. in the Legislature by cajoling and coercing the chiefs if they had been elected first.

It was clear that the Prime Minister intended to win the election by hook or by crook and the expedients he had already contrived to make this possible ruled out any chance of a fair, free and honest contest. Not only were conditions being made as difficult as possible for A.P.C. candidates to stand for election, but rumours were rife that the S.L.P.P. intended to rig both the nominations and the election itself.

Support came for me from a most unexpected quarter, from the heart of the S.L.P.P., in the form of Albert Margai's brother Sam, who wrote in *Unity* of December 24th, 1966:

"Irrespective of our political difference, Shaki, as the Hon. Member is commonly known, is a great and powerful politician who has played a major role in different capacities in the development of Sierra Leone before and after Independence.

"Shaki's background and history are identical to other great statesmen of the world who rose from the ranks to the top, and it is advisable for Sierra Leoneans — young men and women in particular — to know something about the background of this great son of Sierra Leone, Shaki.

"In school, Government service, in the industrial sector as well as founder and Leader of Her Majesty's Opposition Party, Shaki has set a record second to none in Sierra Leone.

"Nevertheless I feel all parliamentarians as well as all Sierra Leoneans owe Shaki a great obligation. Being one of them, I have taken this opportunity to pay tribute to Shaki irrespective of our political differences."

Whether or not it was the Christmas spirit of charity and goodwill that inspired Sam to write so generously of his brother's chief rival, his tribute was printed and circulated under the sign of the A.P.C.'s rising sun along with our Manifesto and played no small part in courting votes in our favour.

On February 17th, ten days before nomination day, the Electoral Provisions Act had been amended so as to raise the deposit made by each candidate from Le200 (£100) to Le500 (£250) and to increase the proportion of the poll necessary for a candidate to retain his deposit from 10 per cent to 25 per cent. It was an ugly calculated trick by the plutocrats. Realising the precariousness of their own position, they were trying to hamstring their popular but penniless opponents. They had in effect imposed a means test on candidates. Few A.P.C. party members had money; most of them were scratching a living, being forced to pick up what few crumbs were left after the big boys in power had had their fill. It was going to be an almighty task finding the necessary money in so short a space of time to place a candidate in each of the 66 constituencies, even though we had the men.

It is one thing accepting a challenge when you know exactly what is weighed against you, when you are confident that each party will stick rigidly to the rules of the game, but it is quite another matter when you try to prepare yourself to match your wits against an opponent of unorthodox technique, when you are uncertain when, how and with what he will strike. As obstacle after obstacle was thrown in our way and every conceivable wile used against us, I became so depressed and disillusioned that I believe it was only my implicit belief that justice must eventually prevail that gave the necessary boost to my rapidly diminishing patience and self-control and enabled me to hold out against pressure to retaliate from my sorely provoked supporters. This would inevitably have led to bloodshed on a massive scale, which was the very last thing we wanted.

From the outset I had objected to the composition of the Electoral

Commission which had been changed since the 1962 elections and was now dominated by Mendes who, I felt, were unlikely to be impartial. In particular I opposed Albert's selection of I.B. Sanusi as Acting Chief Electoral Commissioner on the grounds that he was a staunch S.L.P.P. supporter. But my protests fell on deaf ears, for nothing was done to reconstitute the Commission on more neutral lines.

My doubts of the impartiality of the Electoral Commission were soon confirmed. Indeed, its whole operation proved highly irregular. Contrary to Section 37(8) of our Constitution which stated that the Electoral Commission "shall not be subject to the direction or control of any other person or authority," the name of every Returning Officer was first vetted by the Prime Minister before being officially appointed by the Commission. Two seminars of administrative officers had been held, one in July, 1966, and the other in February, 1967, at which the Secretary to the Prime Minister and Head of the Civil Service had left no doubt in the minds of Returning Officers about what was expected of them during the coming election, namely, to see to it that the S.L.P.P. Government was returned to power.

To prove to their master how eager they were to do his bidding, they returned six S.L.P.P. candidates unopposed before the elections were even held; among them, of course, Albert Margai and his brother Sam. The Opposition candidates, both A.P.C. and Independents, were disqualified on the flimsiest of grounds and all appeals were promptly dismissed by the pro-S.L.P.P. Electoral Commission. The Dove-Edwin Commission of Inquiry which later investigated the conduct of the 1967 elections, described these six 'returned unopposed' cases as scandalous, especially in one instance where the S.L.P.P. candidate was not even a registered voter in the constituency concerned and therefore ineligible to oppose the rejected A.P.C. candidate.

When Albert and five of his party members were 'returned unopposed', there was a resigned acceptance in some quarters of the likelihood of the S.L.P.P. getting back into power. Albert had little difficulty, therefore, in persuading many Paramount Chiefs and Independent candidates to sign a document declaring their support for the S.L.P.P. in the event of their being elected. What many of them cared about was a seat in the House. If in order to secure this it was necessary to give a show of support to one party or the other, what did it matter?

It mattered a great deal to the A.P.C. as far as the Paramount Chiefs' allegiance was concerned because it was necessary to get permission from the local Paramount Chief before a candidate could hold an election meeting in his Province. Wherever his true sympathy may have lain, no Paramount Chief so committed would dare risk displeasing his patron by allowing the A.P.C. to set foot on his territory, which resulted, in some areas, in our supporters being molested, beaten up and arrested. But although our field of operations was strewn with dangers, our message got through. Many of the people were illiterate and unable to read our manifesto, but they knew that the A.P.C., like themselves, was dissatisfied with the mismanagement of the S.L.P.P. Government and was as anxious as they were to get them out. They noted the party symbol of the red rising sun and voted for that symbol even if they had not been able to meet the candidate.

I drew the attention of the Electoral Commission to the fact that the Register of Voters had not been revised since 1965 when it recorded a strength of 1,573,666. They did nothing about this except to shift the onus of responsibility onto the electorate itself by offering for sale printed copies of the Register so that it was up to those whose names were not included in it to take the initiative if they wanted to vote. In view of the fact that it was on this 1965 figure that the voting arrangements had been made, it seemed extraordinary to say the least that a surplus of 14,634 ballot papers had been printed.

After our recent experiences of the lengths to which our desperate opponents were prepared to go in order the win the election, it was not difficult to guess why these extra ballot papers had been ordered, ugly as the realisation was. There seemed no limit to the evil machinations of our rivals.

Evidence that the S.L.P.P. planned to rig the elections was put in our hands by a worried chief who handed a sheaf of ballot papers to the A.P.C. candidate in his area, telling him that he had been given them by the S.L.P.P. and told to arrange for them to be put into the S.L.P.P. candidate's box. Our scouts, hot on the scent by now, discovered similar cases involving Returning Officers, Assistant Returning Officers, Presiding Officers and other officials. Fearful that the extra ballot papers might by found on them by A.P.C. supporters, voters tried to destroy them. One nervous Presiding Officer who drew attention to himself by haunting one of the polling booths, tried unsuccessfully to dispose of his bundle by flushing it down the lavatory, leaving much valuable evidence in his wake for use by the Dove-Edwin Commission of Inquiry.

Election Day was surprisingly calm. There were a few minor disturbances, particularly among the Fulas who, quite understandably, raised objections when over-zealous A.P.C. supporters wanted to search among their flowing robes for hidden ballot papers. In fact the orderliness of the voting was in such complete contrast to the bitterness and viciousness of events leading up to it, that it was difficult to believe that we had had to overcome so many hurdles and booby-traps in order to survive at all as a contesting party. And now there was nothing that any of us could do but await the results and abide by the decision of the electorate. At least that is the way any *normal* election should have ended; but ours proved to be anything but normal for Albert still kept in reserve a few trump cards to play if the conclusion turned out to be, for him, a disappointing one.

For instance, he controlled the radio and television and the main daily newspaper, the *Daily Mail*; his henchmen dominated the Electoral Commission and were instructed to pass all results to Sanusi, the Acting Commissioner, who had installed himself in the Prime Minister's official residence for security reasons because he complained of threats to his person. Could one seriously trust such committed elements faithfully to count and record the votes? After all, such fraudulent practice could be considered by them no more dishonest than issuing extra ballot papers.

There was inordinate delay in publishing the results. The people heard of them via the 'bush telegraph' hours before the official announcements were made; and when these were made public, they did not always tally with those that the people knew themselves to be the correct ones. This led to confusion and distrust — but above all it led to one very obvious conclusion: the S.L.P.P. was out and it knew it, but it was a bad loser; it hoped that by delaying tactics and cleverly putting over the results with an S.L.P.P. slant, a miracle might be achieved in its favour. It was a last desperate straw but one that was seared and useless.

Paragraph 85 of the Dove-Edwin Report assessed the position thus:

"The mode of relaying results to the public seems to be this: 'Keep the S.L.P.P. in the lead', and this went on till the parties drew level at 28 each, S.L.P.P. getting six seats out of this number unopposed."

Paragraph 83 of the Report also disclosed that a member of the Electoral Commission admitted that he had received orders to hold back some of the results.

If it had not been so shameful, this attempt to fool the people might have been laughable, it was so clumsily enacted. For instance, the *Daily Mail* of March 18th, published the state of the parties as S.L.P.P. 11 (which included the 6 uncontested seats) and A.P.C. 10, yet on the 7.30 a.m. news that same morning it was announced that S.L.P.P. had won 11 seats and A.P.C. only 6!

The overwhelming victory by the A.P.C. in Tonkolili had been common knowledge throughout Freetown from early morning, but it was not announced until late that night. The A.P.C.'s victory in Moyamba West never was announced, so badly had it shaken our opponents' morale. But perhaps the most blatant example of inconsistency was when the B.B.C. news, relayed by the Sierra Leone Broadcasting System, announced that with two results to come, the A.P.C. had a lead of two, only to be followed immediately afterwards by the Sierra Leone local newsreader informing the public that with eight seats to be declared, S.L.P.P. had taken 30, A.P.C. 26 and Independents 2.

By Monday, March 20th, the final results had still not been announced and tension was mounting hourly. A large crowd gathered outside the State House in Freetown anxiously waiting for news. Many of them had already anticipated the A.P.C. victory, were dressed in Party red and chanting Party slogans. Students from Fourah Bay College demonstrated with placards protesting against the delay, but there was no violence and no unpleasantness; everything was orderly and the people were in festive mood. Inside the State House the Governor-General, Sir Henry Lightfoot-Boston, had called Albert Margai and myself to a meeting at which he suggested that owing to the closeness of the results, we might consider forming a coalition government. We agreed to meet again the following day after consulting our colleagues.

Immediately I confronted my Party members with the Governor-General's proposal I was greeted with instant, loud and unanimous objections. I did not expect them to feel otherwise. How, they asked, was it possible even to contemplate working with such a man as Albert Margai had proved himself to be? It was unthinkable, they said, that the A.P.C. should associate itself with a party that could sink to such depths of fraud and deception in order to keep itself in power. All were agreed that the A.P.C. had gained a victory against incredible odds and, however small our majority, it was our right and duty to keep faith with the people who had chosen us to lead them. Those were my own sentiments, too.

ABOVE, PEOPLE QUEUE TO VOTE IN THE GENERAL ELECTION OF MARCH 1967 WHICH WAS WON BY THE A.P.C. BELOW, SIR ALBERT MARGAI, THE PRIME MINISTER WHO WOULD NOT ACCEPT DEFEAT, WITH MEMBERS OF HIS LAST CABINET.

ABOVE, A.P.C. SUPPORTERS WAVE AND CHEER AS THE RESULTS OF THE ELECTION ARE ANNOUNCED AND THEY LEARN THAT I HAVE BEEN APPOINTED PRIME MINISTER OF SIERRA LEONE. BELOW, CROWDS OF ANGRY PEOPLE GATHER OUTSIDE THE A.P.C. HEADQUARTERS TO EXPRESS THEIR DISAPPOINTMENT WHEN THEY HEAR THAT ARMY OFFICERS WRESTED POWER FROM THE PARTY WHICH HAD WON THE ELECTION. ARMY RIOT SQUADS STAND BY.

I then returned to the State House with a letter to the Governor-General informing him that after consulting my Party members, I could not agree to a coalition government. As soon as he received this, he wrote to Albert Margai saying that the meeting arranged for the following day had been called off.

Meanwhile four of the newly elected Independent Members of Parliament announced that they would support whichever party won the majority of seats in the House, but that they would on no account serve under Sir Albert Margai. This really put paid to any hopes Albert may have had of out-voting an A.P.C. Government, for without the assured support in the House of the six Indepentent members, the margin between the A.P.C.'s 32 and the S.L.P.P.'s 28 promised to be even wider.

On Tuesday morning, March 21st, I was handed the following letter by the Governor-General:

21st March, 1967.

Dear Mr. Stevens,

I have pleasure in informing you that, in exercise of the powers vested in me under Section 58 of the Constitution, I hereby appoint you, SIAKA PROBYN STEVENS, to be Prime Minister of Sierra Leone with effect from Tuesday, the 21st March, 1967.

Yours sincerely,
H. L. Boston.
Governor-General.

I read and reread the letter. So overcome with emotion was I that tears of joy welled in my eyes. I knew the tears represented the release of years of pentup, held back, feelings and I allowed myself the tears as a natural and human reaction to an experience so charged with historical implication.

The Governor-General decided to take this action without waiting for the results of the Paramount Chiefs' elections which were taking place that same day, in spite of the fact that the Forces Commander, Brigadier Lansana, had twice warned him that a dangerous situation might develop if any appointment were made when neither party had (in his opinion) a majority and the elections (that is, those of the Paramount Chiefs) had not yet been concluded.

The 12 Paramount Chiefs' seats were not contested under party tickets and those who held them were in the House as representatives of their particular districts. Immediately prior to the 1967 general election the secretary-general of my party wrote to the Governor-General seeking clarification of the position of these Paramount Chiefs, asking whether their votes were taken into consideration when determining which party had the majority and whether, once elected, they were bound to side with the party in power or free to opt for the party of their choice. The reply was that it was the duty of the Governor-General not to determine what person had the support of the majority of the members of the House, but to determine what person is *likely to command* such a majority. Paramount Chiefs, he said, must be taken into account as members but they were free to opt for the party of their choice. In practice, however, it had been found that Paramount Chiefs tended to support the Government in power, so to have awaited the results of their election would have had little if any bearing on the state of the parties. Moreover, the chiefs were not popular representatives in Parliament, they were bound by democratic principles to follow a popular lead. The Governor-General no doubt felt also that the dangerous situation feared by Lansana was much more likely to occur if the appointment of a Prime Minister were delayed a moment longer, for the patience of the electorate was clearly nearing exhaustion.

A letter from a Sierra Leonean supporting the action of the Governor-General, published in *West Africa* on May 6th, 1967, pointed out:

" In the British General Election in 1929 the Conservatives lost heavily (from 419 seats down to 260) while the Labour Party gained greatly (from 151 seats up to 288); the Liberals increased their strength slightly (from 40 seats up to 59). It was the leader of the Labour Party (J. Ramsay MacDonald) therefore, although his party did not have an overall majority, who clearly had to be asked to form a Government."

The situation in Sierra Leone in 1967 was clearly analogous. The A.P.C. was the largest party in the legislature. It was certain, thanks to the clear declaration of four Independents, that Albert Margai could not in any case command a majority. There was every indication, on the other hand, that an A.P.C. Government would be able to do so.

I was called to the State House around 3 p.m. on March 21st, to be sworn in as Prime Minister.

I shall never escape the memory of the moment the troops arrived. I had an inkling of what was afoot, of course, I had seen too much evidence of Albert Margai's contempt for democracy during the election campaign to retain any illusions about his willingness to accept the people's verdict. And it was precisely because I suspected that he was suborning elements of the armed forces to intervene on his behalf that I was so anxious for the release of Bangura and other imprisoned soldiers. But I still did not really believe that Margai's partisans would resort to such a terrible remedy. I did not realise that naked lust for power was such a potent force for evil that, for its sake, men would sacrifice all their principles, the well-being of their country and all the great ends they had sought together for years. I could not accept that Sierra Leoneans who served their country in the armed forces would be prepared to jeopardise democracy and national unity when the crunch came. I think it is more shocking when a possibility materialises which one has thought about and dismissed than when a complete surprise happens.

When my first session as Prime Minister with the Governor-General was brutalised by the invasion of hostile soldiers led by an A.D.C. to the Force Commander, I was almost numbed with shock. But I immediately took an inward decision; I would do all I could to avoid violence and bloodshed, even if I had to postpone my vision of my country's future to do so. I was determined that the lives of Sierra Leoneans would not be sacrificed for any ambition of my own. This did not mean I was going to surrender to the perpetrators of the coup, only that I would resist them by better means than naked force. I did not want to take up a bloodstained premiership. I had struggled for freedom and democracy in my country for thirty years. I had learnt patience. I knew A.P.C. party members and supporters would want to resist the coup in arms, but I also knew that it would be in the best interests of the whole country to restrain them. We had overcome before. And even at the cost of a temporary setback, we should overcome again.

All this flashed through my mind in an instant. But for the present, there was an immediate crisis to confront. There were the soldiers. There were the guns.

The Governor-General was standing beside me, but his voice sounded strangely remote. "What is the meaning of this?"

"I am acting on the instructions of the Force Commander, Brigadier Lansana, Sir!", the A.D.C. replied. "My orders are to prevent anybody from leaving the place until the Brigadier and Sir Albert Margai arrive."

Sir Henry almost literally staggered. He moved like a marionette, only imperfectly co-ordinated, as though uncontrolled by his own will, his arms flapping as if reaching out for support. With a sort of embarrassed, baffled dignity he struggled up to his private suite. It seemed a symbolic withdrawal. A resigned retreat.

My mind rebelled against the gravity, the enormity of the moment. I found I was cracking silly jokes with myself in silence. 'Stevens out for a duck. Governor-General retired hurt'. A surfeit of drama was making me feel light-headed, almost reckless. I felt utterly parched — it was the first physical sensation I became aware of after the numbing shock of the coup. I suppose the tension had made me sweat, dried me out. There was not a drop of water to be had — the soldiers had drunk dry the State House iced water supply. Thirst became a symbol of my impotent rage at our captors. When I was asked for a comment for the world's press, I could not say what I felt. The words stuck in my throat. All I could do was try to find some relief from anger and wretchedness in a joke. "The overseas press are on the line, Sir, and would like a statement from you," the Private Secretary said. Checking the impulse to utter a useless Philippic, I replied, "Tell them I am very annoyed indeed. And tell the world that we can't even get a glass of water to drink!'".

After the Governor-General's withdrawal upstairs, the handful of colleagues who were keeping me company waited with me in the Private Secretary's office. We hung around in frustration, awaiting developments. At 5.55 p.m. Lansana announced on the wireless that there was 'widespread rumour, put out by the A.P.C.,' that the Governor-General had appointed Mr. Siaka Stevens as Prime Minister. If the rumour were true, he declared, such an appointment was unconstitutional because the election results had not yet all come in. The rumour, he said, was an attempt by the A.P.C. to ignore the Constitution and seize power by force which would lead to chaos and civil war. 'As custodian of state security,' he had decided to protect the Constitution and maintain law and order. 'From now on the army is in control... '.

Later that evening the results of the Paramount Chiefs' elections were announced; all but two of them, we were told, had declared support for the S.L.P.P. It was interesting to note that this time there was no delay in publishing the results. In fact they had been rushed through in double quick time, for the plan was obviously to add these seats to the S.L.P.P. muster and thus — with ten chiefs virtually forced into compliance — to give the S.L.P.P. a majority.

It was a preposterous situation, one surely unique in a democracy in this day and age. A constitutionally elected Prime Minister arrested within minutes of being sworn in because his ambitious opponent had failed to deceive and force himself upon an unwilling electorate, and was not man enough to accept defeat in the recognised and civilized fashion. This was the behaviour not of a politician but of an irresponsible desperado. His arrogance and vanity blinded him to such a degree that he was incapable of seeing the hoplessness of his position, for neither he nor his boot-licking Force Commander had any support to speak of either from the people or from the soldiers who were for the moment giving a show of protection for them with their tommy guns. His chances of survival under such precarious conditions were minimal.

It was this realisation that kept our spirits up during the long and tedious hours we waited in the State House for something to happen. As the evening wore on we became hungry and I asked the Private Secretary if it was possible to get something to eat. She went off to see what she could find, but all there was in the kitchen was a loaf of bread, and that was stale. The housekeeper had gone home earlier and locked everything up, she explained apologetically. The A.D.C. still clung to his gun but had lost his jaunty cock-sure look and was now a combined jumble of saggy sweat-soaked uniform and greasy metal, hanging from a chair. The rumblings of empty stomachs, however, were increasingly insistent! It seemed funny to feel so hungry in the midst of so many worse afflictions. I felt like a child again, remembering a boyhood ruled so savagely by the tyranny of an almost always empty belly. The A.D.C., no doubt aghast at the prospect of having to hold his own against a hunger march, gave permission to a soldier to go across to the Paramount Hotel to buy beer and sandwiches for us.

Around 7.30 p.m. we were informed that Albert and Lansana would not be coming to meet us after all and we were allowed to go upstairs to the drawing room where we spent the night. It was difficult to get any sleep for I was greatly disturbed by the noise of gunfire. By an oversight, the telephone remained in operation throughout the whole of my two days' detention in the State House, so I was able to keep in touch with what was going on in Freetown. Rumour had it that I was going to be taken outside the city and shot. Because of this, hundreds of my supporters and sympathisers defied death themselves to erect and man barricades across all roads leading from the State House to make it impossible for a vehicle to get through. They made no attempt to fight the troops, they just stood solidly firm and refused to give way or to be intimidated by them. As a result the troops peppered them with tear gas and bullets; there were many casualties, a number of them fatal.

I was deeply moved by this demonstration of loyalty to me and distressed beyond belief that it had led to so much unnecessary suffering. The following morning, in an attempt to restore some measure of sanity to the confused state of affairs, I wrote to Lansana and urged him to let me open the House so that the Members themselves could decide the leadership once and for all. For my part, I would willingly have abided by the majority decision, whichever way it went, if to do otherwise meant anarchy and bloodshed.

Shortly after this, Lansana broadcast an appeal to all newly elected Members of Parliament to proceed to Freetown 'to discuss very important matters in connection with the constitutional government of Sierra Leone'. It was not his wish, he said to do anything unconstitutional.

Very few M.P.s responded. Most of them were only too aware of the plot to reinstate Albert Margai and they wanted nothing to do with it. The methods used had been unconstitutional and they were not prepared to serve another spell under Albert's mismanagement.

Whether I was included in this invitation, I never knew, for at 5 p.m. on Thursday, March 23rd, I was taken from the State House under armed escort and driven to Pademba Road prison. A curfew was imposed immediately afterwards. It was, I mused, not exactly the way I had planned to celebrate my premiership, but then life is full of the unexpected.

ABOVE, STATE HOUSE - MY OFFICE AND OFFICIAL RESIDENCE - WHERE I WAS DETAINED BY THE ARMY OFFICERS PENDING MY TRANSFER TO PADEMBA PRISON. LEFT, SIR HENRY LIGHTFOOT-BOSTON, THE GOVERNOR-GENERAL WHO RECOGNISED OUR ELECTORAL VICTORY AND APPOINTED ME TO SERVE AS PRIME MINISTER.

CHAPTER FOURTEEN

In the Wings

On this third occasion when I checked in at Pademba Road prison I was led by my old friend Decker to a different room from the one I had previously occupied in the Hospital Block. It was, I learnt later, the Welfare Officer's office. It was small and stiflingly hot, having only one window which was placed in such a way that it failed to catch any breeze. Mercifully an electric plug was installed a few days later so I was able to use a fan.

Within thirty minutes or so of my arrival in the prison a commotion in the yard below my room drew me to the window. To my surprise I saw Albert Margai, under guard, being escorted across the compound. It was like meeting Nebuchadnezzar in the lion's den. Half an hour later there was an even greater disturbance when Lansana appeared through the prison gates propped up by a posse of his armed soldiers. At first I thought the prison was being invaded, for excited police and soldiers were swarming in the courtyard and passing backwards and forwards through the normally locked and barred iron gates. Neither they nor the warders seemed conscious of the fact that prisoners, rarely slow to take advantage of such a confused situation, were drifting speedily on the outgoing current.

One hundred and twenty-nine prisoners escaped and, although most were eventually recaptured, one at least remained at large for as long as fourteen months. It was only when he was apprehended in connection with another crime that his unlawful escape from custody was detected. The coup, which began so tragically, had an in-built tendency to farce. If the country had not suffered so much in the course of it, the rule of the comic colonels would have been laughable.

When Albert and Lansana turned up under separate guard in the prison compound, my first thought was naturally that the rule of law had been restored. I expected to be released at any moment. But after what I had already been through I was wary of too much optimism. In fact, I

261

had underestimated the torturous complexity of the situation. Albert had got himself, and almost everyone else, entangled in his voluminous web of intrigue. Everything was an inextricable muddle.

Two days after Lansana had announced his trumped-up charges of irregular and unconstitutional behaviour against the Governor-General and, on the pretext of maintaining law and order, which had not in fact broken down, had assumed control as the self-styled 'Chief Custodian of State Security', the body politic had another convulsive twitch. Three of his officers — Majors Blake, Jumu and Kai-Samba, who were the next senior in rank to Lansana on the active strength inside Sierra Leone at the time — believed that his aim was not to oust the A.P.C. and create a national government, but to impose Albert Margai as Prime Minister on an unwilling people. This they were not prepared to suffer. They whisked both Albert and Lansana into the capacious quarters I already partly occupied at Pademba Road.

With Lansana out of the way, they invited Lt. Col. Ambrose Genda, then in New York, and Lt. Col. A. T. Juxon-Smith, then on an army training course in the United Kingdom, to be Chairman and member respectively of the 'National Reformation Council' which they proposed to set up and which was to be composed of military and police officers. Genda, although a Mende like Margai, Lansana and the three Majors, had been so overtly antipathetic to Margai that he had, some time before, been retired from the army and sent to the United Nations in New York as an Assistant Secretary to the Sierra Leone Permanent Mission.

Genda was, therefore, no longer an army officer but a civil servant and as such did not in fact qualify as a member of the proposed Council, let alone as Chairman of it. The mere fact that the Majors felt obliged to recall these two men showed clearly their sense of insecurity and their lack of confidence in themselves as leaders. They had the disciplined and relatively inelastic minds of military men who have drilled into them from their 'square-bashing' days the fact that they are not entitled to assume any responsibility themselves as long as there exists an officer of senior rank unless they are delegated authority by that officer. They had gaoled their Commanding Officer. Their Second-in-Command, Col. Bangura, had been gaoled by Albert Margai but they dared not release him for fear he would arrest them and restore power to the A.P.C. Genda had not so far been replaced in the army and no doubt the Majors regarded him for practical purposes as being still a soldier. By their reckoning he came next in seniority after Bangura.

But Genda delayed his departure from New York until he could be recalled by what would appear to him to be a firmly established military government which would make arrangements for his travel and give him the assurance that it would be in order for him to return. Meanwhile, rumour had it in Freetown that he regarded the N.R.C. as a temporary solution and that he intended to hand over power to a civilian administration at the earliest opportunity. Whether these rumours had the effect of casting doubts on his suitability as Head of a military government, suggesting at the same time that the majors in Freetown were unwilling to assist a return to civilian rule, must remain a matter of conjecture. What is certain is that shortly after Genda reached London on his way to Sierra Leone, the Majors changed their minds and decided to favour Juxon-Smith as head of their junta. An urgent message reporting their decision reached the Sierra Leone High Commission in London just as Genda and Juxon-Smith were waiting in the V.I.P. lounge at Gatwick Airport, near London, for the scheduled British Caledonian flight which was to take them home. The gist of the message from Freetown was conveyed to them at Gatwick, but the small group of British officials, journalists and well-wishers who had come to the airport to bid farewell to the travellers, did not realise what had happened and went on drinking champagne and treating Genda as Sierra Leone's future Head of Government.

It would appear that Genda himself was in two minds as to whether to return to London immediately, as an ordinary citizen, and await further developments, or step on the red carpet which had been laid for him and fly to Freetown to face the challenge and attempt to reverse the decision of his former subordinates. Eventually, he decided to save at least some embarrassment and to board the plane, still as Head of Government presumptive, with Juxon-Smith following close behind him. I do not know what arguments were exchanged between them during the flight, but it turned out that by the time the aircraft landed in Las Palmas for refuelling an arrangement had been reached whereby Genda agreed to return to London to await developments while Juxon-Smith journeyed on to Freetown to become Chairman of the National Reformation Council and Head of Government.

It would seem that Juxon-Smith managed to prevail upon Genda to submit to the wishes of the N.R.C. in Freetown and shortly after returning to London from Las Palmas he (Genda) was rewarded with the post of Ambassador to Liberia. Juxon-Smith, on the other hand, was known to have greater personal ambitions and could probably

A.T. JUXON-SMITH, THE YOUNG OFFICER WHO TOOK IT UPON HIMSELF TO RULE SIERRA LEONE IN DEFIANCE OF THE WISHES OF THE MAJORITY OF THE PEOPLE.

foresee a brilliant future for himself as ruler of Sierra Leone, perhaps for years ahead.

As for the three Majors in Freetown, but for the military takeovers in Ghana and other West African countries, from which they must have been drawing inspiration and Dutch courage, I am sure they would have been almost grateful to have been relieved of the burden they had taken on, which was far heavier than they anticipated. In their months of power, they showed every sign of cold feet. Unfortunately, they took as gospel Lansana's charges against the Governor-General and his assessment of the situation. This was understandable for, as I have pointed out, they were disciplined soldiers; Lansana was, or had been, their Commanding Officer and their job had never before been to question him or to reason why. Their political metabolisms showed only limited tolerance of novelty.

The pity of it is that in their obvious quandry it would not, in my opinion, have been difficult for members of the judiciary, civil service and other responsible bodies who genuinely had the interests of the country at heart, to have reasoned with them before the arrival of Juxon-Smith, and succeeded in convincing them of the true state of affairs: that it was Lansana, not the Governor-General, who had acted unconstitutionally, and that they themselves were in fact compounding mutinous and treasonable conduct. However, Juxon-Smith arrived and the moment for rectifying the position passed; the tide in the affairs of our nation was not taken at the flood. We got bogged down, 'bound in shallows and in miseries'.

Meanwhile, I was stuck for the foreseeable future in the even firmer constraints of prison. At least I was no longer obliged to eat the prison diet, which — 'extras' or none — was not one of the features of prison life I recall with rapture. Fortunately, my wife was given permission to bring food from home for me three times a day. Even though she was not allowed to see me, the fact that she visited the prison and had herself prepared my food was a source of extraordinary comfort to me. I never allowed myself to become idle. If I was not occupied in reading and writing and making plans for the future, I was teaching myself French and other subjects that I felt would later be of benefit to me.

Decker one day expressed amazement that in spite of my detention I was always so cheerful. What point was there in being otherwise? You have to keep a keen lookout for rainbows or you may miss them when they come along. Never allow a period of adversity to get the better of you. Never surrender to self-pity and bitterness. Your mind has to be alert and positive to take advantage of the turn of events when it happens. People talk a lot about luck. But luck means nothing unless you have the right word to respond to it. Even the worst adversity offers fresh hope, opportunity and challenge to a man in the right mood. I worked hard in prison to keep my own mood right. Above all else, though, I had abundant faith in the future of Sierra Leone, in the will of the people being respected. Never once did I doubt that, however long it took, reason and justice would prevail for the people of Sierra Leone had opted for a change of government and they would not be fobbed off for long with any other than the one they had chosen.

As David Dalby of the School of Oriental and African Studies wrote in the *New Society* of April 6th, 1967: "The defeat of the ruling S.L.P.P. was not unexpected, and certainly not undeserved, and it is to the credit of the people of Sierra Leone that they should have achieved the first democratic change of government in post-colonial Africa. It is even more to their credit that they should have achieved this in the face of Margai's desperate efforts to remain in power."

Although the coup eroded our pride as a democratic African people, it left us some scope for self-esteem. Our electoral system had been proof even against the most determined rigging. We had become the first Black African people to oust an incumbent government at the polls. Though we had seen recourse to unpardonable violence for political ends, we had drawn back from bloodshed at the eleventh hour. Though the army was too easily tempted by power, it had at least shown some political discrimination and a disinclination to ready manipulation by its leaders.

I admit I felt disillusion and despair when the N.R.C. failed to release me at once or show any inclination to restore the Constitution. The N.R.C. tried to justify its existence, as did Lansana before, on the grounds that a military take-over had been necessary to protect the Constitution, to maintain law and order, to prevent bloodshed and to combat corruption, nepotism and tribalism. That there had been no violation of the Constitution by the Governor-General was proved beyond doubt by the Dove-Edwin Commission of Enquiry which was called for the by the N.R.C. itself. There was no question of a breakdown of law and order until Lansana announced his take-over and rumours abounded that I, among others, was going to be quietly disposed of.

The worst moment for me — worse even than the coup — came when the N.R.C. almost embroiled the country in the bloodshed that had been largely avoided during the coup. Public feeling had run very high over the military seizure of power because the A.P.C. supporters who had won the election felt that they had been cheated of their victory by the army. This tension was exacerbated by the shooting, in cold blood, of some forty peaceful citizens. My heart was incandescent with rage and frustration. I knew I could help; but I was forced to chafe behind bars, where my very presence was a focus for inflamed feelings. David Dalby, one of many independent foreign observers of the situation, wrote in *New Society* of April 6th, 1967: "... the imprisonment of Stevens, a popular hero in Freetown and many other parts of Sierra Leone, has given rise to a greater danger of violence than before." All I could do was hope against hope that this might be wrong and that my friends would be deterred from violence by fear of reprisals against me. But it was a weak hope, uttered to myself in helplessness.

With regard to the N.R.C.'s declaration that it would root out corruption, this only emphasised more than ever the total lack of contact with reality of those who sought to govern the people. Those of us who have had experience of such matters know that the most that can be done is to keep on the look-out for this sort of thing and to strike at the ugly head of corruption wherever it appears; but to talk of rooting it out is mere propaganda and the idle talk of the ill-informed. In any case, if the N.R.C. was sincere in its bid to wipe out corruption, one may well ask where its members were when corruption was reigning supreme during the previous two years. Indeed, would the N.R.C. ever have come into existence or have dreamt of staging a coup if Albert Margai and his S.L.P.P. had won the election? Of course not.

With regard to tribalism, I should like to quote David Dalby once again who, in the same article, writes:

" The present tragedy of Sierra Leone lies in the fact that Stevens' government would have been in a strong position to reduce tribal tension. Stevens himself has the advantage of belonging to one of the smaller indigenous tribes, the Limba, and his party draws support from a wide variety of tribes, as well as from the mixed population of Freetown itself. This genuine opportunity to solve some of the problems of tribalism now appears to have been lost, unless the military regime can be persuaded — if necessary by pressure from outside Sierra Leone — to hand back constitutional power to the Governor-General, and through him to the legal Prime Minister. "

Humphrey J. Fisher, of the School of Oriental and African Studies of the University of London, also wrote about the 1967 elections in the *Journal of Modern African Studies* and concluded by saying:

" We may ask again, why did the army take over? In Lansana's case, it was fairly clearly to restore Sir Albert, to accomplish what inefficient election rigging had failed to do. The initial motives of the members of the N.R.C. are less easily defined. The rapid succession of justifications — the Constitution, tribalism, corruption, economic problems — suggest that the army itself did not know why it was in power. "

I was released from prison around 4 p.m. on April 11th, 1967, and placed under house arrest in my Kingharman Road residence. My health had suffered somewhat through the strain of the elections and the tragic aftermath, and I sought permission to leave the country in order to consult a specialist in London. This was granted and I left for England in September. After receiving treatment for an anaemic condition, I devoted my time and energy to acquainting the British people, via Parliament and the press, with the true state of affairs in Sierra Leone. I hoped that this might help to bring pressure to bear on the N.R.C. to publish without further delay the report of the Dove-Edwin Commissin of Inquiry which had been completed and handed to it several weeks before; and to quicken the transfer of power to the legitimate government.

Life was so hectic and so fluid in those days, there seem to be no fixed points on which to hang memories. I find I have to re-read documents, memos and the press to recall what was in my mind. Everyday details of life have been submerged beneath the dominant issues of national politics which dominated my world. As I peruse the old material, something of the heady atmosphere of the period comes back to me.

" The danger of violence and tragedy on a national scale is now real and very serious, " I told the correspondent of *The Guardian* on October 20th, 1967. "The tempers of the people are rising in the towns and villages throughout the country. I am not a seeker after personal glory nor, I hope, am I a vain man. But my information is that the only thing holding off crisis now is my personal request that the civil population should not rise.

"The trouble is," I went on, "that a corrupt regime — the government of Sir Albert Margai — has been succeeded by an illegal regime which is not representative of the public will in any way, shape or form. Distinguished people in public life, such as Dr. Davidson Nicol, the head of the university, have been threatened with detention and forced out of office. There have been threats to the whole college council and its staff by the man who heads the present military regime, Brigadier Juxon-Smith.

"The commission of inquiry headed by Mr. Justice Dove-Edwin, which was appointed by Juxon-Smith himself, with one army officer and one police commissioner on it, has unanimously decided that my party won the election last March, that I was properly sworn in as Prime Minister by the Governor-General, Sir Henry Lightfoot-Boston, and that the present regime is honour bound to hand over to civilian rule now."

Both the former Governor-General and myself wrote to the Chairman of the N.R.C. warning him not to ignore the findings of the Dove-Edwin Commission.

"...it would be in the national interest," I wrote, "that immediate arrangements should be made for the handing over of power to the elected representatives of the people through His Excellency the Governor-General, bearing in mind the points that (a) this is the very urgent wish of the people, and (b) a very dangerous precedent would be created if the electorate (mostly illiterate) became convinced or even suspected that FORCE takes precedence over THE BALLOT BOX in the settlement of our constitutional affairs, and bearing in mind also the fact that when the Dove-Edwin Commission was set up, no less a person than the N.R.C. Chairman himself stated most categorically that *the Dove-Edwin Elections Commission was the most important of all the commissions that had been set up; that the whole world was waiting to hear the results of the last elections; that the ballot box was the life of the country and that the N.R.C. would honour the findings of the Commission.*"

One thing that baffled me was the attitude of the British Government on the Sierra Leonean issue. On November 14th, I wrote to Mr. Dingle Foot, Q.C., pointing out that Sierra Leone was at present a monarchy with Her Majesty the Queen as Head of State, represented in Sierra Leone by a Governor-General. The Royal Sierra Leone Military Forces had seized power from Her Majesty's representative and put him under arrest "and yet," I wrote, "the British Government appears to have recognised his military regime which is openly flouting the Rule of Law". If violence broke out as a result, I stated, the British Government would have to take some of the blame since it was clear that but for the recognition and help which it was giving the military regime, the regime could not last long.

The question of Britain's attitude was more or less answered in the House of Lords when Lord Brockway asked Her Majesty's Government whether they would use their influence to secure consideration by the Commonwealth Secretariat of the Report of the Committee headed by Mr. Justice Dove-Edwin into the circumstances of the last general election in Sierra Leone. In reply, Lord Shepherd, Minister of State for Commonwealth Affairs, took the view that the matter was outside the

Commonwealth's competence, as it was essential not to infringe the absolute inviolability of a member state's internal affairs. But he agreed to give consideration to the idea that the Commonwealth might establish a common institution, analogous to the European Commission, to which appeal could be made against abuses by member states.

The Commonwealth is an association of self-governing autonomous states and the very fact that it has not only survived many turbulent years, but actually grown from strength to strength, is due to the respect shown by each member country to the others regarding the way in which each one governs itself. I agree, and would not have it otherwise, that no Commonwealth member should interfere with the internal affairs of other member countries.

However, it has sometimes struck me that this unqualified acceptance of one another is stretched to a point where military take-overs actually appear to be condoned. Certainly they are not discouraged. Not a word of admonition was uttered, not a frown of disapproval creased the brows of the Commonwealth Prime Ministers when, for instance, those who illegally overthrew by force of arms the constitutionally elected governments of Ghana and Nigeria, took their seats at the conference table and were received in audience by the Head of the Commonwealth. It is not necessary, nor do I advocate it, that in such cases a country so unfortunate should be debarred from Commonwealth membership, for, however difficult one member of a family may be to see eye to eye with, so long as he remains within the family circle there is far more chance of establishing a harmonious relationship with him than if he severs connections altogether.

Nevertheless, I am forced to ask myself whether it would not add to the dignity, prestige and respect of the Commonwealth 'club' to make it a condition of membership that any member country whose legitimate leader is ousted by the bullet instead of the ballot box is temporarily suspended from attending the Commonwealth Prime Ministers' Conference until such time as the constitutional government has been restored to that country. As things stand, the position is in any case most unsatisfactory, for those who force themselves upon a people do not have the mandate of those people to speak on their behalf *anywhere*, let alone at an international conferene.

On November 28th, a press conference was arranged for me at the House of Commons immediately after which I cabled my wife in Freetown: "Just finished well attended press conference in Parliament buildings and a B.B.C. recording. Listen 29th."

The Dove-Edwin Report was finally published by the N.R.C. at the end of November together with a White Paper giving the N.R.C.'s statement thereon. On November 27th, I sent the following cable to Colonel Blake of the N.R.C.:

" Have just seen copy N.R.C. two-months-late statement on Dove-Edwin. N.R.C. statement full of inconsistencies and elementary illogicalities. In public interest suggest you use your influence secure N.R.C. review of whole situation so avoid widespread revolt against N.R.C. flagrant breach of faith as indicated in proposed White paper. For N.R.C. to level accusations not only against Governor-General but against Chairman of your own appointed commission is the height of reckless irresponsibility and impertinence. Beg remind you and other members N.R.C. that severally and collectively all members responsible for contents of White Paper. Sincerely hope common sense will yet prevail even though time running out swiftly."

On December 6th, under the auspices of the Movement for Colonial Freedom, I addressed an audience in a committee room at the House of Commons. Commenting on the Dove-Edwin Report and the White Paper I pointed out that the reaction of the N.R.C., in the face of the overwhelming and corroborated evidence in favour of the A.P.C., was to appoint yet another Commission, this time a 54-man Civilian Rule Committee. "It is my considered opinion," I declared, "that this new Commission is nothing but a time-saving device designed to keep the military regime in power for as long as possible."

The terms of reference of the Committee were to deliberate and advise on the necessity for a new general election; if this was found to be unnecessary, then to devise a method of forming a national government; if an election was advocated, then to work out the stages by which the hand-over should be effected.

"Would it not be a complete reversal of democracy," I asked, "if a patently unwieldy 54-man Committee should be asked to adjudicate, so to speak, on the necessity for a fresh general election, after the electorate has gone to the polls and elected the citizens who should represent them in a new Parliament?" As a politician, I said, I found no difficulty in reading between the lines. "Once it is agreed that a fresh general election should be held," I said, "it would be almost automatic for the N.R.C. to say that *we are most willing to hold fresh elections,*

271

but there is no money. And so the Military Junta would continue in office until God knows when. I say so because it is well-known that the national kitty is nearly empty. ..."

The composition of the Civilian Rule Commitee was, apart from six A.P.C. members, composed entirely of N.R.C. nominees and S.L.P.P. supporters and sympathisers. The A.P.C., which won 32 seats in the elections, was to get equal representation on the Committee with the six Independents, whose only quarrel with the S.L.P.P. had been concerning its now deposed leader, and with the S.L.P.P. which won less seats than the A.P.C. The N.R.C. was to be represented by three members of its Advisory Council and was to select three persons from each of the three Provinces; three Paramount Chiefs were to be selected by the chiefs in each of the three Provinces and one person from each of the twelve Districts was to be selected by the Committee of Management of each District; the members of which had been hand-picked by the N.R.C.

Three days previously I had cabled two of my party members in Freetown concerning the injustice of the representation on this Committee:

" Proposed Civilian Council would be weighted against A.P.C. right from start. Apart from fact that selections done mostly by N.R.C., which has vested interests in points at issue, the six Independents who go on Council are all S.L.P.P. which gives S.L.P.P. twelve votes as a party against A.P.C. six. Also it appears wicked that Independents should command six votes while S.L.P.P. and A.P.C. get only six votes each. Please also note that three Paramount Chiefs from each Province means six votes for Southern areas and three Northern and one representative per district means seven for South and five North.

"In other words representation on Civilian Council from defeated Southern areas mostly S.L.P.P. would outweigh votes from the generally victorious northern areas and, human nature being what it is, defeated areas may well feel that rather than their A.P.C. opponents take power let it go elsewhere. Also what is need for three members from the practically defunct Advisory Council whose members had been originally hand-picked by N.R.C.?"

Re-reading the cable recalls to my mind the unease I felt over the proposed Council and the difficulty I experienced trying to keep in touch from my exile's perch. I felt isolated and helpless. I pointed out in my cable that the Civilian Council would be deliberately weighted against the A.P.C. from the start: the N.R.C. would control appointments; the so-called 'Independents' would be crypto-S.L.P.P. supporters; the proportions in which Independents and rival parties would be represented on the Council would bear no relationship to the distribution of votes at the General Election. The South would be grotesquely over-represented, with twice as many Paramount Chief members than the rest of the country, and a clear majority over the rest of the country of District representatives.

I pointed out that we had no guarantees that even in this heavily biased form the Council would be respected by the N.R.C., which had already turned against one organisation of its own, the Dove-Edwin Commission. The terms of reference of the Council seemed to clash with the declared policy of the N.R.C., which had already indicated that it would not surrender power before another general election. And it was doubtful whether the Council's brief was compatible with the Constitution, which could not be altered without electoral approval.

I was glad of one aspect of the new Council: the A.P.C. was at last to be permitted to organise openly again after a ban on all parties imposed by the military regime. I thanked God for that at least. But I was very doubtful of the wisdom of our taking part in a highly suspicious exercise.

"It is my considered opinion," I cabled my colleagues, "that A.P.C. would be committing political suicide to rush into proposed Civilian Council as at present constituted and with selection of most members in hands of N.R.C." But I was careful to leave the question open-ended. Feeling remote from the pulse of events, I did not want to hamper the freedom of judgement of party colleagues who were on the spot. I relayed my qualms from a distance and left the final decision to them. "Use this cable as you think fit," I telegraphed, "but do not allow yourselves to be rushed on this life-and-death issue. I am entirely at Party's service."

At the end of the day, the A.P.C. decided to take part after extracting firm assurances of the sincerity of the N.R.C.'s intentions. In the event, I think this turned out to be the right course of action. It kept our party in touch with events and gave us a stake in the running of the country. It was conceived partly as a device to keep us out of control; but it also gave us an opportunity to prevent the monopolisation of control by others.

From London, I also fired off a heavy pamphlet salvo against the military rulers. The pamphlet which caused most controversy was entitled *The Military Seizure of Power in Sierra Leone* and was published on November 27th, 1967. In it I pulled no punches in condemning the military take-over and concluded with the following words:

> *Today the slogan in Sierra Leone should be: Immediate return to Civilian Rule or no co-operation with the so-called National Reformation Council which is violating our sacred Constitution and trying to replace the ballot box with guns and bayonets.*

Understandably this pamphlet met with much criticism from members of the N.R.C., among them the Commissioner of Police, William Leigh. The last thing I wanted was to create an antagonistic atmosphere, to sow the seeds of a cold war between myself and the N.R.C. But I did not apologise for, nor retract, what I had written. If the words were somewhat harsh I believed this was the only effective way to get my message through, but I wrote a personal and confidential letter to Leigh on 12th December explaining why I had found it necessary to do what I had done.

" Dear Bill," I wrote.

"Ever since that day (March 21) when, on my appointment as Prime Minister, I had a personal talk with you, I feel sure you would agree that much has happened; the blame for which it would be difficult to lay at the door of any one person or other. In my own case and in regard to my latest pamphlet, *The Military Seizure of Power in Sierra Leone*, about which I understand you have made some comments, I was forced to take this line of action because, among other things, of the terribly long delay on the part of the N.R.C. in publishing the Report of the Dove-Edwin Commission, a delay which created the feeling that the Council was determined to remain in power indefinitely.

"Now that the Report, with a White Paper, has been published, and without committing myself or my party in any way, I feel that in the national interest, I could reconsider my attitude to the whole situation. In this respect, I propose to return home at an early date with a view to making my own little contribution to a solution of the difficulties now confronting the country.

"I think you know me sufficiently well to realise that, as an experienced and responsible politician, I must appreciate that once the constitutional position is restored and a return to civilian rule effected within the ambit of the Constitution which is the repository and safeguard of the rights and liberties of the people, then it would be in nobody's interest to do anything which could lead to a resurrection of bitterness. I can assure you that for my part, I am prepared to do everything possible to see that the hatchet is buried and all sections to the dispute given a fair chance for a fresh start devoid of fear and recrimination.

"I am addressng this letter to you personally because I am more acquainted with you than any other member of the N.R.C. and I know from experience that it is private contacts of this nature which could create the proper atmosphere in which any official action would depend for its success."

I did not, however, return immediately to Sierra Leone, for word reached me that if I did so I would be arrested. Instead I flew to Guinea where I was offered hospitality by President Sekou Toure. My departure from London and non-arrival in Freetown caused much speculation as to my whereabouts. Matchet's Diary in *West Africa* of December 30th, reported from Freetown as follows:

"'Search for PM continues' announced a headline in the *Daily Mail* here. It was referring to the melancholy fate of Harold Holt, the late Australian Prime Minister; but it could have been referring to Sierra Leone. For while some people here find it hard to believe that the soldiers and policemen of the National Reformation Council are ready to return power to the civilians less than 9 months after taking over, there is wide acceptance of the view that if the politicians can now get together, the 'civilian rule committee' which is to work out a method for handover, can present the military with a programme which they cannot reject and which would mean that the last West African country to establish military rule was the first to end it. But if the politicians are to play their part, only Siaka Stevens, leader of the All People's Congress, whose victory at the elections was recognised by the Dove-Edwin Commission, can lead them. And he is still not here, although he left London last week. ..."

I maintained regular contact with my party stalwarts in Freetown, many of whom urged me to return home. But I felt that this would be premature. The people were already keyed up over the possibility of the hand-over of power to a civilian government and the formation of the Civilian Rule Committee at least gave them hope that something concrete was being done towards this end. But for me to appear on the scene before the machinery had been properly set up for a peaceful and orderly hand-over could have wrecked the whole thing as far as we of the A.P.C. were concerned. There was no doubt that I would be wildly acclaimed and greeted with much jubiliation by a large section of the people but this might very well be misinterpreted by the N.R.C. as a breakdown of law and order and so provide them with an admirable excuse for prolonging their rule.

The A.P.C. members of the Civilian Rule Committee were: S.I. Koroma, C. A. Kamara-Taylor, Solomon Pratt, Cyril Foray, S. B. Kawusu Conteh and S. Gandi Cappio. Briefing them from Conakry through the Secretary-General of my party, C. A. Kamara-Taylor, I gave them the following five points to digest:

" 1 There is no need for any 'cap-in-hand' attitude on the part of any of our men," I wrote. "We have the Constitution and, more important, the masses behind us and therefore we can bargain and speak from a position of strength.

2 We should not compromise on any of the important issues such as that of P.M. etc., and for heaven's sake, don't any of you try to bring in topics which are not on the agenda or the terms of reference.

3 When a person on our side starts asking who the other side wants for P.M., I can only believe that such a person is working for other interests.

4 There are strong rumours that one or two of our men are in regular consultation with people on the other sides against A.P.C. interests. So everyone must be careful. Our men and women outside hear more than we, the leaders, can hear.

5 Should the C.R.C. attempt to take any unconstitutional action, our men should have no hesitation in getting out of it, lest the people should say that we were a party to matters against the interest of the Party."

I urged them to be particularly vigilant at this critical juncture and to get everything on record. I followed this up by emphasising the point that none of our men must serve on any Military/Civilian Commission such as obtained in Ghana. "Rule this out completely," I said. "If they want to hand over, let them hand over. If they do not want to do so, then let them not do so. There must be no half measures in this." I was still being pressurised to return immediately to Sierra Leone, but I, personally, did not think it was yet the time to do so.

The Civilian Rule Committee was due to sit on February 21st, 1968. On February 10th, banner headlines in the local *Daily Mail* asked: *11 Days to D-Day — Why is Shaki not Here?* The question persistently being asked, it declared, was: "Why is Mr. Siaka Stevens, who may be expected to play an important role in advising one of the group delegations or settling differences between them, still not here?"

I let it be known to the people that the A.P.C., much against its will, had decided to put in an appearance at the Committee in order not to be misrepresented to the outside world. It was attending, however, only on the distinct understanding that nothing should be done by the C.R.C. which would interfere with the Constitution. By this the A.P.C. meant that the only way in which constitutional civilian rule could be restored in Sierra Leone was by recalling and re-installing the Governor-General as the representative of the Head of State and by handing over power to the constitutionally appointed Prime Minister.

"The question arises," I said, "suppose the N.R.C. continue to refuse to take this line of action and insist on governing the country by guns and bayonets bought with our own taxes? The answer is simple. We, the people, must refuse to work with it. We must show this Army-Police junta that no people or nation has ever been governed without the consent and co-operation of the governed. We must stage sit-down strikes and take any other action short of violence to make these people see their errors. From now on every soldier or civilian who actively co-operates with this illegal regime must realise that he or she is working against the interest of the country, and I hereby issue a special call to Sierra Leonean citizens in the armed forces to show their loyalty to the State of Sierra Leone and not to a handful of officers who are fighting for their pockets and for power. I call upon everyone to realise that to overthrow a subversive millitary clique such as has seized power in our country is a patriotic duty of the first order. To fight against a duly elected constitutional government is subversion, but to fight against an illegally constiuted government is a duty which every soldier and citizen should be proud to undertake."

As regards the A.P.C. delegation to the N.R.C. Civilian Rule Committee, I prepared a statement for the leader to make at the opening session, as follows:

"Fellow Citizens of Sierra Leone," it began

"On behalf of the All People's Congress, I bring you sincerest greetings from the Central Executive of the Party."

After summarising the events of the General Election, my appointment as Prime Minister, and the coup, my statement declared that the A.P.C. consented to take part in the Civilian Rule Committee only out of respect for our fellow citizens and to place on record the formalities of a constitutional return to civilian rule." It went on to state that:

"It is the considered view of the A.P.C., and I respectfully invite you to agree, that in the present circumstances the only constitutional way by which the country can return to civilian rule is:

(a) For the Governor-General to be invited back to Sierra Leone by the N.R.C. to resume his office as the *de facto* as well as the *de jure* representative of the Head of State.

(b) The reins of government to be handed over to the legal government headed by the Prime Minister without any restrictions being imposed as to choice of a government.

"I am further directed to make the point that the A.P.C. is fully aware of the need for the various sections of the community to be represented on any government that is to be formed if the government is to enjoy the confidence of the people.

"I would finally like to remind you that the world being what it is, men and women cannot but have their individual loyalties and prejudices. And it is only in the Constitution that these differences are compromised for the greatest good of the greatest number. If we dare now to tamper with this Constitution without due process of law, we shall not only be endangering our own lives and liberties but we shall be laying a very dangerous precedent for our children.

"I make this statement in the national interest."

As the weeks went by, reports reached me that people were becoming more and more depressed with the drop in living standards and more convinced than ever that despite the appointment of the Civilian Rule Committee, many of the members of the N.R.C. were doing far too well for themselves willingly to loosen their grip on the reins of power. The rank and file of the army and the police were particularly disgruntled when they compared their bread-line conditions with the obvious prosperity enjoyed by their officers.

Bolstered by my reassurance to them that it was the duty of every soldier and citizen to fight an illegally constituted government, a number of NCO's overthrew the military regime on the night of April 17th, 1968, by arresting all their officers and forming what they called the Anti-Corruption Revolutionary Movement. A few days later, under the leadership of Ambrose Genda, whom they recalled from his ambassadorial post in Liberia, and Col. Bangura, who had been released from gaol and was then with me in Guinea, they formed the National Interim Council, installed the Speaker, Banja Tejan-Sie, as 'officer performing the functions of Governor-General' (Sir Henry Lightfoot Boston has already retired from the post on account of ill-health and no new Governor-General had yet been appointed to replace him), and invited me to return and form the Government.

From my position in the wings I had awaited my cue patiently and confidently for thirteen long months. Now that the moment had arrived for me to appear on stage with the full glare of the floodlights upon me, before a vast audience who expected from me a first-rate performance, I began to have doubts about my worthiness for such a leading role.

CHAPTER FIFTEEN

Constitutional Government Restored

I arrived back in Freetown on the evening of April 24th, 1968. Although I had managed to undertake the journey without attracting undue attention, as soon as I stepped into my house news of my arrival spread around town like wild fire. Before long crowds of people had flooded into the compound and penetrated my house, cheering, dancing and singing, some even weeping, as they expressed in their various ways their joy at the end of thirteen months of military rule.

I could not resist a thrill of personal pride at the reception my people gave me. But I knew my homecoming was only a symbol of a great victory for democracy: I had to try not to see it as a personal triumph. What touched me most was the popular nature of the demonstration which greeted me. Here were ordinary men and women of the sort among whom I had lived and worked all my life, taking spontaneous pleasure in their right to choose their own government — the very right which I had devoted my political career to winning for them. Their joy was infectious. I felt a bit more encouraged in a task which daunted me when I set out from Conakry.

Albert Margai flew in from London the following day and on April 26th, I was once again sworn in as Prime Minister of Sierra Leone. On the same day a meeting was held between all members of the A.P.C. and the S.L.P.P., as well as the Independents, who were elected in the 1967 general election, to decide how best we could serve the nation during the very difficult days that lay ahead of us all. One thing was very clear to me: in the critical state our country was in, peace and stability were of paramount importance to its survival as a nation, and we simply could not afford to wrangle among ourselves over party issues. Wounds were already being licked among the S.L.P.P. parliamentary group who had fought angrily at a meeting at which the leadership of their party had passed from Albert Margai to Salia Jusu-Sheriff. In my view this was not the time for bitterness and rivalry; we *had* to pull together at the

280

moment no matter what our personal, tribal or political attitudes.

Although many of my staunchest Party members were against a National Government, I felt that at this particular time in our history the government should be composed of representatives of both political parties plus some of the Independents, in proportion to their representation in Parliament. Only by this means, I believed, could differences be hammered out reasonably, responsibly and privately around the Cabinet table, and effective compromises arrived at. The alternative, publicly to call down fire and brimstone on one's political opponents, could only serve to exacerbate the existing tense situation. The political arena was pretty densely crowded, but I thought it better to make space inside than start trying to throw people out.

At the conclusion of the four-hour meeting I made my first broadcast to the nation as Prime Minister.

" Fellow Citizens," I said, "I am glad to be able to broadcast to you as Prime Minister of Sierra Leone. I am sure that we are grateful to the members of the Anti-Corruption Revolutionary Movement and the National Interim Council for the great part they have played in bringing back constitutional government to this country. Their names and deeds will go down in history.

"All your elected Parliamentarians met today and agreed to set up a National Government. This has not been an easy task but I ask you to believe that it is the best solution in the present circumstances.

"I shall broadcast to you again in greater detail but just now it is my duty to tell you that the best way you can help me, help the Government and the people is by keeping law and order. If you keep the peace and refrain from molesting people and attacking their property, you will have done very well indeed. God bless you all."

After the swearing-in ceremony at the State House I was driven around the city to greet the people as their reinstated Prime Minister. In many places the crowds were such that the surface of solid concrete and tarmac beneath them became totally invisible and all one could see was a swirling, multi-coloured tide of humanity moving as rhythmically as an ocean as body tightly wedged against body responded to the beat of drums and the sound of music. It was a day of great jubilation and I gave instructions that the curfew that had been imposed by the military regime should be lifted forthwith so that the people could celebrate to the full the end of military rule and the seventh anniversary of our Independence which, strangely enough, occurred the following day. I made reference to this in the broadcast talk I gave that evening.

"My dear people," I said. "I believe that it is providential coincidence that the seventh anniversary of the Independence of this our dear country should coincide with the return to constitutional rule. Indeed 'God moves in a mysterious way His wonders to perform.'

"A few months ago the future of this country was very bleak. But today we can say that with the help of the Anti-Corruption Revolutionary Movement and the National Interim Council, we have again been put on the constitutional rails.

"I feel certain that when the history of this country comes to be written the heroic service rendered by these gallant men will get an honourable mention in the records and these comrades of ours can rest assured that we will always remember them.

"Tonight my mind is full and I cannot say much to you. My mind is full because I think that with the appointment and swearing-in this afternoon I have created a world record of being a twice appointed and twice sworn-in Prime Minister. I have every reason to believe that the special circumstances surrounding my appointment might be a portent for the future.

"Obviously there is not much that we can celebrate today. The kitty is empty and I think you will agree with me that what is necessary at this time is that we should gird our loins and prepare ourselves for the strenuous task that lies ahead to put this country on a sound financial basis. Our political independence will not mean much if our economy is ruined.

"Be that as it may, we are grateful to the Almight Allah for the guidance he has given us, without which this country would have been in a far worse plight than it is today. It is for us now, therefore, to resolve to forget the past, to work for the present and to look to the future, so that this blessed country of ours will be able to take her rightful place amongst nations of the world in general. We have it in our power to put Sierra Leone in her rightful place on the map. Let us therefore pull together."

I think that broadcast was a big milestone in my life. It represented my first real chance to speak to my people as I had always wanted to be able to speak to them. It also marked the beginning of a new relationship I would build with them over long years of service as Head of Government and Head of State. I already felt in my heart a half-formed wish to create just such a realtionship, with the hope that God would give me the time in which to do it. I felt I could sense the beginnings of a symbiosis between me, my Party and my people, not for the sake of my own vainglory but for the sake of national unity and a new political set-up which would bring lasting stability. I kept the broadcast simple. I wanted to speak to the people directly, in familiar words and images. I wanted to convey the depth of my emotions in terms everyone could understand. I felt a suppressed exaltation as I prepared my script and read it before the microphone. But, in spite of all the qualms and controls checking what I was saying and how I said it, I think I succeeded in speaking from the heart.

On April 29th and 30th, I announced the names of my Ministers of the new Government. The total number of Ministers and Deputy Ministers was larger by three than the total number in the last civilian Government because, having been obliged to form a National Government, it was necessary to make selections over a wide area, an area representative of the different elements comprising our community. My first Cabinet Members were:-

A.P.C.:
>Dr. Mohammed Forna - Finance
>S. W. C. Gandi-Capio - Interior
>C. A. Kamara-Taylor - Lands, Mines & Labour
>D. F. Shears - Transport & Communications
>J. Hadson-Taylor - Information & Broadcasting
>Solomon Pratt - Development
>S. I. Koroma - Trade & Industry
>S. A. Fofana - Housing & Country Planning

S.L.P.P.:
>S. Jusu-Sheriff - Health
>R. B. Kowa - Education
>S. L. Matturi - Works
>Dr. Momoh Conteh - Social Welfare

Independents:
L. A. M. Brewah - External Affairs
F. S. Anthony - Agriculture & Natural Resources

Paramount Chiefs:
PC Bai Koblo Pathbana III - Minister without Portfolio
PC J. Kai-Kai - Minister without Portfolio
PC J. J. Gaima - Minister without Portfolio

Criticism was levelled at me from some quarters that my Party had more than its fair share of portfolios, but it must be remembered that the two Independent members had already made it clear that they would have declared themselves for the S.L.P.P. but for Albert Margai's leadership of that party, and now that he had been removed from that office there was little doubt about where their sympathies would lie, which increased the S.L.P.P. representation to six against the A.P.C.'s eight.

To compensate for the increase of three in my Government, and in view of the difficult financial situation in the country, I decided we had to set an example of austerity. I reduced my own salary by Le1,000 (£500) per annum and that of Ministers by Le500 (£250) per annum, and announced that proportionate reductions would be made all along the line except for ordinary Members of Parliament whose emoluments would remain at Le1,840 (£920).

A few weeks later, information reached me that people who could not accept the fact that they were no longer in power were trying to get some of the Anti-Corruption Revolutionary leaders to join them in stirring up trouble. They were holding meetings in various parts of the country at all hours of the night and appeared to be getting considerable financial backing from somewhere. I had pleaded with these disruptive elements over and over again through my speeches to various delegations which had visited me and through reports of these speeches in the press, but to no avail. On May 31st, I considered the situation dangerous enough to alert the people and I warned them in a broadcast talk of the presence of these saboteurs of our national effort. None of us could afford to ignore the threat to our peaceful development that such elements posed, and if sweet reason failed to bring them around, then stronger measures would have to be taken.

" The time has now come," I concluded my broadcast, "when, as a Government, we are determined to govern. The time has now come when we must fulfil our obligations to the public in general for peace and tranquility in the land. The time has now come when the people of this country must be given the opportunity to go about their work and to sleep at night in peace. And I want to assure you all, my fellow citizens, that the Government will not shirk its responsibility in this respect. Law-abiding citizens have nothing to fear."

I then called on one and all to be on the alert and to bring to the notice of the authorities anything which tended to disrupt the peace.

The following month news reached me from a reliable source in London that a substantial force of mercenaries of several nationalities were planning to invade Sierra Leone and this necessitated another broadcast warning to the people to be watchful and to be prepared to defend our country whatever the cost. "Eternal vigilance is the price we have to pay for liberty," I told them.

That the invasion did not take place in no way proved that it was never in fact planned. As I have learnt to my cost, those who sought to displace me, my Party and Government, were utterly ruthless in the lengths they were prepared to go to to achieve their goal. The whole success of such an invasion depends on the surprise element and the fact that so much publicity was given to it beforehand, both here and abroad, was enough to deter the most intrepid adventurer.

During the unsettled period of 1968, I was apprehensive not just of the threat to our fragile democracy but also of my own reaction to insecurity. I was wary of going too far, of responding too severely. After struggling against authoritarianism during the previous regime, I did not want to undo my own work. But in retrospect, I think I probably erred on the side of mildness. At the time, of course, I could not foresee how hard it would be to govern in peace. I did not realise that unreconciled elements would try again and again to overthrow democracy. I did not realise how tenacious divisive tribalism would be. I was trying to act with just the right amount of energy and moderation to contain subversion. But later I would often think that harsher action earlier might have pre-empted some of the terrible crises we still had to face.

As a result of election petitions at the Supreme Court, twenty successful S.L.P. candidates in the 1967 election, among them three of my Ministers, had their elections declared null and void on the grounds that the elections had been rigged. This made it necessary to reallocate three of the portfolios and I gave that of Health to J. Barthes-Wilson and appointed Paramount Chiefs J. Gaima and Bai Koblo Pathbana III Acting Ministers of Works and Social Welfare respectively. The total number of Ministers was thus reduced by two, and the declared S.L.P.P. representatives by three.

The first thing I endeavoured to project to the masses was that the new Government was a Government for every section of the community, a Government for chiefs and non-chiefs, a Government for rich and poor and a Government for all tribes. I warned that those who refused to accept the verdict of the ballot box, who believed that the good things in the country were theirs by birthright, who refused to reconcile themselves to the changed conditions of the day and who tried to cover up their wicked deeds against the nation by arousing tribal sympathies, would be firmly dealt with by my Government.

"All men and women are equal in the eyes of the law and in the eyes of our Government," I declared. "While we will not tolerate disrespect for authority, we are at the same time determined to see that the ordinary man and woman is not molested by those in authority." We were determined to see that local native courts were not used to bring suffering on defenceless people, that the farmers and workers received a just reward for their produce and labours, that the chiefdom councils were truly representative of the people and not just selected to satisfy vested interests, that the chiefs put the people before their own personal interests and that the civil servants and the police did their job serving the interests of the nation.

We pledged ourselves to improve the education and training of the young on whom the future of our country would depend, and to see that our women took their proper place in the community, for "no nation can rise above the level of its womanhood," I said. Non-Sierra Leoneans resident amongst us would be given every protection, but my Government would expect them to identify themselves with the national interest and not interfere with our policies.

The main task of my Government on taking office was to endeavour to consolidate the position regarding the army and the police. Security and the maintenance of law and order were vital to successful administration; and the country had to be protected from the danger of another coup. In the short space of 13 months there had been at least three upheavals in the army. When we took over,the entire officer corps, both in the army and in the police, were in detention, and one can imagine the difficulties with which we were faced from the start.

We released 48 of the police arrested after the coup and 33 of these were taken back into the force. The position was not so easy with regard to the army officers who had instigated the coup, for justice demanded that they account for their mutinous and treasonable action in open court.

Another matter, closely bound up with security, that demanded our urgent attention was border control. The ease with which foreigners could enter and leave Sierra Leone was astonishing and consequently smuggling was a very paying concern to those who indulged in it, but an appalling loss of revenue to the country. We took immediate steps to strengthen patrols in the border areas, especially the Liberian border, and reviewed the whole matter of customs posts. With regard to illegal immigrants, particularly in the diamond areas, an all-out effort was launched to drive such strangers away.

Some sectors of the services, that is to say, the civil service, the army and the police, were, for various reasons, not performing their duties in the best traditions of those services. Information and secret documents were being leaked out and our work as a Government was sabotaged as a result. Such behaviour on the part of a few cast a lot of suspicion on many innocent people and created inefficiency in the services generally. This meant that the attention and energy which Government should have given to the execution of the work of government had to be diverted at times to the taking of precautions here and there against people who were working against the interests of the State. I tried to impress upon such people that when they indulged in such activities they were working not only against the interests of the Government but against the interests of the State and the Nation, and, ultimately, of course, themselves.

Agriculture was, still is, and must be for a long time to come, of vital concern to our Government. So much attention had been paid in the past to experimental methods of cultivation that the production of many crops had fallen off alarmingly. I advocated that it was time to move away from the field of experimentation to the field of reality and to concentrate on increasing the production of rice and other necessary foodstuffs. It was the declared aim of my Government to help farmers to grow more and better rice so that we would never again have to import it from abroad; to distribute high-yielding palm seedlings and encourage them to grow better strains of coffee and cocoa and to improve tobacco plants; to increase and improve the cattle population and to develop our fishing resources.

ABOVE, MY TRIUMPHANT RETURN TO SIERRA LEONE TO TAKE OVER FOR THE SECOND TIME THE POST TO WHICH I HAD BEEN ELECTED. BELOW, ADDRESSING PARLIAMENT WHEN IT MET FOR THE FIRST TIME AFTER THE OVERTHROW OF THE MILITARY REGIME.

ABOVE, A CANDLELIGHT PROCESSION IN FREETOWN TO CELEBRATE THE RETURN TO CIVILIAN RULE UNDER THE A.P.C. GOVERNMENT AND, BELOW, A PARTY AT THE WORKERS' UNION HALL IN DAN STREET TO MARK THE EVENT.

ABOVE, A CELEBRATION BY PARTY SUPPORTERS TO MARK THE BIRTHDAY OF THE A.P.C. AT MY LEFT IS THE LATE BORBOR KAMARA, ONE OF OUR STAUNCHEST AND MOST EFFECTIVE PARTY WORKERS. BELOW, PEOPLE OF ALL AGES STROLL THROUGH THE STREETS AFTER A THANKSGIVING SERVICE.

LEFT, MY FIRST BROAD-CAST TO THE NATION AS PRIME MINISTER, BELOW, A VISIT TO THE BENGUEMA MILITARY CAMP SHORTLY AFTER MY RETURN TO SIERRA LEONE.

ABOVE, RECEIVING AT STATE HOUSE A GROUP OF ALHAJIS AND ALHAJAS WHO WISHED TO CONGRATULATE ME ON MY RETURN AND REAPPOINTMENT AS PRIME MINISTER AND, BELOW, A GRAPHIC WELCOME FROM AN A.P.C. YOUTH BRANCH.

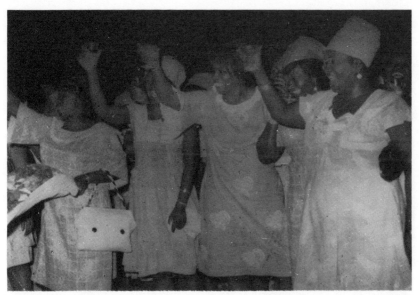

ABOVE, MEMBERS OF THE WOMEN'S MOVEMENT SIERRA LEONE BRANCH GIVE A PARTY IN MY HONOUR A FEW WEEKS AFTER MY RETURN AND, BELOW, WOMEN FROM NYAGUA, IN THE EASTERN PROVINCE, WHO WELCOMED ME WHEN I VISITED KENEMA.

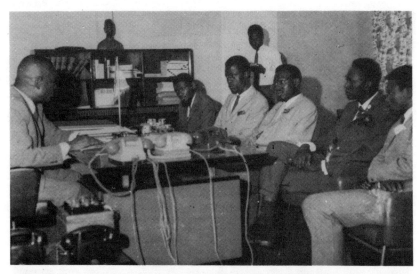

DELEGATIONS FROM ALL PARTS OF THE COUNTRY AND ALL WALKS OF LIFE CALL AT MY OFFICE TO EXPRESS SUPPORT AND CONGRATULATIONS ON MY RETURN. ABOVE, A GROUP FROM THE A.P.C. NATIONAL YOUTH LEAGUE AND, BELOW, FROM THE CO-OPERATIVE UNION OF PORT LOKO, IN THE KAMBIA DISTRICT.

*AS SOON AS PARLIAMENT RESUMED ITS WORK AFTER THE RETURN TO CONSTITU-
TIONAL RULE, MEMBERS OF THE HOUSE HELD A SERVICE OF DEDICATION TO MARK
THE EVENT (ABOVE) AND CHURCH LEADERS CALLED ON ME TO EXPRESS CONFIDENCE
AND SUPPORT (BELOW).*

OTHERS WHO CAME TO CONGRATULATE ME INCLUDED STUDENT REPRESENTATIVES FROM NJALA UNIVERSITY (ABOVE) AND HEADS OF DIPLOMATIC MISSIONS IN SIERRA LEONE, SUCH AS THE SOVIET AMBASSADOR (BELOW).

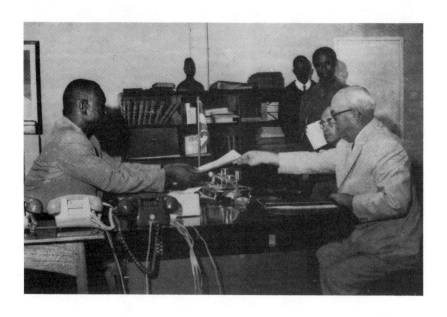

REPRESENTATIVES OF THE SIERRA LEONE LABOUR CONGRESS (ABOVE) WERE AMONG THE FIRST TO CALL ON ME AT STATE HOUSE AT THE END OF APRIL 1968 TO WISH ME SUCCESS IN MY TASK AND THEY WERE FOLLOWED, DAY AFTER DAY, BY HUNDREDS OF OTHER GROUPS, SUCH AS THE ALHAJIS AND ALHAJAS OF PORT LOKO (BELOW).

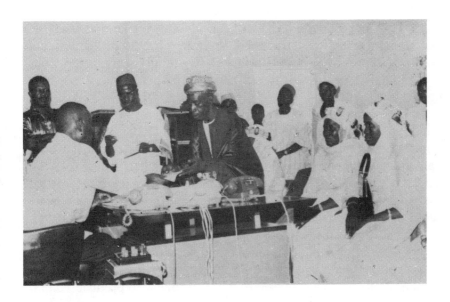

Improvement in agriculture and the living conditions of agricultural labourers would go a long way to solving the problem of the high rate of unemployment in the cities. There was a serious dearth of labour in the rural areas but until conditions for the farming community improved, until more and better roads were built and road transport could operate in the outlying areas, it would be difficult to encourage those out of work in the urban areas to move out into the countryside.

Health, eduation, housing, bridge building, everywhere one looked, something screamed out for urgent attention. Yet where in Heaven's name was the money to come from to finance such development? Previous administrations had left behind them not only an empty till but crippling commitments to pay huge debts and interests on useless pre-financed schemes. For instance, there was the West African Shoe and Rubber Industries Limited (WASRIL) which was first conceived in January, 1964, when certain foreign industrialists proposed the construction of a factory to produce annually some 680,000 pairs of shoes and sandals all with rubber soles.

Thoughtlessly, the previous Government fell for the scheme without considering other alternatives. The organisation which put forward the proposal was the same organisation which executed the project. No tenders were invited, nor were any studies made of similar offers. The final estimated cost was considerably higher than that first quoted and the total construction costs were covered by the issue of promissory notes by WASRIL which were guaranteed by the previous Government to be repaid over a period of five years at 8 per cent interest.

My Government, therefore, found itself with a veritable millstone round its neck. A factory on which Le533,588 (£266,794) had been spent without a single pair of shoes having been produced from it, whose plant and equipment, not to mention the building itself, were found in fact to be incapable of producing the number of shoes envisaged. What was worse, money had to be spent each year on guarding this white elephant from thieves and protecting the idle machinery from deteriorating too badly. Needless to say, the organisation which sponsored the project went into liquidation abroad and ceased to exist.

Secondly, there was the oil refinery. In 1962, the Shell Oil Company submitted a proposal to build a refinery to produce 10,000 barrels a day at an estimated cost of about Le3m., and proposed a 50-50 investment structure between the Sierra Leone Government and the oil company. While this proposal was being studied by the previous civilian Government, another foreign concern put forward a proposal to erect a 100 per cent Government-owned oil refinery of the same capacity, but at a cost of Le6m., that is to say, double the proposal of Shell. For some extraordinary reason best known to the previous Government, it rejected the Shell offer in favour of the latter proposal. In this instance tenders were in fact invited and several reputable firms submitted proposals, one of them actually putting forward suggestions whereby the specification and economics of the proposed refinery could be improved, but by some mysterious exercise of ministerial discretion, the previous Government did not even see fit to get local experts to assist the consultants in the selection of the contractor from among those who had tendered; it appointed a firm of contractors recommended by the foreign concern in question, *who had not even tendered.* By now the contract price had risen to Le6.9m. The foreign organisation appointed not only the consultants to supervise the work, but also the managers to operate the refinery and produce oil after completion of the works.

When my Government came into office the entire operation was a complete shambles and we had to start all over again before we could get the refinery properly completed, tested and working. The refinery would now cost Government about Le7.5m. This would not have been too bad if the refinery could have been operated profitably and at full capacity, but unfortunately investigations indicated that it could only be operated at around 40 to 50 per cent capacity and that even at this level of operation, there would be a lot of surplus products to be disposed of outside Sierra Leone, and a shortage of certain products for local consumption which would continue to be imported. In short, for the next four or five years the refinery would, under the best of management, operate at a loss of well over Le3.5m. Indeed, the indications were that unless we embarked upon financial outlays, it might not start making a profit for six or seven years to come.

Our third headache was the Cape Sierra Hotel; a project that was first conceived sometime in 1960 when it was felt that a tourist hotel would attract visitors to Sierra Leone, bring in foreign exchange and enhance the prestige of the country. The same foreign firm who got the oil refinery contract put forward proposals for the construction of such a hotel at a total estimated cost of around Le1,500,000 (£750,000). The Government of the day was captivated by the scheme and, as it was to be pre-financed, no tenders were invited. A firm of foreign consultants was appointed and the National Construction Company of Sierra

Leone acted both as contractors and as local representatives. The project was declared completed in June, 1967, at a cost of Le1,400,000 (£700,000), yet it was never opened. It stood bleak and deserted at the mercy of the elements for it was said that the sleeping accommodation of 75 beds was not considered to be enough to attract an international tourist organisation to operate the hotel and certain facilities had yet to be added, such as servants quarters, improvements in public rooms and the construction of additional tourist facilities. In addition, the cost of operating the hotel was found to be prohibitive, especially as a tourist industry had not yet been developed in the country. It seems inconceivable that such vital factors were not taken into consideration before such an ambitious project was embarked upon, both by the Government and the contractors. In the event, my Government had to guarantee the repayment of Le1,400,000 with interest over a period of seven years even though the hotel was not earning a single cent.

Another dead loss we inherited was a cement factory. The Sierra Leone Cement Works Limited owed its existence to the same foreign concern when, in 1963, it sold to the Government of the day the idea that if a factory could be established to process clinker and other materials imported cheaply from abroad and utilising local labour, the price of cement would be reduced. At that time, cement was being sold at about 80 cents a bag, and it was envisaged that the operation would result in a reduction of the price to 70 or 75 cents per bag. As before, the previous civilian Government readily accepted the proposals of this particular firm. From the outset the company was a failure. After a number of intricate financial arrangements made with foreign financial organisations, it got itself deeper and deeper in debt. Even though it was not paying its way, it continued to pay a management fee to an outside organisation based on total financial transactions passing through its books, whether or not the management achieved a profit. My Government was faced with guaranteeing the repayment of Le1,500,000 (£750,000) while the price of cement was reaching a prohibitive level and was so scarce that we were forced to import it.

The same foreign concern was responsible for establishing the Metal Assembly Limited to produce metal doors and window frames which should, admittedly, have reduced building costs, introduced new skills and saved some precious foreign exchange. But again, the previous Government invited no tenders for the project and blindly accepted the terms of the same party. The Metal Assembly Limited went the way of all other projects with which this particular firm was involved in Sierra Leone. The company became illiquid and was not even able to redeem Government-guaranteed promissory notes. The accumulated loss when my Government came into power was some Le122,000, though this could well have been considerably higher if the inflated values of the company's fixed assets had been readjusted. And over and above these mounting losses annually incurred by the company, we were faced with the prospect that well over Le500,000 stood to disappear down the metal drain.

With such reckless expenditure there had been nothing left to provide for the vital needs of the country, such as payment of hard cash to the farmers for their produce, and we found ourselves saddled with honouring paper chits that had been given them in lieu of cash.

I went to some lengths to explain to the people why there was no money in the Government coffers and that because of these heavy financial encumbrances, we would not be able to make as rapid strides as we had planned in our development efforts.

" You can therefore understand why we cannot give you immediate promises to reduce school fees," I said. "You can therefore understand why we cannot improve health facilities and build more roads as rapidly as we would like when we have to use one and a half million leones from the taxes we collect every year to pay creditors and to meet losses. But we are not deterred in our effort to arrive at a just and equitable solution to each of these projects," I declared. "We inherited the mess, and we shall spare no pains in ensuring that the various industries are properly reorganised, if at all possible, for the benefit of the country."

Pre-finance should be the very last means to which a government should resort for providing the wherewithal for developing its resources, for it is the most expensive and, where the men in power are corrupt, it is more likely to benefit the negotiating individuals than the developing country. When loans are not readily forthcoming for development, however, a government may have no alternative but to enter into a pre-finance arrangement with a foreign company. But in so doing it is of utmost importance that the schemes envisaged are vital for that country's economic development and will pay their way, such as roads, bridges, harbours and airports which, however expensive to build, are the arteries through which the life blood of a nation flows; indeed, it cannot survive without them. To use pre-finance for anything less, for some unproductive prestige creation, is to erect a monstrous monument to bad planning and inefficient government.

The Ceremonial Opening of the Third Parliament of Sierra Leone was scheduled for June 26th, 1968, but Parliament met earlier on June 5th in order to elect a new Speaker and to swear-in Members. The former Speaker, Mr. Banja Tejan-Sie, was now Acting Governor-General and the man selected to take his place in the House was Mr. Justice Emile Fashole Luke.

The evening before Parliament met there was a real carnival atmosphere, especially in the vicinity of my residence. A candlelight procession of ladies from my constituency, followed by men, women and children from all walks of life, wended their way to my compound cheering and calling for me. Then hymns were sung to the accompaniment of a massed band of schoolchildren; prayers were said and addresses delivered in which I was reminded of the enormity of the task with which I was faced, especially with regard to "restoring the economy of the country, refilling the till which was now empty, finding employment for so many who have been without work and disposing of those in detention".

Replying, I said that I could only pray that the Government would be able to live up to the people's expectations. What else could I say? What promises could I make? With the best will in the world it would be months before we could make any visible improvements, especially as regards the financial situation, and when the belts had to be tightened even more, as they inevitably would have to be before a change could be made for the better, my Government and I would have to face a very testing time. Many people, the majority I would say, tolerate their government only so long as it delivers 'the goods'. They are impatient and demanding, critical and quick to condemn. A government is never praised for a job well done for the feeling is always that it could have done better. If it fails to come up to expectations, the people are merciless. No allowances are made for failure due to Acts of God, let alone for failure due to human error.

A government ought to be regarded as a group of very ordinary men and women fighting against often insurmountable odds to keep the country going. It cannot overcome the laws of nature or economics. It cannot swathe through its problems like a gigantic combine harvester, spewing forth a never-ending supply of the good things of life at diminishing costs. Democracy means educating people's expectations.

I have found that out the hard way. But then my whole life has been composed of the lessons of experience.

As I acknowledged the cheering crowds that night, it seemed that my cup was overflowing. I sniffed the balmy air with pleasure, like a schoolboy scenting palaver sauce on the kitchen range. I felt completely overwhelmed with love for my people, who had come to take on the role my family had for me when I was a child. I luxuriated in emotions that had long been choked out by pressing practical problems. But my joy was tempered with a measure of sadness, for I had lived too long and too close to the realities of life to be deceived by the glitter of success. I was still a peasant and a workaday man at heart. I hated the boss-man mentality. I despised the over-confident and the self-satisfied.

I realised that it was one thing to have arrived at the top but staying at the top was going to be a far more difficult business. At such moments of triumph how easy it is to succumb to flattery, to mistake the empty adoration of opportunists and self-seekers for warm-hearted goodwill, to believe that overnight popularity is for keeps and to forget the fickleness of human beings! Many much more successful men than I had fallen from far higher peaks. How, I asked myself in wonder, had I got there anyway? Shy and reticent, I had never considered myself to be the stuff of which politicians were made; indeed I had never wanted to enter politics. Yet here I was with the yoke of the nation's government firmly on my shoulders and the eyes of a critical people focussed on me, watching every step I took. I could only pray that I could keep faith with them, that the steps I took would be firmly planted, unhesitant and in the right direction, and taken only when careful thought had been given as to where they would lead.

The overwhelming reception I received on arrival at Parliament, both the following morning and for the Ceremonial Opening on June 26th, moved me deeply. The State Opening of Parliament is always a splendourous affair and on this particular occasion the pomp and pageantry were particularly appreciated and applauded because it was exactly two years since the country had witnessed such an occasion. The people turned out in their thousands, all dressed up for the event whether they were ticket-holders for admission into the House, or merely one of the crowd of spectators lining the route. I wore a white suit. I meant it to be symbolic of peace. It was an innocent vanity.

I handed the speech to the Acting Governor-General seated on the Throne. It took him about thirty minutes to read and set out Government's plans for the economic and social development of the country and its stand on international affairs. Government pledged itself to support the principles enshrined in the Charters of the United Nations and the Organisation of African Unity and noted that, as Sierra Leone was a peaceloving country, it would aim constantly to work for the preservation of world peace and the settlement of international disputes by peaceful means.

Government set itself to review the various decrees which had been passed during the previous fifteen months and to repeal those which were inconsistent with constitutional government, as well as to restore the provisions of the Constitution and other Acts of Parliament which had been suspended during that period.

"It is the firm intention of my Government", the Acting Governor-General said, "to abide by, and maintain, the Constitution and the rule of law, to respect the rights of the individual irrespective of race, religion or political opinion, to support an impartial civil service and to uphold at all times the traditions of Parliamentary democracy."

Attention would be given by Government to the preparation of development projects but not, it was pointed out, with a view to prestige enhancement for advertisement purposes; basically these would be for the progressive improvement of the country materially, socially, culturally and economically.

It was the declared intention of the Government to continue the policy of diversifying the economy, to support the efforts being made to form a West African Economic Community and to achieve closer trade and economic links with the neighbouring states of Liberia and Guinea. Government undertook to develop tourism, encourage the co-operative movement and work for a greater participation by Sierra Leonean citizens in the commercial life of the country; to embark on a dynamic policy of increased rice cultivation aimed at producing enough rice for domestic consumption as well as a surplus for export; to promote agricultural development in general and agricultural education in schools, encourage agricultural fairs, conferences and seminars and improve cattle breeding for the production of beef, milk, butter and cheese.

It was the hope of the Government that the trade unions and the employers would put the interests of the nation first at all times and that they would create the right climate for good human relations in industry by showing tolerance and restraint. It recognised the need for a functional transport system and was convinced that an efficient road network was a pre-requisite for social and economic growth. The Government declared its intention to improve the quality of overseas radiophone, give consideration to extending this service to other parts of West Africa and improve the internal telecommunication service; and it undertook to establish more housing estates, improve medical facilities, in particular maternal and child health care, and to concern itself with education as well as the various welfare institutions, such as approved schools, remand homes and prisons.

Concluding the Speech from the Throne, the Acting Governor-General said:

" Mr. Speaker and Honourable Members, the return to Parliamentary Government offers a challenge not only to the elected representatives of the people, but to the whole nation. By accepting my invitation to form a National Government, my Prime Minister has displayed not only political maturity but wise statesmanship. The problems ahead are numerous, but I am confident that with goodwill on all sides, they will not prove insurmountable."

Unhappily, goodwill did not emanate from all sides and before long pockets of violence in some parts of the Provinces caused such havoc and destruction of life and property that on November 19th, 1968, I was forced, in the interest of national security, to declare a state of emergency which remained in force until the following February.

The trouble started during the campaigning for bye-elections in those constituencies where the Supreme Court had declared the recent election null and void. Opposition elements had gone to the extreme length of invoking the Poro Secret Society of the Mende tribe to intimidate the people by spearheading their attacks on towns and villages with an exhibition of Poro activities, including the Poro devil. Apart from anything else, as far as this ancient and respected society was concerned, such behaviour exposed it to odium and contempt.

I had nothing against the powerful Poro Society which had been in existence in Sierra Leone since time immemorial and I considered that the Mendes, generally speaking, were a fine set of people. But, as I said both in Parliament and in my dawn broadcast when declaring the state of emergency, if people tried to prostitute the Poro Society and use it to

305

kill people, destroy property and spread discord in the country, contrary to Poro practices and contrary to the peace and good government of Sierra Leone, then the Government, as the supreme guardian of the peace, was duty bound to step in. Whether it be the Poro Society, Freemasonry, the Church or any other institution, if it were to be used to make trouble in the country, there could come a time when a government would have to legislate against it.

If you make your Poro in the villages or in the bush, that is all right," I declared. "... To come out in the streets in broad daylight with Poro devils is not Poro; it is trouble making; and I am glad to hear that they have arrested two so-called Poro devils."

I believe with all my heart in the African way of life and government. What is African is best for Africans. It is what we have evolved over centuries of experience to meet our own needs and our own conditions. I have tried to put African traditions and African institutions back into our governmental process and structure. I have tried to re-utilise them. I have tried to find new applications for them. In Sierra Leone in recent years, we have not just tried to conserve African traditions — we have tried to use them positively in a genuine African revolution. I felt the abuse of the Poro was a double blow — a blow to political stability, and a blow to our hopes of finding African solutions to African problems.

The tolerance my Government had shown up to now had been mistaken for weakness by our detractors, and I believed the time was well overdue when we had to take a tougher line and to root out with determination the trouble-makers so that the people could enjoy peace and quiet. We would then be allowed to plod on with the business of putting our economy on a healthier footing.

"If any suffering or inconvenience is caused," I declared at the conclusion of my speech in Parliament, "I can only say in Biblical terms: offence may come, but woe to him by whom the offence cometh. I am not the Government. The bunch of people here constitute the Government. It is not one man's property. You can fight me, you can do anything with me, but the A.P.C. Government will stay. There are some people in this world who have what might be called a pathological ineptitude for reality until it is made extremely real; and since they continue to make trouble, we are determined to make the reality extremely real to the people of Sierra Leone."

THE MEMBERS OF MY FIRST CABINET (ABOVE) AND (BELOW) EXPLAINING OUR POLICY AT ONE OF THE COUNTLESS MEETINGS WHICH I ADDRESSED DURING MY FIRST YEAR IN OFFICE.

HOISTING OUR PARTY FLAG AT THE OLD A.P.C. HEADQUARTERS IN 1969 TO MARK THE ANNIVERSARY OF ITS FOUNDATION (ABOVE) AND (BELOW) OUR NEW HEADQUARTERS IN THE STREET WHICH HAS NOW BEEN NAMED AFTER ME.

A VISIT TO THE FISHER STREET MARKET SHORTLY AFTER MY RETURN (ABOVE) AND (BELOW) A WELCOME FROM THE A.P.C. "LIBERTY BOYS".

A VISIT TO KENEMA (ABOVE AND FACING PAGE TOP) AND A TOUCHING WELCOME IN SEGBWEMA IN THE EASTERN PROVINCE (BELOW)...AS WELL AS IN PORT LOKO (FACING PAGE BELOW)

DOCTOR OF CIVIL LAW, THE UNIVERSITY OF SIERRA LEONE.

CHAPTER SIXTEEN

Defying the Assassins

One of my proudest moments was when I received my honorary D.C.L. from the University of Sierra Leone. I know a lot of honours are empty — but there are others which can mean a great deal to the individuals who receive them, either because they are the landmarks of life or because they commemmorate efforts and achievements which are important in themselves. I'm not a man to overvalue paper qualifications. I've known too many good men and women who made do without them and achieved great things for their families and their country. Nor do I greatly favour intellectualism for its own sake; I've fought all my life for democracy in Sierra Leone and do not ever want to see it replaced by technocracy.

All forms of elitism are dangerous and educational elitism has little more merit than any other kind. But education itself is a precious thing to me. I love learning with the sort of pride of possession we reserve for the things we get the hard way. I believe education will help transform the future of the people of Sierra Leone for the better. And like most people who did not get the chance to go to University, I am fascinated by the academic world and treasure the short experience of higher education I was eventually able to enjoy in Oxford.

On a personal level, the honour the University of Sierra Leone granted me commemmorates the sacrifices made by the people back home to enable me to become the first member of our family to receive any formal education. On a broader plan, the Doctorate of Civil Law is an emblem for me of the chance I have been given to contribute to the history of the government of my country. It was not, of course, just a personal honour. It was the University's tribute to what the A.P.C. Government was doing for Sierra Leone, particularly in the educational field. A milestone in the history of Sierra Leonean education had been passed on February 12th, 1969, when the University formally came into being with the fusion of its two older constituent bodies, Fourah

Bay College and Njala University College. My degree was granted at the first Congregation; so it was also a gesture of salute from the new institution to mark its foundation.

Fourah Bay college was founded as long ago as 1827 by the Church Missionary Society for the purpose of training teachers and missionaries. It has a long and illustrious history and has been a profound source of inspiration not only to Sierra Leoneans but to our neighbours in West Africa. Yet up to a few years ago most of our undergraduates opted to read law and medicine, particularly the former. In fact there are so many lawyers in Sierra Leone today that I sometimes marvel how they all manage to keep in business! A certain snobbery used to attach to these two professions; however mediocre their performances might have been, lawyers and doctors were placed rungs higher on the social ladder than the most skilled technicians or teachers.

It is only comparatively recently that the message seems to have got through that, if we are ever to acheive economic independence, we must have our own scientists, engineers, agriculturists, architects, chemists, laboratory technicians and men and women in all branches of technology. In this day and age, society has come to rate a man according to his expertise and the size of his contribution towards his country's economic progress, rather than by the eminence of his forebears, his faultless diction, his social graces and manicured finger nails. Intellectual snobbery is often used to mask a lack of real understanding. "Blessed is he that knows that he doesn't know," I said at the inaugural dinner of the Association of Technologists in December, 1968.

For several years pressure had been brought to bear on Government to found a new college in the Provinces to provide a more down-to-earth education than that provided by Fourah Bay College; which was beginning to be regarded as an ivory tower, out of touch with the hard realities of the nation's most urgent needs. What was wanted was an institution offering technological and agricultural education which would produce manpower capable of undertaking the transformation of rural Sierra Leone. It was with this objective in mind that Njala University College was eventually established in 1964.

The symbiosis of Njala and Fourah Bay in a national university and the award of my Doctorate gave me a chance to reflect on education and also, because the D.C.L. is a degree with which universities generally honour practicioners of the art of government, about the principles on which I would continue to act at the head of my country. I had been thinking about these things for a long time, but I did not want my thoughts to crystallise into dogma. I did not want my reception into the groves of academe to turn my head and make an unlikely ideologue of me!

Education has always been of deep concern to me and the longer I live the more conscious I am of how little of the vast resources of knowledge available to mankind I have been able to tap in spite of my avidly searching mind. I have the greatest respect and admiration for true scholars, those men and women whose minds are absorbed in productive thought and ideas, who seem unaware of their outstanding scholarship and who, because of their natural intelligence, are above the petty jealousies and rivalries of so many of the so-called intellectuals. To my mind, a man should regard his education as a tool not so much for furthering his own personal ambitions, but rather for use in benefiting the community in which he lives. As W. and A. Durant so aptly put it in their book *The Lessons of History*: "Consider education not as the painful accumulation of facts and dates and reigns, nor merely the necessary preparation of the individual to earn his keep in the world, but as the transmission of our mental, moral, technical and aesthetic heritage as fully as possible to as many as possible, for the enlargement of man's understanding, control, embellishment and enjoyment of life." That is why I have always tried to use my influence on educational policy not only to make our schools more numerous, more widely accessible, better staffed and better equipped but also more socially useful. This means a practical curriculum of the sort reformers were already advocating in my childhood and which was to some extent applied in the Albert Academy. We need to stress most and develop most the skills which will help build up sufficiency and prosperity for our people in the coming generations.

The emphasis on the practical is also at the heart of my political philosophy. "Dis nor to question of book, nar sense," I have often said to people who have brought their problems to me. If Sierra Leoneans and Africans generally have a characteristic genius, it is a talent for pragmatism; a way of evolving the best means for a job within the available resources. We construct our solutions on the basis of experience. We are prepared to modify or transform them as necessary. We are not an ideological people by nature and by and large foreign ideologies have borne scant fruit in African soil. I acknowledge my own broad allegiance to some very general political, social and economic doctrines — to democracy, to socialism, to pragmatism, to utilitarianism — but I have always tried, never to be a slave to dogma and I subscribe to these schools of thought only because — and only as far as — they seem to me to correspond to common sense.

During the term of office which began in 1968, I hoped that we would establish the national consensus that had eluded Sierra Leone for so long. Perhaps it was naive of me but I hoped my own political philosophy of pragmatism and open-mindedness would give everybody a chance to contribute constructively to national life and that we could satisfy every reasonable point of view. I forgot that some people are in politics purely for the naked pursuit of power and will never be satisfied even with the most broadly based policies unless they have direct access to power and privilege and patronage themselves. I failed to reckon adequately with fanaticism, which no pragmatism can ever reconcile. And I had no adequate formula to overcome the triablism that so eroded our national morale. The result was that my Premiership was scarred by bouts of opposition violence despite my search for consensus policies. More than once, my life was in jeopardy. More than once I narrowly escaped assassination.

The essential background which makes these terrible events intelligible is Sierra Leone's gradual progress towards republican status. When Albert Margai attempted to force a republican constitution on Sierra Leone in 1967, he was rejected by the whole country because the people were simply not ready for it, and it was mainly for this reason that I opposed him at the time. By 1970, however, more and more of the people began to speak in favour of a republican form of government. Those of us who represented our country abroad often suffered serious embarrassment at international gatherings by reason of our continuing to have as Head of State a representative of our former colonial masters. National pride was also stung by the humiliation of having to submit papers to a foreign monarch for approval and signature, and by the fact that ambassadors accredited to our country, as well as our own envoys sent abroad, had first to be sanctioned by the British Queen. Was this, people began to ask, true independence? When our sister state, The Gambia, became a republic in April, 1970, it seemed to crystallise opinion. It was the general feeling that if we did not follow suit at an early date we would become a backwater among the progressive African states.

"Of all the African states which have gained their independence within the last ten years," I declared at our third Party Convention in May, "only Sierra Leone still retains elements of the monarchical system. I do not propose to go into the reasons why former governments of Sierra Leone did not move over to total independence. Suffice to say that it is for us to make the decision here and now."

Albert Margai's Republican Bill had been passed by the required majority in Parliament in 1966. According to the Constitution, elections then had to be held, which in fact they were, and the same Bill had then to be passed by the requisite majority of the newly elected Parliament before it could take effect. This meant, in fact, that all we had to do to bring about a Republic was to reintroduce the Bill into Parliament and ratify it, which, with the majority of seats we held, would have presented no difficulties. But to my mind the step we intended to take was of such national importance that I believed the whole country had to be totally involved. I therefore set up a Commission, representative of people from all sections of the community, to review the new Constitutional Proposals and to sound public opinion on the issue throughout the length and breadth of the country. When this was done, I planned to hold a general election in November or December, 1970, so that the people would have ample opportunity to vote either for or against a Republican Constitution.

As far as the British Government was concerned, there was no question of its standing in our way over the severance of these last links with colonialism. All we had to do was to make our own internal arrangements and give them due notice of our intention so that the necessary formalities could be effected in Britain.

Within a month of my announcing the A.P.C. Government's intention to go ahead with the matter of a Republican Constitution, a new opposition party, the National Democratic Party, was formed by Hamid Taqi, brother of my Minister of Development, M. Bash-Taqi, and of a former Minister of Information & Broadcasting in my Government, Ibrahim Taqi. Of course, the Taqi brothers were entitled to form a new party if they wished, but I felt there was a smack of opportunism about the new enterprise. They were not really against republicanism in general; there were no valid grounds for objection at that stage, since detailed plans awaited public consultation by the Constitutional Commission. The new party could hardly have any means of generating support except by creating rumours and an atmosphere of prejudice against proposals we had still to formulate. Ibrahim Taqi, who was in London at the time, was asked in an interview by the B.B.C. if there was any truth in the speculation that he might be co-opted into the leadership of the new party.

"Let me make this very clear," he is reported to have said, "that I have been a leading member of the A.P.C. and, notwithstanding the fact that in very recent times I have been removed as a Minister, I believe that we can change the hierarchy of the A.P.C. from the fold of the A.P.C. as a political organisation."

A month later Dr. J. Karefa Smart, one-time Minister of External Affairs in Milton Margai's Government, who had taken no active part in Sierra Leonean politics since, after crossing the floor to join the A.P.C. in 1964, he left for Columbia University, suddenly returned to Freetown from Geneva where he had held the post of Assistant Director of the World Health Organisation. He was met, on arrival, by Ibrahim Taqi who kept the press at bay and drove him off in his car. Rumour had it that he had returned to Sierra Leone to lead the N.D.P. This he denied in a letter to the Editor of *West Africa*, published in that magazine on July 18th. "...I am a loyal member of the All People's Congress (A.P.C.)" he wrote, "and I have no intention of making any contribution to the political life of my country from outside this party..."

Early in August, while I was on a visit to Jamaica, a meeting of the N.D.P. took place at which Hamid Taqi disclosed that he had approached Karefa Smart and intimated to him that he would be formally invited to lead the N.D.P. Karefa Smart was reported to have replied that he had not yet fully made up his mind and wanted time to study the situation. He was anxious, he said to meet with people from all over the country, as well as myself, the leader of the A.P.C., as soon as I returned home.

Karefa Smart came to see me the afternoon following my arrival from Jamaica, on August 13th. He expressed his desire to make a worthwhile contribution to the national effort and wanted to know what I had to offer him by way of a post. I told him that the best course for him to pursue, as I saw it, was to get back into Parliament, but this could not be done without a vacancy being created. With the general elections scheduled only a few months ahead, it would hardly be practicable to hold a bye-election before then. I therefore urged him to wait for the general election.

He was not too happy about this and suggested himself for the post of Governor-General. I was frankly astonished. I knew him to be a close friend of Banja Tejan Sie, and although this fact might not deter him from taking his job away from him, I knew instinctively that there was another motive behind this proposal, as yet unclear to me, and that he would have been utterly nonplussed had I agreed to his request. I explained to him that I had excellent relations with the present holder of that office and would very much like to continue working with him.

I then suggested that he might work for me in the interim as my right-hand man, so to speak, which I felt would in fact be of most benefit to him since he had been off the political scene for six years. He said he would have to consider it and first consult his people. The next thing I knew was that he had reported to the Acting Governor-General that I had offered him the job of my personal secretary!

The interim left me feeling unesasy. I genuinely wanted Karefa Smart to find a proper outlet for his immense talents in the service of the country. I had been proud to have him in the A.P.C. and looked forward to working with him. I had known him a little in the old days, when we were members of the Sierra Leone Organisation Society together, but we had drifted apart politically for a long time after that. He was a latecomer to the A.P.C. He had not, so far, played an active part in the party. We therefore had to get to know each other over again, and for my part I had hoped our interview would be a chance to build a political partnership and friendship in which we could work together for Sierra Leone. In the event, however, the interview disillusioned me, just as it obviously disappointed him. I was alarmed at his impatience, perturbed by the scale of his ambition. It upset me to feel that he was rejecting my efforts to find a just and useful role for him.

On September 4th, 1970, I left Freetown for Lusaka, Zambia, to attend the Conference of Heads of Non-Aligned States and to return a visit which President Kenneth Kaunda had paid to Sierra Leone the previous year. On former occasions when I had been absent from the country I had delegated my duties as Prime Minister and Minister of Defence to the Minister of Finance, Dr. M. S. Forna. On this occasion, however, in keeping with my policy of giving as many people as possible a chance to prove themselves, coupled with the fact that Forna was due to attend a conference abroad within a few days of my departure, I left my ministerial responsibilities in the hands of the Resident Minister, Southern Province, S. B. Kawusu-Conteh, a tried and tested colleague of some years' standing. I made it clear to Forna that this action of mine must in no way be interpreted by him as lack of confidence in his abilities or disappointment in his past performance as Acting Prime Minister. But power can corrupt in curious ways. It makes people self-important. It makes them ridiculously sensitive about status and dignity, like officials quibbling over precedence in a despotic court. It makes them confuse personal grievances with political issues.

On September 9th, five days after my departure, the independent newspaper *Unity* appeared with front-page headlines: *Two Ministers Plan a Showdown. Dr. Forna to Resign?* A *Unity* reporter, it said, trying to confirm the rumour, met Dr. Forna in his office "apparently packing", though he denied that he was resigning. "I have many conferences to attend to," he is reported to have said, "and I would not make such a move as the man for whom I am working is away." It was rumoured also that the Minister of Development, M. Bash-Taqi, might resign. "The cause of the dissention," the report went on, "is understood to be the choice of Mr. S. B. Kawusu-Conteh as Acting Prime Minister. Hitherto Dr. Forna had always acted in the absence of the Prime Minister..."

On September 12th, both Ministers resigned from the Cabinet, despite the absence of 'the man for whom' they were 'working', and they circulated their letters of resignation, addressed to me, to the press. Shortly after this the A.P.C. Executive announced that it had expelled three former Cabinet Ministers — Forna, Bash-Taqi and Ibrahim Taqi — and two other party members. Noting the confusion and potential threats to law and order which had emanated from recent public meetings, Government viewed "with great concern the undertone of subversion and the active attempts by ill-disposed persons to create discord in the security forces" and decided that further public meetings in the existing circumstances and conditions were not in the public interest.

In spite of the well publicised and repeated announcement of the suspension of public meetings, loudspeaker vans toured the city throughhout Sunday, September 13th, noisily announcing that a meeting of the N.D.P. would take place that afternoon. At that meeting Karefa Smart, remarking *inter alia* that he had made several attempts to work with me and had been told he could only do so as a secretary, announced his resignation from the A.P.C. 'for the good of the country'. Stones were hurled into the assembled gathering causing several casualties, and riot police arrived on the scene to disband the meeting and restore order.

... And Shaki Flies Back, proclaimed *Unity.*

As soon as my plane landed that Sunday morning avid reporters flocked about me like so many vultures fighting for a chance to strip the flesh off my bones. What, they asked, were my reactions to the resignations of my two Ministers and to the proposed meeting of the N.D.P. in spite of the ban imposed on meetings?

"I haven't yet seen the Ministers' letters of resignation," I said.

"When these reach me I will study and discuss them with other A.P.C. members before making any recommendations to the Governor-General." I told them that I had come back as a result of what I had heard and what I had read in the London *Times*, that I had not yet had an opportunity to study the situation in the country so was not in a position to say what was wrong or what was right. "What I will say, however," I declared, "is that I feel strongly that if any member of the A.P.C. has anything against the Party or any of its members, he should wait for the forthcoming general election which is imminent. And I want to stress that the Government will not stand for anything that will disrupt the peace and stability of this country. The A.P.C. Government has done a lot to restore peace, unity and stability in the country in the past two and a half years and any attempt to cause unrest will be dealt with drastically."

It did not take long for sufficient evidence to be supplied to me that forces were urgently at work to pitch the country into a state of chaos and confusion. Every possible attempt was being made to discredit me personally and the A.P.C. Government, with accusations of misuse of public funds, of my forcing myself on the people as Executive President before the appeals of those sentenced for the 1967 coup could be quashed by the Privy Council, of my personal ambitions as autocratic ruler, and so forth. I learnt, too, that arrangements had been made the previous week for about 50 or 60 lorry loads of people to proceed to Freetown on Sunday, September 13th, on the pretext that they were to attend an A.P.C. meeting, when in point of fact no A.P.C. meeting had been arranged. Fortunately, somebody had the foresight to intercept these people forty-seven miles outside Freetown. I dread to think what would have happened if this large number of people had arrived in the city to find that they had been misinformed and duped by the N.D.P. Scandalous leaflets and bulletins had been published in Freetown which so involved the army that Government had to issue an official statement rebutting the false rumours.

There was only one thing I could do if effective protection were to be given to the lives and properties of the people and the security of the nation assured, and I forthwith declared a State of Emergency to take effect from midnight on September 14th. In a broadcast announcing the State of Emergency, I declared:

"There are clear indications that a small group of people who want to get into power by every possible means or who have lost positions of authority, are doing their utmost to disrupt the peace and good government of this country.

" ...Bearing in mind the great difficulties which this country has gone through within the last two years and taking into consideration the fact that the country as a whole has been able to rehabilitate itself to the extent that new investors have begun to come in, and bearing in mind the fact that Sierra Leone has been able to earn respect from outside, particularly in the economic field, the Government is determined to see that nothing is allowed to disrupt the peace of the country or to retard development.

"Peaceful citizens have nothing to fear and should go about their normal duties, but I should like to make it clear that if anyone by word or deed tries to stir up disaffection in Sierra Leone, the Government will take the most drastic action in the matter."

As an additional security precaution, the passports of Karefa Smart and his henchmen were confiscated. The same day I announced that the portfolios of Finance, Development and Transport and Communications had been assigned to A. G. Sembu Forna, A. Khazali and E. J. Kargbo, respectively.

On September 20th, Karefa Smart dissolved the N.D.P. and formed a new party, the United Democratic Party (U.D.P.) supported by M. Forna, Bash-Taqi, Hamid Taqi and Dr. Sarif Easmon. Referring to the seizure of the passports of himself and his colleagues, and the declaration of a State of Emergency, he declared in a circular letter touting for members to his new party: "These things, fellow countrymen, have happened even before Mr. Stevens becomes Executive President and they are only a foretaste of what is to come under an Executive President. We wish to state," he wrote, "that our fundamental difference with the Prime Minister is his ambition for unlimited power to be achieved in an executive presidency whereby all powers of the State would be concentrated in his hands. We have decided therefore that the only solution and safeguard to our liberties is the formation of a new party embracing people from all sections of the country..."

On September 22nd, I sought and obtained the Queen's approval to appoint Banja Tejan-Sie, Acting Governor-General, to the substantive rank of Governor-General.

Meanwhile, more and more delegations from all over the country flooded my office daily to pledge their loyalty and support to me and the A.P.C., and many of them brought with them reports of violent clashes between U.D.P. and A.P.C. elements and rumours about plots by the U.D.P. to force me out of office. *Unity* one day claimed that a plot had been uncovered whereby imported ju-ju men had undertaken, for the princely sum of Le28,000, to make me lose the affection of the people and to cause me to become so unpopular that I would decide to resign from office quietly.

On September 23rd, I called a press conference at which I made a statement for the benefit of the public concerning the number of accusations that had been levelled against me during the past few weeks.

" It has been alleged," I said, "that I have caused public funds to be misused in the purchase of army equipment, etc. The answer to this allegation is that all monies spent outside the 1970/71 Estimates had been approved by the Cabinet, and up to the time of the resignation of the two Ministers, there had been no reports of dissent from any quarter.

"In a pamphlet dated September 18th and signed by Dr. Karefa Smart, it is alleged that I was responsible for the expulsion of five top members of the A.P.C. My answer to this allegation is that, as you all know, I was not in this country when the A.P.C. Central Committee took this action. The Central Committee found it necessary in the interest of the Party to expel these men on Friday, September 11th, and I arrived from overseas on Sunday, September 13th. I have, since my arrival, pointed out that the expelled members have every right to appeal according to the Constitution of the Party, and if and when they do appeal, the pros and cons of the expulsion will be thoroughly investigated."

It had also been alleged that I wanted to get myself installed as Executive President of Sierra Leone.

" In this connection," I declared, "let me say that I have never expressed a desire to become Executive President of Sierra Leone and, in fact, as members of the public must be aware, I cannot make myself Executive President. The final decision on the form of Republican Constitution which this country gets rests entirely with the electorate, and the electorate has shown over and over again that they know what is good for them.

"It is true," I continued, "that representatives of the A.P.C. held a meeting in August this year and passed a resolution for an Executive Presidency, but I must point out that such a resolution would need to be endorsed by a full meeting of the National Delegates Conference, which is the supreme body of the Party, before it could be finally adopted by the Party, and I have no doubt that such a Conference would take into consideration not only the views of Party members, but the views of the country as a whole."

I went on to say that if some people wanted to form a new party, "let them do so without trying to find fault where there is no fault." The A.P.C. was bound at all times to take full cognizance not only of the wishes and desires of its members, but of the wishes and desires of the country as a whole in making up its mind on all issues of national importance.

"Speaking personally," I said, "I have enough political experience to realise that I am in duty bound at all times to respect the wishes of the people if my administration is to be successful." I appealed to all members of the public to remember that each one of us had a part to play in the maintenance of law and order in the country and that it was our duty to play that part.

To a question about the allegation made by opposition elements that I was responsible for the outbreak of violence in some parts of the country, I replied that I had never advocated violence and because of this some people said I was soft and even accused me of being a coward when I refused to take certain steps. "I am a man of peace. I do not stand for violence," I declared. "I have been in politics for forty years and it is too late in the day to change. I will not encourage violence in my political career." I assured my audience that violence never paid in the end and said I would investigate reports that A.P.C. supporters, particularly the youths, had been molesting and threatening political opponents in the country.

Asked whether in the interest of peace I would not defer the proposed elections and allow the Government to run its full term of office, I said that I realised that every Member of Parliament, including myself, wanted to enjoy his full five years, but that when there were important issues at stake, in particular issues that involved raising the status of the country, if an election became necessary, we would have to face it.

There was no doubt in my mind that the root of the trouble we were going through was in Government's proposal to acquire a 51 per cent share in all the mining companies in the country and it was becoming increasingly clear that those involved in causing the crisis were being encouraged and financed by people outside Sierra Leone. For instance, two Sierra Leonean students studying in London on Government scholarships were given free air tickets by a foreign firm to return to Sierra Leone. Shortly after their arrival here they announced their resignations from the A.P.C. and said they were joining the U.D.P.

There was evidence that the U.D.P. had appreciable financial resources at its disposal — funds which it would have been virtually impossible for a new party, or even an older one, to raise in such a short time from the contributions of local supporters. On just one occasion they were reported to have ordered 14 brand new Land Rovers and some Volkswagens and vans.

Naturally, we did not and could not object to a political party raising and using funds for the purpose of publicising its policies. However, the danger to the internal stability and security of the country arose from the fact that the U.D.P. interpreted too literally the expression "fighting fund", using their financial means less for the purpose of propaganda than for hiring professional thugs to cause disturbances and physically attack A.P.C. supporters, civil servants and even those entrusted with the maintenance of law and order. Doubting, as they did, their ability to win an election, their strategy now consisted in causing a massive breakdown of law and order in the hope that the confusion would give them an opportunity of seizing power.

By October 8th the situation had deteriorated so rapidly that my Cabinet colleagues and I felt compelled to take effective measures to prevent chaos and loss of life. These were explained in the following statement which I issued on that day:

"I declared a State of Emergency on September 14th, 1970, owing to the tense situation that existed at the time in this country. I did not bring any regulations into force under the Emergency, in the hope that after my declaration, reason would prevail and peace and quiet be restored. This has not happened and following a series of incidents in which people were attacked and wounded, with two deaths, the situation has worsened.

"It has therefore become necessary to adopt urgent measures for the protection of life and property. The measures to be taken are as follows:

a) The United Democratic Party is banned forthwith. The existing Parliament comprises the ruling government party, the All People's Congress (A.P.C.) which was in opposition for some seven years, and the official opposition party, the Sierra Leone People's Party (S.L.P.P.). Since the advent of a third party about six months ago, a party which has changed its nomenclature thrice (S.L.P.O., N.D.P. and U.D.P.), a noticeable change for the worse has developed in the political atmosphere of the country, especially with the return to this country from abroad of Dr. John Karefa Smart, who had been away from Sierra Leone since 1964. It is therefore evident that the emergence of this new political party is responsible for the present unrest and therefore must be banned.

b) The publication of all cyclostyled news sheets is hereby banned, except for publications put out by embassies in Sierra Leone and educational institutions. Government has no intention of interfering with properly organised news media, but there has recently sprung up in Sierra Leone a very irresponsible type of news media which has made it possible for anyone with a typewriter, a roneo machine and a supply of duplicating paper to cover the whole country with the most irresponsible type of information, whether such information was to the detriment of the country or not, and the important point to remember about these publications is that they have very few assets which could be appropriated in the case of judgements against them in legal actions.

c) Certain other measures will be taken in the interest of national security. The operation will be a combined military/police operation. There have been reports about a number of people carrying arms and the warning is hereby issued that if anyone uses arms against the army and the police during the operation, then these security forces will be forced to take appropriate action.

"Parliament will meet on October 19th to ratify the State of Emergency and the measures taken thereunder."

Orders were issued for the arrest and detention of Karefa Smart and the leaders of the banned U.D.P.

Around 10.30 that night one of my security men came to my room and informed me that an officer and an N.C.O., both fully armed, were downstairs demanding to see me. I said I would see them one at a time.

The young officer had, on one or two occasions, accompanied me on visits abroad as an A.D.C., so he was familiar both to me and to my security guards. When my security officer requested him to divest himself of his weapons before seeing me, he laughingly objected. "Do you think I would harm Pa?" he asked.

"Nevertheless ..." said my man, firmly grasping the weapons and taking them from him. Something, he sensed, was very wrong, but although he could not at the moment think what it was, his instinct warned him to take no chances with these two soldiers. Each one of them told me that he had come to report to me that they had already rounded up most of those to be detained and promised to complete the job within an hour or so. I shook hands with them and commended them. It was not until they had left the house that my security officer remembered what it was that was worrying him. He came to me at once and said: "There is something very strange, Sir."

He then told me that only that morning the officer, my one-time A.D.C., had come to my house in civilian clothes saying he was on leave. He had heard, he said, that trouble was expected in the barracks that night and he asked permission to bring his wife and children to my compound for safety. My wife, who, of course, knew him, gave him permission.

"What worries me, Sir," my guard said, "is that there is no sign of his family, nor did he mention to you about the possible trouble in the barracks. Also, if he said he was on leave only this morning, how is it that he is tonight in uniform and detailed to undertake the arrest of these key figures in the U.D.P.?"

How fortunate it was that my security officer had insisted on disarming the two of them and had not allowed familiarity to throw caution to the winds. For I later learnt that the plan, which we foiled, was that by the time the two of them entered my house, reports would be received that a commotion had broken out in the barracks. In the midst of the confusion it was expected this would cause, I would be disposed of by these two men. It came to my mind that the only lie the officer had probably spoken that day was that he was involved in the arrest of the U.D.P. leaders. I am inclined to believe that when he came to my house earlier in the day he was actually on leave and had no idea that he was to be used in the role of assassin that night. He had picked up the rumour of trouble brewing and was anxious to insure the safety of his family and himself. The fact that he did not bring his family to my compound was proof enough to me that, having later learnt of his mission, and realising the bloodshed and chaos that would ensue, the very last place his family should be was in the centre of such activity.

What more wicked and cleverly devised plan could my detractors have evolved than to choose as the man to dispose of me one so familiar to me, one whom I had trusted and relied upon as my personal aid and who would be assured of a welcome reception both by my guards and by myself, his friends. Was the wretched officer of such poor calibre that, despite an order from his Force Commander, he was unable to judge for himself right from wrong, battle against an enemy of the State as opposed to the elimination of the head of the Government of that State and the Minister responsible for its defence? Would he allow himself to be involved in a heinous plot to commit murder and treason? It seemed impossible to believe.

Although that night I had little but the disturbing report of my security officer and my own intuition to give rise to the feeling that there could be treacherous planners at work in our midst and that the two soldiers had actually had an ulterior and sinister motive in coming to see me, I nevertheless immediately reported the matter to Bangura and insisted that he apprehend them and thoroughly check on them. The only action that was taken was a temporary reduction in their rank.

My suspicions were more than confirmed the following morning shortly after seven, when Sembu Forna, my Minister of Finance, arrived at my house to tell me that he had just received a telephone call from a reliable source advising him that a coup was being planned and that he should inform me immediately.

"What is more," he said, "contrary to your instructions, the U.D.P. office is *not* closed and there is a crowd of people there which gives the impression that the job of clearing the place was not thorough enough."

Bai Koblo, who arrived at my house shortly afterwards, confirmed this fact.

The telephone rang and a soldier from the barracks reported that some senior officers were behaving in a somewhat extraordinary manner. I tried to get in touch with both the Force Commander, J. Bangura, and the Commissioner of Police, J.E.N.G. Smith, but they were not available. Then I received a message from the Governor-General to say that he had arranged a meeting at nine o'clock that morning between leading A.P.C. politicians and army and police officers to discuss the present situation in the country and to decide how best the problem of security could be solved.

"Surely, Sir, the initiative to call such a meeting should come from you as Minister of Defence," Sembu Forna rightly remarked.

"I agree," I said. "But don't worry. We'll attend the meeting and we'll put up a show of strength to let them see that we are ready to deal with any situation that may arise. Go at once and alert our people and get them organised. We haven't got much time."

Sembu Forna and Bai Koblo left immediately to contact our supporters and those elements in the army who were known to be loyal to us. It is at times fortunate that the speed at which news and gossip travel from person to person in Freetown equals that at which fire demolishes a straw stack, for within the space of an hour a large part of the city's population was fully geared for action.

My two colleagues then proceeded to the Governor-General's office. As they arrived they met the Permanent Secretary, Ministry of the Interior, and the Commissioner of Police leaving the Governor-General's office. The time was only just after 8 a.m. and Sembu Forna's suspicions that there was something unhealthy being planned for us at the meeting were even more aroused. He wasted no time on niceties and shocked even Bai Koblo by the harshness of his words to the Governor-General.

"We know exactly what is going on," he told him. "And I warn you that you are playing a dangerous game hobnobbing with the army and the police in this way. We are prepared for any eventuality when we attend the meeting, and I may as well warn you that if any shooting starts, not one of us will live to tell the tale."

"All I want is to iron out differences," the Governor-General explained, shocked but managing to retain his poise in spite of it.

"Don't you think that is the business of the Minister of Defence?" Sembu Forna asked.

We arrived at the meeting promptly at 9 a.m., each of us armed and making no secret of the fact.

"And we know very well how to use them," one of our number assured an army officer who appeared worried at the sight of our guns.

We had to wait ten minutes or more for the Force Commander and some of his officers, who swaggered into the room without even apologising to the Chairman for being late.

The Governor-General opened the meeting by stating that the Force Commander and the Commissioner of Police had earlier reported to him a drop in morale of the troops since operations began under the State of Emergency, and he asked the two officers to repeat their report for the benefit of the politicians present. After listening to what they had to say, I made the observation that both of them, by reporting direct to the Governor-General, had side-stepped me as Minister responsible for both the police and the army. This was not only discourteous and out of order, but showed they lacked confidence in me.

"And how is it possible," I asked, "for the morale of the men to drop so suddenly, when the operations were only begun last night? I would like to know in particular why, when the Force Commander went to report to the Governor-General, he did not take with him his second and third in command, Col. Momoh and Major King."

I then called upon Col. Momoh to give an account of the situation as he saw it. He told the meeting that as commander of the major unit in the army, he had not observed any lapse in the morale of his men and that if there had been any indication of this sort, his Regimental Sergeant Major would have brought it to his notice. He said he had no doubt whatever of the loyalty of his senior N.C.O.'s, especially the Regimental Sergeant Major. He concluded by expressing surprise that an officer junior to him in rank, Major Noah, should have gone over his head to make a report of that nature to the Force Commander. Major Noah, bristling with weapons, was at that moment guarding the door of the room.

The effect of Col. Momoh's report on the representatives of the army and the police at the meeting was like that of an electric shock. They stared at him with hostile expressions frozen on their faces, too stunned to utter. I seized this psychological moment to drive home my attack on Bangura and Smith, to operate, as it were, while they were still anaesthetised.

"Neither of you," I declared, "has given me the co-operation necessary for the effective observance of the State of Emergency. And you," I said pointing to the Commissioner of Police, "you have never believed in this operation. You have deliberately failed to attend meetings designed to plan army/police operations and instead of obeying my instructions, you have taken to seeking the advice of the Attorney-General." Their mouths were working as if they wanted to defend themselves, but not a word issued forth from either of them. "If this is the way ..."

At that moment my voice was almost drowned by the shouting and general commotion created by a large and excited crowd and everybody's attention was transferred to the mass of people who had gathered around the State House.

"Those are U.D.P. people who have come to protest," the Governor-General declared.

"On the contrary," Sembu Forna corrected him, "they are A.P.C. supporters anxious to see fair play."

With that everybody rose to see for themselves. Rumour was rife among our detractors that we had imported plain clothes army personnel from Guinea. This was quite untrue, but if it was now the cause of an extra worry line or two on the brows of the service personnel in the room, this was all to the good.

As Noah relaxed his guard to determine the nature of the crowd, Sembu Forna and S. I. Koroma left the room and proceeded into the courtyard to acknowledge the excited people and assure them that we were in control of the situation. Hot on their heels came Noah, his gun at the ready. Sembu Forna turned to face him.

"Let me warn you, Noah, as I warned the Governor-General earlier today," he said. "If any shooting starts these people here are going to have to search for new leaders among themselves, because not one of us will remain alive. We came here today with full knowledge of your plan and well prepared to blow it to smithereens if you try to carry it out."

After that evidence of the support we had, when the plotters came face to face with realities, the meeting fizzled out. The arrogant self-confident attitude displayed by most of the service personnel was now sagging pitifully beneath damp and creased uniforms that all of a sudden seemed too big for their wearers, and their dejection seemed to plumb the depths when the Chairman, their heretofore protector and champion, made an attempt to tidily bring the matters to a close for the sake of the records, by suggesting that a solution to the problems facing us might be found if the Prime Minsiter had a private meeting with the Police Commissioner and the Force Commander.

It was certainly a victory, but one that left a very sour taste in my mouth; the kind of victory, perhaps, that the Duke of Wellington had in mind when faced with a lady's rapturous comment: "What a glorious thing must be victory, Sir!"

"The greatest tragedy in the world, Madam, except a defeat," he replied.

Apart from the dismissal of one or two lower-ranking army officers, no heads rolled as a result of this abortive coup, though one could hardly describe it as a 'coup', a word that carries with it an element of surprise, for we were well and truly prepared for it. Many of my Ministers and party supporters could not understand why I retained the services of those who had plotted against me.

"If the Commissioner of Police and the Force Commander are allowed to remain in their posts, I will never contest the elections," one of them declared.

"And if the Governor-General remains in office you are going to have more difficulties, Sir!" another warned. "He has no personal liking for you. His friends are in the opposite camp."

I was fully aware of the risk I was taking and of the fact that many thought I was far too soft to be in command when I retained in key positions men whose aim it had been to bring about my downfall. However, I still had, even if it was becoming somewhat diminished, a faith in the better side of human nature predominating. I believed that however antagonistic a person might be, it was possible to win him over by affording him another chance, after making it understood that his past behaviour was considered reprehensible. I have never seen the wisdom of making an enemy of a man who could, with patience and tact, become a friend. But it was not easy to explain this to my people. The feeling was that offering the other cheek was all very well in theory, but if practised in conditions obtaining in Sierra Leone at that time, not only the other cheek but the whole head would be grabbed. They saw much more sense in plucking out the offending eye.

Parliament ratified, by an overwhelming majority, the State of Emergency Declaration which I made on September 14th; and on October 23rd I broadcast to the nation to apprise the people of the current situation. I explained that the declaration of the State of Emergency had not been an easy decision to make but that Government had duties and responsibilities to the people and believed that this was the most effective means of safeguarding their interests. Our action had been proved right by the wonderful support which it had got from Parliament, and Parliament, I reminded them, was the supreme governmental machinery in Sierra Leone and representative of the whole nation.

"I am sure that everyone would agree," I said, "that when anxious parents start rushing to school to withdraw their children, as happened in Freetown on October 8th; when schools start shutting down, as happened in Makeni on October 7th; when people start firing shots into the air in various parts of the country; when people start throwing acid at their opponents; especially at a time when treason prisoners are waiting for their appeals to be heard, then it is high time that any Government worthy of its name, took action in the national interest.

"Until a few weeks ago, when a handful of disgruntled and ambitious power-drunk men sought to discredit Government by breeding discontent among the people, the stable atmosphere necessary for carrying out our principal task of nation-building had been well nigh achieved. That stability, however, became seriously threatened by those rebels, and if Government had not acted promptly to maintain law and order, Sierra Leone would have been pitched back into an even worse state of chaos and confusion than that which followed the military take-over of March, 1967. We salvaged precious little from that wreck with which to start the business of government and the creditable stage of development that we see around us today, and of which we can be justly proud, has cost us dearly in terms of effort, determination and sacrifice.

"Fellow Citizens," I declared, "my Party and Government will never stand by and see those years of labour and hardship expended in vain. Nobody — and I repeat — *nobody* — will be allowed to obstruct our forward march toward economic independence. We must be constantly on our guard, for there will be many other power-seeking opportunists who will make promises to lead the nation to 'easy street' overnight. Nobody is going to fool us into believing that there is a short and easy road to achieving financial independence. Economic development is a slow and gradual process — for the most part it is a tedious route march on subsistence rations towards a nebulous goal, for no date can be set for the achievement of economic independence, as was the case for political independence."

I recounted our achievements during the short time my Government had been in power, and stressed the fact that the A.P.C. Government was interested in developing the resources of our country and improving the living standards of the people, but not concerned with power for power's sake or in ideological alignments:

333

" To succeed in our aim there must be an atmosphere of stability and full co-operation from all the people. But if you — the people of Sierra Leone — are going to give your whole-hearted and unstinted support to Government, you must have an accurate understanding of the problems facing Africa today and of the history that created those problems.

"We on the continent of Africa are a people who have suffered untold hardships. To begin with, our personality was crushed and degenerated by the slave trade. Since then we have been humiliated by the massive exploitation of our continent and so long as we — the independent African states — remain balkanised, each individual state of Africa will continue to be so humiliated and subject, economically, to those that exploit us.

"Our aim, therefore, is: Firstly, to redeem the dignity of our race by proudly upholding the ancient and well-tested traditions of our ancestors, rather than blindly aping the customs and mannerisms of foreigners. Secondly, to develop our nation to the utmost so that not only may it be self-supporting, but equipped to aid those African states who are less fortunate. Thirdly, but perhaps most important of all in the context of a Third World, to work for the unification of our continent without which our individual achievements will count for very little indeed.

"Unhappily," I went on, "as many African and Asian countries have learnt to their cost, the colonialism they fought and which they believed they had defeated for good and all, returns in another guise. At first, and to the unwary, this so-called neo-colonialism is unrecognisable. Certain world powers believe that they can only achieve their ambition for world domination at the expense of poor, small and struggling nations in Africa and Asia. Generous aid is offered with one hand, while the other holds the ever tightening noose of control. We in Africa are not interested in political and ideological battles between the great powers. Our whole interest is to develop our countries. But it would appear that certain great powers do not want to leave us alone to settle our affairs the way we, the Africans, understand them."

Reverting to the problems facing us at the time, I said that one of the main aims of the rebel group led by Karefa Smart was to bring about the hegemony of one tribe in the country.

"Government is now in possession of abundant evidence," I declared, "to prove the means by which these people were going to achieve their aims, and on account of this, it was forced to take drastic action against them in the interests of the country.

"When the going was tough in this country between 1964 and 1967, some people thought fit to bale out and proceed to foreign lands on lucrative appointments with all the comforts that went with them, and there they stayed until they judged the soup to be cool enough. After the heavy spadework has been done, now that peace and stability is taking hold and development is underway, they return to Sierra Leone and have the rank arrogance to believe that they are indispensable to the future progress and prosperity of the country, and seek to grab the reins of office with all speed and by all means. Fellow citizens: is this the way intelligent people should behave?

"A significant aspect of the difficult situation through which this country is now passing," I declared, "is the fact that the introduction of the new party in Sierra Leone has coincided with a coup plot within the army. We have the evidence of a junior officer who was engaged in propaganda work for the party. We also have evidence to the effect that one of the ammunition magazines of the army was broken into about a fortnight ago and about 850 rounds of ammunition stolen, some of which have now been recovered. I think you will agree that the setting up of a new party is one thing, but to try to connect such a party with the army is a most dangerous thing to do. Small wonder one of the leaders of the party declared a few weeks ago that the party had moved on to the offensive. Investigations are still going on in this regard, after which appropriate action will be taken; and when you come to hear all the evidence that is available, you will shudder to find how near we have been to disaster."

In conclusion I said:

"It has become abundantly clear to Government that the troublemakers amongst us are being supported with money

335

provided by outsiders whose sole aim is to make our country a puppet and a satellite. We must thank God that we discovered this conspiracy in time, that we have succeeded in breaking and exposing it, and that our country has been saved from the hands of her enemies. We must not, however, rest on our oars. We must keep on the alert. We must keep an eye on our frontiers. The army and the police are doing fine work, but we the people must help and encourage them. *We must have peace.*"

Peace, if one can so call a period of cautious watchfulness, doubt and suspicion, lasted but five months. False rumours were constantly being fed to the people by our detractors in an attempt to cause panic, the most important being that Sierra Leone would be declared a republic on the tenth anniversary of our Independence, April 27th, 1971. I did not pay any particular attention to this. One got used to hearing such things that to waste time and energy refuting them would play into our enemies' hands by detracting our attention from affairs of state. One evening in mid-March, however, I received an urgent summons to a secret meeting at which a friend warned me that false rumours were being spread by both soldiers and civilians that I and my Government were going to force a republic on the people of Sierra Leone and that the soldiers intended to make this an issue for staging a coup. "There is no time to lose," my friend urged. "You must issue a denial of the rumour immediately."

The following day, March 22nd, I arranged for the following statement to be issued by my office:

" There have been increasing rumours that a decision has been taken either by the Government or the Prime Minister of Sierra Leone to declare Sierra Leone a republic on or before April 27th, 1971, when she attains her Tenth Independence Anniversary.

"Government wishes to state that whilst evidence is not lacking that it is the wish of many Sierra Leoneans that Sierra Leone should become a republic in the near future, and that public consciousness in regard to the disadvantages of the present monarchical form of Constitution has been fully aroused, no decision one way or the other, has actually been taken on this matter.

"The general public must be fully aware that a Constitutional Review Commission has been set up to sound public opinion and that the Commission has been actively engaged in this exercise, in order to ensure that any decision finally reached would be in complete accord with the wishes of the majority of the people of Sierra Leone.

"Government wishes to state categorically that neither the Government nor the Prime Minister intends to declare Sierra Leone a republic on or before April 27th, 1971.

"Government feels it necessary to issue this statement not only to dispel unfounded rumours, but also because of man-oeuvres on the part of certain persons with ill-conceived motives who, although fully aware of the earnestness of local aspirations on this matter of a republic, either wish to destroy the spirit and character of the forthcoming important occasion, or to diminish the zeal and enthusiasm with which all patriotic Sierra Leoneans look forward to the Tenth Independence Anniversary celebrations. "

I arrived home from the office that day around 6 p.m. and had barely settled down when a friend 'phoned to say that he had heard very disturbing news about certain activities going on in the army barracks and he warned me to be on the alert. I then called my personal bodyguards and warned them likewise, and sent messages to the barracks that I wished to see the Force Commander and his Deputy. The latter, Lt. Col. Momoh, arrived about 8 p.m.

"I hear that there is trouble brewing in the barracks and that some top-ranking men know something about this. Can you enlighten me?" I asked him.

He looked at me aghast. "I swear to God, Sir, that I know nothing whatever about any trouble," he said with sincerity. "I will return at once and keep my eyes skinned."

About two hours later I managed to get in touch with John Bangura, the Force Commander. By the time he arrived around 10.30 p.m., the Deputy Minister of the Interior happened to be with me, and I invited them both into my study. I told Bangura that I knew about the plot to use the rumour of the declaration of a republic as an excuse to stage a coup and said that this was the reason why I had issued an official denial earlier in the day.

I have rarely seen a man so ill at ease. He kept shifting his position and checking his watch every other minute. My feelings as I faced this

Judas were a mixture of revulsion and pity. Was there no way, I asked myself, of making him see sense, of rescuing him from certain disaster and destruction.

'I am concerned about your divided loyalty between myself on the one side and the Governor-General and Karefa Smart on the other," I told him. "We laboured together to bring back a constitutional government in 1968; we made a good team, didn't we? I had always hoped that I would be able to rely on you to work with me to make that government work. You disappointed me once. I hope..."

"I swear in the name of God and my mother," he blurted out, "that my loyalty to you, Prime Minister, remains untainted. I shall always be grateful to you for what you have done for me and I look upon you as a son regards his father."

I believe at that moment he meant it, but my illusion was immediately shattered when for the umpteenth time he looked at his watch. "Are you in such a hurry?" I asked.

"Er — no, Sir," he replied uncertainly. "It's just that I haven't eaten yet."

I sent for some food for him but when it came he refused to eat, saying that he was on a special diet. I invited him to have a drink and he insisted on a non-alcoholic one.

I proceeded to acquaint him with some of the things I had heard about him that disturbed me, in particular that he had received Le50,000 from Karefa Smart to stage a coup. I expressed my disapproval at the way he had forsaken his legal wife and mother of his children for a younger woman of mixed race, not only on moral grounds but for reasons of state security. My doubts on this score were later confirmed when certain police officers, posing as her admirers, were paid large sums of money by her to get rid of me and install Bangura in my place. She had set her heart on 'flying flag' as the first lady in the land. Ambitious and ruthless women have caused the destruction of many otherwise honourable but gullible men.

"Let us not beat about the bush, John," I said, in a final attempt to win him round. "I know what is going on. I do not fear for myself, but I fear very much for you. If anyone shoots and kills me at my age, my widow might mourn me for a while, but I have lived a long life and there are others who are quite competent to step into my shoes and carry on as if I had never existed. But you, John, you are still a young man. You have a future to work for and a great deal to lose if you stick your neck out and stop a bullet in the process. All I am asking you is to think very carefully before you take irreversible steps which you will later regret."

Again the time check, the uneasiness and the sweat-soaked face. When I tried to continue the conversation, he excused himself and said he had to go because the drink had gone to his head. I stared at the innocuous beverage before him and marvelled, but he was too desperate to notice anything unusual about his remark.

At midnight my friend telephoned again to make sure I was on the alert. I checked that the guards were on duty and prepared for any action, then returned to bed. The next thing I knew was that shots were being fired in the very compound of my house. As I jumped out of bed and threw myself on the floor. I heard a voice ordering: "Fire to the right! Fire to the right!" This was where my bedroom was situated. Bullets peppered the walls and windows of my room and tore the mosquito net over my bed.

People asked me afterwards what it is like to be sleeping peacefully in your bed one moment and the target of a fusillade the next. It is an impossible question to answer because instinct takes over. You become powered by adrenalin. You do not *think* about it in any normal sense of the word, so afterwards you cannot easily describe it in words. Because I was in bed it felt dream-like in a way; half-real, as though part of me was somehow witheld from the experience.

Crawling on all fours, I went into the corridor to check that my guards were all right. They were stationed quietly at various points returning fire only when necessary so as to reduce casualties to the minimum. Their coolness seemed superhuman. I felt a diffused sense of gratitude for it — to them, their officers and God! Suddenly there was a shout followed by shots from my guards, and the lifeless body of a sergeant slumped and fell from my bedroom window through which he was about to climb. Another soldier was shot as he attempted to enter my lounge. I felt sick — less from fear than from horror. The violent death even of a would-be assassin is no pretty thing.

After about thirty minutes of intensive firing there was a sudden peace. Then, in reply to a command to fire, a man's voice was heard to say plaintively: "Sir, I have nothing left." They had run out of ammunition. My nephew, who was on the ground floor, heard one soldier say to his mate: "Thank God the Brigadier himself is here." This he later gave as evidence on oath at the trial.

The presence of Brigadier Bangura, however, was of little comfort without a further supply of ammunition, and now that their magazines were empty, the troops hastily withdrew leaving behind them their two dead comrades and much wanton damage to my residence, but without having succeeded in their deadly objective. We suffered not a single casualty.

I went to inspect the damage, which was extensive both inside and outside the house, and then left to take shelter elsewhere in the city. Around 9 a.m. I was advised that the country was in confusion and realised that I had to make an appearance to convince people that I was unharmed, and to broadcast a statement to explain the situation. To do this I went to the Party headquarters.

" This is your Prime Minister speaking to you in Freetown. I am alive and well, by the grace of God."

I had not got very far with the broadcast when a soldier whom I trusted interrupted me and said with urgency: "Come out of here at once, Sir." It seemed that information had reached him that a further attack was being planned. I immediately left the building with various Ministers and party colleagues and went to my office at Tower Hill where crowds of well-wishers and sympathisers had gathered to greet me.

As soon as I got into my office I 'phoned the Governor-General on the private line we shared and told him that, from what I had heard, Bangura intended to carry on with the coup. I pointed out to him that as Commander-in-Chief of the Armed Forces, it was his urgent duty to intervene and to stop the Force Commander from taking any further unconstitutional action.

After about an hour I felt so exhausted that I decided to leave and try to get some rest somewhere. I had almost reached the bottom of the stairs that led to the entrance to the building when I saw an army lorry pull up at the gate, then another one, and a crowd of soldiers, heavily armed, hurriedly scramble out of them and take up positions to the right and left of the building with their rifles pointing towards it. My guards covered me and pushed me upstairs into my office where I lay flat on the floor. We had barely reached the room before the firing started. Bullets penetrated into my office from left, right and centre. One shot broke the lavatory cistern and burst a pipe so that water flooded the lavatory, the ante-room and, eventually, my office. Before long the carpet I was lying on became like a paddy field and I was saturated.

The telephone connecting me with the Governor-General rang insistently. It was impossible to reach for it was in the direct line of fire. In any case there was no point in him relaying to me Bangura's reply to him. The rifles and machine guns did it for him.

Rapid firing continued at intervals throughout the whole afternoon and I was not able to leave the building until after 6 p.m. By this time I had crawled into the ante-room between my office and the lavatory because there was no window there. Most of the glass in the other windows had been shattered; curtains had been ripped by bullets and hung in ribbons, the wall behind my desk was pitted with holes and an acrid stench of gunpowder and damp carpets pervaded the place.

At 3.15 p.m. Lt. Col. King announced on the radio that the Force Commander had an important message to make. I learnt later that King had not wanted to identify himself, but that Bangura had insisted on him doing so. "Fellow citizens," Bangura said. "Owing to the current state of affairs, the army has been compelled to take control of the situation until further notice. A comprehensive statement will be made as soon as possible. This statement has the full backing and support of the armed forces. Any undue interference will be viewed with disdain."

Later that afternoon, King came on the air again, this time to say that the majority of the men in the army dissociated themselves from the Force Commander's broadcast and that as far as the army was concerned, it regarded my government as the legal authority. It was a most confused situation and the thought went through my mind that if this was a sample of the way our army organised affairs, it was high time that the army itself was reorganised.

Shortly after King's announcement, and when it was confirmed that the loyal elements in the army were in fact in control, the hostile forces withdrew and I was able to leave the building.

It had been a terrifying ordeal. It is bad enough knowing that men are seeking to kill you, but even worse is the knowledge that there are those who, through loyalty to your person, risk injury and death without honour in putting themselves between you and the lethal weapons that are aimed at you. When I saw the lines of sheer fatigue and exhaustion on the faces of my security guards and their state of general dishevelment, tears dimmed my sight. Between us — but largely thanks to them — we had somehow saved the day; constitutional government still reigned and the nation had been spared the setback of another military takeover.

The editorial in *West Africa*, in its issue following the disturbance, had this to say, among other things:

" So irresponsible is the idea of over-throwing civilian governments in Sierra Leone at this time that unless Sierra Leone is simply proving the unhappy maxim that a country which has experienced one coup is always likely to experience another, one fears that civilian political influence might have been at work to secure army support in the desperate bid for power."

There was no doubt in my mind that urgent and serious consideration would have to be given to finding a deterrent to a repetition of assassination attempts and other acts aimed at disrupting the normal order of society. Some means must be found whereby personal power-seekers are kept at bay, whereby the consideration of life, law and stable constitutional government takes precedence over money, possessions and high office.

My mind went back to the lenient treatment I had given the two would-be assassins five months before, whose only punishment had been a reduction in rank; to those who had plotted against me at that time who were allowed to continue in their key positions; to the wretched Bangura who could not have been more clearly a traitor to me had he had the word emblazoned on his chest, yet I allowed him to leave my house to keep an appointment with those who, a few hours later, attempted to shoot me, because I refused to believe he was incapable of a change of heart. As things had turned out, I could hardly blame those among my colleagues who accused me of being soft. Yet this was not the case, and I have already in this chapter explained myself on this score.

Now, however, I had come to the full realisation of the fact — a fact which I had known all along, of course, though I was reluctant to admit it — that university degree or no university degree, college diploma or no college diploma, refinement or no refinement, man can turn brute and it is then that brute force must be used to deal with him. That I did not take such action after similar instances in the past was simply because I was not prepared to employ brute force to back the theoretical power I possessed. However, this time those responsible had to be brought to trial and the guilty punished according to, and with the full weight of, the law. I had learnt to my cost, and to the cost of those who looked to me for leadership, that there was much truth in Shakespeare's comment that "nothing emboldens sin so much as mercy".

*A BROADCAST TO THE NATION IN MARCH 1969 (ABOVE) AND A MOVING WELCOME
EXTENDED TO MY WIFE, REBECCA, WHEN SHE RETURNED TO FREETOWN FROM A
TRIP ABROAD A FEW MONTHS LATER*

MY INSTALLATION AS CHIEF MOTOR DRIVER BY THE TAXI AND OTHER PROFESSIONAL DRIVERS OF FREETOWN IN JULY 1968 (ABOVE) AND (BELOW) ATTENDING AN OFFICIAL FUNCTION WITH MY WIFE AND S.I. KOROMA WHO WAS TO BECOME THE COUNTRY'S FIRST VICE-PRESIDENT. IN THE BACKGROUND IS MY SON JENGO WHO STUDIED MEDICINE IN THE GERMAN DEMOCRATIC REPUBLIC.

CHAPTER SEVENTEEN

Dawn of the Republic

There was no time to absorb the shock of the assassination attempts. I had three jobs of inescapable urgency to tackle: to pacify the rebellious elements in the army; to fill the vacuum in the nation's defences created by the disorder of the armed forces; and to make it impossible for the same kind of threat to national security ever to occur again.

At the time, I remember, I found it hard to prioritise these problems in my own mind. The last of them — eliminating any future possibility of a violent *putsch* — seemed to me to be essentially constitutional. It was no less urgent than the others but could not be so quickly solved. At the most optimistic projection, it would take weeks rather than days — and whatever I did I was determined to do quickly. I felt certain that only fast, decisive action could cope with the emergency. Every instinct told me that national defence was the top priority. I had lived through invasion scares and knew what it was like living from day to day in government with army officers of dubious loyalty, some of them in league with enemies abroad, some of them in foreign pay. In the aftermath of the assassination attempts, I could not be sure that the army would be in any shape to resist foreign intervention. On the other hand, I did not want to rely on outside help to protect our country. We had striven for generations to rid Sierra Leone of foreign dependence. I wanted us to go it alone, if we could, in the crisis we faced. I also wanted to give the army command another chance to do its duty by the people.

On March 24th, the day following the abortive coup, I attended a meeting of Ministers and army officers in an endeavour to restore normalcy and confidence between us. It became disturbingly clear to me that elements in the army command were unreconciled. There was evidence in abundance of their lack of confidence. You could see it in the amount of hardware they carried round with them. I was frankly fascinated by one officer who had no less than three revolvers on his person, and found myself wondering whether, like a juggler, he employed them all at once! Little was achieved, and a meeting was arranged for the following day.

"Whatever you do, don't attend tomorrow's meeting!" a trusted friend warned me on the telephone that evening. I stayed away from that meeting and from the one arranged for the following day, when pleas were made by some of the dissident element for amnesty for all those who had taken part in the two abortive coups.

> "The Prime Minister, Dr. Siaka Stevens, it is understood, was expected to attend the meeting, but he was not there," *Unity* reported. "... The whereabouts of the Prime Minister was not known..."

Few indeed knew where I was, and as time went by a number of people began to express anxiety about me. The Governor-General, many of the Ministers and party members, the Diplomatic Corps and even those who worked closely with me in the Prime Minister's office, sought news one from another as to where I might be. The thing that worried many of them, I was told later, was that it was totally out of character for me to disappear.

"You have so much courage," one person told me, "that the sort of thing you would normally have done on the morning immediately following the shooting was to drive bare-headed in an open car to inspect the damage and assure yourself of the well-being of your staff and of the public in general." That I had failed to do this apparently led some to believe that I had either suffered serious injuries, or that I was not in fact free, that I was being held by my enemies and that the reassuring messages from me that were being broadcast at frequent intervals had been forced from me at gun point and were being relayed to deceive the people. All this was gratifying in a way, but it took more than flattery to make me feel secure after escaping the assassins so narrowly. After the first abortive meeting with the army men, I took an instant decision to re-shuffle my priorities in line with my original instinct. I decided to shelve reconciliation with the army until after the immediate defence needs of the country were met.

The previous December, Parliament had passed a Resolution calling for a Defence Agreement with our two neighbours, Guinea and Liberia. After attending the meeting with army personnel on March 24th, and from the reports I received of the proceedings at the other two meetings, I realised that if ever there was dire need for the agreement to be activated, it was now. The way was wide open, in fact, for enemies from outside — for those, no doubt, who had so heavily financed the abortive uprising — to recoup their losses by attacking us. The position was so critical that I left Freetown for Guinea by car during the night of March 25th, and arrived in Conakry around five the following morning.

After consultations with President Sekou Toure and members of his Government he, as the President of the Republic of Guinea, and I, as the Prime Minister of Sierra Leone, together signed a Defence Agreement under which each country could call upon the assistance of the other in the event of a serious threat to its security.

I knew, of course, how dedicated Sekou Toure was to the task of foiling by all possible means any attempt by non-African interests to interfere in the internal affairs of African states. His constant vigilance in this respect turned out to be fully justified when Portuguese troops and mercenaries invaded Guinea in an attempt to overthrow his Government. Coupled with his apprehensions about foreign interference was a constant preoccupation to maintain the political stability of African countries — a preoccupation which he had expressed publicly many a time and which also found an expression in his unequivocal condemnation of coups and his policy of delaying the recognition of regimes arising from the violent overthrow of legitimate governments.

My public diary reveals what I said about it in the broadcasts and speeches I made on my return. But my feelings were more complex. I was grateful for the friendship of my old comrade, Sekou Toure, who came now to help my people as once he had come to my own aid when I was a dispossessed exile from my country. Of course, I was concerned about how the steps I was taking would work out in the perspective of history. What leader worth his salt would not have these on his mind in the circumstances? People often think that because a man acts fast and makes tough decisions he must be either hard or rash. I can put my hand on my heart and say I agonised over each of the terrible decisions I still had to make in the aftermath of the abortive coup. I got down on my knees and prayed every day during the critical period that God would guide me to make my decisions *right* as well as expedient. And I thank Him that at the end of the day they worked out for the best.

I flew back to Freetown on Sunday morning, March 28th, and shortly after my arrival I broadcast to the people advising them of the step I had taken and the reasons that had prompted me to do so.

"The dissident army men may have their faults," I concluded, "but there is no doubt that financial and big power pressures played, and continue to play, an important part in the recent troubles. Let us find them and expose them for their due rewards."

A short while later, I made another broadcast in which I stressed the fact that the rebel soldiers and politicians had wanted "to confiscate and retain the Government in order to show that brutal force prevails over reason, legality and common sense".

All those who had tried to trample down the legal regime were outlaws and I declared that so long as I was the Prime Minister of Sierra Leone, I would never permit a clique of men without a mandate to assume power. "I would rather die for my country than accept government by brute force," I said.

Even as I ended my speech, announcing that from that very moment the armed forces of both Guinea and Sierra Leone had become as one and were "ready to crush all those who might attempt to destroy peace and security in our two countries", several truck-loads of Guinean troops arrived in Freetown and four MiG jet fighters of the Guinean Air Force flew overhead to assure our people that we no longer stood alone.

Our detractors made a great deal of capital over the arrival of the Guinean troops in Sierra Leone. It was obvious that they did not want to see our small states getting together, but preferred us to remain as small units so that they could swallow us up at will, either politically or economically. The London *Times* of April 2nd, for instance, a reputable newspaper by most standards, produced such an inaccurate report that it even included a picture of a one-time Commissioner of Police here and declared him to be Brigadier Bangura!

" According to Mr. Stevens," the report said, "the reason for invoking the Defence Agreement with Guinea was last week's attempted coup, which was alleged to have been organised by elements of his own army. There is evidence that this is the reverse of the truth, and that the disturbances in Freetown on March 23rd and 24th took place after the arrival of the first armed Guineans in Sierra Leone."

According to the British Broadcsting Corporation, 45 armed Guinean soldiers arrived by helicopter "close to the Prime Minister's residence." This false statement was followed up by an interview with Albert Margai who gave some highly coloured views of a situation with which he showed himself to be pathetically out of touch; in spite of his claim to having 'good contacts'. But I have found in life that there is little point in rebutting calumnies. Better by far to ignore them and get on with the job. Yet sometimes one just sees red and feels compelled to set the record straight.

In some ways, I should much have preferred to fill our defence gap through some sort of co-operative Commonwealth action, arranged through our friends in the U.K. On many occasions in the past, the British have despatched troops to defend ex-British territories, for example, in Kenya and Anguilla, who found themselves in trouble with rebel forces. Yet in 1967, when we desperately needed such help from them, they sent not even a message of sympathy but expected us to sit down with folded hands while the army took over control from the legally constituted government and sacked the Queen's own representative. What more natural thing, then, than for us now to seek the assistance of our brothers on whom we could rely for support, many of them being our own kith and kin, such as the Madingos and the Foulahs? We were in great difficulty, and I am not ashamed to admit it. We had a responsibility to the nation, a responsibility to protect lives and property by whatever means we believed would be the most effective, and Guinea ably and willingly provided those means.

Once the defence gap was bridged, we could turn back to the task of reconciling the army. There was only one way to do it: everyone who supported or sympathised with the *putsch* had to be removed from command. This meant cutting out the rot from the top. It meant taking action against men whom I knew and, indeed, liked. The Force Commander and six army officers were arrested and detained on March 28th. On the following day, March 29th, I wrote the following letter to the Governor-General, Sir Banja Tejan-Sie:

" Painful as the duty is, I have no alternative but to comply with the expressed desire of the Government of Sierra Leone that the following telegram should be despatched immediately under secret cover to Her Majesty Queen Elizabeth the Second ..."

The telegram requested that under the provisions of Sections 26 to 28 of the Constitution, the Governor-General should be relieved of his duties immediately and proceed forthwith on leave prior to retirement, and that the Chief Justice, Mr. C. O. E. Cole, should act as Governor-General until further notice. Approval was received on March 31st and Cole took office the same day.

It was the day Parliament met to review the events of that explosive past week. The most critical period was over and some members might have been excused for feeling like an audience turning up late for a melodrama and seeing only the denouement. But there remained a crucial role for the House to discharge. There were emergency measures to ratify and, above all, there was the constitutional root-cause of our troubles to tackle. I wanted Parliament to re-cast the Constitution in a watertight form that would be proof against factional instability. I told the members that we could live in peace only by keeping the rules of democracy. I denounced attempts to force a change of government by violence, "but, if we go by the rules," I said, "then everybody's time is bound to come". I felt that I was struggling to explain what had happened to myself as much as to my parliamentary colleagues, as I went on:

" The real people who can effectively wield power in this country are so few that each one must have a chance, and if you wait a little you will get your chance. I have been in this game for over forty years and if I enjoy some benefits today, I have to thank the Almighty God. Therefore, Mr. Speaker and Honourable Members, I feel that each one of us has a responsibility to see that law and order are maintained in this country."

I urged the young up-and-coming men to work hard if they wanted to succeed in life. If this world was a place where a person could take another's post by knocking him out with a weapon, nobody would take the trouble to go to school or college, but would merely go and get his gun, shoot a man and take his job:

" In that case," I said, "he will be making a sad mistake, because if a sergeant knocks a man down, a corporal who witnessed it would say to himself: 'So — is it as easy as that?' and will in turn knock the sergeant down and add another stripe to his sleeve. And so on and so on until nobody gets anywhere at all.

"We who happen to have had a little bit of education and a bit of literacy must realise that we owe a great responsibility to those of our brothers and sisters who have not had the opportunity of education; they look up to us and they mould their behaviour by the example that we set. Let us therefore pray God that we do not fail them."

When I sat down again, I felt a little bit of normality had been recovered. I was trying to reach back to a feeling of stability and peace, beyond the recent troubles. I was trying to pick up threads of progress and continuity that the conspiracy against my life had severed and frayed. Parliament responded warmly. Things seems to be resuming their right places again.

On April 7th, Parliament met to ratify the Sierra Leone/Guinea Defence Agreement which I had signed on behalf of the Sierra Leone Government a fortnight before.

"... In this world of ours," I declared, "one can only pick and choose when there is an alternative or when there are alternatives. When you do not have an alternative, then you take whatever presents itself, and anyone here who says that we should not have signed a defence agreement with Guinea is invited to tell us now what we should have done when we found ourselves in the position we were in on March 23rd last.

"Could anybody get up and say what we could have done when, without provocation, dissident soldiers went to the head of Government — leave my personality out of it — at half-past twelve in the morning and rained bullets on the whole building? As if that was not enough, they went again to the office of the head of Government at half-past one in the afternoon and started to shoot. I was not the only person there; innocent people who were earning their living were there as well, and were so shocked that most of them were incapable of moving. ...We feel, Sir, that we have every justification to call other people here to help us. If you cannot preserve yourself you are finished. The only way left open to us was to call on friendly neighbouring African territories for help. We did not call in Germans, or Swiss, or Englishmen; we called our own brothers along the boundary. Sooner or later we will all be one. It is only the demarcation line that divides us."

Some people, I said, had wickedly used the word 'invasion' when referring to the arrival of the Guinean troops.

" The Guineans did not invade Sierra Leone," I declared. "The Guinean soldiers are here on the invitation of the Government and people of Sierra Leone; if we had not brought them in, perhaps quite a few people in the gallery today would not be here."

I gave instances of the behaviour of some of the rebel soldiers. One of them stopped for petrol, impatiently drew his gun and shot the garage hand. Others went to the market, fired shots in the air to cause the traders to flee in panic, then helped themselves to the money and wares that had been left behind. Some even went to an infants' school by my office on the day of the shooting and seized the children's lunch. Much of the world, I said, would rather see an Africa made up of fragmented states than a united continent.

" That is not what we the Africans want," I declared, "We want to link up, and common sense dictates that we must link up so that when one is attacked the others will rise up to assist. Whether we are French speaking or English speaking, the sooner we link up the better it will be for all, Sir."

I gave as an example the many different nationalities of the people who make up the great nation of America:

"If we believe that one hundred thousand Mendes, or two hundred thousand Limbas, or five hundred thousand Temnes can stand by themselves, we will only be fooling ourselves. We *have* to get together so that in case of any difficulty we will be able to call upon our friends to help us out."

It was hoped, I said, that in time the Republic of Liberia would link up with us so that we could begin to lay the foundation for a defence pact that would embrace the whole of West Africa.

Parliament duly ratified the Defence Agreement, but the Opposition staged a complete boycott. Both this and the criticism of the Defence Agreement by Albert Margai in London, showed up the obstructionists in their true colours and exposed their lack of sincerity, for it was in fact Albert Margai who first negotiated for a defence pact with Guinea in 1966. The negotiations took place in the house of a District Officer in Sefadu, but he neither sought nor obtained the full mandate of Parliament to ratify these. As I pointed out to Members: "Albert Margai started this business, and we continued it. And now he is jealous."

Even with the valuable assistance that Guinea would provide under this Defence Agreement, it was clear to me that the future security of our country would depend more and more on the ability of every citizen to participate actively in defence. Government would never be able to provide sufficient funds to maintain an army and police force of the strength necessary to hold our own against an invasion of any size. In many countries a young man has to undergo a period in the forces, even in peace time, to train him to usefully serve his country if the need should arise. In the dangerous situation in which we were placed, I saw an urgent need for our men and women to be trained for defence. As things stood, the very sound of a gun shot sent people flying off in all directions in utter panic. Nobody knew what to do and in the atmosphere of terror and disorganisation, an enemy would have no trouble at all in trouncing us. With a sense of discipline drilled into them, with instruction on how to use weapons, with a clear understanding of their duty in the event of an emergency, ordinary Sierra Leoneans would become a formidable obstacle for any enemy to reckon with.

With the army defused and defence provided for, we could turn to face the constitutional problem posed by the *putsch*. The Constitution had us hamstrung during the crisis. Whenever I thought about the desperation induced by hanging around trying to communicate with the Governor-General while bullets whizzed around shattering the glass and cracking the plaster, I had to call on all my resources of good honour to keep my temper. Even a Governor-General determined to oppose the coup atempt would have been powerless to frustrate it. He would have neither the stature nor the authority to command popular support. Only an elected Commander-in-Chief and Head of State would be in a position to defend democracy against any future *revanche*. In other words, the coup precipitated the need for a Republican Constitution.

Of course, we had long intended anyway to bring in a republic. Sierra Leone had been edging towards republican status since the mid-sixties. Popular support for republicanism was pretty well universal and the Fashole Luke Constitutional Commission was well advanced in its appointed task of public consultation to determine the most widely acceptable form of republican constitution. Now, however, the process, which we had been unfolding gradually, demanded urgent completion. We felt we needed a republic at once — even an imperfect one which would need modification after further public consultation. As it was, democracy lay exposed to the men of violence. By ushering in a republic at once, we could make Sierra Leone safe for democracy.

On January 25th, 1967, the previous S.L.P.P. Government had

given the third reading to a Republican Constitution Bill. The A.P.C., then in opposition, abstained from participating in the proceedings for reasons I have already given. We made it clear that we were in favour of this country becoming a republic, but we found it difficult to participate in voting for a Bill which contained a considerable number of obnoxious clauses which the then S.L.P.P. Government was unwilling to amend.

According to the law which then operated, the 1967 Republican Constitution Bill would have become an effective Act if it was passed at the first Session after the 1967 General Election. It was impracticable for this to be done. Firstly, there had been an interregnum caused by the military seizing power. Secondly, when the civilians ultimately resumed power in 1968, there were far too many more urgent matters to be looked into before the draft Republican Bill was voted upon.

After the 1968 civilian National Government was transformed into an effective A.P.C. Government, we gave serious consideration to the matter of transforming this country from a monarchy into a republic. We made known our intentions and gave everyone the opportunity of putting forward proposals. We would have liked to hold a general election before inaugurating the new Republic, but the emergency conditions of 1971 made it impossible. We decided to proceed to republican status by the fastest and most efficient route and then, with stability re-established, seek the approval of the electorate retrospectively. Of course, we were quite willing to stand corrected by the people, though in fact, at the end of the day, our measures got massive endorsement. Meanwhile, we made known our intention to Buckingham Palace and the British Government and were advised in due course that the Queen had approved the steps we proposed to take and would relinquish her functions as Head of State of Sierra Leone.

We all felt it was very bad luck that the emergency and general shortage of time forced us to fall back on the 1967 Republican Constitution Bill. We were fully conscious of the fact that it contained a number of undesirable provisions, but I made it clear that it was not our intention to retain these any longer than necessary. I assured the people that my government would not take advantage of the undesirable clauses and that we undertook, wherever possible, to allow these to lie dormant in the Republican Constitution until they would be replaced, in the near future, by a popular Republican Constitution.

Parliament met on April 15th to sanction the Constitution (Amendment) Bill, 1971. Referring to the shortcomings of the Bill and its obnoxious clauses, I said that in spite of this, it was the opportunity we needed and we were going to take it. I cannot say I was happy. To have to use a defective, secondhand Bill seemed to tarnish my dream of bringing to my country the full dignity and sense of independence that republicanism represented. I felt I was being forced to sever the last of our colonial bonds with a blunt blade. But politics is a practical craft, or it is nothing. I resigned myself to making the best of a bad job. It was still a great occasion, and a great stride forward for Sierra Leone.

With the amendments to the Constitution approved, one final act remained before Sierra Leone could move to a republican government, the adoption by a two-thirds majority of the House of the Constitution of Sierra Leone. The vote was taken at 12.57 p.m. and at 13.05 p.m. I rose and declared:

"It is my humble duty to announce to the nation that Sierra Leone is from this moment a Republic!"

The whole House, the Members on the floor and the people crowding the galleries, as well as the waiting hundreds packed tightly cheek by jowl in the precincts of the building, cheered and clapped, shouted, wailed and sang, embraced one another, wept and laughed, and fought feverishly to clutch my hand. 'Shaki the hero!' they yelled.

"Shaki the hero," *Unity* reported, "was dressed in a light blue suit, with pipe in hand ..."

Shortly afterwards the Acting Governor-General, Justice C. O. E. Cole, was sworn in as the first President of the Republic and myself as its first Prime Minister. Two days later, on April 21st, I took office as the first Executive President and Justice Cole reverted to his substantive post of Chief Justice.

"My dear people," I said, after being sworn in, "I pray God that I may prove worthy of the confidence which you have reposed in me by appointing me to this office. I shall keep in touch with you, the people, all the time because I know that if I keep in touch with you I shall be on the right road."

I told them that in our changed constitutional position, as indeed in the past, only the wicked and the trouble-makers had need to fear; those who kept on the right side of the law and worked for peace had nothing to worry about and would receive every encouragement and protection from Government.

"We thank all our friends who have helped us up to now and

especially the British Government and people with whom we have had close ties for over a hundred years. We mean to remain in the Commonwealth and we mean to establish new contacts and to make friends with all those who want our friendship and treat us on the basis of respect and equality."

As a republic, Sierra Leone could now well and truly say and mean that she was going to pursue a policy of non-alignment, I said. We lacked sufficient know-how and capital for development and were therefore determined to give every encouragement to those who had these commodities to offer us.

In a later broadcast on the tenth anniversary of Independence, April 27th, I explained in greater detail what the changeover to republican status meant. Although Independence ten years ago released us from the rule of the imperialists, I said, it still left our country under a colonial constitution. Our Head of State remained in London; all our overseas diplomats represented the British Queen and Sierra Leone was the last country in Africa tied to the British monarchy. I declared that it was through no feeling of disrespect for the Queen that we decided to change to a republican constitution, that she remained Head of the Commonwealth, that we intended to continue our Commonwealth membership and gladly acknowledged her as the symbol of Commonwealth unity.

" But we believe that the dignity of Sierra Leone demands that all the institutions of government in this country should be in the hands of Sierra Leoneans and based in our country, that our Head of State be a Sierra Leonean elected by those who represent the Sierra Leonean people."

Parliament had done me the honour of electing me as Executive President for the next five years. It had decided that it was more important to have a President who was working directly in Government for the good of the country than simply a President who appeared only on ceremonial occasions. As President, I said, I was also Commander-in-Chief of the Armed Forces. Every member of the army from senior officers to the most junior recruit now owed his loyalty to me as the representative of all the people of Sierra Leone.

" The task of that army is to defend the State and Nation of Sierra

Leone under its duly elected Government. This," I declared, "is a task which I, as Commander-in-Chief, will ensure is carried out by the armed forces."

I assured the people that the change in Constitution did not endanger any of the democratic rights which we in Sierra Leone had been proud to preserve.

"I have been elected as President for five years," I said. "The present Parliament will complete its term of office in 1973 when the next parliamentary election will be held. You will therefore continue to be represented by a government each one of you has helped to elect. Our system of justice, which protects the freedom of each individual, will be maintained as before. We also have a Vice-President, Mr. S. I. Koroma, who is also Prime Minister. He will lead government business in Parliament, but I as President shall remain the Head of the Cabinet and the Government."

The Government, Ministers, Members of Parliament, civil servants, public officials and armed forces had, I said, been elected or appointed to serve the interests of every citizen of Sierra Leone, irrespective of tribe or class.

"They are the servants, not the masters, of the Sierra Leone people. We are all in office not for the sake of our personal ambitions but in order to make this a better country to live in. ...We are your representatives. We must devote ourselves to the public welfare, not to private careerism. We must set an example to the whole nation by living humble lives, leaving the money-making, property-owning, big houses and cars to those private businessmen whose ambition it is to become rich. We are elected and paid by the ordinary people of Sierra Leone, entrusted with the responsibility of leading them to a better way of life. We must show that we are fit for this responsibility. ...Let us build our new Republic of Sierra Leone into a nation worthy of its people," I declared, "worthy of taking its place in the new progressive continent of Africa."

When I accepted the office of Executive President, I swore that I would faithfully and truly discharge the duties of the office of President of the State of Sierra Leone according to law and that I would support and uphold the Constitution of Sierra Leone as by law established.

I doubt if anybody who has not themselves held such high office really appreciates the weight of responsibility that falls on the shoulders of a Head of State. Whatever action you take, whatever decision you arrive at, whatever words you utter outside the intimacy of your own home, can affect the lives of every man and woman in the country. The first thing I had to learn to do, therefore, was to draw a very definite line between Siaka Stevens the man and Siaka Stevens the President, so that the very human emotions of the first did not at any time encroach upon and influence the bounden duties of the latter. This in no way means that I believe a President must aim to become a heartless machine. He is very much a human being and must needs always remain so. But there are times when I have been faced with the most appalling issues requiring my decision, when pressure is brought so strongly to bear on my personal feelings, that it would be only too easy to shirk the duty of the President according to the law and to allow the actions of the man according to his sentiments to take over.

One case in point was the death sentence passed by the Court Martial on Bangura and three other officers as a result of their part in the abortive coup. I am fully aware that many people were shocked when these sentences were carried out and that even today, much speculation goes on as to what prompted me to allow the law to take its course. There is even a fantastic rumour circulating that I had actually decided to commute the sentences to terms of imprisonment but that certain strong party members had forced me to change my mind. Let me put the record straight here and now. No single person, nor even the demonstrations in favour of the death sentence that filed through the city, had any influence whatsoever on the action I was obliged to take. For me it was a dreadful act. I had to wrench myself out of my own character. I had to shed all the personal feelings and sympathies and emanations of spirit which had accumulated in my own progress as a human being and, in particular, in the course of my acquaintance with the condemned men. But it was not in a personal capacity that I was asked to sign the death warrants. I still felt the moral responsibility in a deeply personal way. But I was able to act out of a sense of duty to my office. The limits of the law very properly restrict the power of a democratic head of state, but — thank God! — they also help him do his duty.

To view the whole thing dispassionately, and leaving personalities out of it, these officers were out to get rid of me not because I was a man they disliked called Siaka Stevens, but because I headed a government which they, or their backers, wanted to oust. Because of their actions, several people lost their lives and the Constitutional Government was all but overthrown. They were tried, found guilty of a crime punishable by death and so sentenced. The sentences were passed on to a Committee on the Prerogative of Mercy which recommended that the law should take its course. These recommendations were then referred to me as Head of State for confirmation or otherwise in the normal way. I confirmed them not in my capacity as Siaka Stevens the man, the injured party and one-time friend of the chief accused, but as Executive President of the Republic of Sierra Leone, of the nation whose people I had sworn to serve. The peace and security of that nation had twice been threatened in the short space of five months and it was my solemn and avowed promise to the people to do all in my power to guard against any future attempts of this kind. There was no question where my obligations as President lay.

A BIRTHDAY CAKE PRESENTED
STATE HOUSE STAFF

*BEING SWORN IN AS THE FIRST EXECUTIVE PRESIDENT OF SIERRA LEONE BY
CHIEF JUSTICE C.O.E.COLE (ABOVE) AND SWEARING IN S.I. KOROMA AS FIRST
VICE-PRESIDENT (BELOW)*

INSPECTING THE ARMED FORCES AT A CEREMONY AT BROOKFIELDS STADIUM WITH BRIGADIER J.S. MOMOH AND FIRST VICE-PRESIDENT S.I. KOROMA (ABOVE) AND AFTER A FRIENDLY DISCUSSION WITH PRESIDENT AHMED SEKOU TOURE OF GUINEA (BELOW).

*THANKSGIVING
SERVICE ON THE 10TH
ANNIVERSARY OF
INDEPENDENCE.*

*RECEIVING AT STATE
HOUSE A DELEGATION
OF PARAMOUNT CHIEFS
AND DIGNITARIES FROM
PUJEHUN DISTRICT.*

*FREETOWN WOMEN
WELCOME ME ON MY
RETURN FROM A
FOREIGN VISIT.*

INSPECTING THE NATIONAL WORKSHOP (ABOVE) AND CONSTRUCTION WORK IN PROGRESS (BELOW).

CHAPTER 18

At the Helm

As I get older I find my mind dwelling more and more on the past. Inevitably my thoughts wander back to the time when Sierra Leone became a Republic. At 1.13 p.m. on April 19th, 1971, I declared the State a Republic after a Republican Constitution had been approved by Parliament and passed into law with a majority of 53 in favour and 10 against. I can remember that as I spoke those fateful, all-important words there were tears in my eyes, for in my own lifetime I had seen my country come such a long way. I was proud to be associated with the struggle that had led to this moment, and that pride was swelled as I listened to the shouts and applause that followed my declaration that April day. There was a long standing ovation but I was so oblivious to the passage of time that I cannot tell you whether it lasted for just seconds or minutes. I can remember looking up at those who piled into the public gallery and being overwhelmed at the thought that these were my people, that the struggle had been for them.

Later that day the British flag was lowered from State House and replaced by the flag of Sierra Leone. Once again there was a tremendous response from the crowds. They shouted 'Happy New Year' and cheered. And like all New Years we were starting off with a clean slate, all of us full of resolutions. The only difference between this and other New Years was that those resolutions were going to be remembered and maintained, and not dropped at the end of the month like a child resolving to give up candy.

That night no one got very much sleep, least of all me. Crowds gathered in the streets and impromptu parties and celebrations went on into the small hours of the morning. In fact, I remember that there was little opportunity to sleep for the whole of that week! Two days later I became the first Executive President of Sierra Leone at a ceremony in Parliament Building. Again I was called on to make a speech. I prayed to God that I would prove myself worthy of the confidence put in me by my people — and that prayer has been with me ever since. I told Parliament that only by keeping in touch with the people at all times could I be sure of following the right path. I also promised to deal firmly with trouble makers — my experience as a policeman had taught me the importance of that — and I realised that if Sierra Leoneans were to have confidence to pursue the building up of their country, they deserved to be able to carry on their lives in peace and quiet, free of trouble and disturbance. When I was a policeman I remember well the pain and unhappiness that just one law breaker could bring to a whole community — and I was not having any of that!

A few days after Sierra Leone became a Republic I had the honour of swearing in the first Vice President and the Prime Minister. After the ceremony Mr. S. I. Koroma and I drove through the streets of Freetown. The pavements were lined with people, and I think that the Vice President was as touched as I was at the crowds' enthusiastic reception. S.I. — as he has affectionately come to be known — is, like myself, a province-born man and has had a long career in politics. Perhaps one of his most striking qualities is his holiness — he is a very devout Muslim — and it is easy to detect the importance of his religion in his everyday life and work. One of the most worrying moments for me and my country was when we heard of his terrible car crash, and the dreadful injuries he sustained. And yet with quiet determination he got better and quickly returned to serving his people, almost as if nothing had happened.

A little more than a week after we became a republic there was yet another celebration. Our tenth anniversary of Independence was marked by public holidays and nationwide festivities. At Brookfields Stadium, which has been the centre of so many important events in the life of independent Sierra Leone, Members of Parliament, members of the diplomatic corps, visiting dignitaries from all corners of the globe, and myself, gathered to watch a march past and parade by the armed forces. I was impressed by the high level of organisation that had gone into the creation of such a special ceremony, and my heart was warmed by the fact that our overseas visitors could see just what Sierra Leone could achieve. Later that evening I gave a grand banquet and ball at State House. I remember it as being a very glittering occasion, with all those present dressed in their best clothes. It was a wonderful climax to what had been a marvellous day, and indeed a momentous couple of weeks. When I finally got to bed that night I could hardly sleep as my head was so full of what had been happening. I felt particularly happy because this was an occasion that could only be remembered with pleasure by me and my people.

I recall my own childhood with such vividness that I am always conscious that the things we do now are providing memories for our children. Without doubt children always remember events of pageantry and display, and I like to think that in years to come mothers and fathers will tell their own children about their recollections of the Tenth Anniversary of Independence. I have always had a strong sense of history, and as an African I have always been aware of the oral tradition of history in our continent. Stories told around the camp fire many years ago are still recounted with the same sense of pleasure in our homes today. In this age of communication by satellite, and even the storing of information in computers it seems essential to me that families still retain their tradition of story-telling and childhood tales. I am glad that Sierra Leonean children were provided with such a dazzling day of events to tuck away in *their* memories!

Thinking back to that year it is natural that events are dominated in my mind by the achievement of republican status. And yet for some reason one visit that I made stands out. Recently I was flicking through my old engagement diaries, and I realised that this particular visit was the very first one that I made outside Freetown after Sierra Leone became a Republic, and I suppose that this is why the opening of Bo Teacher Training College is so fresh in my memory. When I reached Towama I was amazed at the welcome I got. I know that many people imagine that politicians and other well-known people become a little blazé, even jaded, with the ever-cheering crowds. But from the very bottom of my heart I know that there is nothing that thrills me more than the affection and warmth of my people. Whenever I hear a gathering of people cheering it can be guaranteed to send a shiver down my spine!

That was how I felt when I arrived at the Teacher Training College of the United Christian Council. The opening of this college was especially dear to me as I have always been very conscious of the value of a good education. My own experiences have shown me the importance of good teaching. I owe everything to the sacrifices that my father made for me in order to send me to school. But more than that, I owe a great deal to the fact that at those schools I received sympathetic and sometimes inspired instruction. It is only through the establishment of training colleges, such as the one at Bo, that our children will truly receive the benefits of education. Having been brought up in the province myself I know how badly distributed centres of education were. The only way I could have a proper and advanced schooling was to leave my family for Freetown. It pleases me considerably that children in the province can now receive just as good an education as those in what used to be known as the Protectorate, and I think that Bo College, which after all has been running for some ten years now, has had quite a hand in this achievement.

Another event which stands out in my mind in the early days of our Republic was when I was awarded the *Daily Mail's* 'Man of the Decade' honour. The newspaper ran a poll for its readers in order to try and discover who people in the street thought fitted the description of "Man of the Decade", and apparently the response was overwhelmingly in favour of me! I remember saying at the time of the presentation that it would be a very long time before I would forget this gesture, and certainly I still recall the day Mr. Sam Metzger, Chairman of the *Daily Mail*, presented me with the award as if it was only yesterday. Mr. Metzger suggested that I might even become "Man of the Century", and although I was touched with his tribute, I cannot help hoping that with nearly twenty more years of the twentieth century to go there might be other contenders for the title.

A time of great change such as I went through during the establishment of a Republic is always a time for stocktaking, for sorting out one's own ideas and values. For many years all my thoughts were with — and within — my country. There was so much going on in Sierra Leone that I had little opportunity to consider her relationship with the rest of the world. Indeed, I had little time to think about what I shall term the 'theory' of government. For too long the business of the everyday life of my country had taken up each minute of my day.

With the advent of a Republic I felt rather like a man who had just climbed to the top of a hill and taken a few moments to look at the steep incline he has just struggled up, and also turns an eye to the view that lies ahead of him. The view ahead of me was inevitably rather misty, for only a fool will claim he knows the future; nevertheless I could make out the dim outlines of what lay in front of me. I knew that sticking to one particular ideology was not for me, or Sierra Leone.

It is all very well for people in the West to say "I'm a Communist" or "I'm a Liberal", but in the Third World we cannot afford that sort of luxury. We cannot sit in book-lined rooms and discuss with our friends whether Marx was right or wrong, or whether Keynes' theories were of any practical use. We must roll up our sleeves and get down to the matter of raising living standards in Sierra Leone. There are still people in my country who will never be able to read this book simply because we have not yet the resources to educate everyone. There are babies who will never grow into adults because in many parts of the country the drinking water is contaminated, simply because we have not got the money to put these things right. Sometimes it makes me weep with rage to think of what will happen to some of my fellow countrymen merely because of lack of funds. I am a practical man, and I have always realised that the first thing to do in my country is to ensure that our children are educated, well clothed and fed, and that our families have pleasant homes to live in. It is the quality of everyday life that matters to me, not the political beliefs that a man holds.

For this reason Sierra Leone pursues a policy of non-alignment. This sets us free from being a pawn of one of the super-powers and allows us to voice our own individual opinion on world events. I like to think that our policy of speaking out and of expressing what we consider to be the right opinion, rather than an opinion that we have been told to express, has put us on the global map. Sierra Leone has earned a reputation for generating mature and sensible viewpoints, and the voice of my country is a respected one in world affairs. It has always been a matter of great pride to me that my Government was the first to recognise and establish diplomatic relations with the People's Republic of China. The Minister of External Affairs at that time, Mr. Solomon A. J. Pratt, went to Peking, and on July 29th, 1971, a communique was signed, affirming that the Chinese Government and people supported the Government and people of the Republic of Sierra Leone in their struggle against imperialism and colonialism and in their efforts to safeguard national independence and state sovereignty. In turn, my Government affirmed its recognition of the Government of the People's Republic of China as the sole legal Government representing the entire Chinese people. It is difficult to realise now the courage that this decision demanded. The person who makes the first move, particularly when all those around him are against it, must be brave. But my Government and I thought that this was the right decision; we took it, and we turned out to be right. Of course, none of this would have been possible if we had not been firmly non-aligned!

When I have a spare moment and I am able to sit alone with my thoughts — a rare occasion in the life of a president — my mind often goes over the changes that have occurred in Sierra Leone during the last ten years. Living standards have definitely been raised, and I think my countrymen show a confidence and assurance that I did not detect in them before. Today my people are often their own masters, some running their own businesses and many contributing to industry as a whole in Sierra Leone. They mix freely and easily with visiting white tourists and holiday makers; the old antagonisms of the past, if not forgotten, are at least well hidden. Indeed, the coming of the tourist industry is one of the changes that have overtaken Freetown life during the last decade. It never surprises me that Sierra Leone should attract some people for a holiday. I have travelled abroad to many countries, yet when I return to my own country I cannot help thinking that it is the best! The coastal scenery still strikes me, after over seventy years of living here, as spectacular, and with the mountains in the distance it looks truly beautiful.

Whenever I go into one of our hotels and compare them with the ones I have to stay in when I am abroad, I am afraid the patriot in me always awards good marks to our hotels. Some people are very critical of tourism in general. Critics say that the visitors come for a week or two, they stay in their luxury hotels in Aberdeen and probably only see Freetown from a car window, and then they leave as quickly as they come, taking with them a false and distorted view of this little bit of Africa. I admit that it saddens me that many do not take the trouble to find out what Sierra Leone is really like, and yet one must be practical. Those Aberdeen hotels are providing employment for a good number of my people; often the tourists are wealthy and spend their money freely; and fringe services all benefit from our yearly crop of visitors. So, I say to those critics, every penny of foreign currency brought by the tourists can do some good for our people. I have learnt in life that you must always take the rough with the smooth — anything good always has something attached to it which is not so beneficial, and tourism is a case in point.

Our diamond industry, too, has sometimes been the object of criticism. It is a sad fact of life that wherever vast amounts of money are concerned, corruption will always raise its ugly head. Our diamond industry has not been free from such problems, and it has also suffered from undue external influence. But even taking these difficulties into account, it cannot be said that our mineral resources are anything other than an asset. Almost a year after the creation of our Republic, the third largest gem in the world was discovered. I can remember being shown the diamond, which was 969.9 carats, and being completely dazzled by it. I named it the 'Star of Sierra Leone', which seemed to be a most apt title. As *The Times* of London said, it was a "...useful windfall for a country struggling to develop its economy". It saddens me in many ways to think that we had to lose that precious stone to another richer and more prosperous country. But I can take comfort in the fact that I know the proceeds of the sale contributed to a little bit more happiness in the lives of many.

People have asked me about the decision to turn Sierra Leone into a one-party state — a decision which was not taken lightly. After all, the one-party state idea was floated by the S.L.P.P., and was met by almost universal opposition. So why, then, did my government take these steps? I have always said that the A.P.C. is an evolutionary party; as Sierra Leone has blossomed and matured in its new found independence, so the A.P.C. has complemented this growth. It was a decision that came at the right time in the history of my party and the history of my people.

Perhaps it is difficult for the outside observer to realise that the one party system for us does not result in rigidity and oppression, but rather allows us all to work together in the best interests of our developing nation. As I have stressed before, my party does not owe anything to any particular ideology — it is a party of practical aims. Our one party system does not mean that we all have to subscribe to the view of any one political theorist. Within the A.P.C. there are many men and women of all sorts of differing political complexions, and I think it says something of the nature of the A.P.C. that we can embrace them all. The A.P.C. does not stand for communism or conservatism, it stands for Sierra Leone and her people. Anyone who professes to be against the A.P.C. is really saying that he opposes the broad objectives of our Party, i.e. development and the consolidation of our independence, rather than its strategy and tactics which are subject to constant reconsideration at the party level. Since the establishment of the one party state I have the feeling that there is a more cohesive spirit amongst those who strive to build up our nation — and this can only be for the good. I know that it is often thought that opposition is an admirable way of keeping a ruling party on its toes, and while I think this may be the case in Western democracies, I also think that the recent history of Sierra Leone puts us in a different position.

I have spoken before of the luxury of political debate, and I think this must apply to small dissenting parties in African countries such as my own. We have not time to hang around talking — there is too much work to be done. Yes, an opposition party can be a useful means of checking the party in power — the experience of all our people who remember the near-tyranny of the S.L.P.P. shows us that. But it can also be a destructive and useless force for a party committed to the good of the country — and the interests of my people must always come first with me.

My counry has been racked for too long by divisiveness, both tribal and religious, and as I look down my list of ministers I like to see the varied mixture of people that we have. Coming from such a mixed background myself I cannot help but think that this variety somehow captures the spirit of the new Sierra Leone, and unity within my country has always been one of my own main aims, and also that of the A.P.C. My work makes it necessary for me to spend most of my time in Freetown, and although I love our capital, I am always pleased to visit the provinces, and sometimes even go back to the places of my youth.

The eve of my 68th birthday found me travelling to Moyamba for a four day visit, and although I have never shirked from work during my lifetime, it is always pleasant to combine business with pleasure! Visiting old childhood haunts can often be a disturbing surprise: sometimes places one knew and loved as a child are changed beyond recognition. But I am always delighted to return to Moyamba, and to see the improvements that have taken place in agriculture since I was a boy. On this particular visit I was able to talk seriously about the problem of rural migration. This is a problem that every country has to contend with, and we are no exception. The trouble is that folk in the country always assume that the towns hold the key to prosperity and happiness. Of course, this is not the case, and many country people have found that there are no jobs for them in the city, it is more difficult to make friends, and they do not have the support of their families. As often as not these people end up in trouble, and in the end an urban life proves to be an empty temptation.

As it was my birthday the people of Moyamba made a particular effort with their entertainments for me. I was feted with songs and music by the police band, and I received many presents, including an antique church bell, silver coins that were used in Sierra Leone between 1871 and 1910, and a live cow. I was given more birthday cakes than I could possibly have eaten, but was glad to be able to share my anniversary with so many other people.

I have stressed that one of the most striking features of the A.P.C., and indeed of my own philosophy, is the recognition of the need for practicality: it is the only way that a small third world country can survive.

A TETE-A-TETE WITH THE FUTURE GENERATION AT A YOUTH CLUB CULTURAL SHOW IN FREETOWN (ABOVE) AND ARRIVING AT A SCHOOL IN KENEMA (BELOW).

OPENING AGRICULTURAL SHOWS IN VARIOUS PARTS OF THE COUNTRY TO ENCOURAGE PRODUCTION

LAUNCHING THE SELF-HELP SCHEME (ABOVE) INITIATED BY THE FIRST VICE PRESIDENT, S.I. KOROMA, IN HIS HOME DISTRICT AND (BELOW) INSPECTING PROGRESS ON A PROJECT IN MAFORKI

A VISIT TO KAMBIA, THE HOME DISTRICT OF THE FORMER SECOND VICE-PRESIDENT, C.A. KAMARA-TAYLOR (ABOVE) AND OPENING THE S.O.S. CHILDREN'S VILLAGE NEAR FREETOWN (BELOW).

OPENING THE FIRST REPUBLICAN PARLIAMENT IN JUNE 1971 (ABOVE) AND RETURNING FROM A VISIT TO EUROPE IN FEBRUARY 1975 (BELOW).

A VISIT TO SUMBUYA (ABOVE) AND TO WEST GERMANY (BELOW).

And so it has always been my intention to foster strong and healthy friendships with other West African states. After achieving political independence for Sierra Leone it soon became obvious that if this was to mean anything it would have to be accompanied by the ability to be economically independent. For this reason we have played a leading role in ECOWAS and have forged firm links with our neighbours.

Perhaps the firmest link of all has been made with Liberia, our immediate neighbour to the west, in the shape of the Mano River Union. This river forms a boundary between the two nations and has become a symbol to all Sierra Leoneans of co-operation between Liberia and ourselves. I remember well the signing of the treaty establishing the Union. It took place in Malema, Soro Gbema Chiefdom, Pujehun District, and the signatories were myself and the late Dr. William Tolbert, the then President of Liberia. It seems to me that although international bodies such as the U.N. perform very valuable functions, it is important to mend our own fences at home before we can play in any world union. The principal objectives of the Union have been to expand trade between the two countries by the elimination of existing trade barriers. It also seeks to secure a fair distribution of the benefits of economic co-operation. It was established in two main phases, the first of which includes the liberalisation of mutual trade in goods of local origin; the harmonisation of rates of import duties and other financial incentives applicable to goods of local origin, and supporting measures for developing co-operation in the production of agricultural and manufactured products of local origin. Since the establishment of the Union we have seen many co-operative ventures and even the setting-up of scholarships for students. Perhaps most importantly of all, we have seen the Union expand so that it now includes Guinea.

Perhaps one of the most painful memories that I have is that of the trial we were forced to conduct in order to weed out destructive and evil forces within our number. I can scarcely look back on these treason trials without experiencing very strong emotions. Nobody likes to come across such cases of disloyalty as I encountered; nobody likes to know that people they have trusted prove to be acting in the worst possible interests, while all the time professing loyalty. I would not wish such a confrontation with deception on my worst enemy — it is something that nobody should have to go through. But I suppose that it is something to our credit that we *did* come through it, and we survived it only a little conscious of the taste of bitterness that it left behind.

There is also something akin to pride in my memories of the whole unfortunate episode. The trial was conducted in a truly democratic way with justice not only being done but being seen to be done. I know in my heart that every consideration of fairness entered into the proceedings, and I think, in a world that has become renowned for rigged trials, or even no trial at all, Sierra Leone has something of which she can be proud. But, as I have said, the episode is a painful one amongst my many memories. There are some things that one would prefer to forget but should not, because from one's mistakes valuable lessons can be drawn, and there are other memories so terrible that all one can hope for is some sort of partial amnesia. The treason trials fall into that latter category and I hope that as long as I live I shall not be faced with such a problem — for my sake and, more importantly, for my people's sake.

As Sierra Leone has dragged herself onto her own two feet, despite the wreckage left by the divisive political parties of the past, and she has become increasingly able to provide for and attend to her own needs, so I have made it my business that she begins to play her proper role in continental and international affairs. I think that one of her greatest contributions has been to the Organisation of African Unity, and here both myself and my country have been greatly honoured by my recent chairmanship of the organisation. But, of course, my involvement did not just start there — for a long time I have been interested in and have played an active part in the O.A.U.

During my visit to Somalia in 1974 for a summit meeting I was elected as one of the eight Vice Chairmen for the coming year. I was also very pleased to be formally congratulated, along with the late President Tolbert, for my part in helping to settle the disputes between President Sekou Toure of Guinea and President Houphouet Boigny of the Ivory Coast, and the dispute between Rwanda and Burundi. Later during the visit I went with President Jawara of The Gambia to the Youth Revolutionary Centre, founded to provide education and training for orphans and destitute children. I am always most interested in visiting any project connected with children, as my own experiences have taught me the importance of a good childhood. I often wonder where I would be today if it had not been for the sacrifice of my father — I certainly would not be a Head of State! So it seems especially important to me that people who do not have parents who can help them, as my father helped me, should benefit from the open heartedness of the rest of us. After all, the children of today are the citizens of tomorrow and if they are to be honourable citizens, then it must be up to us to provide for their future. Indeed, when I returned to Freetown I urged that a similar scheme should be established. I was also much struck by the Somalian system under which all educational institutions had been called on to take a year's holiday in which to contribute to agricultural production. I even returned with a Somalian proverb which I was able to use in a home-coming speech, "If you want to quench your thirst properly and quickly, then you must drink with both hands". I interpreted this as a call to the people to work hard for national development, and it made a vivid and evocative image to the audience. So I came back from my trip not merely a vice chaiman of the O.A.U., but a person considerably enriched — and certainly full of new and stimulating ideas. The old adage of travel broadening the mind seems particularly true in my own case!

I was also honoured to be present at the two day summit that heralded the setting up of ECOWAS. This took place in Lagos, Nigeria in May, 1975, and culminated in the signing of a treaty linking 15 English and French speaking West African countries designed to standardise tariffs and trade procedures. While I was there I was able to make a number of points. One thing that particularly annoys me is what I will term the negative outlook of many Africans. They have been so influenced by the phrase 'the third world', and by the constant harping on the economic difficulties of our continent that they are unable to be optimistic about the future of their countries — they can only see the struggle and the difficulties. While it is certainly true that there is much development to be done before the quality of life improves for all our population, I think it is also essential to look at the positive side of things, too. I believe, and I stressed this at the summit meeting, that we in the third world are very fortunate, as we have an opportunity to learn from the mistakes of the developed countries. We have before us a clean slate, on which it is possible to draw strong firm lines. And with careful attention to the pitfalls to which developed countries have succumbed, we can create a future that is relatively free of careless mistakes. We have much to be thankful for!

As I look back on my life I realise how grateful I am to all the people who have crossed my path at one time or another, and in some way have influenced or affected my actions — or even changed my way of looking at things. Some of the people have perhaps entered into my life only fleetingly, while others have stayed firm friends for many years. And so I find that in writing this, in recording my own achievements and aspirations, I am really recording my gratitutde to those who have helped me on my way to the presidential post. I would like to mention these people by name, but as I sit here, pen in hand, I realise that they are too numerous, and in any case there would always be the danger that I would accidently leave someone out. Rather, then, than giving a long list of these people, I will merely say that there are, as well as individuals, groups within our country who not only I, but my fellow countrymen have reason to be proud of and grateful to.

The efforts of our womenfolk particularly spring to my mind. In the early days of our struggle against sectional and self-interested political parties, when the A.P.C. was forced to become virtually an underground movement, the women members of our Party played a significant and supportive role in keeping the cause alive. As I look through my engagement diaries over the years since I have been in office, I see the many rallies and seminars the women's section of the A.P.C. have organised, and I feel that much of the support that exists for us in the remote villages of the provinces — at grass roots level — is due to the ceaseless yet quiet determination of our women. It gives me great pleasure to see that many women in Sierra Leone are now being given wonderful educational and training possibilities, and I hope that in years to come our women will compete in total equality with the men. Indeed, already we have women army officers, and, of course, very senior civil servants and diplomats. We now have women Members of Parliament, and I am delighted to see the active role they take in our country's affairs, particularly in fields such as education.

Our youth, too, have played an important part in the making of our Republic. Those who were young men and women at the inception of the A.P.C. are our teachers and doctors and agriculturalists — even our politicians — today. The youth section of the A.P.C. forms an important training ground for the citizens of tomorrow and provides an admirable political education. I am always impressed by the exuberance of youth, and always willing to listen to their ideas. I am pleased to say that I often receive members of our younger generation at State House, and I am staggered by their thoughtfulness and their concern for the future of their country. I often visit schools and colleges throughout the country and I always try to put across to my audiences how very lucky they are to have the educational opportunities that exist today. I try to encourage them to make full use of what is available to them, reminding them that their parents were not similarly blessed with such possibilities for advancement. I think it would be true to say that most of the young men and women do realise that they are very fortunate, and I always feel proud when I attend graduation ceremonies at the number of Sierra

Leoneans who are achieving a high level of education and training. It must also be said that such occasions are full of nostalgia for me as I can always picture my own graduation ceremony all those years ago.

The past few years in Sierra Leone have seen important changes that I am honoured to be a part of. Becoming a republic and a one-party state are significant steps in the history of our country — steps that will prove to be for the benefit of our nation. In a way it seems strange that such big events have come towards the end of my life. I have already had my 'three score year and ten', and yet I find myself not sitting in a chair like most old men dwelling only in the past, but leading a very active and demanding life with my sights set firmly on the present and, indeed, the future. Of course, I have been very fortunate because I have always been strong and healthy, but I am fortunate too because my lifestyle keeps me in contact with such varied and stimulating people. In many ways I have had little time for reflection, unlike most old men, because I have been too busy seeing my people or globe-trotting.

Most of my activities and statements of the past few years have been recorded in a book published by my office in 1981 under the title "12 Years of Economic Achievement and Political Consolidation under the APC and Dr Siaka Stevens". It is my belief that this was a period which, as summed up by the compilers of the book, saw dramatic changes in the Sierra Leone scene and made a profound impact on the nation — politically, socially and economically. I know full well that this belief is not shared at present by some of my fellow citizens who can see progress only in terms of their own living standards and feel it is their birthright to buy petrol at prices subsidised by those who still have to travel on foot.

I am deeply conscious of the fact that the living standards of the majority of our people fall short of their expectations, that the level of employment is lower than we should like it to be and that health and educational facilities leave much room for improvement, especially when compared to those obtaining in the highly industrialised countries.

This book, in which I am trying to recall the highlights of my own life and thoughts, is hardly the place for a detailed analysis of the causes of world recession and other factors which have so seriously affected our own situation, especially since the major oil crisis of 1974. Recently (June 1983) I stopped over in London on my way to the OAU Summit Conference in Addis Ababa. Britain, the country on which we tried to model ourselves after Independence, was in the throes of an election campaign, the highlights of which were the questions of unemployment, higher consumer prices and a drop in the living standards. The number of their unemployed was almost equal to the whole population of our country and the price of their petrol at the pump was higher than ours, despite the fact that Britain is now not only self-sufficient in crude oil but also a net exporter of the product.

Naturally, after heading our Government for just over 14 years, nothing would have made me happier than the knowledge that my efforts had brought complete satisfaction to *all* our citizens and that all their expectations had been fulfilled. However, I am confident that the verdict of history, of the historian who will one day examine the period of the A.P.C. administration in the perspective of our overall development as a nation, will be favourable to us. Measured even now on an all-African scale, I believe our record would appear equally favourable to an objective observer. We are, after all, an emergent nation and nations are not built within the lifespan of one generation. Nor can the progress and living standards achieved by the West European countries over a period of some 200 years since their industrial revolutions, be covered by us in less than two decades. As for nation building, even Moses estimated that it would take forty years of wandering in the wilderness to transform the slaves whom he brought from Egypt into a nation fit to live in the Promised Land. Unfortunately, the Bible does not tell us how high were the living standards of the Israelites during the 40 years spent in the wilderness to achieve a new identity, and a new moral outlook under conditions of political independence. As the compilers of the book to which I referred earlier put it, it was largely as a result of our efforts that "the rule of those tribal kings, colonialists, neo-colonialists and army officers who had exercised power successively since the beginning of recorded history in Sierra Leone, gave way, for the first time, to a democratically elected government of the people. The future historian will also note that during our administration tribal and social friction, political divisiveness, physical confrontation, strife and violence gave way to the rule of law and unity and solidarity in a common cause; sectionalism, regionalism and tribalism gave way to a national consciousness which now transcends ethnic and social barriers.

During the same period social underdevelopment, massive illiteracy, and extreme poverty gave way to appreciably higher social and living standards. Though these standards undoubtedly fall short of the expectations of the majority, they have been recognised as giant steps in the right direction. Primary school enrolment, for example, rose during the period of my administration to 40 per cent of the school age population compared to 30 per cent shortly after I became Prime Minister; secondary school enrolment more than doubled; the number of medical doctors increased by over 90 per cent during the same period; while low-cost housing estates made their first appearance in Freetown.

On the infrastructural level, old-fashioned and dangerous ferries gave way to modern, concrete bridges; footpaths to motor feeder roads, laterite roads, often impassable during the rainy season, to asphalted highways; oil lamps to electric lighting; bacteria bearing brook and ditch water to treated pipe-borne water; shacks and frame houses to modern multi-storeyed buildings. The almost total dependence on foreign vested interests, which political independence from Britain had done little to reduce, gave way to a substantial and growing Sierra Leone share in the management and control of key companies in industry, mining, commerce, banking and insurance. In foreign affairs, virtually exclusive relations with a very small number of traditional partners gave way to cooperation with a broad spectrum of countries around the globe.

If any credit is due for what has been achieved, it should go in the first place to the rank and file of our party, the ordinary men and women, young and old, who elected us to govern the country and who subsequently helped us overcome some of the difficulties and perils which I recalled in the chapters of this book.

Personally, I would neither claim full credit for what has been done, nor apologise for what remains undone. Whatever the temporary difficulties we still have to face — difficulties which I do not wish to minimise — the fact remains that we have built a solid foundation for the future development of Sierra Leone. In this respect, my assessment of our task and the measure of our success are expressed in the summary of the recently published history of our Party, *The Rising Sun*, which was researched and written under the direction of the A.P.C. Secretariat including, of course, its Secretary General. This summary refers to the foundation which we built as one on which "future generations will be able to reply in shaping the economic system and the political institutions of the next stage on the road to national fulfilment".

It went on to explain that "the most important pillar of this foundation has been the unification of the country, the creation of a national consciousness out of disparate and often conflicting ethnic and social outlooks; the weaving of a fabric which, while binding together the many entities of Sierra leone, preserves the features and cultural identity of each constituent group.

"Then came the effort to educate vastly increased numbers of young people in all parts of the country, an effort representing yet another long-term investment which involved sacrifice of immediate benefit for the sake of future dividends.

"Finally, in the economic sphere, building for the future has involved sacrificing part of the possibility of higher living standards, and of some wealth generating activities liable to produce short-term returns, for the sake of infrastructural projects, such as roads and bridges which are needed for the long-term development of the country.

"Future historians will recognise the extent to which the A.P.C. leaders had to compromise, balancing the temptation to satisfy immediate needs with the statesmanlike responsibility of providing for the requirements of the future and erecting the framework needed for their fulfilment."

A fuller account of our struggle and of my own political record will be found in the history of our party to which I referred above and which I regard as one of our many minor investments in the future. Indeed, that book is largely intended to acquaint the younger generation with the efforts of their elders and the history of their own country which, as noted by the compilers, has been closely interwoven in recent years with the history of the All People's Congress Party.

The present book has mainly given me the opportunity to pore over my life, to trace the misfortunes and the successes, and to record the people and places that have meant so much to me. I am lucky that I have had such a full life — I feel that I have enough material to fill not one, but two books! Most of all I am lucky that I have been able to do so much with the life God gave me. Who would have dreamt that an ordinary little Limba boy would have become President of his country? I remember that when I was very young my father would tell me tales of heroic deeds and magical things, of brave boys who killed leopards and returned to their tribes and became chiefs — they were the stories that all parents tell to their children as they drift off to sleep at night. And my dreams would often be filled with continuations of these wonderful yarns my father told. I sometimes feel that I have lived a life like one of these tales, that I have made what seemed impossible and improbable to me as a child come true. And so this old man has much to be grateful for, much to give thanks for, much to reflect on as the years pass by.

OPENING A TRADE FAIR IN KENEMA IN DECEMBER 1975 WITH DR. S.S. MAGONA, CHAIRMAN OF THE SHOW COMMITTEE AT MY LEFT.

WITH THE MEMBERS OF THE A.P.C. CENTRAL COMMITTEE IN 1979 (ABOVE) AND THE PARTY'S CONVENTION AT THE FREETOWN CITY HALL IN THE SAME YEAR (BELOW).

AN EXPRESSION OF WELCOME AND CONGRATULATIONS FROM MEMBERS OF THE SIERRA LEONE LABOUR CONGRESS ON MY RETURN FROM A VISIT TO THE U.S.A. WHERE I HAD OBJECTED TO SOME I.M.F. CONDITIONS IN 1979 (ABOVE) AND LAYING A WREATH ON THE GRAVE OF H.E. CHARLES, ERSTWHILE PRESIDENT OF THE LABOUR CONGRESS (BELOW).

WITH LEADERS OF THE LABOUR CONGRESS AT THE OFFICIAL OPENING OF THEIR CONFERENCE IN FREETOWN IN 1976 (ABOVE) AND IN AN INFORMAL CONFERENCE WITH CONGRESS MEMBERS AT STATE HOUSE (BELOW).

ATTENDING THE O.A.U. SUMMIT CONFERENCE IN MOGADISHU, SOMALIA, IN 1974 (ABOVE) AND THE BRITISH COMMONWEALTH HEADS OF STATE AND GOVERNMENT CONFERENCE IN LUSAKA, ZAMBIA, IN 1979 (BELOW).

AT THE ECOWAS CONFERENCE IN DAKAR IN MAY 1979 (ABOVE) AND AFTER SIGNING WITH THE LATE PRESIDENT TOLBERT OF LIBERIA AND THE LATE PRESIDENT SEKOU TOURE OF GUINEA, IN JANUARY 1979, THE AGREEMENT UNDER WHICH GUINEA BECAME THE THIRD MEMBER OF THE MANO RIVER UNION (BELOW).

WITH PRESIDENT KENNETH KAUNDA OF ZAMBIA DURING HIS STATE VISIT TO SIERRA LEONE IN 1969 (ABOVE) AND WITH PRESIDENT SAMORA MACHEL OF MOZAMBIQUE TEN YEARS LATER (BELOW)

WITH PRESIDENT LEOPOLD SEDAR SENGHOR OF SENEGAL,..

*..WITH PRESIDENT GAFAAR NUMEIRY OF THE SUDAN (ON MY RIGHT) AND LT. COL. MENGISTU MARIAM, THE HEAD OF STATE OF ETHIOPIA (ON MY LEFT) WHEN, AS CHAIRMAN OF THE O.A.U. **AD HOC** MEDIATION COMMITTEE, I PRESIDED OVER TALKS, HELD IN FREETOWN IN FEBRUARY 1979, TO RESOLVE THE DISPUTE BETWEEN THEIR TWO COUNTRIES AND...*

..WITH PRESIDENT SIR DAWDA K. JAWARA OF GAMBIA.

*ADDRESSING AN A.C.P. (AFRICAN, CARIBBEAN AND PACIFIC STATES) CON-
FERENCE IN BRUSSELS ON RELATIONS WITH THE E.E.C. IN SEPTEMBER 1979
(ABOVE) AND, AFTER A MEETING WITH THE PRESIDENT OF FRANCE, M. VALERY
GISCARD D'ESTAING, IN PARIS THE SAME YEAR (BELOW).*

*WITH U.N. SECRETARY-GENERAL DR. KURT WALDHEIM IN FREETOWN IN 1974 (ABOVE)
AND WITH PRESIDENT FIDEL CASTRO OF CUBA WHEN HE VISITED FREETOWN IN 1972
(BELOW).*

A PREVIOUS OCCUPIER REVISITS STATE HOUSE: SIR MAURICE DORMAN, THE BRITISH GOVERNOR-GENERAL AT THE TIME OF INDEPENDENCE, AND LADY DORMAN PAY A COURTESY CALL ON THE PRESENT OCCUPIER (ABOVE) AND, (BELOW) THE VICE-PRESIDENT OF YUGOSLAVIA, MR VCIJETIN MIJATOVIC, MAKES A PRESENTATION.

AN OFFICIAL VISIT TO THE RULER OF KUWEIT, SHEIKH JABER AL-AHMED AL-SABAH, (ABOVE) AND RECEIVING THE PRESIDENT OF HUNGARY, PAL LOSONCZI, DURING HIS OFFICIAL VISIT TO SIERRA LEONE IN NOVEMBER 1973 (BELOW).

SURVEYING PROGRESS ON ONE OF THE MANY DEVELOPMENT PROJECTS NOW COMPLETED UNDER THE AID PROGRAMME EXTENDED TO US BY THE CHINESE PEOPLE'S REPUBLIC (ABOVE) AND A MEMENTO OF A RECEPTION GIVEN IN MY HONOUR BY AFRICAN AMBASSADORS IN PEKING (BELOW).

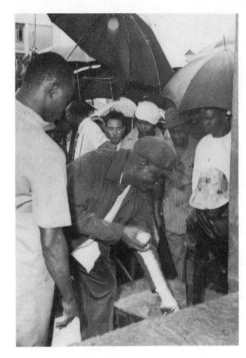

TURNING THE SOIL TO MARK THE BEGINNING OF WORK ON THE CONSTRUCTION OF THE NEW FREETOWN CITY HALL UNDER AN AID AGREEMENT WITH THE DEMOCRATIC PEOPLE'S REPUBLIC OF KOREA (ABOVE) AND (BELOW) THE BUILDING AFTER ITS COMPLETION.

BROADCASTING MY CHRISTMAS MESSAGE TO THE NATION IN 1979 (ABOVE) AND PART OF THE CROWD WHICH WELCOMED ME IN LUNSAR, THE VENUE OF MY EARLY TRADE UNION ACTIVITIES, ON ONE OF MY VISITS TO THE TOWN AS PRESIDENT (BELOW).

CHAPTER 19

A Time to Work and a Time to Rest

Much of this book has dealt with what life has taught me. At 78 I am glad to claim that I am still learning in the school of life and sometimes hardly receiving passing marks. Those who feel that they have nothing more to learn, or are tired of learning, are most probably tired of living. I am certainly not a member of that club, but I am aware of the limitations resulting from increasing age.

The leadership of a country like Sierra Leone is a very demanding job, combining responsibility for the day-to-day affairs of the country and planning for the future with diplomatic work and the performance of ceremonial functions. Moreover, the African tradition being what it is, our people expect their leader to be also the father of the nation, to hear personally complaints and suggestions, to settle disputes, including personal ones, to attend functions, to relieve cases of hardship and often to represent the country abroad. The President of Sierra Leone must be a politician, an economist, a judge, a diplomat, and a compassionate welfare officer, all rolled into one.

Though I can claim a good experience in all these areas and, Thank God, a clean bill of health, I realise that at my age the mind and the body cannot be as agile and resilient as I should like them to be. I can no longer put up with constant late nights and very long sessions at my office. Long debates, long flights and long hours of reading are beginning to tire me.

While I am still anxious to learn from life, the 50 odd years I have spent in politics and public affairs, including the years devoted to the trade union movement, have made it difficult, if not impossible, to find time for the many other interests which I developed over the decades, some practical, some rather academic. I mentioned earlier in this book that I should like to learn a little more about the history, the traditions and the culture of my mother's tribe — the Vai people who were probably the first in Black Africa, outside Ethiopia, to devise their own alphabet and system of writing. I should also like to take advantage of my practical experience of development in an emergent country to analyse in greater depth the problems involved; to identify not only the shortest but also the safest and most acceptable road to development. Finally, I should also like more time to rest, relax, read and meditate, and to look at closer range, with a private eye, not in an official capacity, at what goes on in Sierra Leone, in Africa and in the world.

As I have already indicated in several speeches and public statements, I feel that the time has come when a younger man, possibly one with a different approach to the problems of our country, should have an opportunity of implementing his ideas, and of learning from the experience of leadership, as I have done.

There is also some truth, I suppose, in the saying, *Variety is the spice of life*. Many people in the world, though by no means all, seem to want change, if only for the sake of it. Many years ago we had a strong football team which kept winning the championship and was regarded as unbeatable in the country. In its early days it became very popular and the crowds always cheered it. But one day, with some of its players a little tired or unwell, it unexpectedly lost a match to a weaker team. Some of the spectators were obviously disappointed, but others booed the losing team and cheered the winners, although they had never supported them in the past. I well remember the comments of one of those who had suddenly switched his support from one team to another: "They had enough wins; let somebody else get a chance, let us see new faces on the pitch."

In what is known as the 'western democracies', the two major parties, such as the Democrats and Republicans in the United States, and the Conservatives and Labourites in Britain, usually alternate in power by the will of the same electorate. As I understand it, this is due to the so-called floating voters — a minority of people who always want a change — periodically switching their support from one party to another, and thus bringing about a change of government, though the great majority of the voters remain permanently loyal to the party of their choice or of their social class. The tendency to blame the outgoing government for all the country's real or alleged misfortunes is then coupled with the expectation that the new administration will put everything right. However, like the passion of young lovers, political euphoria is liable to be short-lived, and the greater the expectations aroused by the new government the greater will be the resentment of the masses when these expectations fail to materialise. But this need not be so if the new government takes an objective view of the problems facing the country, presents a realistic diagnosis and prognosis of the situation, accepts full responsibility for the existing state of affairs and makes a real effort to improve conditions rather than to derive political capital from attempts to apportion credit and blame — to receive credit for what it did not do and to find scapegoats for any current difficulties. In this way, if real improvement is achieved in the longer term, the government's standing will automatically rise, and if some problems remain unresolved there will be no bitter resentment on the part of the masses, especially if it can be shown that it has made every effort to solve them.

Thus, like some of the young lovers who continue to enjoy a blissful and meaningful marriage long after the passion of yesteryear has cooled, a leader can turn the euphoria engendered by the change of government into a lasting relationship of mutual trust, mutual respect and mutual dependence between him and the people. It is up to him, of course, to bring about a smooth and gradual transition from the largely emotional motivation of the masses at the time of the change to their active support on objective grounds of patriotism as well as self-interest.

It is my heartiest wish that my successor in Sierra Leone should be able to bring about this transition, avoiding an anti-climax always liable to produce a series of dangerous and destructive shock-waves which the country can ill afford.

It is also my hope that, in the interest of the country and of his own longer term interest, the new leader will resist the temptation, so common in politics in all parts of the world, of attempting to achieve quick popularity by attributing every difficulty to the previous administration. This approach to public relations is bound to lead to demoralisation, controversy and strife, especially in an emergent country where what we need most of all is stability, respect for constituted authority and continuity of government. In Sierra Leone such an approach would certainly be resented by too many people, including, of course, all those associated with what will have become the previous administration.

In any event, sensible and objective people would agree that the interest of the country calls not only for a smooth transition from one administration to another, but also for the new administration to pursue, in broad terms, the policies of the outgoing one — and continue, so to speak, to improve and expand the national structure on the foundation already provided, at the cost of considerable effort, rather than pull down everying it finds and start again from scratch.

The question which remains to be answered, however, is how we should go about selecting the next administration and what is the best method of ensuring a smooth transition.

There are, of course, many ways of selecting the Head of State or Chief Executive of a country, whatever his official title may be. Under the traditional monarchic system, succession is determined by heredity with the sovereign's eldest son (or daughter) automatically becoming heir apparent and eventually assuming the functions of the Head of State on the death or premature abdication of the monarch. For many centuries variants of this system were prevalent not only in Europe and Asia but also in Africa, where some tribes are ruled by hereditary chiefs, though in other tribes the chief is elected or selected by the elders.

The hereditary system offers the great advantage, in theory at least, of eliminating uncertainty about the succession, avoiding bitter and sometimes murderous conflicts between claimants to the succession and, generally, ensuring a smooth transition. However, this system presents overwhelming difficulties, unless certain prerequisites are met. First, the system must be so deeply rooted in the traditions of the people concerned that it is taken for granted and the question of its acceptability no longer arises. This is certainly not the case in our country. Second, the likelihood of the heir apparent being one of the best qualified men to lead the country is generally small. (This may not be a very important consideration in countries where the Head of State plays no active part in the day-to-day operations of government and where, in any event, he can depend on expert advice and guidance of professionals who are not involved in politics and have no axe to grind — which is seldom the case in developing countries.) Since the beginning of history, it would seem, efforts have been made to improve the performance of hereditary leaders by beginning to train them for the job at an early age. These efforts notwithstanding, the number of hereditary leaders whose rule proved disastrous to their countries in all periods of history and in all parts of the world, would suggest that even the most sophisticated type of training for leadership cannot offer anything approaching a guarantee of success.

Besides the fact that the hereditary system would be regarded as anachronistic and regressive in this day and age, the developing nations, faced as they are with seemingly unsurmountable problems, need not only sound and effective chief administrators, but also stimulating and imaginative leadership. Their leaders must be capable not only of managing the day-to-day affairs of the country and ensuring law and order, but also of inspiring confidence at home and abroad; of initiating and pursuing policies required by the circumstances; of uniting the nation and reconciling conflicting tribal, regional, social and economic interests; of perceiving the longer-term development problems of the nation and inducing the masses to accept a measure of sacrifice and self-denial for the sake of the future; of resisting the temptation of immediate popularity at the cost of the next generation. In a nutshell, the leader of an emergent nation must be an astute politician, a realist and a visionary, an economist and a diplomat, a tough taskmaster and a humane judge, above all, a resolute fighter, gracious in defeat and generous in victory. I am not suggesting that all of these qualities can be found in one man, much less that I have been endowed with them. But if a country is to find a leader filling these requirements, or most of them, it is obvious that the search for the most suitable candidate should extend over as wide an area as possible in the hope that somebody approaching the ideal will emerge. In all probability, however, the hour will bring forth the man and he will emerge naturally from the grass roots. The one thing we must guard against and avoid at any cost is the danger of the leadership being taken over by force by whoever happens to command a number of guns. Unfortunately, this type of takeover, known as a military *coup* has been witnessed at some time or other in many, possibly in most, third-world countries, including our own, and even in some European states.

I do not wish to generalise, much less to condemn all those who attained power by such means. There is little doubt that some of the military regimes which came into existence as a result of coups in the past 20 years or so, represented an improvement on their predecessors. Others marked a step backward and a few proved disastrous. None lived up to the promise of eradicating all the evils they had identified, or of turning poverty into prosperity for all.

The extent to which some proved more successful or popular than others has depended partly on the wisdom, ability and sincerity of the new leaders and partly on conditions beyond their control, such as world economic booms or recessions, fluctuations in the prices of their export commodities, or the discovery of great mineral wealth in their countries.

These factors notwithstanding, the dislocation of existing structures, including the economic structure, and the internal conflicts generated by the coups — conflicts which have often brought about a flight of capital and of talented or experienced people — have generally retarded progress and made more difficult the task of the new leaders. Moreover, whatever may be the virtues or otherwise of regimes which came into power by means of military coups, three other facts should be considered.

First, not all the attempted military coups in history have succeeded, though we tend to think mainly of those which did. In fact, the number of attempted coups which failed or were nipped in the bud greatly exceeds that of those which proved successful. In most cases, the failed coups brought about not only the disgrace and, often, the demise of men who necessarily betrayed their oath of allegience and the trust placed in them, but also security measures which affected the rest of the population and the death of innocent citizens.

Second, military coups can be planned and carried out only by the few who happen to be in control of a sufficient quantity of weapons and ammunition, or who are well placed to obtain them. They are not necessarily among the more competent, the more dedicated or the more popular men in the country concerned, or even among the members of their own armed forces, though they may be among the more ruthless or the more violent.

Third, and most important perhaps, violence tends to breed more violence or, to paraphrase the Bible, those who live by the sword run the risk of dying by the sword. Having created a precedent, if one was needed, for the violent or forcible overthrow of a government, and having thus indirectly legitimised this method of attaining power, the leaders of a coup can hardly complain when others resort to the same methods against them. The chain reaction of coups and counter-coups thus created is unlikely to benefit a developing country which needs stability and continuity of government, as much as capital and hard work, to achieve a measure of progress.

A last point which may be worth remembering is that at least some of the military coups we have witnessed since World War II were inspired, if not engineered and actively assisted, by foreign powers to serve their own interests.

If we are to eschew the risks and drawbacks inherent in military coups, some objective criteria, other than heredity, must be devised to ensure that the succession passes smoothly from one incumbent to the next, avoiding the danger of divisive conflict.

In some medieval empires the governership of provinces or colonies used to be auctioned every so many years with the title going to the highest bidder who, having thus become the absolute ruler of the province or country, would proceed to bleed it to death to recover his investment and be left with a handsome profit. Less objectionable methods could include awarding the supreme office to the tallest man in the land, or the one who could run fastest or jump highest. If intellectual standards are preferred, the prize could go to the highest scorer in some intelligence test, or to the one who can solve a difficult riddle or mathematical problem. In very primitive societies, thousands of years ago, the test of physical strength was applied to select the leader of the community with any of its male members being allowed to challenge the leader at any time in single-handed, unarmed combat. Naturally, the challenger had to be a brave man, for while victory would bring him the leadership, defeat would mean certain death.

At the other end of the scale, in the modern western countries, the contest is decided, as we know, by popular vote with all the bitterness and divisiveness engendered by this procedure and the ruinous cost of electoral campaigns. The winner is not necessarily the man or woman best qualified to do the job in the interest of the country, but, more often than not, the one who can rely on the most effective publicity machine, who can raise the biggest funds for his electorial campaign, or, in some cases, cuts a good figure on television.

In Sierra Leone, we decided some years ago that the country could not afford this system and had to be spared its sequels, at least until such time as the national consciousness grows sufficiently deep roots to avert the danger of the recently subdued tribalism and sectarianism again rearing their ugly heads above the national scene. This is why we established the One-Party State and adopted the 1978 Constitution under which the Presidential Candidate of the Recognised Party, elected by the Party's National Delegates' Convention, is the sole candidate at a Presidential election.

The national delegates, representing as they do all segments of the population in all parts of the country, constitute a sort of electoral college. This provides opportunities for competition, but limits the contest to the level of a representative body motivated by national ideals. It also limits to manageable proportions the cost of bitterly fought electoral campaigns on a national scale — a cost which must be measured not only in financial terms, but also in terms of the damage done to internal stability and the unity of the country.

I sincerely hope, however, that our people will adopt the multi-party parliamentary system when the long and painful process of fully integrating and unifying our nation has been successfully completed; when a national consciousness has become firmly rooted; when the vast majority of our people have become educated to the point of becoming not only literate but also trained to understand the economic, technical and other issues involved in running a modern state; when the country has become economically viable and self-sufficient in food; when divisiveness can no longer jeopardize its very existence; in brief, when such a system offers the prospect of being really meaningful.

As far as I can see, and judging from precedents in other parts of the world, the achievement of what I regard as the prerequisites for the safe introduction of a multi-party system would take anything from 25 to 50 years, depending upon world conditions and other circumstances liable to speed up or retard our national development. This means, of course, that some of our more vociferous opponents will not live to see the day when conditions are ripe for exposing the country to the sort of political licence which they demand for themselves, but are unlikely to grant to others under present circumstances.

To give them the benefit of the doubt, I should say that some of those who preach the merits of the western type of democracy just do not realise the dangers and difficulties with which that system is fraught, at least in the case of countries like ours. Should they come to power before the process of national unification is completed and the other conditions to which I have just referred are satisfied, they would soon be faced with the difficulties we ourselves have encountered. Then, assuming even that they will not want to cling on to power for its own sake, they will have no alternative but to re-introduce the One-Party State, lest the whole structure of our society should be torn apart by fratricidal conflict and the State should collapse.

I said earlier that it would take at least 25 years to produce the political and economic climate in which a meaningful western type of democracy could thrive, because this is the lapse of time which, when added to the years since we became independent, corresponds more or less to the life-span of one generation. Most of our adults today grew up under the colonial regime when, to all intents and purposes, there was only one political "party" — the "party" of the white man, represented directly by the District Commissioner and indirectly by the Paramount Chief. Equally important to remember is the fact that the opposition to the established party was generally motivated by personal or tribal considerations, rather than by national aspirations. In simpler terms, the D.C. and his "party" were seen not so much as the unlawful usurpers of the nation's rights, but rather as enemies of the Temnes, Mendes and so on, or as obstacles to personal advancement. The choice was between joining the white man's "party", i.e. the administration, or opposing it. Moreover, opposition to the colonial regime could express itself only in violence and destructive or disruptive activities, such as causing damage to property or sabotaging the economy. This resulted in political militancy or opposition to the government becoming identified in the minds of many people with riotous behaviour and strong-arm tactics.

The concept of fighting hard for a political ideal while subconsciously envisaging the possibility that one may be wrong and graciously submitting to the will of the majority when the battle is lost, has yet to gain general acceptance. Yet, this is an essential condition for the successful functioning of a multi-party system — a condition which also assumes that all parties are motivated by the same national ideal, rather than by sectarian or tribal interests, and, therefore, offer the electorate a choice of methods and personalities, rather than a choice of conflicting an irreconcilable objectives.

Another important prerequisite for a multi-party system seems to be a fairly high standard of living coupled with job security or meaningful opportunities in the private sector. In most western countries, as far as I know, politics is a hobby rather than a profession and virtually all politicians have either private means or good jobs and business opportunities awaiting them when political fortunes turn against them or their term of office comes to an end. In many cases, the acceptance of political office involves even a financial sacrifice. In any event, one's life style is unlikely to change dramatically as a result of either obtaining or losing a political job.

In most African countries, however, the situation is vastly different. Private wealth, however ostentatious it may appear, is generally only skin deep. Family businesses are few and seldom very profitable. We have seen cases of very poor men from villages being suddenly elevated through politics from traditional subsistence farming to cabinet positions. When such men travel abroad on government business, as they often have to, they must necessarily be provided with facilities befitting their status. At home, too, such men must enjoy living standards which would enable them not only to command the respect of foreigners and of their own compatriots (in whose minds competence and authority is often associated with European life styles), but also to perform their jobs as effectively as possible in comfortable surroundings.

Moreover, the African tradition being what it is, men from villages who have achieved prominence in the capital thanks to the support of their fellow villagers, would be expected to reciprocate the help received from their rural constituents, at least by feeding them and looking after them when they arrive in the big city. Frequently, they would also be expected to help them financially, support their applications for jobs or favours and provide some presents for their families.

Thus, when one of these men is elected to political office, he does not merely change his job, but also his life style. His environment is liable to change from what is described as the most primitive (on the European scale of values) to the most sophisticated; from a hut in the village, similar to those in which his ancestors have lived for centuries, to the five bedrooms air-conditioned villa or the five-star international hotel; from the company of illiterate bare-footed villagers to that of world statesmen, millionaires and film stars. The man whose only means of transport may have been his two feet or the crowded Poda-Poda now joins the jet set; his eating and drinking habits change rapidly; his children begin to attend some of the best available schools; his wife is soon converted from country rice and cassava roots with all the chores involved in their processing, to the ready husked, glazed, parboiled imported variety available at the supermarket; almost overnight he is transported not only in space but also in time, spanning the centuries at the stroke of an election.

But the process is hardly reversible. Human nature being what it is, it would be unrealistic to expect a man who has spent some years as an adopted member of the modern, affluent society to return suddenly to a rural African environment which may have remained unchanged since medieval times. Can one tell such a man: "Your time is up; forget all about your government-leased five-room house, your bathroom, your car, your refrigerator, your electronic gadgets; remove your children from the private school and your shoes from your socked feet; tell your wife to forget about the supermarket and go back to the village." In all probability the man will want to cling on to his job by hook or by crook and, if he fails, he is not unlikely to try to return to it by every possible means, foul or fair, regardless of the verdict of the electorate.

In Sierra Leone, as in most other African countries, there is, of course, a small middle class of people, already engaged in business or the professions, who would be cushioned against the traumatic experience of a meteoric rise followed by a meteoric fall. They could and often did rise to political prominence without experiencing a radical change in their life styles. By the same token they could return to their previous occupations without having to suffer severe bruising in the fall from power. However, our whole concept of democracy and socialism has been to ensure that government does not remain in the hands of a self-perpetuating ruling class and that those who represent the people are themselves of the grass roots. In other words, what our party stands for and what most of our citizens expect is not only a government of the people but also one of the people and by the people.

This does not necessarily imply a multi-party state which, as I believe, will become not only feasible but also be put into practice when the social, economic and cultural gaps between the majority of the people and their political leaders is substantially reduced; as it is both in the western world and in the traditional African society where the life styles of the rulers and the ruled can at least be measured on the same scale.

In Sierra Leone and similar countries still in the first stage of their development as independent entities, the attempt to graft a modern state with all its attributes on the medieval base, neglected by over a century of colonialism, has inevitably produced a gap between the so-called educated elite living in the modern age and the masses whose life styles have changed little over the centuries. In Sierra Leone, in particular, this gap was widened by the settlement of the Creoles who provided for a long time the country's educated elite and acquired even a geographical base in the Western Area.

My own objective, and that of the party which I founded, has always been to narrow the social, cultural and economic gaps between the different segments of our population, to make possible their unification and integration and to build a national consciousness transcending ethnic and regional loyalties. Looking back on the 14 years of my administration, I think we have made some substantial progress towards the achievement of our objective. Tribal differences, suspicion and jealousy play a far less important part in our politics today than they did in 1968. Though we were accused, in the early days of our party, of being an alliance between the Temnes and the Creoles, time has proved that this charge never held water. Our Cabinet consists of men from nearly all parts of the country with some of the top jobs having gone to people who strongly opposed us little more than a decade ago and whose ethnic ties might have been regarded as disqualifying handicaps.

At the party level, social, ethnic and cultural differences are not totally unknown. The A.P.C. has become acknowledged to be the party of Sierra Leone.

Our development policy in which we paid special attention to transport, involving the building of many impressive bridges and of hundred of miles of asphalted roads running right across the country, has also helped unify the nation, if only by greatly facilitating the constant movement of people from one area to another, as well as permanent and semi-permanent migration within the country. This, in turn, has brought about a higher incidence of mixed marriages and, hence, of children of mixed ethnic descent who have grown up primarily as Sierra Leoneans, rather than as members of any particular tribe.

Education has also made appreciable progress in the past 14 years with the proportion of children attending schools increasing year after year and, more significantly, this rate of increase has been higher in the Provinces than in the Western Area.

Both the quality and the extent of our education still leave much room for improvement; but we can already predict, with some degree of confidence, that our society as a whole will change significantly as its components change both qualititively and quantitatively.

I know that much remains to be done in the social and economic spheres to achieve a higher level of employment and higher living standards for the great majority of our people, thus narrowing still further the gap between the haves and the have nots, if not eliminating it altogether. Unfortunately, our efforts in this direction which began to show promising results in the mid-seventies, were largely frustrated by world conditions over which we had no control, and suffered severe reverses. This is not the place to indulge in long economic arguments about the merits or otherwise of our economic policies. The facts speak for themselves, but they should be examined in a world context.

Some African countries which were well ahead of us 14 years ago, enjoying the benefits of a more developed economy and higher living standards, are now lagging a long way behind us. Lacking as they do the foreign currency needed to meet even the essential demands of their respective domestic markets, their merchants often travel to Sierra Leone to tap the domestic supplies of our own market, practising an illicit trade as harmful to their own countries as it is to ours.

And despite the difficulties faced by our economy, thousands of our fellow Africans still come to live and work in Sierra Leone, suggesting that, depressing as conditions may be in our country, they are still better than in many others.

As I write these pages, the highly industrialised countries of the world are suffering as never before from the effects of world recession and inflation with the purchasing power of their respective currencies dropping month by month as consumer prices increase on their markets and the living standards of their people decline. In the country which not so long ago controlled more than one third of the whole world, including Sierra Leone, nearly three and a half million people — a number matching the whole populuation of our country — are unemployed. Yet, experts from these countries come to advise us from time to time on how to run our economy. Listening to them one cannot help recalling the Biblical injunction: "Physician, heal thyself." Nevertheless, their advice may well be valid in some cases and has never been ignored by our government. But too much of it has been presented by our detractors as a panacea for all our troubles, which it is not and cannot be. Even though I am not an economist, I probably know the answer to many economic problems which are usually a matter of common sense. However, what looks like an easy problem to an economist may be an insoluble one to a politician who must take into account not only the long-term effects of the medicine, but also its taste — a taste often so bitter as to make it quite unacceptable to the people.

In the light of what is happening in the world today, I am not so sure that we could have done much more than we actually did to cushion the country against the consequences of world recession and deteriorating terms of trade, whatever our critics may say.

Though we may suffer from unemployment and occasional shortages of one commodity or another, none of our people have experienced starvation, lack of shelter, ill-treatment and other sources which have afflicted so many nations in recent years. Nor have we had to sacrifice our investments in the future for the sake of the present.

In the classical economic cycle, booms follow slumps as surely as day follows night and, when prosperity returns to the world, when diamonds adorn more and more feminine fingers, when iron ore and bauxite are in greater demand, when our off-shore oil deposits begin to be exploited to meet a growing world consumption, when our investments in agriculture, infrastructure and education begin to pay dividends, the broad masses of Sierra Leone will enjoy the benefits of the boom. Inevitably, much of the credit will go to the government of the day. What we of our generation have done, and what I trust history and our own people will give us credit for, will have been to provide the prerequisites for the future development of the country, to ensure that Sierra Leone is in a position to take advantage of favourable world economic conditions when they arise, and that the structure of our society is such that the benefits are shared by all.

To some extent, this may suggest the qualities we should seek in the man to be chosen to lead the country in the next stage of our development. I have already described, from personal experience, what the job involves and what, I think, it will continue to involve, in broad terms, for some years to come. This defines, also in broad terms, the basic qualifications to be expected from potential candidates. But, everything else remaining equal, there are differences in emphasis which we may be well advised to bear in mind.

While the priorities of the first 20 years of our state — the consolidation of independence, the unification and integration of the country, the creation of a national consciousness, the expansion of education and the building of a basic physical infrastructure involving foreign aid — were mainly political and diplomatic, those of the next two decades are more likely to be of an economic and organisational nature, involving the expansion of agriculture, an improvement in the financial performance of the mining sector, a higher level of industrialisation, as well as fiscal and monetary policies designed to promote our social objectives. This will call for a bias in these particular directions on the part of whoever may succeed me as President, in the same way as, I think, the past 15 years or so called for a bias in the direction of politics and diplomacy to bring about the necessary social, political and infrastructural foundation on which further development depends.

I have already indicated what I feel should not, or cannot as yet, become the general criteria for choosing a new leader. In the light of these considerations, I have also reiterated my belief that the method we have adopted under our 1978 Constitution is, under the circumstances, best suited to meet our needs at present and for some years to come. Under it (Section 23/1), it is the members of the National Delegates Conference of the Recognised Party — the All People's Congress Party, or A.P.C. — who must elect a new leader of the Party, "and such person shall be the sole candidate in an election for the office of President." It is, of course, my right, as it is the right of any other member of the National Delegates Conference, to nominate a person for the leadership of the Party and to have the nomination seconded by some of my closest supporters.

If I resorted to this procedure my nominee would probably stand a good chance of becoming the Party's leader and, hence, President of Sierra Leone. It has been suggested to me that this would have the advantage of avoiding possible squabbles, manoeuvrings and politicking among potential successors, undoubtedly all of them well qualified, capable and sincere, with some possibly more anxious than I have been to hold the office.

When the Party is ready to elect a new leader, I shall certainly make known my views, D.V. But I will want to be sure that the candidate for whom I would vote receives a good measure of support regardless of my own stand, for it would be wrong and unfair for me to use my influence to promote a man who, however capable, may not enjoy the full support of the masses or may lack the qualities of leadership required in a developing country such as ours. Unfortunately, these qualities cannot always be forecast or identified, any more than one can single out the horse certain to win a race. Naturally, there are favourites, but in politics, as on the race track, many an outsider has won against the hottest favourites — people who had everything going for them in objective terms, but who ended up poor losers, or who, having won the contest, failed to come up to expectations.

Moreover, the people who favoured me and supported me for the party leadership of Sierra Leone were the rank and file of our Party and nation. As is known, none of my predecessors in office favoured me, much less nominated me to succeed them. I can see no reason, therefore, why we should introduce a new system under which the holder of the office sponsors or nominates his successor — a system which, as I see it, would be fraught with serious risks greatly outweighing whatever advantages it may have.

Moreover, without going into details, history in many parts of the world has also shown that even the office holders enjoying the greatest prestige in their respective countries have not always been successful in their efforts to nominate a successor. Thus, heeding the lessons of history, it is only with the greatest caution and circumspection that I shall exercise my rights under our Party's Constitution, and **may the best man win** — the hour will bring him forth.

Looking Back For the past 16 years, while heading the Executive Branch of our Government and dealing with the affairs of State, both domestic and foreign, as well as the affairs of our A.P.C. party, my official daily routine has included:

OPENING AGRICULTURAL AND OTHER SHOWS, SUCH AS THE ONE AT BO:

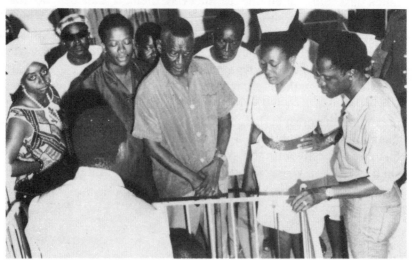

VISITING HOSPITALS, SUCH AS THE CHILDREN'S WARD AT THE MAFORKI HOSPITAL

INAUGURATING DEVELOPMENT PROJECTS, SUCH AS THE DARU AUTO-MATIC OIL MILL (ABOVE) AND A NEW BUILDING AT THE LUNGI INTERNATIONAL AIRPORT (BELOW)

RECEIVING DELEGATIONS AT STATE HOUSE, SUCH AS THE KONO AND MANDINGO TRIBAL HEADMEN

ANSWERING QUESTIONS AT PRESS CONFERENCES

ATTENDING CEREMONIES IN CONNECTION WITH THE CONSTRUCTION OF NEW PROJECTS, SUCH AS THE LIBRARY BUILDING AT MY OLD SCHOOL, THE ALBERT ACADEMY

INSPECTING WORK IN PROGRESS

VISITING ALL PARTS OF THE COUNTRY; INCLUDING MOYAMBA, MY BIRTHPLACE

ATTENDING THANKSGIVING SERVICES

HOSTING RECEPTIONS AT STATE HOUSE

RECEIVING FOREIGN GUESTS, SUCH AS ARCHBISHOP MAKAKIOS, PRESIDENT OF CYPRUS.....

....EMPEROR HAILE SELASSIE OF ETHIOPIA....

....AND THE HON. FORBES BURNHAM, THE PRIME MINISTER OF GUYANA

Even my private life has
acquired a semi-official
character on occasions as
when:

*ATTENDING CHURCH SERVICES
WITH MY WIFE (RIGHT)....*

*OR CELEBRATING MY BIRTHDAY,
FOR EXAMPLE, IN 1974 WHEN I WAS
PRESENTED WITH A REMARKABLE
COLLECTION OF WALKING STICKS
(LEFT) OR....*

... IN 1976 (ABOVE) AND 1979 (BELOW)

AS I LOOK BACK UPON THE 79 YEARS OF MY LIFE, I AM GRATEFUL FOR ITS VARIETY AND ITS RICHNESS, FOR THE CHALLENGES AND SATISFACTIONS IT HAS OFFERED ME, FOR WHAT IT HAS TAUGHT ME, FOR THE HAPPY DAYS AND GOOD HEALTH I HAVE ENJOYED, FOR WHAT I WAS ABLE TO ACHIEVE FOR MY COUNTRY, MY PEOPLE, MY FRIENDS AND MY FAMILY. AND NOW, I AM....

Looking Forward to having more time to:

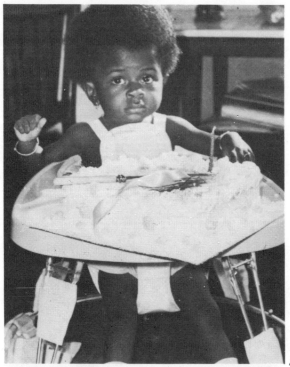

SPEND WITH MY FAMILY,

LOOK AFTER A GARDEN,

426

READ AND WRITE,

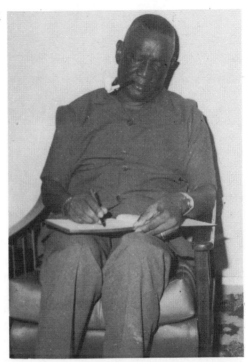

...AND RELAX.

EPILOGUE

The title which I chose for this book speaks for itself. It was life and the process of experience that taught me the most important and relevant parts of what I know today.

This is not to deride the usefulness of a conventional education at various levels. We all can and should learn from others willing to impart their knowledge to us, whether in the classroom, the auditorium, the laboratory, orally or through their writings. We should attempt to acquire even a very small fraction of what other men and women have learnt and discovered through the centuries in all fields of knowledge, especially in the ones in which we are interested, and to which we feel we can make our own contribution.

But I strongly feel that much academic knowledge is liable to remain useless unless it is combined with experience - the experience which enables one to assess the relevance of the acquired knowledge, or parts of it, in a given situation, to select what is applicable, to modify it as may be required by circumstances, and then to apply it in the light of one's instinct and judgement, in the light of what life has already taught us.

Like any educational institution, life teaches only those who want to learn from it, and many are those who stubbornly refuse to absorb the lessons it so freely offers, relying exclusively on formally acquired knowledge rather than attempting to combine it with their own experience.

Some of our young men and women returned from abroad with impressive academic qualifications but proved totally incapable of adapting their knowledge to circumstances, of making it relevant in our environment. I am sorry to say that in some cases neither they, nor the country, could benefit from their education. A few have remained convinced that Sierra Leone and its people should change, if only to enable them to apply successfully the theories that they had been taught.

These Sierra Leoneans could be compared to a few of the expatriate experts and advisers whom we have had over the years; experts who firmly believed that their advice would have produced miracles if only our people and our country had been different from what they are. I deliberately said "a few of the experts and advisers" for many have shown a more flexible and pragmatic approach to our problems and a deeper understanding of our people.

428

Over nearly two and a half decades of independence, for example, we have been advised by well-meaning or interested "experts", both foreign and Sierra Leonean, to spend our meagre resources on projects and sophisticated equipment which, however useful elsewhere, did not always fit our requirements and could not be effectively used by our people.

At the time of writing these pages we suffer from an imbalance in our foreign trade resulting in a shortage of foreign currency, an ailment which we have in common with many other African and developing countries. A classic remedy which foreign advisers have urged us to apply - a remedy which has undoubtedly proved successful in other circumstances - is to promote exports and penalise imports by drastically devaluing our currency. In our country, it is argued, producers of export commodities, such as gold, diamonds or coffee, receive, in real terms, less than world market prices for their goods - a situation allegedly amounting to a disincentive to increase production. At the same time, the experts argue, officially imported goods are subsidised in effect by virtue of the prevailing rate of exchange, making it possible for ordinary people to buy essential commodities at prices which, in real terms, are indeed lower than those obtained on the world markets.

According to the knowledge and logic of the foreign experts, reversing the situation, that is making imported goods more expensive in local currency while increasing the gross income of miners and other producers of export goods, would help balance our foreign trade by increasing the volume of our exports and reducing the volume and, therefore, the cost of our imports. If we paid a bonus to our exporters of gold and diamonds (as some other countries do to promote their respective exports) instead of expecting them to sell their goods through official channels for admittedly less than what they could get on the world markets, we might even find that some goods are smuggled into our country to benefit from a higher price here, rather than out of it. Naturally, this is a tempting thought.

I am not an economist, but what life and my knowledge of our people have taught me is that the level of production of most of our export goods will not increase significantly as a result of higher prices. But a significant increase in the prices of basic imported goods, on which much of the population depends for their day-to-day existence, would inevitably result in higher wages to make up for the increases and, consequently, in greater inflation. For, unlike in some other countries, the living standards of most of our people are so low that no downward adjustment could be contemplated or tolerated and any attempt to bring them down would be fraught with the danger of political destabilisation. Moreover, the consumers of imported goods are far more numerous in our country than the producers of export commodities who, incidentally, would also be affected by the higher prices of imported items which they consume, cancelling out the effect of the higher income they would receive for their efforts and making nonsense of the incentives supposed to promote a higher level of production. Nor, of course, would our suppliers in the industrialised world benefit from a reduction in our imports which would only bring them more unemployment.

Unfortunately, it is not only foreign experts who tend to be carried away by figures and what appears to be irrefutable logic, ignoring the complexity of the human factor and delivering their definitive verdict as if the people expected to apply their theories could be programmed like computers.

Some years ago many of our people became incensed by the high and rising prices of imported commodities, including what many regarded as essential items. It was well known, of course, that both the importers and the distributors of these items were making substantial profits at the expense of our consumers, despite the so-called competition among the various businessmen. Moreover, it was also known that our importers, most of them expatriates, could not or would not order goods in sufficient quantities to secure the lowest prices from their suppliers abroad.

In the circumstances, it stood to reason that if a state-owned corporation or organisation were to buy the essential goods in bulk, directly from producers or manufacturers abroad, and distribute them directly to the public through its own retail network, on a non-profit basis, by-passing not only the importers but also the wholesalers, retailers, and other middlemen, prices to the end consumer would be appreciably reduced.

The logic of the argument seemed irrefutable and, moreover, the theory was reported to have been borne out in practice in many countries where consumer cooperatives had proved successful. Though I had some intuitive reservations at the back of my mind, I could not but subscribe to what seemed to be so obvious a solution to our problem by supporting the establishment of the National Trading Co., or N.T.C. as it became known, - a state-owned enterprise enjoying the full financial and moral support of our government. In theory, at least, the N.T.C. should have been able to compete so successfully with private enterprise as to drive the "sharks" out of business and eventually achieve a virtual monopoly of trade in specified areas. For once, both socialist and capitalist economic analysis concurred in leading us to expect this outcome.

In practice, however, the result of our venture vindicated neither. It is now obvious that even though the venture may not have been a total failure, it certainly did not justify our confidence and its benefits fell very short of our expectations.

Some would still argue that the idea was basically good and would have offered the anticipated benefits if only this or that had not happened, or if some people had not acted as they did. I fully agree with this analysis, but what life has taught me is that what actually happened was not as unpredictable and unlikely to happen as some people would like to think, regardless of the measures we may have taken to prevent it from happening.

We have now accepted the relative failure of the experiment, put it down to experience and written off the financial losses which, in the event, were not unbearable. For if life has not yet taught me how to avoid making any mistakes, it has taught me at least to recognise them and to desist from persisting to advance along an uncharted road which may turn out to be more treacherous than appearances suggest.

In political matters too we have had our share of advisers and well-wishers, some more sincere than others. They too have often failed to realise that not everything that glitters is gold; that social and political doctrines, however attractive in theory, cannot be applied in practice if they do not take into account the reality of the society in which they are intended to operate. An architect can choose the materials best suited for his design. A politician must choose the design best suited for the material at his disposal - the people he wishes to serve.

I do not dispute the advantages of some political theories, nor the fact that they may have been successfully applied in this or that country. But life has taught me that one man's meat can be another man's poison - one of the few adages which my own experience has often confirmed. At one end of the scale we have always had those who want us to copy faithfully the western type of democracy; at the other, those who would like us to emulate the Marxist system as it functions in some countries. Both groups can produce fairly convincing arguments, but neither has bothered to assess the chances of successfully reproducing a working model of the original in our circumstances; and both have conveniently ignored what would happen if we ended up with a broken down parody of the original - a parody resulting in untold dislocation, hardships and bloodshed.

Some of our African leaders, too, appear to have swallowed hook, line and sinker the political and economic theories propounded by foreign doctrinaires, including theories which are known to have failed in other countries, and have attempted to apply them in Africa at their own risk and at the expense of their people.

Some of these leaders are no longer with us but I knew them well. I have not the slightest doubt about their patriotism, their sincerity and their selfless and relentless efforts to do everything in their power to improve the welfare of their respective peoples, to uphold the dignity and sovereignty of their countries and to promote the freedom and unity of Africa. What may be open to some doubt and what has been questioned by some of their own nationals is whether the methods and policies which they adopted in good faith to achieve their lofty aims were workable in practice and appropriate for the purpose.

Whatever the answer to this question may be, the fact is that the situation in many African countries today, especially the economic situation, falls far short of expectations and has been almost unanimously recognised in some cases as very serious. What could have gone wrong? Can drought, world recession and other natural and man-made calamities beyond our control provide the whole answer?

Anthropologists tell us that Africa was the cradle of mankind. It has certainly been inhabited by intelligent human beings for far longer than most other parts of the world. The countries which are now faced with serious food shortages and other enormous difficulties were able to feed themselves for millions of years, long before the human race began to settle in Europe and America. Though still suffering from neo-colonialism, our countries are no longer subjected to the shameful and blatant exploitation experienced during the colonial era. Most of them now benefit from a measure of foreign assistance which was unknown until about 25 years ago.

Could it be that some of the doctrines and theories imparted to us in good or bad faith by non-Africans since the new age of independence may have proved more lethal than the bullets we used to receive in the more distant past?

In the exact sciences researchers test a theory in the laboratory and, if the experiment fails, they either try again, using different methods, or conclude that the theory was wrong. All they stand to lose is their time and effort. In politics, economics and other areas directly affecting the lives of human beings one cannot take such risks; one cannot resuscitate the thousands who may have died or been sacrificed in the process of attempting to make a dream come true; one cannot offer adequate compensation to those who were led to believe that the unattainable could be attained if only a sufficient number would willingly shed their blood on the altar of an untested theory.

Hardly any bank nowadays would risk its money by financing a project before reliable feasibility studies have established its profitability. Would it not be wise for ordinary people to insist on political and economic feasibility studies before agreeing to risk their freedom, their livelihood and even their lives on projects fraught with the danger of ruining their countries and subjecting a whole nation to greater hardships and frustrations than those which a reckless minority had fought to remove.

What has often baffled me in history is how many good and sincere people have struggled selflessly for years only to bring about, in objective terms, the very opposite of the lofty ideal which they had set out to attain.

Historians sometimes attribute these tragic failures to "unforeseen developments" or to circumstances beyond the control of those foolhardy leaders who, giving them the benefit of the doubt, attempted to put everything right without envisaging that something could go wrong. A wise and prudent man would know that though the sequels of some political changes cannot be predicted with any degree of accuracy in an area where one deals with imponderable human factors, one could predict with certainty that unpredictable situations may arise. What life has taught me is to aim at the most desirable, hope for the best, but always expect the unexpected and never rule out the worst.

In my own view, however, the tragic failure of some attempts to solve a wide and complex range of problems with a magic wand is often due not so much to the unpredictable as to the inadequate ground work done by those who spend so much time visualising a bright future that they are left with too little time to study the past and analyse the present. Yet, in social and political edifices, the future can only be built on the foundations of the past and within the framework of the present.

Sometimes, I have the feeling that even when they try to analyse the present, some politicians, or would-be politicians, fail to do so objectively, lest a fair assessment should jeopardise their aspirations and explode their theories; or else, they reject anything that does not fit into their subjective analysis. Nor would they always assess objectively the experience of others in similar circumstances, especially if some aspects of that experience tend to contradict their pre-conceived pattern.

I am not suggesting that the experience of others should always be a determining factor. But totally to ignore the effect of policies which have proved counter-productive in similar situations could be as dangerous as to follow blindly a course of action simply on the ground that it is supposed to have been successful elsewhere.

Life has taught me to make my own judgements in which the experience and example of others carry some weight without ever becoming decisive; it has also taught me to distinguish between wishful thinking and real thinking for practical purposes; to divorce emotions (which we all have) from the sober assessment of reality and, occasionally, to express the former while acting only on the basis of the latter.

In the political field, I have learnt that if people are to participate in the implementation of policies these must relate to their traditions, their natural talents, attitudes and propensities. Conceiving policies which, however desirable, go against the grain of the people, or are out of keeping with their experience, and then rely on persuasion, compulsion or so-called education to change the people so as to make the policies acceptable and applicable, is what I would regard as a recipe for failure; except, perhaps, in the very long run, by which I mean centuries rather than decades.

What life has taught me is to observe and try to understand people, assess their attitudes and aptitudes, their qualities as well as their inherent weaknesses and to accept both as part of reality; to appreciate that some of their basic instincts, good or bad, are too deeply rooted in pre-history to be significantly changed, except in the very short term, by fine rhetoric, coercion, decree, Act of Parliament or even Revolution; in short to see people as they are and not as some would like them to be or imagine them to be. Finally, in the light of what life has taught me, I have learnt to be tolerant and patient and neither to expect too much from people nor to look down upon them or to underestimate their ability and potential.

In practical terms, especially during the latter years of my political career, this has led me to discourage policies and legislation which, however desirable in theory, might prove counter-productive because their successful implementation or enforcement would depend too much on the competence, dedication and integrity of people who may not always prove up to the envisaged task.

By the same token, life has taught me to favour methods which, though perhaps far from the theoretical ideal in a modern society, are more in keeping with the traditions of our people, their culture and their instinctive approach to the solution of problems. In this context, it has also taught me to distinguish between the desirable and the possible, to make allowances for human nature, to blend firmness with compassion and, above all, perhaps, always to remember that no one is infallible. This leads me always to allow for the possibility of my own judgement being wrong, as well as that of my closest associates.

There was a time when, like most young men, I had an unshakable confidence in my own views. Life has taught me to recognise my mistakes in all humility and to revise my judgement whenever the evidence calls for such a course. In other words, life has taught me that no education is ever complete and that the essential lesson of life is that one must continue learning from it to the end of one's days.

One of the things which I have learnt throughout my life is that, however strong and confident one may feel, there is a limit to how far one can go it alone. We are all prone to face crises in our health, our endeavours, our emotional lives and our careers. Occasionally, we are bound to feel that we may have taken the wrong turn and are walking along the wrong path. Past mistakes make us conscious of the risk of future ones and of the dangers which have claimed so many victims. This is especially so in the case of politicians and leaders who are conscious of the fact that a possible error of judgement on their part would affect not only their own lives but also those of their fellow citizens whose number may run into many millions.

There are situations when one feels that, despite one's confidence and apparent power, one is at the mercy of forces which one can neither understand nor control - forces which reach beyond one's experience. Something which life taught me in my early childhood and has been teaching me ever since is that if one is to avoid the danger of succumbing to these forces, one needs guidance and strength from without - a permanent anchor which can help one keep on an even keel in fair weather and save us from floundering in a raging storm. To me, such an anchor is God, although I accept that some people may give their anchor a different name.

I am convinced that God's help is freely available to all those who genuinely seek it. Rejecting it, I feel, is not a sign of strength, but one of extreme presumption bordering on reckless folly, for history is yet to identify the man or woman who never made a serious mistake and never needed moral and spiritual support from a superior force outside his or her comprehension. But life has also taught me that what most of us can expect from God is strength and guidance rather than miracles.

While life has taught me that no one is infallible, it has also taught me that no one is invariably wrong and that there is often a good deal of truth and merit in what may appear at first sight to be a load of nonsense. This has led me to listen more attentively to what others may have to say, to learn from what life may have taught them and, if possible, to put it to the test.

I am certainly not an opponent of change. In fact I spent much of my life fighting for change and reforms which appeared to many to be radical, or even revolutionary. I fought for the rights of our mineworkers because I knew that their working conditions could be improved as a result of resolute action on our part. I fought for the full sovereignty and independence of our country because I knew that our goal was within our reach and that our aspirations could be fulfilled if we went about in the right way. I fought for a more equitable social order in our country and against its domination by people from any particular region, tribe or social class because I knew that this too could be achieved, providing a healthy foundation for further development.

I remain convinced that there is much room for change and improvement in every sphere, and not only in Sierra Leone. The world has been changing ever since its creation and will undoubtedly continue to change, for better or for worse.

In fact, the world in which we now live differs vastly from the one into which I was born and grew up as a child. Much of what we see today in our homes and in our streets and which we take for granted would have been unimaginable in my own youth. Real hunger, as we experienced it at times, is now virtually unknown in our country. Though housing is still a problem no one need die of exposure to the elements or walk barefoot. Clothing is no longer the major problem that it was. Infant mortality and death from curable diseases has been greatly reduced. Education has become available to the great majority and certainly to those who really want it. Electricity and piped water, both still unknown in my early childhood, are enjoyed by a constantly growing number, including virtually all those who live in our major towns and cities.

How many of those who so frequently and vehemently complain about the efficiency of our public transport, the shortage of government cars or the cost of petrol are conscious of the fact that their grandfathers, or even their fathers, had to walk barefoot along miles of forest paths and risk their lives in rickety canoes to cross rivers now spanned by concrete bridges.

In the more distant past people lived in a fairly static civilisation and died in an environment almost identical to the one in which they were born. They did not realise that change was possible and, therefore, did not clamour for it. The extent of the changes which I have witnessed in my lifetime exceeds by far anything that happened in the previous 500 or even 1000 years. Nowadays the craving for change seems to have become addictive and the faster the rate at which some people witness it, the more they want to speed it up.

What life has taught me is the importance of trying to distinguish between what can be changed rapidly with a good chance of success, what is subject to slow change or evolution, and what should be left alone because it is not ripe for change or because it is so rigid and brittle that any attempt to change the status quo would involve too great a risk of disintegration and a waste of effort, resources and human lives.

Moreover, even a change that appears to be both possible and desirable can never be guaranteed to be successful. This, I believe, applies not only in politics and economics but also in other spheres. I have seen machines which had to be written off as a result of attempts to improve their performance, servicable houses which collapsed in the course of modernisation, farmers and businessmen who ruined themselves in the process of expanding their operations or making them more profitable, and people who died or were crippled after surgery intended to cure them.

Unfortunately, I think, these considerations are often ignored by those who, having taken a quick look at our situation and the structure of our society, immediately decide that everything is fundamentally wrong and should be changed forthwith. I very much hope that life will eventually teach them its realities as it has taught them to me - realities which are not always pleasant or easy to accept. I have now learnt to accept them with serenity rather than resignation and this is perhaps the most important lesson which life has taught me - a lesson which guides not only my approach to politics and to my personal affairs, but also my attitude to life itself and to its inevitable end.

For this lesson I also owe a debt of gratitude to the American poet William Cullen Bryant (1794 - 1878) whose *Thanatopsis* made a profound impression on me in my youth, though it was only in more recent years that I began to appreciate the full significance of his words:

> *So live, that when thy summons comes to join*
> *The innumerable caravan, which moves*
> *To that mysterious realm, where each shall take*
> *His chamber in the silent halls of death,*
> *Thou go not, like the quarry-slave at night,*
> *Scourged to his dungeon, but, sustained and soothed*
> *By an unfaltering trust, approach they grave*
> *Like one who wraps the drapery of his couch*
> *About him, and lies down to pleasant dreams.*

APPENDICES

APPENDIX I

TOP SECRET & PERSONAL   22nd August, 1972

His Excellency President Idi Amin,
Presidential Palace,
KAMPALA,
Uganda

Dear President and Brother,

I am Siaka Stevens, aged 67, President of the Republic of Sierra Leone, West Africa, a former British Colony which got its independence in 1961. I have a trade union background.

    I am writing to you on a very delicate issue because among other things I realise that one of the fundamental tenets is that no nation should interfere in the internal affairs of other nations. But the world today is getting smaller and smaller by reason of air travel so that whether we like it or not, the nations of the world are bound to intermingle. We have to intermingle for reasons of health, we have to intermingle for environmental reasons, etc., etc.; so that it is my view that when things take place in one part of the world, more especially in one part of Africa, it is the business of other African nations to do their utmost to see whether something ought not to be done about the matter.

    African nations today are committed to the development of Africa as a whole. We are committed to give every help possible to one another for the general development of the Continent, and that is why African nations as a whole are going all out to struggle for the emancipation of our fellow Africans in the oppressed parts of Africa such as South Africa, Rhodesia, the Portuguese territories, etc.

    It is in this spirit that I venture to write to you in personal and highly confidential strain and I sincerely trust that you will treat this communication as such. If for any reason you do not think it worth while, then do relegate it to the wastepaper basket and don't think of it again. My country is thousands of miles away from yours and the reports which have reached us are the reports which have been presented by newspapers and other mass media of information which are not under our control, so that it may well be that there are discrepancies or exaggerations in the details which have been passed on to us.

Roughly speaking we have been informed that your Government is arranging for a wholesale exodus of Asians from Uganda. The Asians to be deported fall into such categories as Asians with British passports, Asians with Uganda citizenship and others; in fact we understand that no Asians are exempted.

I realise to the full that the action which your Government is now taking is intended to protect indigenous African interests, which is all to the good. The first duty of any Government is to protect the interests of its indigenous people and there can be no doubt that the intention behind your move is laudable.

As a result of the political background of my country, Sierra Leone, we have from the very beginning had to accommodate a conglomeration of the various tribes of West Africa as well as displaced persons from Nova Scotia, America, the United Kingdom and other places, and this situation created tremendous difficulties for us, difficulties which we have been able to surmount little by little as the years have gone by. The situation in your country now seems to be that thousands of Asians have to be expelled from Uganda, many of whom, I understand, were born in Uganda, while others have been granted Uganda citizenship by the Uganda Government. Well, Mr. President, no human being is responsible for the place of his birth or for his parenthood. None of us is responsible for the circumstances of his birth and to decree that a human being should suffer statelessness and economic ruin because of the circumstances and place of his birth or for somebody else's past mistakes, is a terrible sort of suffering indeed.

Now, General Amin, we have all as former colonial territories suffered a lot at the hands of our former British overlords and if today we should try to retaliate for the evils which have been done to our people and our countries we would have very little energy left for our development. This is not to say that the overlords did not bring some good to some parts of Africa.

It must also be noted that there is hardly a State in the world today which has not suffered or benefitted from the incursion of strangers either by war or otherwise. Almost all the civilizations of the past have been built up in this way. The great American nation is built up of strangers from various parts of the world. The great Russian people are a conglomeration of different nationalities such as Armenians, Turks, Slavs and Mongolians. And, as I said earlier on, as the world gets smaller and smaller, tighter and tighter, by reason of air travel, this "mixing up" of people will get more common as the years go by. It therefore seems to me that this question of minorities is a matter which cannot be erased by a stroke of the pen.

It seems to me also that as long as minorities are kept in their proper proportions and in their proper place, they could well contribute to the national development. It is accepted today, even among the great Powers, that no nation, no people can live unto themselves. We can well remember reading from our history books the days when the Romans came into Britain with their civilization and culture.

It is against this background, General Amin, that I should like you and your advisors to consider the proposed expulsion of Asians from Uganda with the idea that the indigenous people should take the place of the people to be expelled, take their place in business, in industry and in other professions. Permit me to express my humble opinion that people cannot be legislated into business or industry; there has got to be aptitude, training and other essentials. I remember some years ago here in Sierra Leone when a Paramount Chief expelled some Lebanese traders from a certain town in the Provinces where the Lebanese owned two or three shops. The natives in the surrounding villages had been used to travelling the one or two miles to this centre to dispose of their produce and buy their wants, such as tobacco, kerosene, etc. The expulsion of these Lebanese traders from this station made it necessary for the local people to travel four or five miles with their produce on their heads to get to the nearest trading station. It was these very natives who formed a delegation to report the Chief to the District Officer. In the end the Chief recanted and the Lebanese traders returned to the station. I was one of those who at the time admired the Chief for the stand which he had taken but it was found later on that the laws of economics do many a time take priority over the laws of politics.

It may well be, Mr. President, that some of those who are now rejoicing to see foreign traders expelled may later on find that at this stage of their development they may not be able to fill the economic vacuum that will be created.

The businesses and professions which these aliens have built up have been built up over a long period of years and it seems to me that if they are to be replaced this should be done by a system of phasing, while the local people are given intensive training in the required directions.

It may well be that being thousands of miles away from Uganda I am not in a position to give proper consideration to the various facets of this tremendous problem, but it seems to me that if you follow a course of "hanging heads" with your advisors and enjoining them to give free expressions of opinions, as well as negotiations with the nations whose people are to be expelled, and even more consultations with the O.A.U., then I believe that a way can be found to ease the strain and tensions which are bound to arise not only with the people who are to be expelled, but with their States of origin and with other Governments which are bound to be affected by this wholesale exodus.

I am writing to you, General Amin, as brother African to brother African, and if you do not agree with the points I have made, please forgive my intrusion; and be assured that it is within the context of general African development and welfare that I have ventured to write to you.

Most of Africa in its present stage of development badly needs outside help in the form of capital and expertise and the laws of economics, like the laws of health, know no boundaries. I feel certain that with education and training we Africans will eventually be able to take our proper places in the economies of our countries, while at the same time allowing for an appropriate number of foreigners to take their place alongside our people in the general development of our countries.

With fraternal greetings, dear Brother,

I remain,

SIAKA P. STEVENS

APPENDIX II

A West African Worker at Ruskin

SIAKA STEVENS

My brief sojourn in Ruskin College has been one of the happiest periods of my two score years of existence.

I had come to this institution of learning with nothing like a warmth of feeling for Europeans because, in Africa, almost all Whites look down on Africans; they keep aloof from us and go about with an archangelic air of superiority. In the workshop, on the works or in the office, whenever issues crop up in which an African is pitched against a European, the conclusion is a foregone one -- the European cannot be wrong. I was brought up in an atmosphere in which I could not think about the District Commissioner without thinking of the Jail House. The very few Europeans who push the 'curtain' aside and try to befriend us, to know how we feel, do so at their own peril. **Socialism is not for export! Colonial affairs are not party politics!** These and such-like ideas seem to prevail in the minds of the average colonial European. Socialists, Trade Unionists, Conservatives, they are all the same in their dealings with us.

So you can understand what the trend of my thoughts was when I found myself, one of two West Africans, amongst a host of Europeans, men and women, at Ruskin.

In short, I was prepared for a 'frying-pan to fire' situation.

But those blokes, those Ruskinites, they confounded me. They beat me hands down with surprise. From the word GO it was one grand atmosphere of cordiality and helpfulness. They drew me out of my self-imposed silence and treated me as one of themselves. I doubted their sincerity at first, but how genuine it was!

From the Principal, with his rich, sonorous voice, his ready availability at all times and his willingness to help, right through the whole staff, they were all so tactful and helpful.

The student body was a grand lot: Englishmen, Scotsmen, Welshmen, Irishmen and Americans. How wonderfully we all mixed. Communists and fellow travellers seized every opportunity to discuss the grand millennium when the workers will rule the world. Socialists were always advocating hastening slowly and so on. They taught me how not to go to bed before one in the morning, how to hurry back for a second helping at table, and how to make do with little.

The lecturers took charge of my head and the students of my heart, and I dare say I gained a good deal in both cases.

Nothing lasts for ever and so my Ruskin days have come to an end, with me wishing I had come earlier. Over for me of course but not for the young men and women at home in Sierra Leone whom I shall tell of my great find.

But even as these thoughts cross my mind, even as I think of the many valuable contacts and friendships I have made here, one thought keeps rearing its ugly head, one question keeps repeating itself to me in different forms:

How is it that the Europeans here are so different from the great majority of those who go out to us in the colonies? What changes them so? Do they realize the harm they are doing? How can they ever really know us and understand our feelings when they are so 'far away' from us?

I am trying to find the answer and you, the reader, must try too.

In these days when the world is being divided into 'camps', Great Britain, in spite of colonial sins of omission and commission, still has enough time, but just enough time, to win the sympathy and support of a great mass of people in West Africa *if only,* as the late Bapu Gandhi of blessed memory used to say, *if only Britain would get up from our heads and walk by our sides.*

*(Reproduced from **New Epoch,** Ruskin College bi-annual magazine, No.1 1948)*

Index